Community Organization
and the
Canadian State

286 - 306

Community Organization and the Canadian State

edited by

Roxana Ng
Gillian Walker
and
Jacob Muller

Garamond Press

Toronto

A publication of Garamond Press

Garamond Press
67A Portland Street
Toronto, Ontario M5V 2M9

Copy editing: Melodie Mayson-Richmond and Ted Richmond
Design and production: Phoenix Productions
Typesetting: Journal Production Centre, Carleton University
Printed and bound in Canada

Canadian Cataloguing in Publication Data

Main entry under title:

Community organization and the Canadian state

Includes bibliographical references.
ISBN 0-920059-47-3

1. Community organization — Political aspects —
Canada.   2. Community organization — Canada.
3. Community power — Canada. I. Ng, Roxana, 1951–
II. Walker, Gillian. III. Muller, Jacob.

HN110.C6C65   1990   307.1'–971   C90-093405-0

Acknowledgements

Grateful acknowledgement for excerpts from:

"Native Women in Reserve Politics: Strategies and Struggles" by Jo-Anne Fiske to be published in the *Journal of Legal Pluralism*, special issue on Socio-Legal Status of Women, forthcoming 1990.

"Management of Urban Neighborhoods Through Alinsky-style Organizing: Redevelopment and Local Area Planning in a Vancouver Neighborhood" by Jacob Muller, originally published in *Community Development Journal*, Vol. 20, 2, 1985, pp. 106–113; titled "Management of Urban Neighborhoods Through Alinsky-style Organizing." Reprinted by permission of Oxford University Press.

"The Politics of Minority Resistance Against Racism in the Local State" by Daiva K. Stasiulis, originally published in *Ethnic and Racial Studies*, Vol. 12, 1, January, 1989, pp. 63–83; titled "Minority Resistance in the Local State: Toronto in the 1970s and 1980s."

"Policing the Gay Community" by George Smith, originally published in the *International Journal of the Sociology of Law*, Vol. 16, 1986, pp. 163–183, titled "Policing the Gay Community: An Inquiry into Textually-Mediated Relations." Reprinted by permission of Academic Press.

The Other Face of 2,4-D by John Warnock and Jay Lewis © 1978. Published by South Okanagan Environmental Coalition, Penticton, B.C.

Contents

Part 3: Community Struggles and State Regulation

Conclusion

Bibliography

Contributors

ANNE BULLOCK is a doctoral student in the Sociology Department, Ontario Institute for Studies in Education.

LINDA CHRISTIANSEN-RUFFMAN teaches in the Sociology Department of St. Mary's University.

KARI DEHLI is a post-doctoral fellow in the Sociology Department, Ontario Institute for Studies in Education.

JO-ANNE FISKE teaches in the Sociology Department, St. Mary's University.

DONALD GRADY teaches in the Sociology Department, Acadia University.

SUSAN HEALD teaches in the Sociology and Anthropology Department, Wilfrid Laurier University.

MELODY HESSING teaches in the School of Criminology, Simon Fraser University.

JACOB MULLER teaches social sciences and co-ordinates the Human Service Workers' Program at Northwest Community College, Terrace, B.C.

ROXANA NG teaches in the Sociology Department at the Ontario Institute for Studies in Education.

BARBARA ROBERTS teaches Women's Studies at Athabasca University.

JAMES SACOUMAN teaches in the Sociology Department, Acadia University.

ALICIA SCHREADER has an M.S.W. from Carleton University and an M.D. from McMaster University. She is completing her internship at Ottawa General Hospital.

GEORGE SMITH is a research officer in the Sociology Department, Ontario Institute for Studies in Education.

DAIVA STASIULIS teaches in the Department of Sociology and Anthropology, Carleton University.

GILLIAN WALKER teaches in the School of Social Work, Carleton University.

Preface

This book owes its inception to a dinner among the three editors in a Toronto restaurant in the summer of 1983. One of the editors jokingly suggested that the other two should organize a session on community organizing and the state at the 1984 Learned Meetings so he could present a paper. What resulted were three sessions at the Canadian Sociology and Anthropology (CSAA) meeting, one on Women and the State, and two on Grassroots Community Organizing and the State. The sessions were enthusiastically received, both by the participants and the audience. The idea of putting together a collection of readings based on these sessions therefore included input from the original participants: Marguerite Cassin, Kathy Cram, Diana Ralph, Marie Sakowski, Dorothy Smith and Alicia Schreader.

As we developed the theme(s) for the book, some papers were dropped because they did not conform to the themes, and new ones were included because they did. All the contributors went though several rounds of revisions based on the editors' comments and comments of the collection by anonymous external reviewers. Earlier drafts of the Introduction, ideas of which now appear in bits and pieces in the Introduction and Conclusion, were sent out to all the contributors for comments.

The editorial process was a protracted and difficult one because we were dispersed across the country and communications among the editors, and between the editors and contributors, were slow. We were all overcommitted and overworked. Due to the marginality of some of us in the higher educational system, we initially received minimal institutional support and acknowledgement for our work. However, friends, colleagues and comrades were generous with their encouragement and support. Among them, Errol Sharpe tops the list in prodding us on and in providing advice on the many aspects of manuscript preparation. Kari Dehli, Daiva Stasiulis, Philip Corrigan and George Smith gave us extensive feedback on earlier versions of the Introduction. Jennifer Thompson spent many hours compiling the integrated bibliography and inputting it into different computers. Marilyn Marshall, Dean of Social Sciences at Carleton University generously made available the invaluable assistance of Else Brock who created the final manuscript. Our gratitude goes to them, to Christina Thiele of the Journal Production Centre at Carleton, who was responsible for producing the camera-ready version, to the people at Garamond Press and to Melodie and Ted Richmond for meticulous copy editing. Finally, we want to thank each other for not losing faith, even at times when the project seemed completely impossible, and for sustaining each other during its lengthy birth.

Roxana Ng, Toronto, Ontario
Gillian Walker, Ottawa, Ontario
Jacob Muller, Terrace, B.C.

January, 1990

Introduction

Problematizing Community Organization and the State[*]

Jacob Muller
with Gillian Walker and Roxana Ng

This book arises out of practical and analytical concerns for those of us involved in various ways of doing what is generally referred to as "community work." These concerns arise out of our relation to the Canadian state, its bureaucrats and officials and the different levels of government. We do not wish to put forward a purely theoretical exercise. Rather, we see this collection fundamentally as a *political* project serving in concrete ways to direct our understanding and to help us as we attempt to transform local "communities" in response to changing political and economic realities.

The selection of papers collected here represents an attempt to extend the general assumptions about what makes up community organizing and community development. We have put together work which includes a variety of activities which may or may not fall under the rubric of "community work." Authors explore the character of the interaction between different kinds of community organizing efforts and "the state." There are inquiries which question the assumed role of women in the community and the struggles of native and immigrant women in particular. In addition, there are "case studies" which deal with community job creation programs and community organized struggles—involving a neighborhood, the environment, anti-racism, the gay community and a fishing community—in relation to Canadian state rule. These diverse studies portray the complicated nature of forms of community organiz-

---

[*]We do not use the terms "problematic" or "problematize" merely in their ordinary sociological sense. Instead, we want to direct attention to questions which have not been posed at the theoretical level before, or to a set of puzzles which need to be explored in the everyday world.

ing and resistance (hence "community organization") in relation to state authorities.

Our aim, in drawing together work which documents differing organizational efforts, is to arrive at an understanding of (a) how state forms serve to divide working people in their attempt to struggle for democratic participation and an equitable share of the product of their labor in Canadian society, and, (b) how those of us involved might work strategically, in different arenas and locations, to improve and transform the conditions of our lives.

Community Organization

The concept community organization is used in this book instead of other possible terms such as community work or community development.[1] This is done to draw attention to the various kinds and forms of organizing that are examined which use the term "community." Thus, community organization is used as a general term highlighting different ways in which groups of people may constitute themselves in various historical contexts using the notion of community.

What our contributors share then, in presenting their understanding of a particular organizing effort, is that they all make use of the concept "community." Yet, though the various contributors use the term, there is no agreement as to what "community" actually means. Because of this, we treat the notion of community as a problematic that requires investigation. Some authors adopt what we have labelled the standard definitional approach while others challenge the meaning of the term. The dilemma in defining community and community organization is not, however, confined to the contributors of this selection. It is one which can be identified as more general within the field. As such it requires some clarification and amplification here.

What we mean by a standard approach is the most common method of understanding "community" which proceeds by defining and redefining the concept.[2] This orientation generally includes a number of features. The most salient of these is the focus on a given territory or space as encapsulating the common needs of those who live or work there.[3] Residents of an area may identify issues affecting their lives and organize for or against change, in opposition to or support for urban development, or in relation to concerns over economic needs and the revitalization of a local work force and industrial base.[4] These issues and others such as the need for adequate services and resources have been identified as aspects of the definition of community.[5] Needs such as these also unite people around a common interest or shared concern which may not be related to

geographic community

functional community

geographical boundaries. This too would qualify as "community" and we frequently hear the term used in this way to identify particular interest groups such as the "business community," the "gay community" or the "educational community." The general concern of analysts who employ this approach is to develop a set of criteria for defining a "community" and to demonstrate that these criteria exist. How a "community" arises in the first place is usually left unexamined or relegated a minor role.

This common definitional approach offers a truncated and disconnected view of people. Residents of one geographical area may be considered separate or distinct from those in another locale. Similarly, those individuals sharing an interest, for instance, in an educational context, are taken to be separate from others. The relationship to any other group of people at the local or national level[6] is left unexamined. At best an analytical correlation[7] is presented without examining the historical and empirical conditions. The problem that needs to be addressed then is the kind of knowledge and ideas that separates out, indeed disorganizes, different aspects of people in their everyday lives.

A major reason why this approach continues to exist is because it aligns both theorists and organizers with the analysis and practices of those who govern within the state.[8] Precisely how this connection to ruling practices occurs is a key question investigated by our contributors in their particular studies.

This prevailing view of community should not be rejected outright or characterized as irrelevant. It is not only present in the work of contributors but also serves as a significant rallying call of solidarity among friends and neighbors.[9] A particular neighborhood or an "ethnic community" may unite against those officials proposing to alter or discriminate against the existing character of the "community" (however defined). This may take the form of neighborhoods or anti-racist campaigns against city hall, or major political community action against different levels of government.[10] As such it clearly has a common-sense usage that provides a sense of identity, belonging and purpose for people whose lives are otherwise characterized by isolation and alienation.

The dominant mode of analysis in the community discourse, the definitional method, will continue to be used until its proponents forsake it. There exists, however, a general alternative approach. Some analysts use concept of community descriptively and try to comprehend the social relations or forces involved in establishing such a phenomenon.[11] They seek to understand social production and reproduction.[12] Such an analysis may focus on the workings of the family, capitalism and "the state" in shaping the development of local relations. The emphasis is on the class character of capital, wage labor, and women's relation to the social reproduction of daily life, be it in education or community care. Commentators who take this position consider as relevant the way in which the state and its various bureaucracies administer and regulate the needs of production and consumption (directly or through the labor market) and how those in government manage day-to-day activities so that capital accumulation may continue uninterrupted. Challenges against the drive for profits may be organized by people based on their everyday needs.

Those who use an approach which challenges the standard use of community are also concerned with the transformation of the state and civil society. Particular efforts have emphasized not only the importance of class relations[13] but also the fundamental relevance of women, Quebec, racial groups, aboriginal people, gay people, etc., in any analytic efforts.[14] Given the rich diversity of people, cultures, and nations in Canada, it is not surprising that a general analytical consensus showing us how this social world interrelates and coheres, does not exist. Indeed, it has been suggested that the search for one universal meaning is fruitless and we may need to accept many meanings of community.[15]

Contributors to this collection reflect in their orientation both of the positions identified so far. Indeed, creating various organizational forms may sometimes involve using different and overlapping definitions and approaches. There is certainly no uniform agreement in this field on what constitutes "community" which would clarify this dilemma. The aim of our inquiry in this volume is to investigate aspects of this problem in order to determine what suggestions can be made to advance our understanding of organizing work. This is an important problematic because those of us involved in this field want to know whether or not "community" can be used as an oppositional base from which to challenge "the state." If so, we need to know how "community" can be used in ways which do not correspond to and align us with the organizational practices used by the state to manage and rule.

The State

The previous section has started to highlight an analytical and empirical thematic for this collection: that "community organization" in Canada cannot be considered without reference to the role of "the state." "Community" has been presented as a general problem to be investigated by the various contributors in analyzing their particular organizing efforts. Just as the use of "community" is problematized so is the use of the term "the state." The point of this section then is to explore the use of the concept "the state" as it has been taken up in the extensive literature on the subject.[16]

The common use of the term "the state" is summarized by Ng,[17] who argues that this concept is generally used to refer to a machine or a set of apparatuses that performs different functions for the ruling or dominant classes on behalf of capital. This has led analysts to assume that the state is "over and above people." Despite the fact that this view makes it difficult to relate the state to the lived experiences of people, it continues to be the prevailing usage and is adopted by some of the contributors in this book.

Analysts who view the state as being "over and above people" have also tended to see the state as static, isolated and fragmented. For instance, in trying to understand Canada's social formations, the use of the term "the Canadian state,"[18] while quite important, nevertheless conveys the sense of an object with a completed process, which seems suspended in time; it suggests that the state in Canada is a monolithic force. Thus, the various national forms within Canada, such as the English, French, Inuit, and Native nations,[19] are not treated as part of a continuing struggle in Canada's social formation.

Further, some analysts begin by rejecting any social reforms that are initiated by state authorities, including vehicles such as "citizens' participation" programs. Methods of participation lead us into a complicated area covering diverse issues, different time periods, various levels of government, and having different organizational forms (e.g., advisory boards, legal tribunals, involvement in planning and policy preparation). It is not possible simply to reject these state initiatives and activities since certain reforms, services, jobs, etc., are necessary. Indeed, in some instances (i.e., the need for paid jobs), community groups have insisted on equal involvement with government bureaucrats by raising "citizens' participation" as a rallying banner for local residents.

Perhaps the most salient assumption made by analysts who use the common view of "the state" is that their analyses somehow relates to community organizations. They do not, however, show how this is the case.[20] The general tendency of analysts has been to view the state in terms of controlling functions (through governance, bureaucracy, and coercion). Those who seek to shape or influence these functions from without are understood to be in conflict with those who govern.[21] How these social interactions of coercion and protest relate empirically is left unexamined. If we are ever to understand those who rule, it is necessary to focus on how such activity is actually carried out in relation to those being governed.[22]

Challenging the standard use of "the state" are analysts who view the state as a struggle between classes or a set of social relations. They see the state as legitimizing certain courses of action, thereby making alternate forms illegitimate and organizing how people relate to one another.[23] Some of the contributors to this book adopt this orientation. We, as editors, do not intend to offer a new definition or theory to explain the state. Whether the contours of the state conform to those identified in the standard approach, or are better explained by those who present a challenge, is a matter to be explored. There is no consensus among commentators on the use and meaning of "the state,"[24] just as there is none among commentators on "community." Both uses of the state mentioned previously exist in the discourse and in this collection.

In advanced capitalist societies, state rule has increasingly taken on the role of mediating and intervening in civil society as part of the provision of the infrastructure essential to the continual accumulation of capital.[25] State authorities actively organize and manage the economy and the work force through the provision of special grants and tax shelters to business and industries; they monitor the work force by developing educational and training programs; and they facilitate and regulate labor supply through various forms of legislation, including immigration policies and unemployment insurance. As well, managers of the state play a central role in putting into place a set of coercive structures and apparatuses designed to alleviate potential unrest to ensure the smooth growth of capital. In this way, "the state" occupies an essential place in the constitution and organization of the working class through various interventive and regulatory mechanisms. Indeed, the state managers and administrators continue to expand their functions and their formal legal and bureaucratic organization.[26] The use and understanding of the term "the state" must be able to take these aspects into account if successful challenges are to be organized. Indeed, an understanding of how "the state" operates to transform class issues and political disaffection into problems that can be dealt with through an expanded "social problem apparatus" of professionals and bureaucrats is essential to all class-based oppositional organizing.[27]

Illustrations of the extension of state rule can be found in the areas of patriarchy and racism, to mention only some of the salient, component features of ruling in Canada.[28] Those in government have, in turn, started to recognize these problems and have developed strategies for "re-dressing" them (job creation programs targeted for women, multiculturalism, programs for immigrant women, etc.). This has allowed government officials, their managers and bureaucratic representatives, to insert themselves increasingly in the lives of various communities. These are important areas for analytic investigation. How these everyday activities of ruling are carried out in relation to community organizations needs to be analyzed and understood. This collection of papers begins such investigations; *Part 2* in particular addresses the extension of social and regulatory mechanisms into areas previously not integrated into state rule.

The issue of the relation between broad social structures and the everyday level at which people live their lives is often characterized as the "macro" and "micro" problem where the two levels of understanding do not meet or are deliberately kept separate. That is, the "macro" analyses of the state (e.g., capitalist logic of production in general) do not necessarily relate to the "micro" analyses of everyday work activities.[29] This area is also investigated by some of our contributors who seek to show how the mandated courses of action by the state are held in place. Precisely how this interrelation of local and "macro" operates needs to be addressed if there are to be advances in this problem area. Indeed, the inability to bridge this gap is of some significance if community organized challenges to state rule are to benefit from analyses of the state.

There is, then, no clear consensus among analysts in general or among the contributors to this book about the nature of "the state," including "the Canadian state," and the way in which this concept is used. Some contributors conceptualize the state as being over and above people, while others refer to a set of social relations. In this collection, therefore, we take the usage of the term as a problem to be investigated empirically. This involves examining the work of different levels of state officials from the various departments and programs, and how they have and are increasingly inserting themselves into the everyday lives of people to regulate production and reproduction.[30] There is a pressing need to understand their impact on the various forms of community organization in order to be able to challenge them. The view of the state as problematic is illuminated by the case studies in this book. An evaluation of "the state" is made in the conclusion where we look at how "the state" works, historically, in different sites and regions, and at various levels.

Community Organization and the State

The focus of the contributors in this book is on the relation between the different forms of community organizing and the Canadian state. The aim is to understand empirically how this interaction works from the perspective of those involved in different kinds and forms of community organizing. Our overall intention is to probe beneath the surface of the community organizations and their relation to the Canadian state. We want to show *how* the different kinds of interactions, agreements, conflicts, struggles and confrontations have led to the general kind of community organization and state involvement that analysts and activists take for granted. This also involves our contributors in revealing the oppressive existing conditions and contradictions in which they find themselves in their work.

We need to come to terms with the different kinds of community organizing taking place in relation to the state. A striking resemblance exists between the various forms of community organizing taking place and the routine administration of state authorities, be it in community economic development, community job creation programs, ethnic and immigrant communities, the women's community, the gay community, the environmental community, or a fishing community. The problem here is not simply one of discovering the relationship between these forms of community organizing and the different government practices, but also of explaining how they are and continue to be entwined. These are aspects which are drawn out of the "case studies."

The descriptions of different kinds of organizing included in this book also raise the dilemma of characterizing the sorts of reform strategies that are effective or ineffective with the various levels and kinds of government personnel. Contributors raise concerns over the use of such techniques as participation in government programs, making demands on or for particular state services, and outright resistance to government policies and programs. In other words, how do certain methods of local organizing come to be understood as successful for those involved with the Canadian state, while others are characterized as unsuccessful. The diverse methods of Canadian state regulation (the ideas or knowledge behind them and the practices they carry out) are also of particular interest since they relate to an array of community-organized challenges (both ideas and practices) in different settings. The state anticipates and regulates the administrative efforts of community groups. This process of regulation may include stipulations to community organizations around state funding, court and legal restraints, as well as the use of the police including the secret police. The general problem investigated here concerns the kind of state regulation imposed on community challenges. For example, do community-organized challenges around social reproduction issues (such as education or anti-racism) have fewer restraints imposed on them than issues pertaining to production (such as in a fishing community)? Indeed, is it possible for community organizations to successfully challenge state repression? What is the role of Canadian nationalism in managing community organizations? These are some of the problems addressed in this collection.

One important implication of the individual inquiries assembled here concerns the potential for building an egalitarian and democratic cooperative movement for social and political change within Canada's social formation. Is such a movement possible, given the array of community organizing efforts? Does it even make sense to organize such a movement using the knowledge that is assumed in constructing a "community" in relation to the state? What might be the response of state officials to building such a movement? These questions also raise the problem of the extent and limits of state regulation which needs to be considered.

In drawing together these papers we have not attempted in any way to be comprehensive, simply to present a range of available experiences. There are glaring omissions, the most significant of which is the absence of any studies from Quebec. We are aware of the lively climate of political activism and social action that exists there, but material documenting this has not been accessible to us. The complex relations between both francophone and anglophone Quebeckers and the different levels of government operating nationally and in the "province" is a study in itself, and not one which we have been able to represent here.

We have, in our organization of the collection, deliberately avoided putting women's issues in a separate section, although the reader will notice that many of the papers deal explicitly with women's experience and women's issues. These issues and experiences are taken up in relation to the more general problems (for example, conceptualizing "the community" and "the state") and processes (for example, the extension of bureaucratic and coercive mechanisms) that we have identified. Our organizational strategy is consistent with our call for re-examining concepts and categories (such as the community and the state) which have served to limit, rather than open up, our ability to explore the lived realities of people's lives in different localities. We feel that gender, race/ethnic and class relations cut across, and are very much a part of, the general problems of community organizing.

Logic and Organization of the Book

Since we intend this book to be both an analytical and political exercise, we encouraged the contributors to retain their presence as much as possible in the stories they are telling us. They were urged to clarify their own location and involvement in the activities they describe, so that the reader will gain some appreciation of the process through which the activists/analysts develop their perspective and strategies.

To facilitate reading of this diverse body of material, we have grouped the papers into three sections according to the problematic of community/state relation discussed earlier in the *Introduction*. *Part 1* of this book explores this relationship by examining the concept of "the community" and its relationship to different levels of "the state." The questions raised in this section include: How does the term "community" come about? To whom does it refer? What people and whose work are subsumed under the term? How can the current usage of the term be challenged?

All the authors whose work appears in this section challenge the concept of "community." They are all feminists who have been and are active in the women's movement and other forms of community politics. Not surprisingly, their studies are on women's work and women's relation to "the community." Walker argues explicitly that if we take the standpoint of women, we begin to see that the emergence of the notion of "community" is linked to the separation of the workplace from the household with modern forms of capitalist development. While men increasingly come to dominate the public world of work, in productive activities, women's work is relegated to the household and reproductive activities.

Dehli's research on the interaction between parents and schools at the turn of the twentieth century reveals the gendered and class character of parental involvement in the schools. Middle class women's work, which was later incorporated into the organization of the school as the school-community relations department, has rendered invisible the gendered and class nature of community work. Similarly, Bullock exposes the myth of "community care" in the contemporary context to show how the notion of community, as used by state officials and adopted by the public, subsumes and masks the work that women do without pay. The papers in this section challenge the taken-for-granted usage of "community" and raise alternative perspectives for us in using the term and in participating in social actions.

Part 2 of the book entitled, *State Funding, Bureaucratic Relations and Community Activities*, investigates historical developments in the interactions between "the community" and "the state" in a number of regional and social contexts. Understandably, since these studies document a variety of experiences which occurred at different times, in different social and political settings, and in different regions of the country, the narratives and the authors' perspectives are very diverse. In spite of these differences, however, two major themes emerge.

First, with the progressive development of corporate capitalism and the consolidation of (male) power in the state, social life in different settings—on the "reserve," in small isolated communities, in women's groups and ethnic groups—become increasingly objectified, rationalized and routinized. This theme emerges most clearly in Roberts' study, in which she traces the work of female immigrationists between 1880 and 1920. The other papers echo the development of new ruling practices described by Roberts, and explore the contemporary forms of these practices as they pertain to funding, social and employment programs, many of which are directed at women.

Second, many authors argue that while "the state" is not a neutral body, neither is it completely controlled and dominated by the dominant classes. Certainly, pressures from below (from women, immigrant, and aboriginal groups, for example) have made an impact on social policies and programs, and on the way in which state officials conduct their business with community groups. The authors in this section, then, begin to identify ways in which space can be created within the state apparatus to respond to the needs and demands of subordinate groups. In tracing the history and development of specific programs and groups, the authors also pinpoint some of the tensions and contradictions of working within the confines of state-funded programs.

Part 3 of the book entitled, *Community Struggles and State Regulation*, documents various kinds of community efforts in confronting the state. It is interesting that "the state" is targeted as the enemy when people experience disruptions in their everyday life: when developers threaten the existing arrangements in an urban neighborhood; when racial tension escalates in the city; when industry threatens the living environment; and when the interests of fishermen clash with those of the fishing industry. In each case, "the state" becomes the mediating force in disputes between capital and local citizens. And in each case, "the state" responds differently. These studies pinpoint two things. First, they identify the specific workings of different levels of the state in Canada. Second, they shed light on the different kinds of issues and activities which can be accommodated compared with those which are suppressed by force. They provide concrete examples for activists waging struggles on different fronts to aid in unravelling the intricate dynamics of state power and organizing collective action.

Finally in the *Conclusion* we, the editors, attempt to synthesize the lessons learned from the studies presented in terms of the major problematics of the book. What do these stories tell us about the nature of "the community" and "the state" in Canada? What is an adequate account of the relation between the community and the state which can encompass the diversity of people's experiences? On the basis of the accounts presented, how may we develop alternate ways of thinking and working in our different work sites which do not negate our experiences and the experiences of others? In the end, then, we share with the reader our thinking about these questions as a way of moving our collective struggles forward.

NOTES

1. See Brian Wharf (ed.), *Community Work in Canada*. Toronto: McClelland and Stewart Ltd., 1979.
2. See David W. Minar and Scott Greer (eds.), *The Concept of Community*. Chicago: Aldine Publishing Co., 1969; David B. Clark, "The Concept of Community: A Re-Examination," *Sociological Review* Vol. 21 (3), 1973, pp. 397–416; A. Dawley, *Class and Community*. Cambridge, Mass.: Harvard University Press, 1976; Hubert Campfens (ed.), *Rethinking Community Development in a Changing Society*. Guelph, Ont.: Ontario Community Development Society, 1983; Roger S. Ahlbrandt Jr., *Neighborhoods, People and Community*. New York: Plenum Press, 1984; Patrick Mullins, "Community and Urban Movements," *Sociological Review* Vol. 35 (2), May 1987, pp. 347–369.
3. See D. Chekki (ed.), *Community Development: Theory and Method of Planned Change*. New Delhi: Vikas, 1979; Mike Miller, "Community Organization USA: The View from the Movement," *International Journal of Urban and Regional Research* Vol. 5 (4), 1981, pp. 565–572; Susan Wismer and D. Pell, *Community Profit: Community Based Economic Development in Canada*. Toronto: Is Five Press, 1981; W. Woodworth, *et al.* (eds.), *Industrial Democracy: Strategies for Community Revitalization*. Beverly Hills: Sage, 1985; Kathryn Troy, *Studying and Addressing Community Needs: A Corporate Case Book*. New York: Conference Board Inc., 1985; Stewart E. Perry, *Communities on the Way*. Albany, N.Y.: State University of New York Press, 1987; D.C. Reitzes and D.C. Reitzes, "Alinsky in the 1980s: Two Contemporary Chicago Organizations," *The Sociological Quarterly* Vol. 28 (2), 1987, pp. 265–283.
4. See, for example, A. Downs, *Neighborhoods and Urban Development*. Washington, D.C.: The Brookings Institute, 1981.
5. Such as, W.H. Form and D.C. Miller, *Industry, Labor, and Community*. New York: Harper and Brothers, 1960; W. Kornblum, *Blue Collar Community*. Chicago: University of Chicago Press, 1974; P. Abrams (ed.),

Work, Urbanism and Inequality. London: Weidenfeld and Nicolson, 1978; F.K. Harmston, *The Community as an Economic System.* Ames, Iowa: Iowa State University Press, 1983.

6. One critique of community organizing, that there is no link made between local and national community, is advanced by Wini Breines, in *Community and Organization in the New Left: 1962–1968.* New York: Praeger, 1982, p. 146. If local community organizations want to be successful, then this is dependent on the degree to which they align themselves with or reflect national social movements according to Robert Fisher and Peter Romanofsky (eds.), *Community Organization for Social Change: An Historical Perspective.* Westport, Conn.: Greenwood Press, 1981.

7. Edward Knop, "Alternative Perspectives on Community Impacting: Toward Complementary Theory and Application," *Sociological Inquiry* Vol. 57 (3), Summer 1987, pp. 272–291; J. Lustig, "Community and Social Class," *Democracy* Vol. 1 (2), 1981, pp. 96–111.

8. On the general relationship of the various community approaches and the management of a city (or "local state"), see Cynthia Cockburn, *The Local State: Management of Cities and People.* London: Pluto, 1978; Warren Magnusson, "Urban Politics and Local State," *Studies in Political Economy* 16, Spring 1985, pp. 111–142.

9. See Martha A. Ackelsberg, "'Sisters' or 'Comrades'? The Politics of Friends and Families," in I. Diamond (ed.), *Families, Politics and Public Policy.* London: Longman, 1983, pp. 339–356, especially p. 347; J. Mallenkopf, "Neighborhood Political Development and the Politics of Urban Growth," *International Journal of Urban and Regional Research* Vol. 5 (1), 1981, pp. 15–39; E. Ross, "Survival Networks: Women's Neighborhood Sharing in London before World War One," *History Workshop* Vol. 15 (4), 1983, pp. 4–27.

10. See, for instance: G. Craig, N. Derricourt and M. Loney (eds.), *Community Work and the State*, London: Routledge and Kegan Paul, 1982; M. Loney, *Community Against Government*, London: Heineman, 1983; M. Loney, *The Politics of Greed*, London: Pluto, 1986; F. Lesemann, *Services and Circuses: Community and the Welfare State*, Montreal: Black Rose Books, 1984; R. Lees and M. Mayo, *Community Action for Change*, London: Routledge and Kegan Paul, 1984; J.R. Short, *The Urban Arena: Capital, State and Community in Contemporary Britain.* London: Macmillan, 1984.

11. For instance, Stephen E. Barton, "The Urban Housing Problem: Marxist Theory and Community Organizing," *Review of Radical Political Economics* Vol. 9 (4), 1977, pp. 16–30; S.S. Duncan and M. Goodwin, "The Local State and Restructuring Social Relations: Theory and Practice," *International Journal of Urban and Regional Research* Vol. 6 (2), 1982, pp. 157–185.

12. Barry Bluestone and Bennett Harrison, *Capital and Communities.* Washington, D.C.: The Progressive Alliance, 1980; Barry Bluestone, "Deindus-

trialization and the Abandonment of Community," in J.C. Raines, *et al.*
(eds.), *Community and Capital in Conflict*, Philadelphia: Temple University Press, 1982, pp. 38–61; Harry C. Boyte and Sara M. Evans, "Strategies in Search of America: Cultural Radicalism, Populism and Democratic Culture," *Socialist Review* Vol. 14 (3), 1984, pp. 73–100; M. Castells, *The City and Grassroots*, Berkeley and Los Angeles, California: University of California Press, 1983; S. Lowe, *Urban Social Movements*. London: Macmillan, 1986.

13. J. Cowley, *et al.* (eds.), *Community or Class Struggle?* London: Stage 1, 1977.

14. D. Roussopoulos (ed.), *The City and Radical Social Change*, Montreal: Black Rose Books, 1982; Marlene Pierr-Aggamaway, "Native Women and the State," in J. Turner and E. Lois (eds.), *Perspectives on Women in the 1980s*, Winnipeg: University of Manitoba Press, 1983, pp. 66–73; A. Tanner (ed.), *The Politics of Indianness*, St. John's, Newfoundland: Institute of Social and Economic Research, 1983; Constance P. deRoche and John E. deRoche (eds.), *"Rock in a Stream": Living with the Political Economy of Underdevelopment in Cape Breton*, St. John's, Newfoundland: Institute of Social and Economic Research, 1987; Jean Panet-Raymond, "Community Groups in Quebec: From Radical Action to Voluntarism for the State," *Community Development Journal* Vol. 22 (4), 1987, pp. 281–286; Steven Epstein, "Gay Politics, Ethnic Identity: The Limits of Social Constructionism," *Socialist Review* Vol. 17 (3 and 4), 1987, pp. 9–54; Nancy Adamson, Linda Briskin and Margaret McPail, *Feminist Organizing for Change*. Toronto: Oxford University Press, 1988.

15. This argument is made by Raymond Williams, "Toward Many Socialisms," *Socialist Review* Vol. 16 (1), 1986, pp. 45–65.

16. It is not the purpose of this project to engage in a theoretical debate about "the state." Nor is our interest in arriving at a definite theory. As part of the overall aim of this book, the focus here is to begin investigating how managers and administrators of the state actually go about doing their duties in relation to the various forms of community organization. The emphasis is on the kind of assumptions that analysts make about those who manage the state in Canada, without offering yet another summary of the literature on the state.

17. See Roxana Ng, *The Politics of Community Services*. Toronto: Garamond Press, 1988, p. 89.

18. Leo Panitch (ed.), *The Canadian State: Political Economy and Political Power*. Toronto: University of Toronto Press, 1977. A more recent review of the literature on the state has been done by Paul Stevenson, "The State in English Canada: The Political Economy of Production and Reproduction," *Socialist Studies/Études Socialistes*, 1983, pp. 88–128; and Vincent diNarcia, "Social Reproduction and a Federal Community," *Socialist Studies/Études Socialistes: A Canadian Annual*, 1984, pp. 196–210.

19. See for example, Leroy Little Bear, Menno Boldt, and J. Anthony (eds.), *Pathways to Self-Determination: Canadian Indians and the Canadian State*, Toronto: University of Toronto Press, 1984; N. Dyck (ed.), *Indigenous Peoples and the Nation-State*, St. John's, Newfoundland: Institute of Social and Economic Research, 1985. On the more general question of the relation of society and the state, Clastres argues that "it isn't possible for the state to arise from within primitive society," in his *Society Against the State*. New York: Urizen Books, 1977, p. 181. For a summary of the discourse of the state in anthropology, see Christine Ward Gailey, "The State of the State in Anthropology," *Dialectical Anthropology* Vol. 9 (1), 1985, pp. 65–89.

20. See the work of A. Cawson, *Corporatism and Welfare*. London: Heineman, 1982; A. Cawson and P. Saunders, "Corporatism, Competitive Politics and Class Struggle," in R. King (ed.), *Capital and Politics*. London: Routledge and Kegan Paul, 1983, pp. 8–27.

21. For example, see Charles Bright and Susan Harding, "Processes of Statemaking and Popular Protest: An Introduction," in C. Bright and S. Harding (eds.), *Statemaking and Social Movements*. Ann Arbor: University of Michigan Press, pp. 1–15.

22. One such example is by Patricia Morgan, "From Battered Wife to Program Client: The State's Shaping of Social Problems," *Kapitalistate* 9, 1981, pp. 17–39.

23. Ng, *op. cit.*, p. 89.

24. See also Bertrand Bodie and Pierre Birnbaum, *The Sociology of the State*. Chicago: University of Chicago Press, 1983.

25. In reference to the Canadian government and state policies surrounding fishing, Clement makes the general argument, "It would be difficult to find any aspect of fishing not regulated and/or subsidized . . ." in his *Struggle to Organize*. Toronto: McClelland and Stewart, 1986, p. 59.

26. See, Jeanne Kirk Laux and Maureen Appel Molot, *State Capitalism: Public Enterprise in Canada*. Ithaca: Cornell University Press, 1988; Marjorie G. Cohen, *Free Trade and the Future of Women's Work*. Toronto: Garamond Press, 1987.

27. See Morgan, 1981, *op. cit.*

28. Eileen Boris and Peter Bardaglio, "The Transformation of Patriarchy: The Historic Role of the State," in I. Diamond (ed.), *Families, Politics and Public Policy*, London: Longman, 1983, pp. 70–93; Zillah Eisentstein, "The State, the Patriarchal Family, and Working Mothers," in I. Diamond (ed.), *Families, Politics and Public Policy*, London: Longman, 1983, pp. 41–58; M. Eichler, "Women, Families and the State," in J. Turner and E. Lois (eds.), *Perspectives on Women in the 1980s*. Winnipeg: University of Manitoba, 1983, pp. 113–127; Frances Fox Piven, "Women and the State: Ideology, Power and the Welfare State," *Socialist Review* Vol. 14 (2), 1984, pp. 11–19.

29. John Holloway and S. Picciotto (eds.), *State and Capital: A Marxist Debate*. London: Edward Arnold, 1978.

30. The argument that the state is a relation of production is made by Philip Corrigan, Harvie Ramsay and Derek Sayer, "The State as a Relation of Production," in P. Corrigan (ed.), *Capitalism, State Formation and Marxist Theory*. London: Quartet, 1980, pp. 1–25. See also Philip Corrigan and Derek Sayer, *The Great Arch*. Oxford: Basil Blackwell, 1985.

Part 1:

Community and State:
Problematical Concepts
and Relations

Reproducing Community
The Historical Development of
Local and Extra-Local Relations[*]

Gillian Walker

The Problem of Community

This paper seeks to locate concepts such as "community" and "community economic development" in the broad historical and structural context in which they have been developed, rather than treating them in the conventional way as descriptive terms which pose some problems with regard to accurate definition or usage. I wrote it first as a way to pull together reflections and readings that would provide a framework for thinking about "the community." This was a practical concern which arose for me as I attempted to work with community groups and teach courses in community work and models of community. It became a compelling concern when I began to confront issues that relate particularly to the increasingly popular area of community economic development.

My need to problematize these terms arises from a recognition that the way the discourse (that is the work, talk and textual representation which is shared, circulated, practised and taught) on community development and organization takes place makes it difficult to see and think about issues that relate to gender, class, race and indeed, the actual definition of community itself. I was alerted to this difficulty by trying to fit my own experience as an activist and organizer in the women's movement into the theoretical framework available in the discourse on community in the early 1980s. The conventional literature was often written

---

[*]Leslie Bella, Richard Cawley, Ted Jackson, Maurice Moreau and the students in the 1986 Models of Community Seminar at the Carleton University School of Social Work made helpful comments on the first draft of this paper. My thanks goes to them and to my co-editors of this volume, for their input and suggestions.

in a manner so abstract as to render neutral, objective and gender-free every concept or activity involved. The massive mobilization of women around political and social issues and the extensive organization of alternative services and structures such as sexual assault centers, transition houses, health collectives and women's studies programs which came out of the consciousness raising of the early movement days did not, according to mainstream community discourse, take place in the community. Nor are the daily concerns of women who must hunt for suitable housing, childcare, quality schooling for their children regardless of ethnic origins, and safety in the streets, present as a discernible feature of the discourse. What then, I had to ask myself, is "the community" and who inhabits it?

These concerns were magnified when I came to consider the rapidly emerging focus on community economic development. Though virtually invisible, women are assumed to be present in the community, in families at least. The economy, however, is identified with the workplace and with skills and attributes which women and men alike have learned to see as male-oriented. The "economy" has been conceptualized as somehow separate from and outside the community; current strategies are concerned with putting it back, developing business and industrial concerns centered and maintained at the local level. In doing so, community economic development threatens to reproduce in the community the divisions of class, gender and race which have their roots in the organization of wage relations hitherto divorced from notions of home and family.

To find a way of addressing these concerns involves me in problematizing each of the concepts which make up the term. The concept of "community" has properties which provide a way of thinking about and working which selects out a particular understanding of the actual, everyday activities and situations of people's lives and theorizes them in a way which then obscures any other understanding we might come to. To approach the term "economic" in a way which does not "take as explanation the very thing which is to be explained" (to paraphrase Marx), is to begin to question a social organization which splits off and treats as separate the social, political and economic aspects of people's lives. This approach presumes a division of public and private and assigns differentiated power and value to each sphere. Although I do not propose to devote time in this paper to a consideration of the properties of the term "development" *per se* I want to point out that, as critics have noted elsewhere,[1] "development" assumes a number of highly ethnocentric and androcentric values about the quality and superiority of "progress." This implies that societies not organized on an industrial model and in capitalist forms are necessarily backward, primitive and undeveloped.

I want to take up the terms from my own location as a woman, for women, outside the discourse which has been put together from the relevancies of those who construct it, who occupy positions which implicate them in the ideological processes of ordering, administering and ruling society. It seems that we cannot divorce notions of community, or indeed economy, from a broader frame of reference without thereby losing the significance of the situations people face at the local level in their daily lives. In arguing that these are problematic terms I hope to show that the way we conceptualize certain features of our social organization as concerned with "community" and others with "economy," provides for practices and courses of action which not only obscure any other approach but also silence and render invisible (or of limited and particular visibility) women and other marginalized groups.

This is a different approach from one which studies marginalized populations to discover how to reinsert them into the discourse on community. It seeks to explicate our marginality in terms of the broader historical processes which have determined both the marginalization itself and our ability to conceptualize and comprehend it in our everyday experience. To understand how this can be so involves an understanding of how that ideological method of thinking is organized and has its basis in material existence, in changes in capitalist forms of production and regulation, and their impact on our lives at the local level. A recognition of the broader framework obscured by notions of community provides us with potential directions for how we might see and act differently, and implies different aims and strategies for those concerned with social action and social change at the local grassroots level.

Antecedents of Modern Notions of Community

I do not propose here to undertake an elaborate exploration of the impact of the development of externalized modes of production, regulation and control which would more fully account for the ideological features of class rule.[2] For the purpose of this paper I have used available historical work[3] to sketch in the briefest linaments necessary to make an argument about the antecedents of modern notions of community.

Whereas concepts of public and private realms have been with us from the time of the Greeks, foraging and hunting-gathering societies did not have these distinctions. In these societies, kinship systems insured survival and provided for the enforcement of social obligations. Political authority was seldom situated beyond the boundaries of the tribe or caste and systems of representational decision making were rare. Leaders tended to be those who were best able to accomplish the activity to be undertaken; authority and power resided in ability. This was not seen as a political matter; it implied responsibility rather than privilege. Both men and women in such systems could potentially occupy leadership positions and be fully involved in decision making and organization.[4]

Agricultural forms of productive enterprise allowed for different notions of property, possessions and the production of surpluses which could lead to the acquisition of wealth. Collier suggests that it is under such circumstances that politics—"the representation of one group by another, or the power of one group or class over another" comes about.[5] It is in this form of productive organization, Engels and others have proposed,[6] that we see women emerging as a form of property, as possessions valuable for their ability to produce the next generation to whom property can be passed. Their sexuality must therefore be controlled to ensure the legitimacy of heirs. Yet, even here women are integral to the productive enterprise, not just for the maintenance of kinship ties and inheritance patterns, but also for their work in producing the subsistence and surplus on which the mode of production is based. Women under such systems are often farmers and traders in their own right, and little separation exists between the public and private at the social and economic levels, even where political systems may become increasingly centralized and organized on class lines dominated by men.

The most familiar form of this mode, from which many of our traditions and institutions arise, is that of the feudalism of medieval Europe. It is to this form, or to a romanticized version of it, that early exponents of the ideal of community life tended to allude. Feudal relations were of necessity built on mutual obligations, interdependence and bonds. These relations created often complex webs of obligation that articulated the local to the central in terms of the rights of liege lords to claim goods, taxes, services and fighting men from their vassals. The production unit was that of the household, and divisions of labor which existed between women and men were not ones which strictly segregated women from the production and trading of subsistence and surplus. Political forms tended to exclude women from certain aspects of the public domain except in exceptional circumstances. Women of the dominant class, however, often had access to and wielded power by virtue of their position in the familial organization of economic relations and as managers of large productive enterprises centered in the household. The organization of such households extended beyond immediate family to include kin, retainers, apprentices, craft workers, farm workers, and so on.

As capitalist forms developed, initially in very localized sites of production, expansion of market needs led to an increasing centralization of economic control in the mercantile centers where finance and trading were focused. The centralization of economic control was closely tied to a political apparatus which sanctioned and supported it. It can also be seen to have its social correspondence in the centralization of the activities of the dominant classes.[7] The rise of capitalism and the breaking down of the rigid social relations of feudalism led to a situation where class boundaries were permeable and the acquisition of wealth allowed for an expanded middle class, the upper echelons of which rivalled the older aristocratic upper classes in wealth and power. This led to a time of intense reordering of the internal stratifications of the ruling class and an intensification of the centralized nature of its locus of power. What we can see in Western cultural forms in the late eighteenth and the nineteenth centuries is the increasing differentiation of the urban and rural with the characteristic juxtaposition of the squalor and sophistication of the city and the bucolic innocence of pastoral life, the separation of "town" and "country." Comedies of manners, novels and biographies focusing on style, form, fashion, "the season," the making of successful marriages and the doing of "good works" show how the so-called private (social) world, which appears to modern sensibilities as trivial, silly and riddled with pretensions and snobbery, was intricately connected to both economic and political structures and largely managed and produced in the activities of women of the dominant classes.

What was accomplished here in a lasting manner that can be seen in societies influenced by European and particularly British models is part of an increasingly translocal organization of the dominant classes. Members of these groups may own property, industrial plants, land holdings and so on in particular areas but they send their children to schools and universities outside the area, and travel to other dwellings and to fashionable centers for business, social, leisure and cultural activities. Whereas once the base of wealth and power lay in landholdings or local industrial sites, in the late twentieth century control is increasingly concentrated in corporate and transnational conglomerates centered in the finance capitals of the world. Working-class people may move between locations in search of work (and thus may be part of the increasing "mobility" often cited as a feature of Canadian life) but their employment and living patterns tend to be restricted to the local level.

It is also the development of capitalist forms and the breakdown of feudal bonds that, as Smith suggests, externalizes relations of interdependency into generalized, yet distinctive relations of exchange between money and commodities. In this process the individual is constituted as a free agent in market relations, whether as capitalist or as wage laborer. In destroying feudal relations and creating the autonomous individual, capitalism also creates the conditions for a civil society operated through democratic processes.[8]

Smith points to two difficulties which prove to be barriers to the full experience of equal participation in democratic processes. One is the class differences which underlie and radically modify the social and political effects of egalitarian principles and forms of government. The other is the recognition, disclosed by taking the standpoint of women that: "The universe of individuals thus created is a universe of men and not of women."[9]

The separation of household and workplace that took place during the process of the industrialization of labor and the relegation of women and their domestic labor to an increasingly privatized "home" means that the constitution of the individual worker, like that of the wage, conceals an actual relation between domestic labor and the individual worker in the productive process. This presupposes an organization of women's work in the home which thus appears as personal services to the worker which are not directly articulated to the market process.[10]

Recent analyses from a Marxist-feminist perspective have developed this understanding of women's domestic labor and its relation to their participation in the paid labor force. While such an analysis illuminates the situation of wage labor for women and men, it does not sufficiently account for the different and specific relations of middle-class women and men. Here the individual, participating in the appropriation of the means of production, also has to be "reproduced" on a daily basis through the domestic labor performed in the home. This presumes relations based on what Zaretsky has called "the individual family"[11] where the individuality of the wife as a civil person is subsumed under the person of her husband. As the transfer and consolidation of capital ceased to depend entirely on transgenerational mechanisms of marriage and inheritance and was organized in corporate, specialized, capital-holding trusts, joint stock companies and so on, the relation of women to the family and "the internal structure of appropriation and the relation of domestic labour to these have also been modified . . . [A] radical separation between the company or corporation and the . . . middle class family emerges."[12] Under these newer forms of economic organization, property relations are increasingly externalized and divorced from the local organization of household, family and community. Middle-class women become subordinate to or invested in the occupational career of a husband, which provides them with the means to maintain status for themselves and their children. This in turn involves a relation based on control of appropriate space in which to raise children and the development of suburban locations in which the features that mark and maintain class relations can be reproduced.[13]

State Intervention

What becomes apparent in the foregoing discussions of the development of capitalist forms is that although capitalism is characterized as being a mode of production, the mode of production is itself underpinned by processes of reproduction considered merely "natural" and left largely untheorized by political economists until taken up in recent feminist work.[14] This theoretical lacuna results in a conception of economic forces as somehow being neutral, objectified and gender-free, yet at the same time a male preserve.

In the tensions surrounding production and reproduction we see the roots of what Ursel describes as a fundamental contradiction in capitalism, that between the short-term interests of the extraction of surplus for immediate profit and accumulation, and the long-term interests of the dominant class and society as a whole in the reproduction of the conditions under which such extraction of surplus can take place.[15] In other words there is nothing intrinsic to the production-for-profit system that allows for the costs of maintaining the living situations which are necessary for people to continue to produce. In theory at least, and in fact in many cases, both historic and current, when a labor supply is used up or worn out, capital can move on to or import fresh sources. Ursel argues that it was only certain periods of chronic shortage of labor which brought about the recognition of the need to regulate the appetites of the market in the long-term interest of the survival of the system.[16]

The process of regulation involved the increasing intervention of government and the creation of "welfare state" policies designed to ameliorate some of the more gross excesses of short-term production imperatives in favor of longer-term conditions favorable to the continuation of a stable and adequate workforce. An analysis of the complex relation of different mechanisms of government and state formations to aspects of this regulating role at the international, national, provincial and regional levels is beyond the scope of this paper. What is important to take into account here is a way of understanding state relations and practices which will allow us to see that although the state is not a neutral arbitrator between competing interests, as liberal democratic philosophy would have us believe, neither is it merely a monolithic apparatus for coercion and social control.

Welfare provisions designed to improve the conditions under which the capitalist enterprise goes forward have often been won as the result of fierce and continued struggle on the part of organized labor, reform groups and other constituencies. The terms of the struggle, however, have been laid down and, in the main, controlled by state practices. These practices include the objectified ideological forms through which conceptual processes provide for policy initiatives and actions.[17] The forms of individual and organized participation sanctioned by the state as part of the "legal relations revolving around the idea of citizenship and the mechanism of the contract"[18] are also instances of such practices.

The importance of the capitalist state, as Duncan and Goodwin and others[19] have pointed out, lies not so much in what it does but in how it does it. The operational features of democracy, such as the franchise and representative parliamentary politics, transform crucial socio-economic relations and differences between social groupings (such as those of classes, sexes and races) into legal relations between abstract, atomized and supposedly individual, equal and identical citizens. This form of citizenship is most developed in social democratic welfare states where at least a tendency toward political equality is present. To deny this tendency would be to posit a "crude ideological determinism where the ruling class simply and easily fills the heads of the working class with its own ideas."[20] Notions of citizenship which separate social relations from political relations are essential to the operation of the capitalist state.

Forms of representation and participation have been in existence, of course, since pre-capitalist times. The issue, in relation to an understanding of current notions of community and state is: whose interests are represented in a system in which presumptions of individuality and individual rights of citizenship subsume, under legal relations and ideological forms, divisions of class, sex and race. The state or, perhaps more accurately, various state formations,[21] are key constituents of a ruling apparatus and play a key role in the formulation of the organizational and conceptual practices through which ideological hegemony is achieved.[22]

Contemporary theories of the nature and operation of the capitalist state are frequently concerned with discussions of the autonomy or lack of autonomy of differing levels of government from other parts of the ruling apparatus, especially those which control the major economic institutions.[23] What seems to me to be important to understand in the context of community development is that the state, centralized at a national level or decentralized and possibly more autonomous (or open to influence) at the local level must mediate, negotiate, order and ultimately rule over those arenas which have been divided into the social, economic and political. The state must perform its tasks where these arenas intersect, in the everyday local world in which people exist as actual, embodied subjects and where they carry out the daily activities in which they produce and reproduce themselves. These are activities that are directly organized in terms of gender, class and racial dimensions, though state policies and practices obscure such structural divisions. An understanding of both what the state does and how it does it would seem therefore to be fundamental to an assessment of both the constraints and possibilities for action and change at the local level.

Rethinking Community and Community Economic Development

My attempts to understand the historical processes which have led to the development of current uses of terms such as "community" and "community economic development," has involved us in an inquiry into how advanced capitalist forms of economic organization structure both the material features of our lives—how we earn a living, where and how we live and so on—and the way our lives are ordered and controlled. How this structuring takes place is not immediately visible in the ways we have developed and been taught to understand our lives. What we take for granted as natural, eternal arrangements of society, such as "community," "family," "the economy," are in fact specific results of the organizational process which construct these arrangements as such but which are themselves obscured from view.

To grasp this in terms of our understanding and experience of community, family, economy and the like, we need to see the relation of the local, where we live our "embodied" lives, to the extra-local. This involves more than an attention to central state and governmental forms. It involves understanding how society is ruled and how the world economy is organized from abstracted, extra-local points. Included in the process are multicorporate and transnational institutions operating at a local level to gather power and profit extra-locally and to provide conditions for capital production. This form of ruling actually organizes, disorganizes, reorganizes people's lives both geographically and emotionally. The relation of the state and different levels of government to this process is thus a complex one. The imperatives and relevancies of the state have to be understood; municipal and regional governments have particular interests in managing the "local," and national governments must co-ordinate it with the demands of a national economy and an internationally-organized system. Governmental forms may be more or less centralized or decentralized, but corporate forms are only centralized in a global sense, which gives them their extra-local character.

I am not meaning to suggest here, of course, that we do not live our lives in certain very specific relationships to each other and in particular locations, but only that the form these relationships take is given shape and determined by the broader structures. Feminist research and scholarship have been instrumental in tracing the influence of these broader structures on the directly experienced aspects of our lives. We have come to understand that the family is not just the natural and inevitable way for women and men to live together and raise children, but is also an institution which formalizes the work process involved in reproducing the relations of class and gender in a capitalist system. We have also been able to see that individualism and individual rights are not merely natural expressions of human existence but the specific outcome of material conditions which have developed in such a way as to deny, or rather perhaps to conceal behind rhetoric, the fact that these rights do not apply equally to all.[24]

It is also possible to see that our lives are not in any simple way organized communally. In fact, they are structured by wage and commodity relations and by ideological forms so that common features are actually experienced individually and the commonality of the features of that experience are obscured. Individuality, the "individual family," the legal relations of supposedly equal, identical citizens, methods of participation and franchise via the electoral system and so on, all reinforce this social isolation. This structuring of atomies, or individuals, arises out of the so-called free market requirements for labor power and produces not only the requirement for democratic and representational rights but also forms of democracy that are in fact controlled by those in power. The economic organization is responsible for the fragmented, isolated and alienated character of so many people's lives. Most emotional satisfaction and fulfilment is relegated to the so-called private realm, through consumption of leisure and pleasure commodities and most of all through intense personal relations within couples and families, all of which are deemed to compensate for the manifold denial of human needs in the service of profit.

The particular form of the family as we know it is one mechanism whereby social needs for interaction, interdependence and relatedness are taken into account. It is the family, and more particularly the work of women within the family, that is charged with providing both the production and experience of individuality (within the framework of gender, class and race) and the care required by those not able to look after themselves. Increasingly, as welfare state provisions designed to relieve the household of total responsibility break down or are dismantled, more and more caring functions fall to the family, ostensibly as part of a network of personal concern represented by "the community" in which "the family" is located.

Here, at last, we can begin to put in place an understanding of community that goes beyond the natural acceptance of the term as describing a geographic area or functional interest group. We can trace the concern with community to the same source as the breakdown of particular feudal or feudal-style relations and the emergence of social relations based on a wage economy. The term itself, in the sense in which we have come to use it, arises in the deliberations of philosophers and early sociologists such as Comte and Tönnies and relates to concerns with ways to replace or create forms of connectedness and social cohesiveness in the face of the upheavals and massive social dislocation engendered by the industrial revolution.[25] It has developed in a number of ways, both through the work of sociologists and allied academics concerned with definition, meaning and uses, and in the work of reformers and organizers concerned to put in place organizational forms at the local level which would provide ordered, rational and hopefully humane living conditions of the poor and working class.

The ideological properties of the term community stem from what it provides by way of both conceptual and practical co-ordination; ways of thinking about and working with the fabric of people's lives that name rather than explicating their experience. Disputes over the definition of community can thus be seen to be disputes over what is to be named as such, not over what is actually explained or made evident by the term.[26] My argument here is that this mystification arises because of the disjunction between the actual and the abstract which the conceptual work of professionals mediates and transforms. This ideological usage of the term community has been the stuff of top-down efforts by the state and various related apparatus to put back at the local level what capitalist forms abstract. This is done out of a necessity to "capture," to organize and administer local aspects of people's lives, loyalties, connections, living arrangements, in forms that can be managed and related to, such as citizen participation, the formation of interest groups, self-help projects and the like. In doing so, however, state formations are responding not only to their own imperatives for the management of dissent and the manufacture of consent, but also to the claims that people make to create their own connections and organize to meet their own needs out of adversity, necessity and self-interest. This can be seen as an expression of what Gough identifies as the contradiction of a welfare state which simultaneously embodies tendencies to enhance social welfare, to develop the power of individuals, to exert control over the blind play of market forces; and tendencies to repress and control people, adapting them to the requirements of the capitalist economy.[27] So at best "community" appears as a contested category which provides for an arena of struggle over those needs of people which fall outside the workplace.

An analysis of the ideology of community from the standpoint of women and from the kind of critical perspective put forward by Bryson and Mowbray and others[28] suggests that the notion is part of a socially-constructed, abstract and rationalized method of ruling which, while it does not represent an organized elitist conspiracy to bamboozle, is in fact a mode of domination in the interests of the continued accumulation of capital and those in position of ownership and control. The notion of community, when presented in the neutral, objective, apolitical, ahistorical manner of ideology, obscures under the guise of individual and group interests the whole network and structuring of people's lives in terms of class, gender and racial features that are embedded in particular relations of production. It also depoliticizes issues, or excludes those which are unequivocally political in nature.

In terms of gender, even a brief look at the discourse which surrounds community indicates that the notion is as saturated with gendered features as any other aspect of society and that its seeming neutrality discloses, as elsewhere, a male perspective.[29] This is despite the fact that women have been an integral part of community at every level of leadership, participation and presence and have through their work in the family, a particular relation to the local setting.[30] Wilson even goes so far as to suggest that:

> . . . 'community' is an ideological portmanteau word for a reactionary, conservative ideology that oppresses women by silently confining them to the private sphere without so much as even mentioning them. Moreover it attempts to confine them, or at least implicitly to define them, at the same time as economic policy and social change, pushes them into the public sphere of paid work and yet simultaneously removes the last state props that supported them in their work in 'the community', that is, in the family. As a first step towards a greater understanding of what

women's position in the community actually is, I suggest we abandon the
word community altogether—it is only one of the veils of illusion in which
we are cocooned.[31]

This concern with the effects of "community" as ideology on our ability to conceptualize the "private" realm returns us to the initial questions raised about notions of the economy. We are dealing with an economic organization which subsumes and subordinates women's work in the home and the labor force, and with terms which interfere with our ability to recognize this fact. Given this analysis we can see that the basic assumptions of movements such as that of community economic development must be questioned and examined rigorously before they are embraced as an unproblematic solution to the local impact of current shifts and changes in the capitalist system.[32]

Such an examination must also include a discussion, not undertaken in this paper, of the role of community workers and consultants who provide the interface between state concerns and grassroot struggles.

As it stands now, community economic development appears as an attempt to restore various forms of small commodity capitalism to a local level of control through a variety of mechanisms such as community-owned development corporations, worker co-ops and so on. This, in some major ways, could provide for a reconceptualization and reconstruction of the social, political and economic arenas and better understanding of their integral connectedness. The boundaries between public and private, macro and micro, would need to be challenged and dissolved, however, if a genuine reconceptulization of work to include the work of women and the situation of other marginalized groups were to take place.

What has been raised here is a series of questions, rather than a set of solutions to the dilemmas posed by the need to understand concepts such as "community." The discussion does, however, indicate some possible directions, strategies and areas for exploration. At the very least it proposes a role for those of us with the opportunity to reflect and analyze, in the critical task of redefining from the base rather than from the top-down, the implications of movements such as community economic development. This reconceptualization must take place if strategies designed to promote economic democracy are to avoid the pitfalls identified here in this consideration of what such terms by definition include and exclude. For women the strategies indicated would further embrace the need to organize together and in alliance with other social movements concerned with peace, the environment and so on. Existing socialist forms of political and economic organization have not radically altered women's situation, for reasons, I would argue, that relate directly to the focus on production and the maintenance of the dichotomies of public and private that beset capitalist forms. This paper is intended to open up a dialogue among those with concerns in the area of community development who want to take part in raising the critical issues for the future of our work as activists and organizers.

NOTES

1. In particular the work of Adele Mueller and Alice de Wolff of the Ontario Institute of Studies in Education has helped my understanding of the ideological properties of development philosophies and practices, particularly in relation to women.
2. D.E. Smith, "Women, Class and Family." In *Women, Class, Family and the State*. Toronto: Garamond Press, A Network Basics Book, 1985.
3. *Ibid.*, A. Bullock, and G.A. Walker, "Historical Themes, Trends and Values." Unpublished mss. (Ottawa: Carleton University, School of Social Work, 1984; K. Dehli, "Community Work and Schooling in the Toronto Board of Education." Unpublished Master's Thesis. O.I.S.E., University of Toronto, 1984; E. Zaretsky, "The Place of the Family in the Origins of the Welfare State." In *Rethinking the Family*, edited by Barrie Thorne with Marilyn Yalom. New York: Longman Inc., 1982; K. Collier, *Social Work with Rural Peoples*. Vancouver: New Star Books, 1984; E. Wilson, "Women, the 'Community' and the 'Family'." In *Community Care: The Family, the State and Social Policy*, Alan Walker (ed.). Oxford: Basil Blackwell and Martin Robertson, 1981.
4. K. Collier, 1984, *op. cit.*
5. *Ibid.*, p. 31.
6. Engels proposed this in *The Origins of the Family, Private Property and the State* (Moscow, Progress Publishers, 1968). See also E. Zaretsky, *Capitalism, Family and Personal Life*. London: Harper Colophon Books, 1976.
7. Here I am using class in a rather loose, descriptive manner which acknowledges the internal stratifications and divisions but recognizes overall Marx's notion of class as a relation to the mode of production.
8. Smith, 1985, *op. cit.*, p. 9. It should be pointed out here that Marx considered this to be a positive and necessary step toward the development of a free alliance of individuals under socialism.
9. *Ibid.*, p. 10.
10. *Ibid.*

11. Zaretsky, 1982, *op. cit.*

12. Smith, 1985, *op. cit.*, p. 12.

13. D.E. Smith, "Women, the Family and Corporate Capitalism," in Marylee Stephenson (ed.), *Women in Canada*. Toronto: New Press, 1973.

14. Marx along with most 'male-stream' theorists tended to see the family as a natural unit outside the realm of production. Feminists of different persuasions have taken this up in different ways, but in general agree on the importance of recognizing the form of the family as socially structured and integrally connected to the productive process.

15. J.E. Ursel, "Toward a Theory of Reproduction." *Contemporary Crisis* 8, 1984, pp. 265–292.

16. *Ibid.*

17. For an explication of one such process see G.A. Walker, "Burnout: From Metaphor to Ideology," *Canadian Journal of Sociology* 11 (1), 1986, pp. 35–55.

18. S.S. Duncan and M. Goodwin, "The Local State and Restructuring Social Relations," *International Journal of Urban and Regional Research* 6(2), 1982, p. 163.

19. *Ibid.*, and also London Edinburgh Week-end Return Group, *In and Against the State*. London: Pluto Press, 1980.

20. *Ibid.*

21. P. Corrigan and D. Sayers, *The Great Arch.* Oxford, New York: Blackwell, 1985.

22. This refers us to the thinking of political analysts such as Gramsci who note the educative role of the state and allied aspects of the ruling apparatus such as schools and the media in bringing about a dominant understanding of how society is constructed and operationalized which enlists us in complying with and collaborating in our own ruling. A. Gramsci, *Selections from the Prison Notebooks*. New York: International Publishers, 1971.

23. This is well summarized in the work of Ng and Klodawski. (R. Ng, *The Politics of Community Services*. Toronto: Garamond Press, 1988 and F. Klodawski, "Accumulation, The State and Community Struggles: Impacts on Toronto's Central Area, 1945–1973." Unpublished Ph.D. Thesis, Queen's University, 1985).

24. Work in the areas of psychiatry and psychology shows that the very structure of individual personality is fundamentally gendered in ways which disadvantage women, ethnic groups, etc.

25. See for example the work of Bullock, in A. Bullock, "Community Care of Severely Handicapped Children at Home: A 'Moment' in the Organization of Women's Work." Unpublished Master's Thesis, Carleton University, 1986; and Wilson, 1981, *op. cit.*

26. This is well covered in R. Plant, *Community and Ideology: An Essay in Applied Social Philosophy*. London: Routledge and Kegan Paul, 1974.

27. F. Klodawski (1985, *op. cit.*) has a particularly useful and penetrating

discussion of the state and local relations in urban, municipal settings, which is too extensive to detail here.

28. See L. Bryson and M. Mowbray, " 'Community': The Spray on Solution," *Australian Journal of Social Issues* 16(4): 255–267, 1981; K. Dehli, "Out of the City Trenches: Some Notes on Analysis of and Practice in Communities." Unpublished mss. Toronto: O.I.S.E., Department of Sociology in Education, 1983.

29. Bullock, 1986, *op. cit.*; R.A. Brandwein, "Toward Androgyny in Community and Organizational Practice," in *Women, Power and Change*, edited by A. Weick and S.T. Vandiver. Washington, D.C.: National Association of Social Workers, Inc., 1982; and Wilson, 1981, *op. cit.*

30. *Ibid.* and Brandwein, 1982, *op. cit.*

31. Wilson, 1981, *op. cit.*, p. 55.

32. G.A. Walker, "Community Economic Development: Self Help Capitalism or Oppositional Base?" *SPAN: Canadian Review of Social Policy* 13, 1985, pp. 65–71.

Women in the Community:
Reform of Schooling
and Motherhood in Toronto[*]

Kari Dehli

Introduction

The term "community" and most forms of community intervention, have assumed the presence of women in the family as available providers of care, nurture, services and particular forms of organizational labour. Women have been, and continue to be, the crucial "cement" holding the community together.[1] Nevertheless, apart from some very important contributions by the women's movement and feminist activists, recent community work strategies in Toronto have for the most part ignored women's experiences in the family and community as starting points for practice.[2] Instead, the work of women in the community is quietly assumed and practically confirmed. In this way community work takes a gendered character.

In this paper I will illustrate how this gendered character of community work has come about and how it works in a particular context. I argue that community work can be understood through detailed empirical analysis of its practices, and the material and historical conditions in which these particular practices arose. My illustrations are drawn from the Toronto Board of Education, which has employed twenty-three community workers since 1975.[3]

The organization of community work around schooling, in the context of a fairly politically progressive school board is perhaps peculiar to Toronto. We could expect in such a context, where community work is focused on parents of children in school, that much of the work would

[*]I want to acknowledge the financial support of the Social Sciences and Humanities Research Council of Canada which makes it possible for me to carry out this research.

explicitly take up questions starting from the experiences of women as mothers. With some isolated exceptions, this has not been the case in this school board. Trying to understand why this is so, even when the majority of community workers are women, has led me to investigate empirically and historically the formation of institutional relationships between parents and schools, and of what is properly considered mothers' responsibilities.

The paper is based on several sources of information and inspiration. For thirteen years in Toronto I have been actively involved in community work, both as a paid worker, as a volunteer on boards of directors of community organizations, and as an interested activist. In 1983 I carried out research for my Master's thesis by interviewing, observing and participating in the activities of community workers employed by the Toronto Board of Education over a seven-month period. Since the Spring of 1985 I have been doing documentary research in the same school board's extensive archival collection. I have focused on documents of the Toronto Home and School Council, established in 1916, as well as on the activities of members of that Council who were elected as school trustees. What I am looking for are the ways in which patterns and assumptions of interaction between parents and schools came to be structured according to a sexual division of wage and domestic labor, including the organizational labor involved in creating and maintaining community. In the conclusion of the paper I suggest that the work of women in Home and School associations historically can be understood as part of women's work in the social organization of class relations and local state formation.

Contemporary Community Work in the Toronto School Board
Community work practice in the Toronto Board of Education since the mid-1970s has proceeded on the assumption that children have two parents, and live in nuclear family households. The other key assumption is that communities actually exist in the world, and not simply in the imagination of policy makers. Based on these assumptions, the Board also assumes that sets of parents within a local area or "ethnic" grouping can represent a community's interest in relation to schooling. Thus, communities are ascribed agencies through forms of representation. In a recent document produced by the coordinator of the Toronto Board's community work department its practice and mandate are described as follows:

> Since 1975, the School-Community Relations Department has worked to increase the involvement of all communities, particularly ethnic commu-

nities, in the Toronto school system, and to service the needs of school and administrative staff in relation to these communities by providing assistance in the development and maintenance of parent groups at the Local School, Area and City levels.[4]

In the policies and practices of community work in this school board, a starting point of the experiences of women as mothers has either not been considered at all, or has been seen as an impediment and counterproductive to the goals of community work intervention.[5] Beginning with community as a unit, a consensus is assumed to exist within it. The job of community workers is to mobilize or develop—whichever the case may be—*parents* to define and build on this consensus, not to explore fundamental contradictions. And yet, community workers agree that it is "mostly mothers" who come out to events and meetings which they organize.[6] When trustees, administrators and community workers talk about the potential benefits of "parent participation" in children's schooling, and about forging a new "partnership" between parents and teachers, it is Mother who is implicitly assumed to be the partner. A document of the community work department referring to a "Partners in Learning" discussion in a Toronto school, states that parents will have "shared what they do to help their children learn; what the *opportunities* for learning are in the home; what the obstacles may be." Teachers, on the other hand, will have "shared ideas about how to help children learn within the home situation: how to use T.V. well; the importance of setting a time for children to read; the importance of sleep and nutrition; how to use the local library and to get books in their own language."[7] All of these may be evaluated as good activities for parents to engage in with their children. Leaving aside such judgments for the moment, what I want to focus on here is the embedded assumption that someone is there, in the home, with time and energy to take up good suggestions on how to supervise and support the child's learning. The ordinary practices of teachers and community workers confirm that this someone is almost always presumed to be the mother.

During interviews with community workers and through observation of different types of meetings—local school, area and city-wide—I became aware that fathers are sought out (or select themselves) for more public and political tasks, such as representing parents on School Board committees. One community worker, a woman, recognized this as a problem,

> The mothers we work with . . . we're not very good at valuing this work. It's still seen as mothers' work. They are struggling to get men involved. Then it will be of higher value. That's not good.[8]

Such recognition was rarely stated by these community workers. For the most part they could not take up "gender" as a central relation around which to organize their work. Nor could they take up the subordinate position of women in the family, or their work as caregivers as relevant in their practice. This is more than ironic as the practices of these community workers presume and depend upon maintenance of the nuclear family form. Taken as a unit, mothers and fathers are thought to act together in the best interest of their children. One community worker, a woman said, "I can't see women's rights as mine. What are they talking about? I don't see it as separate woman, man and child. We're all together."[9] Such comments become more than statements of political beliefs, when we discover that these workers, through their work, have come to know a great deal about the often painful realities of family life of the people with whom they work. Another worker, also a woman, was aware of considerable male violence against women in one of "her" communities. Yet, she felt quite unsupported in her efforts to do something about this. She tried to organize a morning discussion group where these women could discuss their oppressive experiences. But she hastened to add that her "real agenda" was to connect these women to "school stuff" and not "just talk about problems at home."[10] Violence against women in the family lies outside the boundary of what constitutes community work in this case. Recognizing and dealing with this could potentially shatter the already fragile organization of communities through the schools, and challenge the presuppositions of a consensus latently "there" to be developed.

How can we begin to understand the fragmentation of community work practice, such that only a limited part of people's experiences can form the basis for organizing and development? Rather than attempt to locate responsibility or cause with individual community workers—who are doing an outstanding job under very stressful and politically pressured circumstances—I have tried to explore the question historically. In doing so I want to keep in mind that community workers employed by a local school board are working for the state, here the local state. Their work is circumscribed and shaped by existing policies, administrative procedures and structures. There is, as well, a long history of changing practices and discourses about schooling, parenting and proper relations between the two, which have become embedded in the institutional relations of this state organization. Exploring the institutional relations surrounding community work does not negate the participation of community workers as active agents. However, it strikes me that much community-work literature has focused primarily on the work as a set of techniques or tools to be taken up by individuals without much regard for the specific conditions in which the work is to be carried out.

Women and School Reform, 1915 to 1930

As Cynthia Cockburn (among others) has shown, local state institutions such as schools are central in the lives of women.[11] Women consider it an ordinary part of their work to negotiate with housing authorities, welfare offices, obtain daycare services and deal with children's schooling. How has it come to be taken for granted that women are there to hold family and community together? The history of local organizing and reform work by women in and around the City of Toronto public schools, focusing on the period from 1915 to 1930 may provide some answers to this question. Many local state practices pertaining to mothers were put together during this time. In so far as schooling is concerned, between 1916 and 1930 local organizations around many Toronto schools were created by women in the form of home and school associations. During this time a city-wide council to coordinate and propagate the efforts of "Home and School" was established. Organizing efforts were undertaken by women—mothers and a few teachers—and were closely linked to broader movements for urban and social reform, which advocated: peace, women's suffrage, child welfare, public hygiene and greater government efficiency and accountability. The questions I want to explore here are the specific problems in the relations between mothers and schools which they identified and tried to address through their reform work. I am also interested in finding out who these women were, who founded or joined Home and School associations, and what their relations were to other organizations in the city.

By way of situating these questions historically it is helpful to keep in mind that the introduction of compulsory school attendance in Ontario in 1871 constitutes an important mark in the relations between mothers and schooling of children.[12] Compulsory attendance for all children can be seen as a state measure aimed primarily at the urban lower classes, ensuring that their children would stay off the streets, and benefit from organized and supervised instruction. As Houston[13] has pointed out, the Ontario School Attendance Act was not immediately and practically enforceable, but it could be used selectively to intervene in particular cases. From relatively limited beginnings (in terms of resources and personnel at the disposal of school boards), the practical consequences of compulsory attendance were extended in the first decades of this century. Practically the responsibility for ensuring regular attendance rested with the mother, although the father was legally responsible. Men were presumed to be engaged in waged work, while women were assumed to be homemakers and child carers. The realities of family life in the working class were then, as now, quite different.[14]

Women involved in Home and School associations took up the enforcement of regular attendance as one of their main and persistent organizational preoccupations.[15] Agreeing with dominant views on family life and education within early 20th century urban and social reform movements, they considered the proper nurturing and development of children as vital to the creation of responsible citizens, and thus to the survival of Canada as an efficient nation state. The introduction of "progressive" reforms in school was feared useless if the home, and particularly the mother, failed to provide the proper preparation of children before school, and complementary support for regular attendance during the years in school. One of the early leaders of the Toronto Home and School Council explained,

> We have faith in this movement because the home and the school are the rock-bottom foundations of individual and national character, and if these forces do not unite in their efforts to produce the right sort of citizenship the future of this country will fail in its responsibility. I believe in education that educates, education not only for the child but for the adult.[16]

And further,

> We must cultivate and elevate home-life if we would make our nation strong and secure, for as the home is so will the nation be.[17]

Although these women, who formed the first council of Home and School clubs, were not the first or only group to identify problems of citizenship and nation-building, they took up these questions in particular and practical ways, focusing on what, in their eyes, was the critical link between mothers and school. The women who were involved in this work were largely Anglo-Saxon and respectably middle class. One notable exception to this generalization was Ida Siegal, a prominent activist in Jewish education within public schools in this period. Early leaders of the Home and School Council—such as Ada Mary Brown Courtice, Caroline Brown, Edith L. Groves and Mrs. K. Johnson MacTavish— were from, or married into, solid, albeit not always wealthy middle-class families. Caroline Brown was one of the first generation of women in Canada to enter the medical profession. Courtice was the widow of an editor of *The Christian Guardian*; she was a methodist, active suffragist and peace campaigner and had organized and run her own private school in Toronto.[18] Edith Groves had been a teacher in the Toronto public school system, until she married a school principal. Brown, Courtice and Groves were all elected trustees of the Board of Education. Groves became the first woman to chair the Board, and had a school named after her (now Heyden Park Secondary School for girls, the only single sex school in the Toronto public school system).[19]

For these women, and women like them, social and urban reform movements of the early 20th century offered opportunities for political involvement at a time when women were still fighting to obtain the vote. Women who owned property in their own right had been able to participate in School Board and City Council elections for some time. Augusta Stowe Gullen had been elected to the Toronto Board of Education before the turn of the century.[20] Moreover, reform work related to education and child welfare enabled an extension of women's "natural"—even superior—abilities, beyond the confines of the private sphere of the family. This reform work with children was seen as an important mission for women. In the words of Ada Courtice: "To start little children on the right road of general efficiency seems to me the greatest thing women can do."[21]

Like so many of the early 20th century reformers they believed firmly that education was the key to much-needed change. They also believed that they held a valuable and correct knowledge of how "to start little children . . .." Their contribution consisted of ensuring that this knowledge was transmitted to children in schools, and to women—mothers—who did not, in their judgment, already possess it. Home and School Council members themselves took up the second aspect of this reformative educational work, among mothers of soon-to-be or already pupils of Toronto schools. In many ways this work among mothers resembles what we now call community work. In fact, the creation of a "social spirit" in every neighborhood was closely associated with the education for efficient motherhood.[22]

The neighborhood or community was idealized in contrast with the disorder and chaos of urban life. Social reformers, such as those involved in Home and School work, were appalled by the social conditions of the city. They campaigned for public health measures and provision of clean and reasonable housing. Adding to their anxiety was the apparent concentration of "strangers" in the rapidly growing City. The Toronto Bureau for Municipal Research posed the question in 1921: "How shall we deal with the stranger within our gates?" After complaining that "hordes of aliens" from South and central Europe had "poured into our midst," the article goes on,

[T]he community, as a community, has done practically nothing, beyond what it does for the native born, either to understand the alien or to effect a fusion between the native and alien cultures.[23]

Home and School associations represented one form of concerted action among women to shape "community" out of what was perceived as dangerous urban chaos. Before the organization of the Home and School Council in 1916 there were nine local associations in the City, the oldest being the Rosedale Art League started in 1896. By 1921 there were 33 clubs (including four in separate schools), in 1926 there were 54, and in 1930 there were 70 Home and School associations affiliated with the Toronto Council.[24]

The school was an ideal focal point of community in as much as all children were compelled to participate, hence all parents had to ensure their children's school attendance. A female teacher speaking at the March 8, 1921 meeting of the Council was reported to have made a strong plea for schools to be "used for community work," as school buildings belonged to "all citizens irrespective of creed, race or class."[25]

While the creation of a Home and School association around every city school was the goal, particular populations and areas warranted special organizing efforts. In June 1917 the Council established a committee to "study the question of interesting the non-English speaking parents in Home and School work," while it was noted in November 1919 that the "New Canadian Districts in our City" should have special meetings.[26] It is difficult to determine how the "non-English" or "New Canadians" responded to efforts to organize them. But the work must have been difficult, maybe even controversial. An entry in *The Story* a few years later records that an "Extension Committee" was formed in 1925 specifically to carry out programs in "downtown schools, where it seemed impossible or inadvisable to have Associations."[27] It was in these schools that the children of recent immigrants and the poor attended.

A substantial portion of the work with "foreign" adults revolved around broadly defined ideas of citizenship. Evening classes in English and Citizenship Education were offered through the Board of Education and through the Council's own efforts, often in cooperation with the Neighborhood Workers' Association (a group of early social workers). On the topic of citizenship, members of the Council's Citizenship Committee were reported to have addressed 184 "church, school other groups" during a three-month period in 1926![28]

This education for citizenship was not only directed towards "aliens," but also to women who had recently gained the franchise. The Council took on the task of ensuring that women exercised their new responsibility with intelligence. In November 1917 a call went out to all local associations, as well as to religious congregations, to pray for women to receive Divine Guidance "in the performance of this new duty and that they may be enabled to continue to work harmoniously and unitedly for matters concerning home, school and national welfare."[29]

The Home and School Council joined with a number of other groups in their efforts. Originally the Council was formed by the Education Committee of the Toronto Local Council of Women (a chapter of the National Council of Women of Canada). Quickly, formal affiliations were established with the Toronto Women Teacher's Association, the Ontario Education Association, the Children's Aid Society, the Central Ratepayer's Association, the the Neighborhood Worker's Association, and many others. After a few years the Council became an "inside" organization of the Toronto Board of Education, meaning that they would have free access to the use of school space, and would be invited to observe board and committee meetings.[30] Individual supporters or associates included Dr. Horace Britton, Director of Toronto's Bureau for Municipal Research (established in 1914), Professor Peter Sandiford, Professor of Educational Psychology and Director of Educational Research at the Ontario College of Education, University of Toronto, and Dr. Helen MacMurchy, the first Director of the Child Welfare Division in the federal Department of Health. Meetings of the Council were frequently held in the Social Services building of the University, and later in the administrative offices of the Board of Education.[31]

Cooperating with these and other prominent organizations and individuals was central to the reform strategies of Home and School women. The work they carried out in local associations and at the city level was in many ways clearly political. In their records there are frequent references to all-candidates meetings and expressions of congratulations to winning candidates in school board elections (especially when these were members of the Council). While there is criticism from Toronto's conservative school trustees in the 1980s that parent organizations have become unduly political "under the influence of" community workers, the records of the Home and School Council suggest that these were originally very political organizations. Then, as now, candidates in school board elections benefitted from the provision of public forums where they could present their views. Moreover, the Council itself actively promoted candidates who supported their aims.

There were important advantages accruing to the Council and member groups from having candidates they supported elected to the School

Board. Referring to the work of Edith Groves and Ada Courtice, a passage from the 1922 section in *The Story* states it well:

> In the days of small things it meant much to have official recognition from such women and their advice and influence at executive meetings were very valuable.[32]

Working in local Home and School clubs was not in itself sufficient to accomplish necessary changes in schools or families. Central, political coordination and leadership were as necessary then as they are now.

Training Women for Motherhood

While citizenship was a central concern, a related and increasingly important endeavour throughout the 1920s, was the education for parenthood. For all practical purposes parent education was aimed at women as present or future mothers. Women in general had a moral duty to exercise the franchise intelligently and according to their maternal instincts. Mothers, however, had an additional moral and national duty to develop their sons and daughters for citizenship and efficiency. Throughout the 1920s it appears as though the organizational emphasis shifted more and more towards the training of girls and women for motherhood. Explicitly, political efforts were pushed in the background at the beginning of the 1930s. Although this tendency was not without modifications, it represented an important shift from reforming social conditions to educating individual mothers.

Kindergartens were thought to be an excellent way of drawing mothers into the work of the school. Early on in the Council's work, calls went out to headmistresses of kindergartens to invite mothers for tea, thus laying the ground for cooperation with the school, and for development of local associations. It was thought that mothers could pick up many useful ideas about child rearing from watching what went on in the kindergarten. Other direct and indirect methods were also employed to reach mothers.

During the early 1920s Toronto experienced a serious depression. Unemployment was high, wages were low, housing was scarce, crowded and expensive. Frequently all able members of working-class households, including women and children, were engaged in wage labor to ensure the survival of the family.[33] In response to this situation, after a request from the Toronto Trades and Labour Council, Home and School women engaged in direct relief work in targeted schools. They collected and distributed clothing and milk to children in need. While members, such as Ida Siegal, worked tirelessly as chair of the Physical Welfare Committee, there are indications in the Council minutes that relief work was not an end in itself, but a means to "stir up new Home and School Clubs as both incentive and need were present."[34]

Elsewhere the provision of relief was described as a means of maintaining regular school attendance among children of the unemployed. Importantly, relief was only given after a personal visit by a nurse to each child's home verified that the need was real and that the parents could not afford to pay for milk.[35]

There is a strong sense that although members recognized the harshness and injustice of the City's social conditions, the actions they took assumed that education and self-improvement was the way out of poverty. In particular for women, there were repeated assertions that what was needed was household management based on scientific principles, thrift, fresh air and moral virtue. Some women were thought particularly needy. Thus, the Council encouraged translation of the City Medical Health Department's pamphlets into "Jewish [sic] and Italian."[36] A prominent Toronto reformer, and City Medical Officer of Health, Dr. Charles Hastings, told an enthusiastic Council meeting in 1921 that,

> malnutrition of the children in our city schools means not so much that the children are suffering from an insufficient quantity of food, but from food which is not properly selected and does not tend to produce proper development.[37]

Teaching mothercraft to women and domestic science to girls seemed a logical response. Indeed, council members advocated vociferously for the expansion of domestic science in elementary as well as secondary schools. The focus here, however, is on the educative and organizational activities directly addressed to women who were already mothers. According to Ada Courtice, mothers could and should play a critical role in the advancement of education, but they needed to learn.

> If the women of Ontario will study and understand the methods of present-day education with a view to making their girls capable, happy masters of their own problems . . . then we will be helping to advance progressive education in Ontario.[38]

Several Home and School clubs organized home visiting teams, often in collaboration with a teacher or a nurse. Parent education seminars, lectures by a roster of lay or professional experts, distribution of "mothercraft" and child welfare brochures and magazines, as well as child study circles were organized in collaboration with local clubs. After the St. George Institute for Child Study was established at the University of Toronto in 1926, the Council could draw on the scientific knowledge of its faculty and graduates. The Institute, in return, used the organizational base and skills of middle-class women in Home and School associations to develop child study circles. These were used not only to impart knowledge to mothers, but also to gather empirical data from mothers who were trained to observe their own children as would "amateur scientists."[39] To add to this work the Council opened two Saturday, pre-school clinics in 1929, one in the North and one in the West end of the City, both in cooperation with the Child Welfare Council. These were centers for physical examination of children, which were later expanded to five clinics.[40]

A final example of the Council's educative work is the weekly Home and School column in the *Globe and Mail*, started in 1930. These columns announced upcoming meetings of local Home and School clubs, as well as meetings, lectures and so on, organized by the Council. It also included reports from selected meetings written by Council members. Obtaining such a regular column in one of the City's daily newspapers speaks to the extent to which Home and School organizations had become accepted. It also speaks to the competence of the women involved. By the beginning of the 1930s it appears that this type of maternal community activity had been thoroughly integrated into the social organization of City schools and neighborhoods.

Implications for Current Community Work Intervention

As we can see, the organizational activities of Toronto's Home and School Council women were varied, extensive, and apparently, quite successful. Many of the reforms which they advocated, and the views which they espoused, were taken up by other organizations including the Toronto Board of Education. The point here is not to prove that these women necessarily were the first or even the only ones to introduce reforms in education of children and adults. But rather to keep in mind that they, as with many of today's education reformers, were part of much larger movements for change.

In terms of the specific changes which they tried to promote in the relationship between mothers and schools, it is important to note how their work and views became institutionalized in the school board's organizational practices. The question of regular school attendance became a responsibility for essentially female social workers employed as attendance officers from the mid-1920s onwards. The Council (along with others) had promoted such a strategy, believing that women could do the job better than men because they took the "home view." The work of attendance officers involved frequent visits to the homes of children who did not come regularly to school. In the home they would impart expert advice on child management to mothers with a great deal of moral as well as legal authority.

The education of "New Canadians" in English and Canadian ways has long been integrated in the Toronto school system. It is not a coincidence that the recent forays by the Toronto School Board into organized community intervention has focused primarily on "ethnic" communities. The language is now one of multiculturalism, and teaching is done in languages and cultures other than English (or French).

However, an important difference between the two periods ought also to be very apparent. In the early phase of Home and School organizing, the active leaders started with an explicitly stated ideology of motherhood and maternal duty, coupled with a range of arguments about the value of science in almost all areas of life. Women as mothers were their starting point, and it was this starting point which provided them with a particular legitimacy as "experts" in the related areas of child welfare and education. Their vision of a good mother—available and interested in her child's education, ready to support the efforts of the school, able to take part in a local Home and School club—has become the not so hidden referent against which all mothers continue to be measured. Immigrant and poor women, women in "fatherless" households, are now, as then, found wanting, and subjected to various forms of assistance and intervention.

As the reform movement progressed, the real differences in the experiences of women—differences from those of men, and differences between women bassed on class and race—were increasingly glossed over as Home and School women, and the reform movement they were part of, became integrated into the institutional relations they had been trying to change. The Council's emphasis shifted from reform of schools, to education of mothers and increasingly localized organizing activity. In the process a whole apparatus of professional experts was created in and around schooling to deal with children's physical and mental health, determine deviations from "normal" development, establish special classes, and counsel mothers on how to better carry out their responsibilities. Middle-class women quickly entered these new professions, which provided a logical alternative to teaching and nursing for educated women seeking employment. But, although women took up "front-line" positions as social workers, counsellors and the like, the professions were controlled and managed by men and tied to state institutions.[41]

School Boards can be seen as part of the local state formation in the sense that, by legal authority and public financing, they represent the locally organized management of the one legitimized form of socialization of children. Schooling is compulsory in Canada, and the organization and delivery of formal, institutionalized education have tremendous implications for adults as well as children. The work of Home and School women in the early 20th century can be understood, in part, as attempts to change society through reforms in education of adults as well as children. Whether society changed as a result of their activities is doubtful, and the point here is not to "prove" whether it did or did not. What I have tried to show is that the two primary social institutions which they were concerned with, the family and the school, were brought into stronger and more formalized relations with one another. I would suggest that as a result of the kinds of reform activities engaged in by Home and School women, women were drawn more closely into the sphere of state control and intervention. How mothers related to their children was increasingly taken up as a legitimate concern for the school. As a result women were, in many ways, becoming accountable to the local state for their mothering practices. "Voluntary" organizations by and for women around local schools represented one avenue for integrating and scrutinizing mother's work in a context of sociality and neighborliness among women. Home and School clubs were not overtly controlling but represented, nevertheless, very particular forms of mothering and housework as normal and good. The resemblance to the dual character of community organizations around schools in the 1970s and 1980s is strong.

Boards of education were reorganized and bureaucratized during the early 20th century. Rationalization based on scientific management methods was supported by urban and social reformers, including Home and School women. The organization and delivery of teaching were to be based on "facts," the work of educating was divided into discrete parts to be done by "experts." During the early decades of this century there were important shifts in the discourses of school reform, from concerns with philosophy and goals of education to measurement and efficiency of school provision. The women in Toronto's Home and School Council were actively involved in this period of transition. Ironically, they contributed to a de-politicization of their own reform work, as administrative practices were put in place to implement the reforms they were asking for. Thus the question of attendance, for example, was transformed from a large moral and political urgency into a practical matter for school social workers in relation to a limited number of "problem" families. Similarly, a whole range of testing services and special education classes are in place to take care of students who "deviate" from the "norm," while the norm itself is not on the agenda of parents' organizations.

The history of apparently neutral and technical reforms introduced during the last fifty years in Toronto displays a strong class and gender character in their practical consequences. Surveys of who goes to special education classes, who is streamed into vocational schools, and who drops out, persistently reveal the systematic patterning of "objective" decisions. It is also clear that it is primarily the mothers in recent immigrant, "ethnic" or working-class areas of the City who encounter the apparatus of social workers, psychologists and special education "experts."

The Toronto Board's recent community work intervention strategy is inserted into these complex relations. Although community work was initiated by left-wing trustees who were responding to very real pressures from parents in the "Inner City," the practice of community work is severely restricted by the administrative and political environment of the School Board. It is difficult to see how it could be otherwise as long as community workers are directly paid and supervised by the local state. Matters which are very real in the lives of immigrant and working-class men, women and children are "out of bounds" or too controversial to take up. The ways in which issues are addressed are embedded in institutional practices of long standing. The proper channels are complicated and frequently used to stall any initiatives from parents' groups. It is "best" to leave difficult (read political) decisions to experts or to elected trustees. In the meantime, parent organizations ought to remain at the "community level," where they can do good work for the school, and provide a sense of belonging in our fragmented city.

Holding the community together continues to be women's work, but now that assumption has become so entrenched that it cannot be questioned within an otherwise progressive community work practice. It is my view that the past history of relations between Toronto mothers and schools does provide us with some insight into why this is so. Perhaps, too, something can be learned from the ways in which the early women reformers were gradually incorporated into the management of the School Board. The outcome of current struggles over community work and parent involvement could lead to the exact opposite of what conservative trustees have in mind. By refusing to continue the integration of parent participation in school decisions, these trustees may well, inadvertently, ensure that the organization of parents will remain politicized. If the organization of parents is initiated outside the institutional parameters of the Board, it may even be possible to explore alternative ways of thinking and doing community work, ways which may support and develop communality as a challenge to familialism.

NOTES

1. Elizabeth Wilson, "Women in the Community," Marjorie Mayo (ed.), *Women in the Community*. London: Routledge and Kegan Paul, 1977.
2. See for example, Donald R. Keating, *The Power to Make It Happen: Mass-based Community Organizing: What It Is and How It Works*. Toronto: Green Tree Publisher Co., 1975; James A. Draper (ed.), *Citizen Participation: Canada, A Book of Readings*. Toronto: New Press, 1971, which has one article on women; and Brian Wharf (ed.), *Community Work in Canada*. Toronto: McClelland and Stewart, 1979.
3. I want to stress that this research is at a very early stage, and that I do not want to make claims about generalizability at this point or in this short paper.
4. Charles Novogrodsky, *A Report Prepared for Ontario Ministry of Education Conference "Together We Are Ontario"*, Constellation Hotel, Toronto March 19–21, 1986, p. 1.
5. School Community Relations Department, Toronto Board of Education, *Interview Notes*, 1983.
6. *Ibid*.
7. Christie Public School, January 21, 1985, "Partners in Learning," Appendix A in Novogrodsky, *op. cit*.
8. *Interview Notes*, 1983.
9. *Ibid*.
10. *Ibid*.
11. Cynthia Cockburn, *The Local State: Management of Cities and People*. London: Pluto Press, 1977.
12. Bruce Curtis, Work in Progress.
13. Susan Houston, "The 'Waifs and Strays' of a Late Victorian City: Juvenile Delinquents in Toronto," in Joy Parr (ed.), *Childhood and Family in Canadian History*. Toronto: McClelland and Stewart, 1982.
14. Michael Piva, *The Conditions of the Working Class in Toronto, 1900–1921*. Ottawa: University of Ottawa Press, 1979.
15. Toronto Home and School Council, *Minutes*, 1916–1930, Toronto Board of Education Archives. Hereafter these records will be referred to as *Minutes*.
16. Ada Mary Brown Courtice, quoted in Toronto Home and School Council, *The Story of the Toronto Home and School Council, Through the Years*

1916–1936 (1936), p. 10, Toronto Board of Education Archives. Hereafter this document is footnoted as *The Story*.

17. *Ibid.*, p. 8.
18. Terry Crowley, "Ada Mary Brown Courtice: Pacifist, Feminist and Educational Reformer in Early Twentieth Century Canada," *Studies in History and Politics* (1980), pp. 75–114.
19. *The Story.* See also two collections of poems by Edith Groves, *The Kingdom of Childhood*. Toronto: Warwick Brothers and Rutter, 1925, and *Everyday Children, A Book of Poems*. Toronto: the Committee in Charge of the Edith L. Groves Memorial Fund for Underprivileged Children, 1932, with an introduction by Dr. Helen MacMurchy.
20. Honora M. Cochrane, *Centennial Story The Board of Education for the City of Toronto 1850–1950*. Toronto: Thomas Nelson and Sons, 1950.
21. *The Story*, p. 4.
22. *White Paper No. 47*. Toronto: Bureau of Municipal Research, April 29, 1921, n.p.
23. *Ibid.*, No. 43, January 14, 1921.
24. *The Story*, p. 44.
25. *Minutes* (March 8, 1921).
26. *Ibid.* (June 1917, November 1919).
27. *The Story*, p. 20.
28. *Ibid.* p. 23.
29. *Minutes*, November 19, 1917.
30. *The Story*, p. 47; Cochrane, *op. cit.*
31. *Minutes*, 1916–1925.
32. *The Story*, p. 19.
33. Piva, *op. cit.*
34. *Minutes*, May 18, 1921; September 21, 1921; March 15, 1922.
35. *The Story*, p. 15–16.
36. *Minutes*, June 11, 1917.
37. *Ibid.*, February 1, 1921.
38. *The Story*, p. 8.
39. For an interesting account of the development of child study circles in the United States, see Steven Schlossman, "Before Home Start: Notes Toward a History of Parent Education in America, 1897–1929," *Harvard Educational Review* Vol. 46, No. 3, August 1976, pp. 436–467. In another article Schlossman demonstrates the connection between corporate foundations and the child study movement, see Schlossman, "Philanthropy and the Gospel of Child Development," *History of Education Quarterly*, Fall 1981, pp. 275–299. Mary L. Northway, a long-time teacher at the St. George Institute for Child Study in Toronto, makes clear that this Institute, too, benefitted from a financial contribution from a philanthropic foundation, the Laura Spelman Rockefeller Foundation. See M.L. Northway, *Laughter in the Front Hall*. Don Mills: Longman Canada Ltd., 1966.

40. *The Story*, p. 28.
41. James Struthers, " 'Lord Give Us Men': Women and Social Work in English Canada 1918–1953," *Historical Papers*, 1983.

Community Care:
Ideology and Lived Experience

Anne Bullock

Introduction

This paper is concerned with how a textually-mediated understanding of the term "community," shared by mothers of severely handicapped[1] children and the Government of Ontario, organizes women's work so that it complements the process of de-institutionalization.[2] The textual work[3] on community and conceptual practices that give rise to it[4] can reinforce the invisibility of women in "the community" and contribute to the belief that their concerns are less "progressive" than those often taken up in community organizing.[5] In the meantime, the women's work as care-givers in the community expedites the fiscal and administrative priorities of the state, as I hope to show here.

The promotion of community care of severely handicapped children at home by the government and by families themselves on the basis that it is more "natural" and humane is a good example of how our taken-for-granted understanding of community as "something positive" prevails, even when it fails to live up to those beliefs and expectations. Provincial governments, which are responsible for funding services and programs for retarded people, must do so at the same time as they overhaul the entire social welfare system to make it more cost effective. In Ontario the work the women do caring for their handicapped children is becoming more highly organized, and requires a greater expenditure of emotional and physical labor on their part to bring it into line with the management objectives of the provincial government. The dominant belief that community care is preferable to institutional care[6] on the basis of "humanitarian" motives offers a way for the government and families to think about the very different issues at stake for them in providing for the children's needs or, indeed, the needs of all severely handicapped people.[7]

My personal experience with community care began in 1980 when I set up a parent relief program for parents of handicapped children. The program was one of 32 funded that year by the Ontario Ministry of Community and Social Services (COMSOC) to arrange short-term care of the child so that families could take a break from constant care. There is a growing body of research on respite care[8] that indicates its effectiveness in helping families "adjust to" or "cope with" the difficulties of care, thereby averting "family breakdown" and the need to seek a long-term institutional placement for the child. I had often heard families express a desire for such support, and this seemed a promising start for my work— finally the ideas of the provincial government and of families were "in synch" with each other!

Earlier, a brief stint as a ward counsellor in a provincial retardation facility had left me committed to de-institutionalization and firm in the belief that community living—with the necessary program and service supports in place—was the answer for retarded persons, their families and workers like myself who wanted to work with them for change.[9] The Parent Relief Program afforded me the opportunity to see what community care at home looked like close up. It didn't take long to sense the gap between the rosy ideas many of us had about care at home in the community, and the unremitting physical and emotional labor the women were drawn into in order to care for their children in accordance with that ideal. Moreover, it became clear to me that giving families time off from care did not address the underlying causes of stress, family breakdown or the resulting institutionalization of children that parent relief programs were created to alleviate.

The observations in this paper are drawn from my thesis research which included personal interviews with women looking after their severely handicapped children at home, an analysis of selected textual work on community, and an analysis of selected government documents that describe, promote and organize community care of mentally handicapped people. By beginning with the experience of care-givers, it is possible to compare the lived experience of providing care in the community with the textual version of community which ignores, transforms or glosses over the material details of that experience.[10] What is happening to the women in this situation alerts us to the way in which people's lives get organized to meet needs that do not originate in the local setting[11] which, in this case, we recognize as "the community;" and how their desires to have their handicapped children live at home are shaped to fit "ruling interests and practices"[12] rather than their own.

The Parent Relief Program I set up shifted the focus from the context of care—the fact that it was women who bore the major responsibility for it, and how they came to be in that position—to maintaining the women in their "roles" as care-givers. This was not done intentionally. Yet dealing with the problems of care instead of the system which produced the problems made the personal costs borne by the women secondary except as they influenced the possibility of an out-of-home, government-financed placement being needed for the child. It is generally agreed by families, government and various experts that such placements are to be avoided at all costs. The need to provide relief to care-givers, however, is indicative of the fact that community care is not "natural" or easy to organize; it signals the implicit coercive aspects of such programs for women.

Historical Notions of Community

Most of us don't stop to consider that our ideas about community are a historical construction which originates from idealizations developed by philosophers and sociologists in the 19th century.[13] The idea of community began as a critique of the social relations of capitalism and provided an alternative to them.[14] The characteristics of the pre-capitalist societies, which stood as the "models" for community, came to serve as indicators for the social health of their own society. Over time, these indicators become reified and are held up as standards for social relationships,[15] incompatible with the constantly changing needs of capitalist society[16] at the present time.

The 19th century accounts often used the "nomenclature of the family" to describe "community"[17] and relied on a particular understanding of its nature and organization as well as the location and value of women's work.[18] By the mid-19th century, changes in the organization and work of the family within capitalism had begun to separate home from work life. "The family," over a period of time, became identified as a "haven"–the place where people could experience the face-to-face relations and stable environment associated with "community," but which capitalism made more and more difficult to attain. The family became, in a sense, the repository of pre-capitalist values.[19] The possibility of experiencing the material and emotional comforts of family life came to rely more and more on the work of women in a privatized household in a particular relationship with a man, outside the sphere of paid work. The ideological accounts of community failed to include the fact that in "real life" the creation of "family life" involved work to which women devoted all or part of their energies, depending upon their need to con-

contribute financially to the household. Women were central to the notion of community because its relations depended implicitly on the labor of women in individual households.

Initially the "ideal" woman and family were bourgeois and required the material resources available only in bourgeois families. This changed as bourgeois women themselves promoted their views among working class women. At present, although the ability of women to reproduce the "ideal" continues to vary according to material resources, this is less obvious as the images become more abstract and are circulated more widely[20] via schools, the advice of experts, popular media, etc. The same thing has happened to the notion of community. Its material basis fades into the background and its ideologically constructed attributes, especially those associated with its intimate, supportive and integrative side take precedence. This is one reason why the term "community" is such a powerful descriptor of care at the present time, but also why community care, as a course of social action, is of such importance for women. Its most positive attributes are actually found in "the family." These characteristics, in the last 150 to 200 years, have been more and more the product of the invisible and taken-for-granted labor of women.

The conflation of "family" with "community" turns the notion of community into a bundle of contradictions—it is "public" and "private," collective and individualistic all at the same time. We need to be aware that ideas about community that fail to take account of its social organization within a society that is, by definition unequal, are doomed to reproduce that inequality in practice. Thus the most progressive or humanitarian of projects can be subverted to non-humanitarian interests in the sense that ordinary human concerns take second place to keeping capitalist society on track.

Community Care, State and Family

The implementation of community care policies for various institutional populations has been supported by conservatives who see this move as a step toward reducing government involvement and spending in social welfare areas, and by liberals who argue that community living restores the basic rights of which residents of institutions are often deprived.[21] The ideological construction of community, in disciplines like sociology and social work where it is a specialized area of study, provides for the possibility of improbable alliances of this sort. It has also allowed the provincial government and families with retarded dependents to "team up." This construction makes the concept of community care recognizable to ordinary citizens, even when the policy and the lived experience of it are at odds with each other.

When families with mentally handicapped dependents use the term to describe the work of care, they are not referring to an abstraction but to real situations and people. Although families of care-givers share a common experience and have similar needs for support, the form and organization of that support differs according to their individual requirements. It is difficult in practice to make hard and fast predictions about how easy or difficult it is for them to have, or not have, the child at home all the time. The provincial government, on the other hand, must attempt to categorize and deal with the needs of its various constituencies in some systematic way as part of its work.[22] How it does this is shaped primarily by the on-going changes in capitalism[23] but is also affected by its struggles with those constituencies. COMSOC's desire to economize by cutting back on institutional care or by eliminating it altogether could not very easily be imposed if the families of residents or others connected with their welfare were opposed to these ideas.

While institutional care and now "community care" can be seen as attempts to formally organize care for individuals unable to provide for their own needs, families have also done their share of this work. Long-term care of dependent people has not been exclusively "public" (state-provided) or "private" (family-provided) in the last century. There are some underlying assumptions about community/family that have remained fairly consistent in both the public and private arenas, and these have implications for our understanding of women's work in the community. The 19th century institution was intended to be organized as a substitute family form in an attempt to serve as a "model community."[24] This is still a model in certain forms of institutional care, especially for children.[25] The notion of the public/private, collective/individualistic community has been very much a part of the history of care of retarded people in Ontario and has provided for actual practices intended as courses of government action at various points in time.

In the late 1920s and early 30s, there was considerable support for returning institutionalized children to their families.[26] The reasons for the interest then, as now, centred mainly on cost benefits and the benefits to the children. Home care was characterized as a responsibility "which must be faced and dealt with by the community."[27] The success of this idea, however, relied on the efforts of individual families, and in particular the mothers, who would provide for the child's subsistence and, more importantly, carry out training programs to make the child more independent, easier to care for and hence a less likely candidate for the institution. The critical position of the mother as the intermediary between child, family and a host of "outsiders" whose expertise could make the child more independent and the mother's work easier, although not an issue at that time, is important now when much the same thinking informs a very different set of social and material circumstances.[28] As well, the government faces a very different set of pressures to deal with the high costs of long-term institutional care in some publically acceptable manner.[29] Finally, the way in which the care-giver "role" is understood to be "natural" to women, even by women themselves, and the manner in which the work of child-care is assumed to be an expression of individual maternal devotion unrelated to the larger world[30] have each provided, via textual discourses, not only an understanding of women's work as central to community but also a logical basis for state organization of that work, even some 40 years later.[31]

In the case of care of mentally handicapped people, the Williston Report, which served as a catalyst for de-institutionalization[32] and was widely hailed as a progressive piece of work by government and families alike in the 1970s, stated:

> True social care implies sharing in responsibility by the community in assisting parents in carrying out their part in looking after a child to the best of their ability.[33]

The way in which the private family is treated, in this and other works, as the backbone of community care is very striking. Looking back over the past 15 years, that is exactly how de-institutionalization and community care have worked out, especially for families with a severely handicapped child.

Today access to the most important government-funded support services and allowances is determined by the severity of the handicap.[34] Children at greatest risk of being placed in an institution are the prime target group for assistance. While this arrangement may indeed help some families, it does not say much for the government's commitment to making care of mentally handicapped children easier for their families regardless of the degree of the handicap.[35] This distinction on the basis of government-defined priorities has the potential to cause divisions between families, who end up competing against each other for various resources. The parent movement began after the Second World War when families lobbied the government to provide local schooling for their children as an alternative to institutional placement for educational purposes. These lobbying activities provided a basis for the establishment of a network of local associations and the creation of a provincial body. The associations played a significant role in the development of more progressive and humane arrangements for the care of mentally handicapped persons both inside and outside institutions. The majority of children "returned" to the community in the 1970s as part of de-institutionalization were returned to the care of their families, or, when their families were not able to provide for them, were taken into the care of Children's Aid Societies.[36] In spite of this outcome, the assumptions on which the provision of care by women are based were not questioned by the provincial government or by the associations.[37] The treatment and understanding of community and family as one and the same in writings on the subject contributes to this. In fact, the use of the term "community" by "the state" at the present time to describe women's unpaid work in maintaining dependent people, shows how the "return" of certain forms of care formerly provided by "the state" to "the community" (understood as "family," and in which the labor to produce the care is performed by women at no cost) has been accomplished by the state through it's documentary work. The increasing reliance of the state on community care to solve some of its financial problems cannot be seen as wholly manipulative nor intentionally directed toward the subordination and economic dependence of women. Those who create state policy understand "community" and women's work in the same way as do academics and various experts. Increasingly, families come to understand it in the same way.

For example, various aspects of community care are facilitated and monitored by social workers who are often responsible for the "relational" work with the dependent person's family. Our equation of community and family care, and our belief in the benefits of it for children in particular, are second nature. These ideas are prevalent in social work practice literature. The following is an example from an influential book on home-based services for children whose special needs ordinarily make them candidates for out-of-home placements

> The inherent integrity of the family as the primary care system must be at the core of social policy development, and there must be built-in safeguards against harm to that system . . . [because] nothing takes the place in our lives of the oldest institution known to man: the family."[38]

Comsoc draws on the above book in a policy paper entitled: "The Nature and Effectiveness of Family Support Measures." [39] The paper stresses the effectiveness of "natural" support networks in preference to institutional care. In practice, comsoc has been supporting care in the family through funding initiatives which cover costs of special equipment, and programs and services not available through the existing service system. A COMSOC media release states that this initiative keeps the family functioning more easily[40] and coping. It also states:

> This is a good example of how we can keep a child at home for about $7,000 per year instead of institutionalizing which is extremely costly.[41]

There is certainly nothing secretive about COMSOC's aims, yet the ideological understanding of "family" mutes the import of the message. Indeed, families (and mothers) echo those same ideas. Here is what one of the women I talked to said about the decision to have her handicapped daughter live at home:

> I just don't think there's anything the same about institution or group home care and care at home. It just devastates me to think of a child being dumped in a place other than a home—whether it be their own home, a foster home or adoptive home—but a place where there are parents, siblings and extended family. . . .[42]

My discussions with the women show the disjuncture between their lived experience and the ideology of community care. At the same time, the belief that out-of-home care is "dysfunctional" and costly and should not be supported has resulted in a kind of self-fulfilling prophecy with regard to many living alternatives. The women are right—they can provide better care, and it certainly is cheaper than a lot of the available options. On the other hand, this is not solely the result of mother-love, the family or the "community experience," although any or all of these can be beneficial to the children and other family members. Rather it is the result of a complex interaction between material circumstances and people's thoughts and feelings, and the shaping of these according to long-term ruling interests.

Not every family is in a favorable position to meet the material or emotional needs of the child. No matter how much "the family" wants the child at home, it is the mother who will bear the responsibility for care, and she will have to do her work with very little help from "the community." My research indicated that the women could not count on the amount or kind of support they received from their partners, other members of the immediate family, extended family, friends or neighbors or even the formally-organized, COMSOC-founded community support programs.[43] Ironically, meeting the child's needs in a community setting requires the women to reproduce a miniature institution in the home where they must learn and carry out the skills of a team of professionals (in addition to their "ordinary" work as wives and mothers).[44]

Even an examination of that direct care is insufficient, because the work the women do coordinating the attention the child receives from specialists, teachers and so on must also be considered. It is especially in these last areas that the intensification of the women's work is most evident and the effects of ruling practices are most visible. The women have more work to do, not only as a direct result of de-institutionalization, but also because of general cutbacks in areas such as education and health, since their children now use these "community" services. They are also required to develop the ability to interact with the state on its own terms by developing proficiency in "ruling practices" and the discourse of ruling as a condition for participating in government programs of community-based support.[45]

Care of the child can also affect the mother's opportunity to work outside the home, although the expenses of community care at home can make two salaries a necessity, even in middle-class families. The following statement was made by one of the women I interviewed:

> . . . a lot of people ask me why I work and why I'm not at home. I'd love to be at home—not full time—certainly I have a career and I've worked very hard for that . . . but I can't financially afford to stay home and keep my kids living with me.[46]

The effects of cut-backs in health care services for the women's work are evident. Hospitals are able to "do" less these days for all of their patients, but they are especially hampered in their efforts to meet the needs of children who need one-to-one supervision on top of medical attention. Hospital stays for the children, which are often frequent, may involve the use of restraining devices because there is no staff to provide that constant supervision. If the use of restraints is unacceptable to families—and it usually is—then they must make arrangements for supervision that *does* meet their needs. If they can afford to, families often hire somebody to do the job, but in many instances mothers simply add hospital supervision to their other tasks and organize their time so that they can be with their children at the hospital.

There are comparable situations in schools. It is clear that this facet of the child's experience of community life also gets put back on families, as schools find their efforts to provide for the child curtailed. The families I talked to consider integrated schooling part of the community care ideal and have struggled to get their children out of segregated environments. This option has some drawbacks however, and a number of families have expressed mixed feelings over such moves. While the child may benefit socially, there are clear indications that education cut-backs have reduced or re-deployed essential support staff, leaving classroom teachers with considerable supervision responsibilities. It is almost impossible to meet a handicapped child's needs under these conditions. Teachers and students suffer, as do mothers, who know better than anybody how vulnerable their children are without that support.

How "Community" Benefits the Government

Although it is difficult to estimate what the government saves in dollars through de-institutionalization, the areas where savings could be made are not too difficult to identify—for example: being able to abandon the projected construction of at least 6,000 institution beds[47] to meet requests for more space, and reduction of direct care staff in institutions (1,163 people were slated for lay-off as part of COMSOC's 5-year plan).[48] At the same time, community-based programs continue to operate on small budgets.

In the case of the Parent Relief Program, the low wages paid to the women who work as relief providers and the restriction of relief time to 21 days or 504 hours per year help keep program costs to a minimum. The estimated annual cost for institutional care is between $35,000 and $40,000 per child per year.[49] If the organized rest made possible by Parent Relief Programs contributes to even a handful of families being able to care for their children at home, these families will have more than repaid the government investment in funding them.

Home community care of severely handicapped children raises questions of "class." The women I interviewed formed a homogeneous sample, although the striking similarity between them in education, composition of their families (all were two-parent) and income was not intended. The fact that they came forward to be interviewed can be considered a finding in itself.[50] The women did not see themselves as affluent, yet they often stated in the course of our conversations that they felt fortunate to be spared the stress that comes from inadequate or uncertain income and the effects of this on looking after the child.

Where the women worked outside the home, their education and training in areas like teaching and nursing gave them access to some of the better-paying jobs available to women. As well, that same education and training provided them with essential skills for looking after a severely handicapped child. They are able to understand and follow the directions they receive from physicians, teachers and therapists, in addition to being able to relate care of the individual child to the broader issues of normalization and de-institutionalization.

It does not require a lot of imagination to see how difficult it would be for a mother to reproduce the ideal family/community if she lacked the necessary material resources and opportunity and/or ability to organize her paid and unpaid work. The various accounts of de-institutionalization and community care actually assume that a middle-class lifestyle, which offers a greater possibility of having the necessary resources, is the norm. As mentioned earlier, the inability to grasp the concept of community care as it is defined by the government, may work against lower-income families getting their share of support (limited as it is for all families). It also appears that severely handicapped children are continuing to come into the care of Children's Aid Societies, much as they did in the 1970s when substantial numbers of children were returned to the community[51] and when alternatives to home-care other than large facilities were almost non-existent.[52] A 1984 newspaper article entitled "CAS Program Frees Disabled Children From Institutions," stated that institutionalized children were being placed in foster care when it was not possible for them to be returned to their own families. The article noted that institutional costs range between $60 to $100 per day while the per diem rate for foster care is $20.[53]

A Politics of Care

The notion of a "community" that relies on "the family" for its existence is a contradiction. Community implies an egalitarian social organization that benefits all of its members. "Family" implies a privatized, hierarchical and gendered work organization that does not equally benefit its members and that also foments differences among families who are thought to comprise "the community." This appears to be the basic contradiction which provided for the ideological construction of community to begin with, and which has been compounded in particular ways and in particular social periods ever since. Implementing the ideals of community would require a corresponding weakening of family ties.[54]

The organization of women to work as care-givers appears to affect them in different ways, although no group of women actually benefits from the current arrangements—if care of severely handicapped children at home serves as any indication. My research shows how middle-class women must intensify their labor to reproduce the ideals of community in the face of diminishing resources—in terms both of what is required to care for the handicapped child, and what is required to maintain the standard of living for the family as a whole. It also suggests that working-class women may be subjected more to the intervention of Children's Aid Societies when they are unable to provide what is defined in the community as "proper care." In both instances, community care has not increased the options for families, but instead has been organized at the expense of alternative non-institutional living arrangements. Community care of dependent people is also contributing to the proliferation of new low-paid or volunteer jobs for women. In some instances, cutbacks in state services such as health and education contribute to their availability for this work; the availability of other women is the result of a lack of "formal" work experience or relevant training that would give them access to work outside the "female job ghetto."[55]

Long-term changes in the responsibility of caring for dependent people require a greater understanding and appreciation of the work of care and of how it fits into and is a part of the organization of the labor force as a whole. This is especially important when the labor force is in a constant state of change, as it is in our society. An ideological version of community care, in this case the organizing of the care of handicapped children at home by their mothers, may be implicated in a larger reorganization of the labor force[56] in which state practices serve to mediate between the needs of capital and the reproduction and maintenance of people.[57] The home care of severely handicapped children affects a relatively small number of women and thus provides only a glimpse of a possible "larger picture." There are, however, indications that the work of a growing number of women is being organized around the provision of care to a growing number of people defined as dependent. Care of the elderly is the most obvious example but it is not unique.[58]

The state organization of women's work as care-givers in the community militates against developing a politics of care. The reliance of the state on an ideologically constructed family/community category to meet its own financial and administrative priorities reinforces and deepens the forms of inequality mentioned earlier—particularly those arising out of gender. Women are not only bearing the brunt of the state's requirement to divest itself of expensive long-term care responsibilities; many of them are also rendered more dependent on a male wage as a result—even middle-class women. That economic dependence can be more "silencing" than even the "invisibility" of the work itself.

The gains made by women in recent years have been predicated on their speaking out about their oppression. Women who care for dependent individuals at home in the community are in a vulnerable position, especially when this care limits their chance to take paid work. They may feel compelled to "put up with" more rather than risk the loss of the resources they already have—whether these come from a male partner or the government. While requiring men to devote a greater share of their time to the work of care can have short-term benefits, it is unlikely to produce substantive changes in the responsibility for long-term care. As things now stand, that reversal of roles represents a poor economic bargain for the majority of families, as men usually earn more than women. It is not in the interests of families to alter the more "traditional" division of work if this is going to affect their ability to provide for a dependent family member. The politics of care would require an examination of the position of men in the economic order and of the belief that the ability to care is a female trait: this involves changes for both men and women.

We know that subordination and economic dependence have contributed in the past to the stereotypic view of women as conservative or difficult to organize.[59] We can see in this paper how this can still be the case as women attempt to retain a shred of control over their work as care-givers. We need to develop a politics of care which takes these various facts into account, and challenges the structure of a society that gives rise to inequalities on the basis of gender, class and race. With the benefit of hindsight,[60] we can see that single-issue campaigns that failed to recognize these forms of oppression as an integral part of capitalism worked, in the long term, against the interests of those the campaigns were supposed to help.

Working for Change

The struggle between families and the state over the definition and location of appropriate care of retarded people indicates that struggles with the state are not necessarily a lost cause. Activities of parent-lobby groups like the Ontario Association for the Mentally Retarded (OAMR) made the general public more aware of the plight of retarded people in institutions and the government more aware of their special needs. Even though community care serves "the state's" needs better than the needs of families right now, the task of learning to live with our differences in this society has inched forward. Unless, however, groups like OAMR consider the relationship of women's paid and unpaid work to their efforts and how the state shapes this work, community care of retarded people will be at the expense of women, as "families" are implicitly or explicitly expected to provide it in accordance with government policy.

The bleak outlook at the moment does contain some "rays of hope," but only if we struggle to break down the distinctions between men/women, paid/unpaid work and so on. The work of mounting and organizing collective struggles is difficult. As social workers involved in various aspects of community care and organizing, we have an important role to play in this. We are in a position to "connect" individuals or groups who, along with care-givers, have an interest in care. In the case of community care of severely handicapped children these forces might include unions who have lost workers as part of de-institutionalization, teachers or nurses who are hampered in their efforts to provide the specialized services the children need, and associations for the mentally retarded or other advocacy groups. We can also support care-givers by recognizing that care is work. The assumption that it is "natural" can serve to oppress women; we should instead be working to empower them by pointing out how care is a part of the larger social, political and economic context.

The degree to which we are open to these possibilities in our work, and effective in using them for change rather than practicing in accordance with ideological notions of "community" or "family," depends upon a critical analysis of the meaning of organizing terms and concepts as well as a recognition of how those meanings can provide for "ruling"—in this case through government de-institutionalization policy which describes, promotes and legitimates community care at home that is based on women's labor in privatized families.

NOTES

1. It is difficult to describe the children's disabilities so that they are readily understandable to the largest number of people without resorting to labels, such as handicapped and retarded, that have negative connotations. My use of this language is not intended to be disrespectful, although I realize that it can be interpreted in that way.

2. Ontario Ministry of Community and Social Services. "Three Decades of Change: The Evolution of Residential Care and Community Alternatives in Children's Services," Policy Development, Toronto, 1983. To summarize, de-institutionalization refers to: (a) the systematic de-population of retardation facilities; (b) the creation of community-based services and programs consisting of alternative living accommodation such as group homes, the provision of programs that increase the "retarded" person's capacity for independent living or enhance the ability of the individual's family to meet that person's needs and, most recently, the creation of Parent Relief Programs to give families a rest from care.

3. Texts refer to words or images that exist on a fixed material from without the speaker's presence.

4. Dorothy Smith, "The Ideological Practice of Sociology," *Catalyst* 8, 1974, pp. 39–54.

5. Jalna Hanmer, "Community Action, Women's Aid and the Women's Liberation Movement," in Marjorie Mayo (ed.), *Women in the Community*. London: Routledge and Kegan Paul, 1977.

6. For example, see Ontario Ministry of Community and Social Services, 1983, *op. cit.* and Wolf Wolfensberger, *The Principle of Normalization in Human Services*. Toronto: National Institute on Mental Retardation, 1972.

7. People who are severely mentally handicapped typically require life-long assistance in meeting their physical, social and intellectual needs. This fact distinguishes their care from that of other groups like the elderly, and raises different issues for the government in organizing that care.

8. For example, L. Wikler and D. Hanusa, "The Impact of Respite Care on Stress in Families of Mentally Retarded Children." Paper presented at the American Association of Mental Deficiency, San Francisco, 1980.

9. The philosophy of normalization, which became popular in Canada in the 1970s, redefined retardation and argued for the integration of retarded people into the community. The person most intimately connected with its development and promulgation was Wolf Wolfensberger, an American, who was appointed as a visiting scholar in mental retardation at York University during this period.

10. Smith, *op. cit.*

11. Dorothy Smith, "What it Might Mean to do a Canadian Sociology: The Everyday World as Problematic," in *Canadian Journal of Sociology*, Vol. 1 (3), 1975, pp. 363–376.

12. "Ruling practices include those activities involved in organizing and economizing on the costs of reproducing capital;" Marie Campbell, "Managerialism: A Class Phenomenon in Nursing." Paper presented to Canadian Sociology and Anthropology Association Session on Marxian Analysis of Professional Occupations. The Learned Societies Conference, University of Montreal, May 29, 1985.

13. Robert Nisbet. *The Sociological Tradition*. New York: Basic Book Publishers, 1966.

14. Raymond Plant, *Community and Ideology: An Essay in Applied Social Philosophy*. London: Routledge and Kegan Paul, 1974.

15. Lyn Lofland, "The 'Thereness' of Women: A Selected Review of Urban Sociology," in M. Millman and R. Kanter (eds.), *Another Voice: Feminist Perspectives on Social Life and Social Science*. New York: Anchor Press, 1975.

16. Gillian Walker, "Working Paper: Capitalism and Community," unpublished Manuscript, School of Social Work, Carleton University, Ottawa, 1986.

17. Nisbet, *op. cit.*

18. Lofland, *op. cit.*

19. Michele Barrett and Mary McIntosh, *The Antisocial Family*. London: Verso Editions, 1982.

20. Dorothy Smith, "Women, Class and the Family," in R. Miliband and J. Saville (eds.), *The Socialist Register*. London: The Merlin Press, 1983.
21. Andrew Scull, *Decarceration: Community Treatment and the Deviant — A Radical View*. London: Polity Press (2nd Edition), 1984.
22. See Cynthia Cockburn, *The Local State*. London: Pluto Press, 1977 and London Edinburgh Weekend Return Group, *In and Against the State*. London: Pluto Press, 1980. One aspect of state work is the maintenance of "the welfare state."
23. London Edinburgh Weekend Return Group, *op. cit.*
24. Eli Zaretsky, "The Place of the Family in the Origins of the Welfare State," in B. Thorne and M. Yalom (eds.), *Re-thinking the Family: Some Feminist Questions*. New York: Longman, 1982.
25. Barrett and McIntosh, *op. cit.*
26. Harvey Simmons, *From Asylum to Welfare*. Toronto: National Institute on Retardation, 1982.
27. *Ibid.*, p. 126.
28. Scull (*op. cit.*), argues that de-institutionalization required the welfare state structure and ideology.
29. See Scull, *op. cit.* and Ian Gough, *The Political Economy of the Welfare State*. London: Macmillan Publishers Ltd, 1979.
30. Dorothy Smith, "Women, the Family and Corporate Capitalism," in Marylee Stephenson (ed.), *Women in Canada*. Toronto: New Press, 1973.
31. The advent of the welfare state was critical in this change and is central to an understanding of women's paid and unpaid work, since it assumed a family composed of a bread-winner male and dependent female. As well, many women depend on state funds for their livelihood either as state employees or recipients of state allowances.
32. Simmons, *op. cit.*
33. Walter Williston, "Present Arrangements for the Care and Supervision of Mentally Retarded Persons in Ontario." Ontario Department of Health, 1971, p. 14.
34. See, for example, Ontario Ministry of Community and Social Services, "Guidelines of the Special Services at Home Program." Toronto: Operational Support Branch, 1984.
35. Families whose children are less severely handicapped face their own set of difficulties, often around issues of access rather than care *per se*.
36. Simmons, *op. cit.*
37. In the discussions on de-institutionalization, little is said about the growing number of families affected because their children were not considered eligible for admission to institutions after the requirements were "tightened up." In that sense, de-institutionalization is a very misleading term. It stands for a finite process and implies that when institutions are empty the project will be complete. It does not take into account that more and more children do not appear on institution records.

38. Sheila Maybanks and Marvin Bryce (eds.), *Home-Based Services for Children and Families: Policy, Practice and Research.* Illinois: Charles C. Thomas, 1979, p. 11.
39. Ontario Ministry of Community and Social Services, "The Nature and Effectiveness of Family Support Measures in Child Welfare." Toronto: Policy and Program Development Division, 1983.
40. Ontario Ministry of Community and Social Services, News Release. Communications Branch, 1982, p. 3.
41. *Ibid.*, p. 3.
42. Anne Bullock, "Community Care of Severely Handicapped Children at Home: A 'Moment' in the Organization of Women's Work." Unpublished Master's Thesis, Carleton University, 1986.
43. *Ibid.*
44. Anne Bullock and Marie Campbell, "Community Care: An Analysis of Gendered Ideology-Bound Ruling Practices." Paper presented to the Canadian Sociology and Anthropology Association Session on Women, Ideology and the State. The Learned Societies Conference, University of Manitoba, June 1986.
45. *Ibid.*
46. Bullock, 1986, *op. cit.*, p. 139.
47. Simmons, 1982, *op. cit.*
48. National Institute on Mental Retardation. Toronto: News Release, September 1984.
49. *Ibid.*
50. Bullock (1986, *op. cit.*), especially section on methodology.
51. Lillian Keys, "Developmentally Handicapped Children and Adolescents Currently in the Care of the Children's Aid Society of Metropolitan Toronto and Related Issues," Toronto, 1977.
52. See Ontario Ministry of Community and Social Services, "Three Decades of Change . . ." (1983, *op. cit.*) for the statistics.
53. Pat Bell, "CAS Program Frees Disabled Children from Institutions." *Ottawa Citizen*, December 27, 1984.
54. Barrett and McIntosh, *op. cit.*
55. Patricia Armstrong, *Labour Pains: Women's Work in Crisis.* Toronto: The Women's Press, 1983.
56. Insight arising out of a conversation with my thesis advisor Gillian Walker, June 1986.
57. Jane Ursel, "Toward a Theory of Reproduction," in *Contemporary Crisis* (8), pp. 265–292.
58. Nancy Guberman, "Behind Recent Social and Fiscal Policy in Quebec: A Re-definition of Motherwork by the State," paper prepared for the Workshop on Motherwork, Val Morin, Quebec, 1985. Guberman's analysis indicates that the maintenance of various dependent groups (especially unemployed youth) is a matter of increasing concern to the provincial gov-

ernment. "Family" and "community" are coming to the fore in the name of everything most positively associated with both, and Guberman argues that their use serves to re-organize motherwork.

59. Dorothy Smith, *Feminism and Marxism: A Place to Begin a Way to Go.* Vancouver: New Star Books, 1977.

60. Zaretsky, 1982, *op. cit.*

Part 2:

State Funding, Bureaucratic Relations and Community Activities

On the Contradictions of State-Sponsored Participation:
A Case Study of the Community Employment Strategy Program in Labrador, Nova Scotia and Prince Edward Island*

Linda Christiansen-Ruffman

Introduction

The Community Employment Strategy (CES) experiment in the mid 1970s was one of the few state-sponsored community participation programs in Canada. Originally conceived as part of the federal-provincial social security review, CES received federal Cabinet approval for a three-year developmental phase on August 8, 1974.[1] Because of an extensive evaluative program, CES offers us a unique opportunity to examine the ideological practices and activities of a community participation program developed and sponsored by the state. This paper focuses on the implementation of the Community Employment Strategy in three provinces with the aim of gaining insights into participation, the state, and contradictions of state-sponsored participation programs.

Although CES was implemented in two "communities" in most provinces, the CES experiment on Prince Edward Island, in Labrador and in Nova Scotia form the empirical base of this paper because they are most familiar to me. No claims are being made that these initiatives exhaust the empirical or theoretical possibilities for implementing the program, nor that they are representative. Nevertheless, their diverseness is instructive and the experiences of each program can be analyzed comparatively to facilitate our understanding of state-sponsored efforts.

I became familiar with CES during 1975–78 while I was working as

*This paper was originally prepared for presentation at the 19th annual Meeting of the Canadian Sociology and Anthropology Association, June 8, 1984 at the University of Guelph, Ontario. I wish to thank Michael Keyes, former Federal Coordinator of CES in Nova Scotia, and the editors for comments on an earlier draft.

a consultant on a sub-contract with DPA Consulting, then called Development Planning Associates, under contract with Canada Employment and Immigration, then called the Department of Manpower and Immigration. As part of a very detailed process and outcome evaluation, interviews were conducted with individuals involved, or who might have been involved, in all aspects of the program by one of the dozen members of our multi-disciplinary evaluation team. Within the bureaucracy interviews were conducted at all levels (with the exception of the federal deputy minister), and the research team had access to correspondence and internal memos relevant to the program. As well, I and other members of the research team were participant observers at key meetings within CES. While the analysis which follows is informed by the data gathered for the two year process and outcome evaluations,[2] it does not use this information directly but focuses at the institutional and program orientational level. CES becomes an occasion for grounded theory.

Originally, CES was an occasion for designing an innovative approach to evaluation research. I had been invited to become involved with writing a proposal to evaluate CES in each of these provinces because of my years of active (and continuing) involvement in community issues and my earlier research on citizen participation. We designed an evaluation methodology consistent with the CES ideology, one which recognized government and community representatives as equal partners in all phases of the CES experiment and its evaluation. Representative evaluation committees consisting of community representatives and government bureaucrats were established to give advice and to receive reports. Although a methodological discussion on this project is beyond the scope of this paper, some of the consequences of this methodology will be discussed in the analysis which follows.

The paper has two major analytic foci. First, it describes the ways in which state-sponsored community participation was actually implemented in three provinces, focusing on how citizen participation was conceived and structured by governmental officials within CES. Second, it analyzes the contradictions of state-sponsored community participation which were evident in the CES experiences. The paper concludes with a speculative evaluation of state-sponsored participation and its potential for transforming the state.

The Community Employment Strategy Experiments

The Community Employment Strategy (CES), a state-sponsored experiment in community participation, had as its aim the design and delivery of employment-related programs and services through involvement of community representatives along with federal and provincial bureaucrats. Its formal objective was "to open up employment opportunities for persons experiencing particular and continuing difficulty in finding and keeping satisfactory employment and who consequently rely on some form of transfer payment for most or all of their income."[3] In fact, CES had several objectives:

□ to open employment opportunities;
□ to bring the "community" into the process of identifying and resolving their own employment-related problems;
□ to develop an innovative strategy of delivering employment-related programs;
□ to coordinate existing government programs.

The CES projects in all provinces shared these official objectives.

The processes of establishing CES programs in each of the provinces was roughly similar. In November 1974, each province was officially invited to participate with the federal government in the development of CES by selecting two sites where CES might be implemented on an experimental basis.[4]

Structurally, all provinces had a full-time federal CES coordinator who was employed by the Canada Employment and Immigration Commission (CEIC). Each province had a part-time provincial coordinator. In Prince Edward Island the position was held by the Director of the Manpower Resources Division in the Provincial Department of Labour. In Newfoundland he was with the Department of Manpower and Industrial Relations, and in Nova Scotia he was with the Department of Social Services. In all three provinces, one of the first tasks was the designation of two communities which would be the focus of the CES experiments. Eventually CES staff was hired at the local level to relate to these communities and the community associations which were established and/or designated. At the provincial level, in all three provinces a Federal-Provincial Work Group was eventually established consisting of state officials from a number of potentially relevant governmental departments at both the federal and provincial levels. In all three provinces, the federal and provincial coordinators were responsible for implementing CES under the overall direction of the Steering Committee containing their bureaucratic superiors. In Nova Scotia, the Steering Committee consisted of only two persons, but more were involved in Newfoundland and Prince Edward Island.

As will be apparent in the next section, in spite of the similarities in program objectives, in directives from the CES office in Ottawa, in structure and in initiation process, the three provinces interpreted the objectives of CES, combined the components and structured the implementation of the program quite differently. To a large extent, the differences hinged on various conceptions of and commitment to community participation by the federal and provincial bureaucrats who were involved.

Differential Implementation of CES Experiments

In examining the CES experiments in the three provinces, it was difficult to recognize that the same program was being implemented. Several factors within CES allowed and in fact contributed to the diversification of implementation modes. An important background factor was the diversity of ideologies and understandings of participation which allowed for different interpretations of community participation within CES. Moreover, the design of CES was largely conceptual. The guidelines that existed were not narrowly prescriptive and there were few rules or implementation strategies.[5] Since it was an experiment, both the definition of the problem and the means of solving it were seen to be emergent. Thus, state officials within each of the provinces were able to shape the implementation of CES, and this ability was strengthened still further because the original conceivers of CES at the federal level were no longer with the program and the new bureaucrats at that level did not share a clear or consistent vision of the program.

The different implementation modes of CES within Atlantic Canada were not formalized but evolved in part because of the ways in which the program was conceived by the individuals and governments involved. The concept of community participation and the organizing abilities of the federal and provincial coordinators created major differences. One may begin to appreciate the differences in programs, and the possibilities and limits of state-sponsored participation, by examining the way in which the various objectives of CES were conceived and the way in which the operations were structured at the provincial and local levels.

Prince Edward Island

In Prince Edward Island the provincial coordinator had originally been involved at the federal-provincial level in formulating the program parameters of CES. He began his job full of enthusiasm about CES because of its experimental nature, its innovative potential and its promised large budget. Financial cutbacks in the program began to reduce provincial enthusiasm. Provincial energy for CES effectively dried up when the federal government refused to allow the continuation of the province's plan to involve the community through the board of what would become a crown corporation aimed at employment generation anywhere in the province. The interim CES board, with individuals from the business community who were to participate in that crown corporation, was disbanded. The budget and program potential were not seen by the provincial officials as large enough to warrant any definite cooperative enterprise, and provincial officials were not enthusiastic about going through a planning exercise involving a number of different departments or the community.

In Prince Edward Island CES was eventually implemented in the two ends of the province—the eastern part of King's County and the western part of Prince County. Existing community boards, the Regional Service Centre Advisory Boards, were utilized for community involvement, but CES was never a very high priority for these Boards. Although they formally made a decision to accept CES as one of their responsibilities, they were not imbued with a vision of CES and its potential. They gave advice, often in a *pro forma* way through correspondence, but they did not see a responsibility for initiating, soliciting or even actively supporting proposals. The CES staff at the local level, a field worker, was employed on short-term contracts by government, not by the community boards, and the community's role was for the most part passive. The Board did not control a budget or have any real authority. On the few occasions where one of the Boards did attempt to participate in a proactive way— such as when the Eastern Kings Board established a sub-committee to develop a strategy—the effort was subsequently ignored by the federal and provincial bureaucrats on Prince Edward Island, by the Federal-Provincial Work Group and by the CES officials in Ottawa. Although the community was asked for advice, authority remained within the state structure.

In spite of a fair amount of organizational chaos and a lack of clear objectives, CES on Prince Edward Island quickly developed a number of employment projects including renovation of a school house for a thrift shop, a housing repair project, a training program, park development and an oyster co-op. CES on Prince Edward Island was also supposed to develop an employment strategy with the community to govern the selection of projects and to coordinate the delivery of employment-related programs among federal and provincial departments. In fact, drafts of the strategy were written primarily by the Prince Edward Island based federal bureaucrat. Ultimately CES staff in Ottawa were directed to help him write a satisfactory document, and their acquiescence to their superiors further helped to underscore the lack of community involvement within CES in Prince Edward Island.

In Prince Edward Island the strategy and structure of CES were least well developed compared to other provinces. In spite of a minimal amount of community involvement, however, employment projects, a strategy and eventually a Federal-Provincial Work Group were set up. The final strategy objective was to support and complement the employment objective of the comprehensive development plan by focusing on the seasonally unemployed as the target population. Unfortunately, most of these projects were short-term and did not address the defined problem of seasonal employment; in fact their short-term nature and timing contributed to seasonal employment. It is one of the ironies of CES on Prince Edward Island that when CES was in the greatest organizational chaos, it delivered the greatest number of projects.

Labrador

In Newfoundland, the Labrador Straits region from L'Anse au Clair to Red Bay was one region where CES was implemented.[6] This relatively isolated region consisted of eight small fishing communities with an average population of 275 (in 1975) situated along a barren coast and connected only by ferry or airplane to the Island of Newfoundland. In establishing CES, the federal and provincial coordinators helped to set up the Community Employment Strategy Association (CESA), locally known as the Committee, with two elected representatives from each community and one member from each relevant organization such as the Southern Labrador Development Association, the Welfare office and the Women's Institute. A new organization was created even though a regional development association (Southern Labrador Development Association, or SLDA) already existed with a similar representative structure.[7] A local CES coordinator from the region was hired by a committee consisting of two local representatives, the federal coordinator and the provincial coordinator, and she began to tackle some of the major development issues of the region—(e.g., the inadequate ferry)—and to do feasibility studies for alternative industries in the area–(e.g., a bake apple liquor). On the ferry issue, for example, the community organizations did not hesitate to use "the political route" and sent a delegation to Ottawa when the ferry operator's license was being reconsidered. With the help of a Memorial University Extension Worker skilled at community development, CESA along with SLDA and Fisheries Committees in each community began to work on a development strategy. With SLDA, CESA established a community priorizing process to assess short-term employment projects, and this process favored employment-related projects consistent with the development strategy.[8]

In Saint John's, Newfoundland, meanwhile, the federal and provincial coordinators had established a Federal-Provincial Work Group with representatives from a number of federal and provincial departments. No one from CESA or the Labrador Straits area was represented officially on this body. From the officials' viewpoint, the Federal-Provincial Work Group was to be the major decision-making and planning body. A number of the CESA members and the Local Coordinator resented being excluded from decision-making, especially in what had been promoted as a community program. One indicator of the resulting tensions between community and state officials surrounded the evaluation. The Federal-Provincial Work Group established a committee to interact with our evaluation team, which was comprised of the CES federal and provincial coordinators and two other state officials but no community representatives and no local coordinator. From the officials' perspective, the evaluation reports were for them and could be changed at their insistence and withheld from community members and the local CES coordinator. As evaluators we saw ourselves as reporting to the three partners to the CES process—the federal government, provincial government and the community.[9]

Compared to CES on Prince Edward Island, the components of the process in Newfoundland and Labrador were more clearly focused on strategy development and more adequately integrated. The coordinators initially encouraged the community and enlisted the community's energy into CES, but they lacked the skills and knowledge to forge a government-community partnership. The community had what it saw as its own organization, but control of major decisions and of its budget remained with the state.

Nova Scotia

In Nova Scotia two very different communities were selected by the government as sites for the CES experiment—residents of one of the poorest and most isolated counties, Guysborough County, and single-parent families in Halifax. In both cases the federal and provincial coordinators helped to establish a community board which was conceived to be in partnership with the state officials in developing a community employment strategy. The community boards in Nova Scotia, unlike those in the other two provinces, were given their own authority and their own resources, attributes considered necessary by the federal and provincial coordinators if community participation was to have any substance. The community boards had a staff which was employed by and reported directly to them. The community boards also had a relatively large budget and some ability to control monetary expenditures.[10] Thus, unlike Prince Edward Island and Labrador, the community associations were able to gain a fair amount of authority over their affairs and to feel they had a stake in the state-sponsored program.

A Federal-Provincial Work Group in Nova Scotia was established and then changed to make it more consistent with the goal of attempting to facilitate the emerging plans and strategies of the community boards. In contrast to the other two provinces, the Nova Scotia Federal-Provincial Work Group was structured explicitly to be supportive of a state-community partnership. In the first place, both staff and board from the CES community were full members of the Work Group. More importantly, the Group was oriented explicitly to be a resource and not a decision-making body. As quoted by Keyes, the preamble of the April 15, 1976 Federal-Provincial Work Group procedure document states that:

> Local Boards [are] responsible for identifying, planning, and implementing economic and economically related strategies and the Federal-Provincial Work Group providing where necessary, assistance in community organizing, contacts with financial and business institutions, cutting red tape, economic development and so forth. . . . The responsibility of the Work Group within this framework is to fill a general supervisory, consulting, assisting role.[11]

The structure of the Federal-Provincial Work Group was consistent with bottom-up rather than top-down planning and embodied the idea of shared authority between community and state. The Work Group structurally recognized the community and the community's potential expertise in identifying and planning employment opportunities which were relevant to local community conditions.

The relationship between the Federal-Provincial Work Group and the community in Nova Scotia was considerably different from that in the other two provinces. In Prince Edward Island, there was no recognition of a community presence and the designated regional social services board was not involved enough in the program to ask for participation. In Newfoundland, community representatives attended meetings only by invitation. The community's right to participate was not recognized, in spite of eventual protests from CESA. In both of these provinces, program action was seen as originating and decisions made within the confines of this committee of state officials. There was no change in top-down authority. Thus, unlike the Nova Scotia CES, these structures were not established to take into account and jointly address the multiple objectives of CES.

In this section we have seen how a state-sponsored community participation program can vary quite considerably both in its concept of participation and in its structure, even within the same general program. Although a detailed description is beyond the scope of this paper, it should also be pointed out that CES in Guysborough, Nova Scotia was a successful CES experiment. It did create a number of full-time small businesses, including the Mulgrave Road Theatre Co-op, which provide employment and tangible proof of the feasability of the CES strategy. Moreover, the community board, led by the chair and with unofficial support from the federal and provincial organizers, refused to change its focus on the need for employment creation in the local community rather than training, despite considerable pressure from the federal department, whose mandate was oriented toward the retraining of individual workers. After CES terminated as a federal program, the community organization was successful in gaining cabinet approval for a proposal from Mulgrave, Guysborough, Canso Development Incentives Ltd. (MGDIL) for a $500,000 capital reserve community revolving fund to support small business enterprises in the local region. It essentially became a community development corporation.[12]

The differences in community participation between Prince Edward Island, Labrador/Newfoundland and Nova Scotia occurred mainly because of the differing community organizational skills and experiences of the coordinators.[13] The Nova Scotian coordinators had considerable previous experience with community organizations. One had organized tenants in urban ghettos and had an excellent understanding of power; he was able to recognize and willing to exploit opportunities to develop CES as a community-based program. Unlike federal and provincial coordinators in other provinces, in Nova Scotia these individuals saw themselves as organizing not only the community but the state bureaucracy in meeting the multiple goals of CES. In accomplishing the complex organizing tasks, they made ideological use of the idea of community participation with their bureaucratic superiors and incorporated the idea of a community-government partnership both in their rhetoric and in their practice. They also believed in the importance of the CES experiment, supported its potential promise with their energies and held a vision of community participation as potentially transformative of the state structure.

Although there were inevitable tensions between the community and the state representatives, these potential conflicts, especially in the Guysborough situation, were utilized constructively. For example, there were tensions surrounding the evaluation in Nova Scotia when the state officials wanted priority review and the evaluators refused, insisting upon community partnership. The supposedly legitimate community emphasis of the program was used by the coordinators, in the evaluative process, against attempts by the larger state bureaucracy to insist upon its "normal" control-oriented practices which exclude the community.

Contradictions

Both the relatively successful example of community participation in the CES experiment in Nova Scotia and its relative failure in the other two provinces point to contradictions within state-sponsored community participation. In this section, we will highlight several empirically emergent contradictions which appeared in the implementation of CES during the evaluation period. These contradictions, in turn, may be related to features of a governmental hierarchy which has perhaps outlived its usefulness.

Contradictions in Priorities and Rewards

State-sponsored community participation leads to contradictions in priorities and rewards because of fundamentally different orientations of community participants and government bureaucrats. The government bureaucracy is not accustomed to treating individuals or communities as important. The lack of priority given to community was most clearly apparent in Prince Edward Island, where the early stages of CES were marred by conflict between levels of governmental bureaucracies. The federal and provincial government officials were each attempting to realize their version of CES and/or to retain control of the program. The community aspect was essentially ignored.[14] Similar battles among government officials between and within jurisdictions marked Federal-Provincial Work Group meetings on some occasions in the other two provinces. What was important was defined in bureaucratic terms which often had little to do with the community.

Even when community representatives were present and articulating their perceptions, it was not uncommon for community priorities to be compromised because the rules were seen as being made by government officials. For example, certain elements of the community strategies were rejected because they were not seen to be within the mandate of the government departments involved. Even in the case of Guysborough, where the community strategy ultimately prevailed, the strategy was rejected at first because it was seen as being outside the department's mandate. Reflecting the attention to community priorities in Guysborough, the composition of the Federal-Provincial Work Group in Nova Scotia was changed so that it would be more consistent with the

Guysborough strategy.[15] In most circumstances, however, the processes governing the activities of state bureaucracies had little to do with the process of working with the community.

Government bureaucracies have clear parameters and explicit sets of rules governing their activities. Although CES had several stated objectives, each was stated singly and many of the bureaucrats treated each objective as requiring unique sets of activities. They also wanted to ensure something measurable was happening (e.g., number of jobs), and they were accustomed to using monetary resources to get results. Although CES had goals both of jobs and of community involvement, ideas about community process were regarded as irrelevant to the goal of producing jobs. It was easier for the bureaucrats to use money to produce jobs.

The result of focusing on discrete priorities in this way is that the unanticipated consequences of actions on other priorities go unrecognized, to say nothing of the effect on unspecified community values. Within CES on Prince Edward Island, normal bureaucratic priorities and rewards resulted in an inverse rather than a direct relationship between community effort in the program and financial rewards. When Prince Edward Island's CES program was not working well according to everybody's account, for example, the Ottawa bureaucrats did not insist on participation or process. Instead, they followed their bureaucratic instincts and sent project money supposedly "to get something going." They were apparently oblivious to the fact that from the standpoint of promoting public participation, this was the worst thing they could do. When the community began to respond with a few of its own initiatives, it was told that there was no more money left. The bureaucrats had now changed the rules to prevent hastily conceived "make-work" projects, the very type which they had helped to initiate. The inappropriateness of the governmental response to these circumstances underscores the contradictions inherent in state-sponsored participation. In fact, within the evaluation period of CES programs in these three provinces, the more a community participated in planning a strategy and the more they did what the program asked them to do, the fewer the monetary resources they procured from CES. At least this tended to be the case within CES programs in the short term.[16]

Contradictions Within the Partnership

According to the rhetoric, citizens and government within CES were supposed to act cooperatively and in partnership. In fact, however, the partnership was one-sided with the government controlling tremendous resources in terms of money, infrastructure, information and expertise. The community associations, for example, relied ultimately on government money to pay their staff, to finance their operations and to support employment-related projects. The reality of inequality on these dimensions was part of the taken for granted structure which "everyone knew." This reality of resource inequality contradicted the idea of a partnership and formed the background of interactions between government officials and members of the community association and staff.

The government-community partnership was clearly not balanced in terms of the contributions of the two partners. In Prince Edward Island "the community" was structured into the CES experiment in such a way as to have almost nothing to bring to the partnership and no basis to counteract the power of the bureaucratic structure. In Nova Scotia, on the other hand, "the community" had some control over its own resources. Moreover, "the fact" of community expertise, on which CES was premised, was highlighted and structured into the community-state relationship within the Federal-Provincial Work Group. The "community," thus, had a source of legitimacy and expertise of its own which it could bring to the partnership and which allowed for some mutuality of relationship in its "partnership" with the state.

To the extent that a community organization gained some autonomy, however, it came into immediate conflict with the felt necessity of "responsible bureaucrats" to assert total control and to exclude all outsiders and unnecessary contingencies. Since CES was a governmental program and since the federal and provincial coordinators were supposed to be "in charge," both in their own view and in the view of others within the governmental structure, there were severe pressures to keep the community under control. A community totally under control, without autonomy, however, could not be a partner. In the more successful programs, therefore, issues of power and control frequently arose.[17] As the community associations gained in strength and ability to work together, almost inevitably some tensions arose between the community association personnel and governmental officials.

In negotiations around a possible partnership between the government and the community within CES, the various CES experiments handled these dilemmas, tensions and contradictions quite differently. As mentioned above, in Prince Edward Island, the community was never treated as a partner; the two designated community organizations were not very involved with the program; and hence issues of power and control rarely arose. In Labrador, the federal and provincial coordinators began to establish a community organization which would permit a partnership. Once the community organization began to experience itself as capable of independent action, however, the "state control response" was activated. The coordinators attempted to regain control by stifling community initiatives and undermining the paid community staff. Their lack of experience with community organization may be contrasted with that of the Nova Scotia coordinators who persisted in the establishment of viable, community organizations.

The two organizations in Nova Scotia differed somewhat in the extent to which they achieved "partnership" with governmental officials. In the experiment with Halifax single parents, the governmental officials and community board and staff never established a good working relationship and on some occasions the "state control response" dominated their relationship.[18] In Nova Scotia's Guysborough experiment, however, the governmental officials and community board and staff eventually reached a situation of trust necessary for a partnership and developed a shared vision. Subsequently the governmental officials closely associated with CES attempted to organize the bureaucracy to accomplish the agenda necessary to realize that vision.

Even in the Guysborough situation, however, the state control response frequently interrupted attempts to establish a working relationship. The idea of confidentiality became a major issue on several occasions.[19] Some governmental officials considered all information to be privileged and for the eyes of the state alone. They considered it illegitimate to share information with anyone outside of the bureaucratic structure. The federal CES coordinator in Nova Scotia was reprimanded for "giving away information" to the community. On the other hand, he could argue that the idea of a partnership required sharing of information and "insider" knowledge.

Contradictions between Community Participation
and Bureaucratic Functioning

State-sponsored community participation also sets up contradictions with the usual norms of bureaucracy. Bureaucratic impersonality and rule-guidedness is functional for impartial and ordered administration of government programs. The realities of dealing with citizens, especially those living at a distance or working during the day, creates numerous practical problems for the bureaucrat. For example, hours of work had to be modified considerably to be "on hand" when citizens were available. Individual governmental officials were not rewarded for their consideration of the partnership; for example, when they scheduled meetings outside of office hours and when they travelled to out-of-office meetings to meet the requirements of community volunteers, sometimes they were negatively sanctioned. The hours which federal and provincial coordinators spent in travel were often not counted as work, and when bureaucrats took day-time hours off in exchange for the fifteen and sixteen hour days they were working while in the field, colleagues in the bureaucracy often thought that they "were getting away with something" and not "putting in the right hours of work." The state bureaucracy with its routinized work day, tended to ignore the invisible time away from the bureaucracy, and it had few mechanisms for rewarding the difficult, immeasurable organizational work which was being done.

The norms of bureaucratic impersonality were challenged by the involvement of governmental officials with the community. From the CES experience, the inappropriateness for communities such as Guysborough of some governmental rules, programs and procedures could not be avoided. The government, however, did not intend to reward innovation and questioning, and this placed governmental officials working with the community in impossible situations. If governmental officials did become advocates of citizen concerns, they put themselves in a highly visible and vulnerable position and risked being transferred. Serving citizen interests violated the norm of lack of personal commitment; trying new ways violated the norm of routinization; and becoming involved and caring for the community violated the the norm of impersonality. Working with members and staff of the community association to develop new, innovative solutions to community employment problems was clearly not the normal business of a state bureaucrat. Innovative use of programs to suit special needs of a community created problems and hindered the smooth flow of state affairs. At one stage of the program, some officials were threatened with law suits because rules were not being followed. A number of governmental officials put pressure on the coordinators because it was clearly easier for a government bureaucracy to function without community participation.

Contradictions of State Competence and Incompetence— the Crisis of Top-Down Expert Planning

On the one hand the state commands and is seen to command tremendous resources. It has at its disposal, for example, expert planners. One of the goals and implicit realities contained in CES is that "the community" has expertise to contribute meaningfully and uniquely to planning solutions and ways of dealing with its future. The almost inevitable strain between some expert top-down planners and "the community" as planners may be conceived as a struggle for control or as a struggle for priority which has been discussed above.

On another level, however, the existence and recognition of citizen expertise challenges the existing structure of top-down planning and the sanctity of expert knowledge and hence points to a major contradiction within the state apparatus, if not society itself. This contradiction was graphically illustrated within the Newfoundland/Labrador CES. As mentioned before, the community and government bureaucrats tended to disagree on a number of items including whose task it was to write the community employment strategy for Labrador Straits. What happened is that both parties attempted to write a strategy and both relied on some outside help. In Labrador, despite inter-community rivalries, members of community organizations such as CESA, SLDA, the fisheries committees and the agricultural committees worked together and wrote a relatively comprehensive and integrated strategy with the help of the local Memorial University extension worker. The bureaucrats and expert planners, on the other hand, were less successful. They enlisted the help of a consultant who solicited information from the representative of every department involved in CES and literally reported each view. The bureaucratic divisions among departments and competing federal-provincial jurisdictions prevented a comprehensive plan from emerging. Although any top-down structure is designed to appear comprehensive if one is sitting on top, in practice the fragmentation into departmental jurisdictions and the lack of a grounded community focus prevented a comprehensive vision. The government officials in Newfoundland were reciting their departmental priorities when they were supposedly planning a development strategy for the community; people living in the eight small communities in Labrador were not part of their focus. Analytically, the community was "apart"—and the bureaucratically organized parts could not reconstruct a viable, comprehensive and sensible plan for the whole.

In spite of the tremendous differential in material resources available to the state compared to those available in Labrador, the community-based planning process performed more competently. And there were structural reasons for this. In spite of few material resources at the community's disposal, the community had its own knowledge and expertise. The persistence of competency, responsibleness and trustworthiness at the community level belied the state's "normal" orientation of mistrust and its low opinion of its citizenry. Moreover, the planning exercise in Labrador graphically illustrates that despite more expert resources, the governmental system of planning does not and is likely not able to work at the community level. It clearly challenges the nature of expertise and of top-down planning.

The Transformative Potential of Community Participation

The contradictions inherent in state-sponsored participation may lead one to suggest its abandonment, or at least the abandonment of state-sponsored participation programs. Recognizing, however, that contradictions are inevitable in our society, one might instead focus on the nature of the contradictions implicit in state-sponsored participation and the transformative potential of the practice. The struggle for participation focuses attention on some of the problematic features of government organized bureaucracies, and the practice of the Nova Scotia CES made visible one of the directions of this transformation.

In Nova Scotia the Federal-Provincial Work Group consisted of bureaucrats from both federal and provincial government departments as well as the community board chairpersons and paid staff. It was organized by the federal and provincial coordinators not as a decision-making body but as a facilitating body. Over the two years or so of its meetings, the governmental officials involved began to orient their attention to the needs of the community and to talk about how their departments' programs might be useful—or how certain information might be helpful in putting together a proposal or doing a feasibility study. Although there was some friction over federal versus provincial jurisdiction and over the territoriality of one department compared with another in the beginning, this territoriality of jurisdiction and departments tended to be minimized as attention became focused on helping to solve community problems.

The extent of this cooperative and facilitating orientation was quite clear when an Ottawa bureaucrat responsible for CES came to Halifax. He was accustomed to the usual hierarchy and obviously felt that he, as a representative of Ottawa, the senior government, had the most authority and power. He did not consider it appropriate that anyone from the community was a partner at a decision-making meeting and went into the meeting to negotiate with the other relevant bureaucrats. The bureaucrats who had been part of the Federal-Provincial Work Group began to point out the inappropriateness of the Ottawa bureaucrat's orientation. They argued that a community representative should be involved and began to teach him the importance of focusing on the community. As a result of the CES process in Nova Scotia, and consistent with the community orientation ideologically endorsed within the CES, this federal bureaucrat began to act, albeit haltingly, with a new orientation toward his role. Rather than attempting to control the organization, he began to try to use his influence among other Ottawa bureaucrats to find resources necessary for implementing the CES Guysborough community economic strategy.

The community orientation of CES in Guysborough began to transform this small sector of CES from a typical top-down bureaucratic orientation, emphasizing control and preventing creative and community-oriented activity, into an organization focused on and committed to the delivery of resources and support for community initiatives. By focusing directly on community needs as embodied by people who saw themselves as representing the community, some of the bureaucratic inflexibility and petty departmental territoriality came to be superceded. A more creative process of bottom-up planning began to be instituted in spite of the pressure from within the bureaucracy as described above.

The emerging potential within the Federal-Provincial Work Group was never entirely realized. The CES experiment was cancelled, even before the evaluation was submitted and studied. Some of the positive dynamics recognized as existing in Guysborough and in a few other CES projects became components of a new CEIC departmental program, Local Economic Development Assistance, LEDA. The transformative components, however, were apparently not incorporated in the new program. Indeed, this could be read as further evidence of the triumph of state control.

Conclusion: The Contradictions of State-Sponsored Participation

In the implementation of CES in the three provinces a number of contradictions in state-sponsored community participation became apparent. Because participation often involves struggle and some change in the power and decision-making structures, the very existence of state-sponsored participation programs is somewhat of a contradiction. The state structure, which is organized to govern through its authoritative decision-making structures, does not normally foster ideals of power-sharing, especially in the centers of power.[20]

It is not surprising, therefore, that in spite of community advocacy of citizen participation, individuals and groups are often skeptical of citizen participation efforts which are sponsored by the state. Even people who have been participation advocates are afraid of being co-opted by participation designed to serve state interests and not arising out of the community's needs and struggles. State-sponsored participation is open to manipulation and co-optation and to wide interpretation of the nature of participation itself. It may deflect people away from the important issues. Skepticism of state-sponsored participation tends to be supported in the writing of contemporary political economists. For example, Loney argues that: "Overall government funding and involvement in the voluntary sector must be seen as a conservatizing force."[21] Although the skepticism is well justified, it is my contention that Loney's sweeping statement is not useful analytically and is politically misleading and defeatist. We must begin to examine the conditions under which state-sponsored participation in fact allows greater community control.

Analytically it is useful to recognize the multiple contradictions within state-sponsored programs, including both their controlling and conservatizing tendencies and their progressive potential. In fact, one might argue that at the basis of the contemporary state is rooted the ideological legitimacy of participation[22] as well as the structural forces of hegemonic control which oppose participation.[23] If we adopt both of these concepts of the state, we will notice that their implications are contradictory; hence these two concepts together may help us to make sense of some of the contradictions apparent within the CES experiments. Some readers, accustomed to the "either/or syndrome" which dominates Western thought, may protest that only one of these two concepts of the state is "correct." I would argue that the concepts are not logically contradictory because they can be seen as being at different levels of analysis. Adopting these two concepts simultaneously allows us to see that at the basis of the contemporary state is rooted the ideological legitimacy of participation as well as the structural forces which oppose participation.

For an activist, confronted with the contradictions of state-sponsored community participation, two opposite conclusions might be reached. One possible conclusion is that state-sponsored community participation is a contradiction in terms, that it exploits the community and that it is not worth the effort either of the citizens or bureaucrats involved. The second, and opposite conclusion, is that state-sponsored community participation, although extremely difficult, is important for the increased involvement and better results of community-based planning, and ultimately, for transformations within the state.

The experience of CES and the diversity of its implementation would lead one to adopt the second option. This would underline the importance of citizen participation to transform the existing power of the state, to mitigate the worst abuses of departmental territoriality and to focus state policies more directly on communities which, ideally, bureaucracy is designed to serve. While agreeing with functional analyses of the current state system such as that of O'Connor[24] which focus on the ways in which the state serves capitalists' interests, and recognizing the existence of the state control response, it is important for activists not to adopt the conservative stance implicit in such analysis and not to allow their inaction to contribute to legitimizing functions of the state which are against the interests of local communities and ordinary citizens. Community participation and its capacity to focus both objectives and process on diverse individuals and on the communities which it is designed to serve has a transforming potential. In fact, it contains within it a very different concept of power.

The diversity of CES indicates the difficulties, the contradictions and the possibilities of state-sponsored participation. As the oppressiveness and inappropriateness of our large-scale, centralized attempts to solve society's problems becomes more glaringly apparent, and our ability to destroy the world becomes increasingly part of the world's consciousness, it is my view that an ideology and practice based on community participation is increasingly necessary, appropriate and possible.

NOTES

1. The origin of CES may be traced directly to the federal-provincial Social Security Review; more specifically, it was one of five strategies contained in the "Working Paper on Social Security in Canada" presented in April 1973 by the Federal-Provincial Working Party on Employment and contained in the paper "Toward an Employment Strategy." On August 8, 1974 the federal Cabinet approved a three-year development phase for CES, and the Department of Manpower and Immigration was made the responsible government department. This department was subsequently reorganized into the Canada Employment and Immigration Commission (CEIC), and the senior official who chaired the Federal-Provincial Working Party on Employment was appointed to chair the CEIC. With extensions, CES continued until March 1979, when it was said to be a victim of financial restraint.

2. See Development Planning Associates Limited, *Labrador Straits Community Employment Strategy*. Prepared for the Canada Employment and Immigration Commission, the CES Coordinators, and the Communities in Labrador Straits, 4 volumes, 1978; Development Planning Associates Ltd., *Evaluation of the Community Employment Strategy in Prince Edward Island*. Prepared for Canada Employment and Immigration Commission and the Joint Federal-Provincial Manpower Needs Committee for Prince Edward Island, 5 volumes, 1978; and Development Planning Associates Limited, *Evaluation of the Community Employment Strategy in Nova Scotia*. Prepared for Canada Employment and Immigration Commission and the Nova Scotia CES Research and Evaluation Committee, 6 volumes, 1978.

3. Canada Employment and Immigration Commission, *Community Employment Strategy 1976–1977*. Ottawa: Supply and Services Canada, 1977.

4. Even before this, the process had begun in Prince Edward Island. In October an official from the CES secretariat in Ottawa, CES-O, had described CES at a meeting of the Joint Federal Provincial Manpower Needs Committee, the senior policy group in Prince Edward Island which was given ultimate responsibility for CES on Prince Edward Island and thus called the Steering Committee. Letters of understanding concerning CES on Prince Edward Island were exchanged in January 1975. A federal coordinator was appointed from CEIC; the position became full-time on April 1, 1975. The Provincial CES coordinator was part-time as he also held the position of Director of the Manpower Resources Division in the Provincial Department of Labour. A similar process of initiation took place in the other provinces.

5. Indeed, it is likely that the originators of CES would have argued that clear implementation strategies would have been inappropriate because they would have undermined community development efforts. It is one of the contradictions of state-sponsored participation that bureaucratic rules tend to inhibit community efforts and yet most state officials are not skilled or knowledgeable enough to implement community programs without such rules. Even programs fortunate enough to have "committed" government bureaucrats in the first generation tend to falter over time as the bureaucratic hiring process tends to emphasize skills valued by the bureaucracy and inappropriate to promoting participation.

6. The other CES location in Newfoundland, on the Port au Port peninsula, was evaluated by another consulting company.

7. The two organizations tended to work cooperatively and their existence was the beginning of a non-competitive working regional orientation among the highly independent and relatively distinct communities. As might be expected, there were intense inter-community rivalries over, for example, the placement of a fish plant.

8. One feature of the development plan formation and the subsequent priorizing process was the extent to which it marginalized women and women's projects. The plan was mainly developed by men and it mainly related to the fishery. In response to a call for short-term employment generating projects (Canada Works), both men and women had submitted projects. The men's projects tended to be funded; the women's projects were not. One reason for this decision was the plan. The other reason was the perception that women should not be paid for labor which they would do anyway. The same, equally applicable argument, was not made concerning men's labor or men's projects.

In the following year the women in one community submitted a project to renovate a community building since this type of project had been and was funded. While this shows women's enterprise and the presence of a strongly felt women's culture, it nevertheless indicates how in the so-called developed world, women must compete in a men's world to receive benefits such as government grants.

9. Eventually the evaluation process broke down over the issue of control and the evaluators wrote a report submitted to all three parties.

10. In fact, single parents in Halifax were targeted in two geographic areas of the City, and astute community negotiations resulted in both the North End and the Spryfield area having its own coordinator, staff and budget.

11. Michael J. Keyes, *The Politics of Guysborough Community Employment Strategy Association (C.E.S.A.) 1975–1980: An Experiment in Rural Job Creation and Retention.* M.A. Thesis in Public Administration, Dalhousie University, 1980, p. 57.

12. See *ibid.*

13. Comparative analysis of the implementation of CES at the three sites indicates that the differences are mainly attributed to the individuals involved, a finding not common in contemporary sociological analysis. The individuals were working within specific structural constraints, but there was enough flexibility even within this government program to organize the process very differently. Such a finding tends to support the importance of an action-oriented theoretic approach and the efforts of activists, at least in the short term.

14. In fact, this tendency for those in power to convert new initiatives for their own purposes has been observed on a number of occasions by the women's movement. With considerable frequency, a resolution concerning women's rights will be changed into the "more general case" to suit other political interests. If women and other disempowered groups are not careful, ultimately their initial concerns are forgotten.

15. Keyes, *op. cit.*

16. Although this was true in the short term, in fact the CES participation efforts which did work at planning later received resources from outside of CES. For example, CES was relevant to the Coastal Labrador DREE agreement and to the Guysborough community revolving fund.

17. It may be that community participation within CES had even more problems with control than in other departments of government because of the elaborate systems of accountability and the highly rigid rules within CEIC: A number of informants experienced with the operation of government departments have mentioned having found CEIC, the federal department administering CES, to be most bureaucratic of all departments; one consultant called it "a bureaucratic nightmare."

One should not be surprised at the highly developed and rigid system of control within that department since, in some ways, that department is one of the leaders in state control. Its major function is to control those who do not "fit in" because of their immigrant or unemployed status. One could imagine the department having developed elaborate systems for treating such people harshly, impersonally and non-sympathetically as a way of protecting the state against undesirables. CEIC also has upgrading programs to train marginal people in skills required to be "proper" Canadian citizens. Another and supporting reason for the elaborate and rigid bureaucracy in CEIC is the large number of people processed by the department. In dealing with large numbers efficiently, bureaucracy must not pay too much attention to individuality or to question the routinized tasks. (See also Ng's paper in this collection).

18. Both Halifax and Guysborough within Nova Scotia shared approximately the same amount of power over staff and resources. The community boards and coordinators in the two places were roughly similar in their ability to understand the need for resources and community control. The difference appeared to be that the community representatives in Halifax distrusted state power and their ability to work in partnership with the state. They had little expectation of creating a highly successful program, little energy compared to the staff and board in Guysborough, and no clear vision of a transformed world. Their political sophistication and their other life responsibilities led to a degree of alienation from the program. They worked extremely hard and conscientiously for long hours, but within the parameters of what they thought was possible, compared to the community actors and coordinators in Guysborough who tackled what jaded reason might have argued was impossible.

19. The issue of confidentiality is not unique to the CES experience. It has been raised on other occasions when community members have attempted to become part of a planning process. For a description of this process in a hospital planning exercise, see Linda Christiansen-Ruffman and Janis Wood Catano, "Resistance to Consumer Participation Among Health Planners: A Case Study of BONDING's Encounters with Entrenched Ideas and Structures," *Resources for Feminist Research*, Vol. 15 (1), 1986, pp. 21–23. A similar process was reported by a female member of a political party. When women struggle and finally gained representation on the committee which made appointments to boards and commissions, that committee reportedly no longer met. In fact, confidentiality generally becomes an issue when people gain access to information normally under organizational control. The organization, or the state, fears the misuse of information by people it cannot control in terms of jobs, salaries, etc. The community in this case takes on the position of stranger, as one who cannot be trusted. Even when community members gain access to one set of structures, they often find that those in control simply shift "important" information and decision-making to a different arena.

20. It is not surprising, therefore, that we find ideas of participation more attractive to politicians early in their terms and that we find participation schemes most common in the more peripheral government departments where additional authority vis-à-vis their more powerful colleagues may be derived from involving the people.

21. See Martin Loney, "A Political Economy of Citizen Participation," in Leo Panitch (ed.), *The Canadian State: Political Economy and Political Power*. Toronto: University of Toronto Press, 1977, pp. 446–472, especially p. 454.
22. See, for example, Carole Pateman, *Participation and Democratic Theory*. Cambridge: Cambridge University Press, 1970.
23. See, for example, Rianne Mahon, "Canadian Public Policy: The Structure of Representation," in Leo Panitch, 1977, *op. cit*, pp. 165–198 for a discussion of the state as an organizer of bourgeois hegemony.
24. See James O'Connor, *The Fiscal Crisis of the State*. New York: St. Martin's Press, 1973.

Ladies, Women and the State:
Managing Female Immigration, 1880–1920

Barbara Roberts

Introduction

Members of women-to-women services or community groups in the 1980s sometimes worry if they are doing the right thing, knowing that their efforts help the state to manage dissonance and pain in people's lives which, properly nurtured, might turn to dissent and lead to social change to their benefit. The women activists and immigration reformers of our great-grandmothers' generation examined here, ladies of the ruling classes who imported British domestic servants to build the Empire by working in Canadian kitchens, had few such qualms. They believed that on the whole, their interests, the interest of women immigrants, and those of the government coincided. They, therefore, expected the men in government to support their projects by giving them government grants and access to such information, services and facilities as existed. In turn, the ladies did the work, provided program development, management, delivery and staffing. This partnership was mutually beneficial (although lopsided) for several decades until the senior partner (the government) changed the rules to meet its new needs. Throughout, the women who were the objects of the ladies' services were helped and managed: recruited, selected, shipped, received, and distributed into their niches. Although the context and details are quite different from those of our time, and the rules have changed somewhat, there is much that is familiar.

This paper examines the kind of work done by these women of the ruling class (hereafter "ladies"), and how they organized themselves in relation to those men who managed the Canadian state between 1880 and 1920. It focuses on how the ladies organized working class, single women from other countries into becoming domestic servants, and illustrates some of the issues encountered by these ladies in dealing with immigration policy and practice, including securing government grants, resisting government control of the work, managing record keeping and reporting practices, and handling relations between members of staff and the board of management who ran the ladies' projects.

My sources are documentary: the papers of the Women's National Immigration Society and of the Immigration Department, held for the most part in the Public Archives of Canada. My own interest in these ladies and their Society stems from four sources: my experience as an immigrant to Canada; my involvement in various grassroots feminist organizations; my interest in immigration history and ethnic and women's studies; and my commitment as a feminist historian to uncover women's heritage. On a less abstract plane, I also wanted to know if we could adopt any of the methods used by the ladies to reclaim from the government larger amounts of our tax dollars so that they might serve women's interests rather than those of the government.

The experiences briefly described here of the Women's National Immigration Society and of Eliza Corneil illustrate the increasing intervention of government in immigration between 1880 and 1920. During the course of these four decades, the government became involved not only in managing female immigrant traffic, but in regulating the activities of the ladies' organizations which had long been recruiting, screening, selecting, receiving and settling single women immigrants in Canada. These ladies' groups had done important work in supplying the labor markets of the Empire, with minimal government support or interference, since the middle of the nineteenth century. From the early years of the twentieth century, the ladies spent inordinate amounts of time and energy scrambling for government grants; their efforts relied heavily on the personal and class influence of their male affiliates. By 1920, the management of female immigration had been taken over by professionals employed or controlled by the Canadian government. This pattern of increasing state intervention suggests that the intensification of government control over immigrant and other women's services is not a new phenomenon, but existed in the early decades of our century. More research is needed to trace the ruling processes of government in their historical particularities as they articulated the everyday activities, both organizational and individual, of women in different classes in this period.

The Historical Context
Between 1880 and 1920, Canada changed from a rural agrarian nation to

an essentially urban industrial one. It has often been described as a period of nation building. Two types of nation building took place during these years. The first was economic, and involved the development of a national system of manufacturing, building national markets, the intensification of agricultural production and resource exploitation, and the provision of systems of communication, transportation, and administration necessary to support the efforts of government and entrepreneurs. The second was the creation of the human nation: the building of the communities and the society of Canada. The latter was both contingent on the former and a part of the former. The work of women was fundamental to both.

Women reformers were very much involved in immigration. Part of their interest stemmed from the difficulty they experienced in finding domestic servants for their own homes. This difficulty persisted despite the fact that most single women immigrants to Canada were domestic servants, domestic service being the major occupation for single women at that period. Nevertheless, more than self-interest motivated these reformers. They felt themselves called to participate in the great work of nation building, and it is in this context that their work must be seen. Much of the work of Canadian women reformers has already been detailed, and more is in the process of being explored.[1] The work of these reformers in the nation building efforts of this period is particularly fascinating because of the questions it raises about the relationships between sex and class groupings, nationalism, maternalism, racism, and about the aims, limitations, effects and accomplishments of reform in general and women's reforms in particular. In no sector of the women's reform movement are these questions brought more sharply into focus than in the sector of the immigrationists—that small group of women who concerned themselves with supplying and supervising a stream of immigrant women to Canada.

Whatever else Canadian women reformers have been (such as upper-class urban dwellers), they were generally quite patriotic. Most women reformers in this period were apparently proud of Canada's development and optimistic about its future. Although it was not until nearly the end of the nineteenth century that Wilfrid Laurier proclaimed the twentieth century to be Canada's, immigrationist reformers had long been working on the assumption that this was so. The government and big business agreed that a vigorous immigration was a necessary means to build the Canada of the future, although they did not always agree upon who should come here to do the building. For the immigrationist reformers, the problem was not so complex. Whether they discussed female immigration as a remedy for the shortage of household help, or as a necessary component of building the Empire strong and true in the Dominion, they aimed to build a community of which anyone could be proud. Canada was to be a British country, founded upon the moral, patriotic and racial influence (and unpaid labor) of British wives and mothers in Canadian homes.

The immigrationists often spoke of themselves and were spoken of by others as Empire builders. They saw themselves as providing a vital service to the nation as well as to the women immigrants whom they helped select, ship over, supervise, place in jobs, and start upon their mission in the life of the nation. These reformers were ready to cooperate with anyone who seemed to share their goals and was willing to go along with their methods. They were particularly pleased to work with government and business interests, in a variety of projects in which their priorities all seemed to coincide. There was seldom serious conflict between these parties. Women immigrationist reformers did not see their interests or goals as in conflict with those of government or business, and only at times did they see a conflict in method. By the same token, business and government were pleased to avail themselves of the services of the immigrationists, and for the most part were cooperative as long as they did not have to pay too high a price in money or inconvenience for the work that the ladies were eager to do. On the rare occasions when the reformers wanted to use methods or carry out programs that were too expensive, government and business were likely to become less enthusiastic partners. Despite the generally amicable tone of the relations between the three parties, however, the immigrationists were not equals in the decision-making aspects of the partnership. They did not, in the end, command the resources of the other two, and had not the means to enforce their preferences. Instead, they had to rely on personal influence derived from their class position, lobbying male relatives and friends who did have political power because they held political office or owned large and powerful enterprises. This was decreasingly effective as the twentieth century progressed.

By 1920 the situation had changed considerably from forty years earlier. Canada was urbanized, industrialized and modernized. Work was performed differently, and women worked increasingly in occupations other than domestic service. British women were less susceptible to the blandishments of the immigration societies and the lure of Canadian conditions. Changes in the British economy had virtually cut off the supply of the relatively desperate but respectable and experienced single women workers upon whom the immigrationists had largely depended. Immigration work was taken over by professionals who often were employed by the government, followed approved procedures, and had bureaucratic priorities. The immigration of British domestics became a part of the Empire Settlement Scheme, mapped out by the British Colonial Office and the Canadian federal government. The Canadian Department of Immigration established a Women's Bureau to oversee the female immigrant traffic. It was no longer necessary to support the ladies' notions of how to do nation building and the importance of women-controlled services for women in order to buy the use of the reformers' facilities and services. By establishing an independent women's council of representatives from a variety of women's reform groups to oversee the provision of these services, the government put in place an administrative framework following its own preferences and priorities, to deal with particular issues in the immigration of women. The government managed the reformers by giving them free rein in distributing funds to women-run female immigrant reception facilities, while at the same time protecting itself from pressures to integrate women reformers' priorities into its policies and proceedings.

Immigrationist reformers often provided cheap social service agencies for the federal government. The unpaid or cheap labor of women established, maintained and operated an extensive and effective network designed to meet the needs of women immigrants, and to provide services and facilities to make the immigration experience possible as well as more comfortable. Without the work of these reformers, immigration would have been an even more trying experience for the single women who came here from the British Isles. Even after the advent of steam made it profitable to eliminate some of the worst horrors of the Atlantic crossing, travel by steerage was not comfortable. Getting off the ship, through the immigration procedures and onto a train with money and baggage intact could be a formidable task for someone who did not know what to expect, exactly where to go, to whom to speak and whom to trust. And once on the trains the problems were not over. Train travel for immigrants could be dreadful in the 1880s, so much so that at one point the head of Canadian Pacific ordered that respectable second class passengers, especially women, could travel in first class cars at no extra charge in order to avoid the rough company and cigarette smoke of loggers and laborers.[2] Conditions improved in the ensuing decades but never to the point of great comfort.

It was the presence and work of the women reformers that helped make these transitions bearable for some women immigrants. Escorting parties to and on ships, meeting immigrants at the docks, helping them collect belongings, taking them to quarters, providing a safe and pleasant place to rest, meals to eat, and other women to talk with, finding jobs, offering a place to meet friends and socialize during time off, or, in the case of women going on to the Northwest, handing them from one link on the reformer chain to the next—these services were useful, whatever their other effects. Most of them were financed by a combination of private contributions of time, materials and in some instances money, as well as government grants from municipal, provincial and federal bodies. Much of the work was centered in homes for the reception of female immigrants, such as that of the Women's Protective Immigration Society (WPIS) in Montreal. The work of the WPIS provides an interesting example of the early patterns of cooperation between immigrationist reformers and the federal government, and the transition of the management of immigration work from the private and personal to the public and bureaucratic domain.

The Society

The Women's Protective Immigration Society (WPIS) was founded in 1881 in Montreal under the patronage of the Princess Louise, wife of the Canadian head of state, the Governor General. The women who founded this society were the wives and daughters of families which were among the most important in the city and the most powerful in the country. Their men were the owners and directors of the industrial, commercial and financial enterprises that were seen as synonymous with the nation—railroads, steamship and other transportation and utility companies; many kinds of industrial and manufacturing plants; banks, insurance companies and other financial and commercial institutions; and a broad range of other powerful interests. These women were mostly but not entirely of British origin, and were of different political and religious affiliations. Some were related by descent or marriage; all were linked by their class and sex. These ladies saw themselves as an influential group called to do important work and to play a significant role in the expansion and building of the young nation. They were feminists in that they believed that their interests as women were more important than their religious and political differences; in fact they refused to allow any sectarian religious element to enter their work, and in Canada of the 1880s that was a radical stand. They were maternalist in their assumption that single women immigrants needed moral guidance and protection which they, as upper-class women and feminists, were uniquely qualified and called to provide. These ladies were accustomed to being taken seriously. They were politically adroit, and of course very well connected. Thus, for a time, they usually got more or less what they wanted.

They wanted little. The first year of the Society they requested but did not receive a $1,000 federal grant. The second year, they opened a reception hostel on Mansfield Street in Montreal, and got the federal grant to help run it. At this time, there were virtually no other facilities for the reception, protection and distribution of single women immigrants in Montreal. To pay the WPIS $1,000 was cheaper for the government than to provide decent facilities of its own. The money bought the government the facilities and staff necessary to do the job; the ladies got the status of a quasi-government agency. Both sides were very pleased with the bargain. To consider this transaction in the context of the times, it is helpful to realize that in 1887 the total spent by the government on immigration was $313,891. The $1,000 granted that year to the WPIS was the only money given to any agency to deal with female immigrants. About 2% of all English immigrants entering Canada in 1887 were assisted by the WPIS for an expenditure that represented only about three-tenths of a percent of the total immigration budget.[3]

In the ensuing years the WPIS worked closely with its main sending agency, the British Women's Emigration Association (founded in the mid-nineteenth century by a group of English feminists who saw emigration as an immediate alternative and long-term supplement to the struggle to get increased occupational opportunities and a living wage for women), and with other groups in the British Isles. As well, the Society assisted women sent out by emigration agents or coming on their own. The Canadian section of the female immigration network began at the dock at Quebec City which was the main port of entry at that time. Women immigrants who were travelling in groups (known as "protected parties") would be under the care of a matron responsible to the sending agency while on board ship. All other women immigrants were said to be "unprotected" if they were not under the care of a designated person such as an older family member, responsible male or older female, or matron. The protected women would be handed over to the WPIS representative at Quebec City; the other women also would be gathered up (if they were willing) by her and included in her care. The responsibility of the WPIS representative was to see that all these women were safely delivered to friends, family or, in the case of domestics, employers. Those women going on would be sent to the WPIS Home in Montreal. (After 1897 there was a sister institution in Winnipeg, after 1906 in Toronto, and later in major cities all the way across the country from Halifax to Vancouver, all set up and run by women reformers interested in female immigration.) Travel to Montreal and points west was by train, and often not very comfortable. Parties of women under the care of the Society would be escorted on trains by a woman; others often were not. In all cases they were met at the train station in Montreal and taken to the WPIS Home, where they could rest until they were sent to jobs or put back on the train to go west to family, friends, employers or other women's groups who would repeat the process until the immigrant arrived at her destination. At least this was the way the network operated in theory.

In fact, the network appears to have worked surprisingly well. In the early years when the WPIS was virtually the only organized group doing this work, fewer immigrants were going to the West and Northwest. When the flow of traffic became heavier, the women's organizations had become better organized in their work and were more or less able to cope with their particular part of the immigration process—or so it appears from the records. The WPIS Home was a multipurpose institution (as were its sister hostels across the country). It served as hostel, placement agency, complaint bureau, social center, and post office box for newly arrived women immigrants. Those women who were between jobs or who needed a holiday could return to the Home for varying periods. This served a useful purpose for the WPIS, as immigration virtually ceased during the winter and thus the Home was almost empty of women much of this time. The managers decided to use it as a boarding home for women, most of whom were their "old girls." The exact procedures of the WPIS changed over time, as immigration increased, train schedules improved, other ports became more widely used, and other facilities became available; but the main outlines remained the same.

Most of the women who worked in this female immigration network were unpaid. The arrangements varied from one Home to the other, but in Montreal, the Matron and domestic staff of the Home were full-time paid employees responsible to the ladies of the managing committee of the Society. To handle the paperwork involved in these institutions, there was a Secretary who was often a volunteer, and perhaps a clerical staff of one. In Montreal, the paperwork was done mainly by the ladies of the Society. In some instances a woman working as a matron escorting immigrants to various parts of the Empire might remain in a Canadian Home for a period of months, work in the Home, then return to her original work. Sometimes matrons were unpaid. Although the principles upon which this network were based had originated in Britain in the middle of the nineteenth century, decades of practice in female migration reform work led to some variety in the arrangements that might be made in a particular case.

Struggle for Resources and Control

Despite the fact that most of the women working with the Home in Montreal were unpaid, money was a constant problem for the Home. The income and expenditures of the Home varied somewhat from year to year. The federal grant was usually about half the annual income of the Society. The province contributed a fixed sum ($500), and a like amount was raised by boarders' fees. Donations did come in but seldom reached the amount of federal or provincial grants. The federal grant gradually increased over the years from the initial $1,000 annually to a high of $2,000, but it did not keep up with the increasing costs of the Home. By the end of the first decade of the twentieth century, the Home was trying to cope with its share of the boom in immigration to Canada. While it is true that far fewer women passed through the hands of the Montreal Society as trains began to go directly from the ports of entry to Toronto and the West, sizeable numbers still stayed at the Home. In the years just before the outbreak of the first World War, over 800 women annually stayed for 24 hours or more. By this time, prices of everything had increased. The federal grant paid for the food and laundry costs in these years, but no more. The operating costs of the Home had to be met by other means. The Society argued that since it was performing a needed service for the government, the government should pay for it.

For some years the story of the Home demonstrates a recurring struggle to wrest a larger grant from the federal government. Although relations between the Home and the government were amiable in nearly all other respects, there were several distinct periods of conflict over the grant: around 1895; between 1897–1906; and during the 1914–18 War. The 1895 problem was short-lived and easily solved. The federal grant was cut in half that year, probably because the appropriation for immigration had been cut by one-third.[4] It was restored the following year. The Society had written letters of protest, but it is not clear if these had any influence or indeed were necessary.

The second conflict was protracted and more complicated. It bears detailing as an example of the use of influence, a study in political tactics, and an example of the limits of cooperation between government and the reformers. In 1896, the WPIS held a conference on female immigration in connection with the annual meeting of the National Council of Women of Canada. The conference was held at the YWCA, and presided over by Lady Aberdeen, founder of the National Council of Women and wife of the then Governor General. At the conference the WPIS and its supporters proposed a "national system" of immigration and an improvement of their current procedures for its management:[5] women's committees in various parts of Canada would manage female immigration in much the same way as did the WPIS and its sister organizations. The national system would include authorized agencies in Great Britain, in touch with the receiving and distributing centers in Canada. The conference also suggested changes in government policy, such as the promotion of concentrated rather than scattered settlement of the Northwest, to improve health and social facilities available for women. The proposal was based on considerable experience with female immigration managed by the system then in use by women immigrationist reformers. In effect it asked for a more systematic approach to the problems of settlement (especially as they affected women) by the federal government, and envisioned an expansion of the present work done by women reformers within this more systematic framework.

Implementing such a national system of immigration would mean considerably increased responsibilities for the Society. More money would be needed. Since the expanded work of the Society was for the benefit of the nation, the federal government was the appropriate source for funding. Mrs. Gillespie, its current President, wrote to Clifford Sifton, new Minister of Immigration, to ask for $10,000 to set up receiving Homes in Winnipeg, Calgary, Regina and Vancouver.[6] Sifton refused the request. The Society meanwhile went ahead with various parts of its program. Its name was changed to the Women's National Immigration Society (WNIS), to reflect the increased scope of their work. In 1897 the Society moved to larger quarters and applied for a bigger grant to cover the increased costs of the new work—which it did not get. The ladies implemented what new practices they could without funds. The Society convinced one of the steamship companies to advance passage money to carefully selected women, to be repaid out of wages the women would earn once established in Canada. The Society would supervise the repayment and guarantee the company against loss.[7] The following year the Society intended to use its hoped-for grant increase to finance an expanded version of this scheme, whereby the Society itself would advance the passage money.

Lobbying for Expanded Funding

To avoid a repeat of previous rebuffs from the government, the Society decided to campaign to get more grant money rather than rely upon polite requests. The first step was to send a formidable delegation of ladies to Ottawa to call upon the Minister.[8] Lady Shaughnessy and Mesdames Andrew, Allan, Barnart, Clouston and Gillespie expected to find a ready ally in Sifton. He was the architect of a comprehensive and large-scale program of nation building, based on the rapid and efficient population of the Canadian West by experienced agrarian settlers from the U.S., Britain and Europe. Sifton was not restrictive about the national origins of these settlers (although Americans, Britons and Western and Northern Europeans were preferred), as long as they were ready and willing to farm the prairies under difficult conditions without making a fuss. He was willing to spend large amounts of money to recruit and support the importation of desirable new Canadians. Other Canadian officials were more "racialist" in their outlook and did not like Sifton's "sheepskins," as the well-known sturdy peasants in sheepskin coats, often Slavs, were called. They preferred to recruit from the more Western races. But both factions would have agreed that the British women with whom the Society dealt were desirable immigrants.

Whatever Sifton's reaction to the delegation, he was unwilling to pay more money to the Society when he already got its services for only $1,000 a year. He sent out Frank Pedley, his new Superintendent of Immigration, to tell the ladies the bad news. Pedley explained that the government at present got lots of immigrants for free, and was thus reluctant to increase the grant. He said that the Society must consider the help that it got from the immigration agents of the Canadian government in England as part of its support from the government. The Society countered by reminding Pedley that its associates in England were in fact doing the work of the government agents—for free. The Society thus deserved to be better compensated for this work, if they were going to continue to do it. However, the government did not change its position.[9]

The President of the Society thereupon wrote directly to Sifton describing in complete and careful detail the origins and operations of the advanced passage scheme, and the methods, affiliations and merits of the WNIS.[10] The letter was dealt with by Jasper Smart, Sifton's assistant, who had formerly praised the work of the Society and implied that there would be official support for it.[11] Smart wrote to Pedley, "Of course you understand that nothing can be done" and Pedley dutifully communicated the refusal to the ladies.[12] Undaunted, the Society next recruited support and allies. Gillespie wrote to a number of prominent and influential men, describing its work and reiterating its long years of service to the nation. They were constantly being thanked and praised, she said; now they wanted more generous concrete support. Funds would be sensibly used; the social and political connections of the ladies (which were clearly described) would guarantee that. Lastly, the letter justified the appeal for government funding. The Home was supported by the government, and thus should not be expected to need donations; "it is not a charitable institution." Copies of the letter were sent to the Minister and to a number of other politicians.[13] Shortly thereafter the ladies called on Israel Tarte, at that time Minister of Public Works and a long-time supporter, who urged them to escalate their campaign.[14] The next step was a petition. It was a letter of support for the work of the Society signed by various Montreal representatives in both federal and provincial levels of government, including such men as Tarte, Dandurand, Monk, Bickerdike, Guerin, and Roddick. Copies were sent to the Prime Minister, the Minister of the Interior (immigration) and other members of Cabinet.[15] The appeal failed again.[16]

By 1902 the Society was in dire straits financially. It got a rent cut from Sir Thomas Shaughnessy, the owner of the house in which the Home was located, and continued to press for increased funds.[17] Ellen Barnard wrote on behalf of the Ladies' Committee to Laurier reminding him of Gillespie's earlier letter (to the prominent men), and explaining that each day it became more evident that the present grant was inadequate. The ladies warned that the work of the WNIS was "of such benefit to the domestic welfare of Canada—especially in the Northwest where servants are almost unobtainable—. . . without more means at our command it will be almost impossible to continue." Inadequate funding meant that "we are crippled in our work." This letter too was signed by supporters.[18]

Barnard next wrote personally to Laurier, outlining the campaign thus far, and describing a number of conversations with Cabinet Minister Tarte about the project and his support for it. In this letter she attributed Sifton's refusal to fund the WNIS to his Northwest-centered parochialism ("chacun preche pour sa paroisse"). She referred to Tarte's promise to "help us all in his power," as well as to her own hope for recognition of their work "in a substantial way, as we are willing to devote time and energies as heretofore."[19] This too produced no results.

In February 1903 the Society got up a petition outlining its twenty years of work, the value of its service, and its problems in continuing to provide its services as costs had increased so tremendously. It asked for a $2,000 annual grant. The petition bore the names of 68 very prominent Montreal men, and was also signed by others whose names do not appear in the WNIS records. This petition was sent to Ottawa and followed by a delegation of ladies to visit the Prime Minister. Laurier was finally persuaded to increase the annual grant to $1,500. Deputy Minister Smart wrote to this effect in April 1903, attributing the increase to the "increased service performed" by the Society.[20]

Victory was sweet but not long to be savored. The WNIS experienced terrific problems in collecting the increased grant. It was only after a series of letters from the WNIS which led to the discovery that there had been clerical errors and procedural bungling in the Department, that the money was finally collected—after nearly two years had elapsed.

The political setting in which immigration work was carried out was abruptly changed in 1905. Sifton offered Laurier his resignation over a dispute concerning the educational rights of the French Canadians in the Northwest—in effect Sifton was against them—and Laurier surprised Sifton by accepting it. Deputy Minister Smart resigned as well. The new Minister, Frank Oliver, did not like Sifton or his policies and procedures and did not appear willing to spend money so freely on immigration matters. The Society was caught in the reassessment that followed. The Department authorized only $1,000 for the fiscal year 1905–06.[21] There ensued a struggle with Scott, the new Superintendent of Immigration. Polite persuasion failed. Next, a copy of the letter confirming the authorization of the increase to $1,500 was sent to Scott, accompanied by thinly veiled threats to use the influence of the Society's supporters, and to call personally on the Minister.[22] Finally, a prominent lawyer, G.W. Stephens, corresponded with Oliver, asking him to take a personal interest to see that "the agreement entered into between the government and this society" was carried out.[23]

Scott refused to move until he was provided with a complete list of all of the 650 women brought out by the Society in the past year, including names, origins, arrival dates and present addresses.[24] This request was considered unprecedented and quite unreasonable. Scott had taken the position that a grant must be applied for anew each year, and that no guarantee existed that it would be given each time.[25] Thus the increase granted in 1903 was meant to apply to one year only. Internal memos indicate that Scott was equivocating, but it is not clear where the initiative came from—Scott himself, the Assistant Deputy Minister, the Deputy Minister or the Minister. Scott implied that in order to get a grant each year, the Society would have to supply detailed information on its activities for the past year.

Stephens refused to get the information for Scott and told him quite bluntly that the Prime Minister and Minister of the Interior had agreed to the grant and it was not necessary to justify it all over again: "The ladies are being practically held up by a piece of bad faith on the part of someone and this kind of business is not calculated to enhance the popularity of the present government." Stephens ordered Scott to send a cheque and stop temporizing. Scott did.[26] From that time until the War, the Society had no more problems with its grants. It is interesting to note that the Montreal Society was the only such group that was successful in fighting its grant cuts. The increase that the Society had won in 1903 was automatically passed on to the Winnipeg Home, the only other one established at that point. So was the cutback in 1905. The ladies in Winnipeg were never successful in restoring their lost grant; they lacked the combination of influence, political skills, and persistence that so greatly aided the WNIS of Montreal.

Society and Staff Relations

The employment of Matron Eliza Corneil illustrates the impact of changing relations between immigrationist reformers and the federal government. Corneil, born in Quebec in 1829 of English Protestant descent, was appointed in 1888 by the Women's Protective Immigration Society in Montreal and Quebec City to "look after . . . joint interests and . . . to meet, care for and forward" all of the immigrants entering Canada at Quebec, then the major port of entry, who were going on to the Society in Montreal.[27] At the same time the Department of Agriculture (which was responsible for immigration at that point) also appointed her as a "quasi-agent" of the Department. This was done to avoid making her "simply an officer of the Department for which we should be responsible. . . ."[28] The Department "hired" her for the Society and paid her salary, but not directly to her.[29] Instead, her cheques were sent to the head of the Society in Quebec. Thus, Corneil could be closely supervised by the Society, and while she was on the government payroll she was not really a government employee. On the other hand, her quasi-official standing reassured the Society "that her authority will be recognized by the other immigration officials."[30] They need not have worried.

Her official designation was Matron of the Quebec Immigration Office, Women's Protective Immigration Society. Her salary was $50 monthly, plus living quarters in Quebec during the immigration season. During the midwinter months when the harbor was closed, she went to Halifax on immigration work; there she received a housing allowance.[31] Other perks included free railway passes while on government business and sometimes on leaves home.[32] Her primary duties were to "meet, care for and attend to" all women immigrants sent out to the various Societies from their sister network in Britain;[33] additionally she ran the Louise Embankment Immigration Building which housed her quarters, the offices of the immigration officials and services, plus several furnished bedrooms for the accommodation of women awaiting job placement, or families who were forced to stay over for some reason. Further, she looked after women and children immigrants in general, conferred with the government agent or appropriate local organizations about problems of indigence and the like, took care of sick people or sent them on to hospital, and in some cases arranged funerals, took care of temporarily parentless children, and performed other similar tasks. She was described in an understatement as a "most valuable worker;"[34] she provided almost the only services offered by the government in the 1880s and 1890s at the major Canadian port for women immigrants coming across the Atlantic.

In 1892 the responsibility for immigration was transferred from Agriculture to Interior and Corneil was transferred too. She was described by Interior officials as the holder of the office of Matron for the Department and as working for the Society.[35] This cosy, if somewhat irregular relationship, typical of the ties between these Societies and the federal government at this time, was soon to be regularized. Although this process was in accord with the general trends towards bureaucratization and professionalization of immigrationist reform work, it was immediately precipitated by procedural problems caused by poor communication between the Society representative, the Department, and Corneil. In February 1893, Dominion Government Agent Clay reported with some annoyance that Corneil was having problems because she had not been paid for two months. Clay felt that he would have to pay her if the Department did not. "If Mrs. Corneil is . . . employed by the Department," and was to receive some of her instructions, at least during the time that she was in Halifax, from the government agents, he could not "understand why her cheque should go to [the WPIS's] Mrs. Macpherson of Quebec to be endorsed." Why she could not get her salary like "the rest of us" Clay did not see, particularly since she had previously had problems with this odd arrangement. "Why should she depend on Mrs. Macpherson for her cheque any more than other people?"[36] Thus one of Corneil's co-workers challenged her special status and the irregular arrangement between the government and the Societies. In this particular instance, Macpherson had not left clear instructions about where to send the cheques while she was on her holidays in England and Corneil was working in Halifax. The normal procedure was for the Department to hold the cheques pending notification from Macpherson.[37] The Department changed its procedure after receiving Clay's complaint and sent Corneil's cheques to Clay to deliver to her,[38] presumably not requiring endorsement. Macpherson was not pleased with the new policy. The ladies of the Society would no longer have control over Corneil's activities, methods, level of performance, if she no longer had to submit a report to them in order to get her paycheque. Lacking these regular reports, there was no way to be sure that she managed the female immigrants properly to promote the aims of the Society. While she had belatedly written the Department to send cheques directly to Corneil during the holiday trip, Mrs. McPherson insisted she "would like it altered through me" again upon her return to Canada, "as it gives me control over her and, the mistake before has been giving control to the Matron; it has never succeeded and since I had it altered we have had no trouble, and then Mrs. Corneil is 'obliged' to come up and report me everything. . . ."[39] Nevertheless, the cheque continued to go directly to Corneil. This innovation represents a significant change in the ability of the ladies to control each step of the process, hence in relations not only between Society and staff, but between Society, women immigrants, and the state.

The lines of authority became less blurred over the next few years as the old procedures clashed with the new bureaucratic norms. For example, in 1894 Corneil overstayed her leave. She had had to apply for it like other members of the Department; however, she had not followed appropriate procedures to request an extension. She had thought that Macpherson would recall her when she was needed again. Corneil explained to the Department that her "motherly feelings" had caused her to stay with her children longer than she had intended. She asked that her salary not be docked for the extra time off.[40] The Deputy Minister told her rather sharply that since she was on the regular establishment list of the Department and got her pay from the Department, it was quite outside Macpherson's jurisdiction to grant an extension of her leave or other concession not within the rules of the Department. While the Department wished her to follow Macpherson's advice about how best to carry out her job in dealing with women immigrants, she was to consider herself "on the staff of and under the control of" the government agent at Quebec. Corneil had in the meantime told the agent that she had assumed Macpherson would take care of getting her an extension.[41] The old methods of informal arrangements and personal relationships, as well as the lines of communication, were no longer appropriate or adequate to the task. It is also worth noting that Corneil's family relationships appear to have been considered good reason for a lengthy, indeterminate visit by the WPIS, but not by the government.

Corneil occupied a favored position in the government service. She received paid annual holidays of several weeks' duration, and when necessary, paid sick leave. She was well liked by her fellows, both public servants and unofficial associates. She was appreciated by the reformers with whom she worked; the Halifax Local Council of Women were quick to write to the Department expressing their concern that there might be plans to replace her, when they heard that the Department was checking references for a Matron at the new Halifax Immigration Building.[42] Shortly thereafter, government officials at Halifax asked to borrow Corneil for several months to help them set up the new building. They needed her to get services established and instruct their new matron: she would be a great help, they said.[43] The agent to whom Corneil was now responsible at Quebec wrote in 1901 noting that, although Corneil was 71 years old, she was still very good at her job, and the agent wanted an assistant to help her. The job had become even more demanding as immigrant traffic had greatly increased, and "when large numbers of immigrants of both sexes remain overnight in the building, I consider an assistant matron to be necessary."[44] An assistant matron was duly hired. Thanks to string-pulling by influential friends in her home town (the usual way to get a government job at that time),[45] Marie du Tremblay began work as Assistant Matron in May 1901, at a salary of $35 monthly.[46]

Du Tremblay's relations with her superiors were more formal and less friendly than Corneil's; the former was far less well treated, supported, or tolerated. Her experience is more typical of what women employees of the Immigration Service could expect over the next few decades, and represented the new regime for staffers of the bureaucracy which replaced that of staffers of the Society. As Corneil got older, problems at Quebec grew. In 1903 a new official toured the building and was furious to find that some upstairs rooms, presumably occupied by immigrants, were filthy. He ordered the matrons to divide the work and see that this did not happen again; he demanded an official report on the matter.[47] Shortly after, du Tremblay complained that she needed a raise; Corneil was 78 years old and spending most of her time in her room, leaving her assistant to do most of the work. Moreover, the workload had greatly increased due to a growing flow of immigrants. Besides, she added, she had to pay for her children's education.[48] The request was denied. The official, angry at the dirty rooms, had apparently taken a dislike to du Tremblay, and consistently opposed a raise in her pay.[49] It was not until considerable influence had been brought to bear on the Minister himself that a raise to $40 was approved.[50]

After 1908 Corneil's annual leaves were longer and more frequent. Various proposals were made to the Department about a successor. Du Tremblay's friends pushed for her promotion, while others, like the Anglican Bishop of Montreal, and the British Women's Emigration Association (BWEA) (the main immigrationist network which sent women emigrants all over the British Empire) opposed it. The BWEA wanted an English woman appointed;[51] the Bishop wanted Corneil pensioned off and replaced by someone who would go aboard the ships and enquire as to the moral character of the women immigrants, as well as carry out Corneil's other duties which he thought Corneil was too old and du Tremblay too inefficient to do.[52] The Medical Superintendent at Quebec wanted a trained nurse to succeed (or assist) Corneil, to take temperatures of the immigrants daily to avoid outbreaks of disease, that is, if a trained nurse could be hired at the same salary as Corneil.[53] Corneil hung on. In 1915, she was still in her post at the age of 86. Near Christmas time, there was a rumor that she had resigned. She wired the Department, "Did not resign and have no intention of doing so."[54] At this point records of Corneil disappear into the abyss. Perhaps she remained at Quebec, getting older and older, until she was the oldest public servant in Canada. Perhaps she is still secreted in a corner of the old Immigration Building. Whatever her personal fate, she does represent a rather unusual example of patterns of cooperation between government and immigrationist reformers. In her career experiences can be seen some of the trends characteristic of female immigration reform work between the 1880s and the end of the First World War. She came in when the government was using organizations like the Women's Protective Immigration Societies to carry out its female immigration work in Canada. She went out (one presumes) at the end of the period of private and somewhat irregular arrangements to deal with this work. Literally millions of immigrants came in to Canada during her period in office. During these years, the foundations for both the modern nation of Canada and the modern practices for female immigration work had been established.

Transition to Modern Practice

The Society lost its favored position during the First World War, when it was politically outflanked by a rival group of male clergy men who finally succeeded in getting half of the Society's grant to fund the work of the rival enterprise. The Society had closed the doors of its Home during the war, and the male-directed group had control over the traffic for a brief interlude. This situation changed in 1919 when female immigration work was reorganized after discussions between government officials and women reformers.[55] A Council of Women, composed of representatives from the various women's hostels, and women's reform organizations and clubs active in immigration work (as well as from some provincial governments), was established to manage institutions and establish and carry out policy relative to female immigration. All funds earmarked for the work were given to the Council to portion out. Each group had to apply to the Council for its grants, rather than to the government. This had several effects. It lessened the ability of an individual group or society to put pressure on government officials. It appeared to give women's groups the power to control resources necessary to carry out their activities. To a certain extent, this power was real. However, the government still had the power to determine how much money would be given to the Council—the size of the pie, as it were. The Council merely determined how large a piece of the pie each applicant would get. This method set up competition between women's groups for funding; previously, a larger grant given to one group did not necessarily mean that another group got less, as there was no firm ceiling set on total funds for female immigration societies' work. It is worth noting that this new method of allocating a total grant to a central body (albeit no longer a non-governmental one) to be distributed among women's groups is more or less followed today by the federal government, in the operation of Secretary of State Women's Programs which funds the bulk of women's projects. Members who distributed grants through the Council would also have liked to have adequate funding, but had little influence to get their total allotment increased. A major difference, however, is that state control over the work of the Council and over the Societies was at that time comparatively poorly established, in part because the Council was not completely integrated into the state apparatus.

The passing of the WNIS marked the end of the period in which personal influence of individuals was a viable way for these women reformers to get money and cooperation from the government. The material conditions of the female immigration work in Montreal had changed tremendously in these several decades. In the early days, the WNIS was all that existed to care for respectable female immigrants. Thus the government was willing and even eager to support the Society and affiliate with it in the work. The Society was welcomed as long as it delivered necessary social services cheaply, and its feminist and maternalist eccentricities (such as the insistence that the work must be carried out under the control of women, and that female immigrants must be carefully controlled and watched over at every step of the immigration process) were tolerated so long as they did not cause problems for the government. Then, a number of factors coincided: changes in governments or in officials; changes in the number of facilities available to care for female immigrants; changes in the numbers to care for (due to the decrease in women going through Montreal because of improved transportation or the war). It was no longer necessary or expedient to give the WNIS what it wanted. The WNIS was cheap at $1,000 a year, but not at $2,000, at least in a period of cheese-paring policies. The government was willing to use the Society only so long as the Society provided the best alternative. It was a relationship based less on agreement upon the principles which ought to govern female immigration than on expediency. The relationship was determined on the one hand by the extent of the ladies' power to get the government to do what they wanted it to do, and on the other hand by the limits of the needs of the government to use the ladies to do what it wanted done.

By the early 1920s, immigration work was far more in the public domain. It had become professionalized and bureaucratized, and was thus much harder for lady reformers and their supporters, however influential, to manipulate. Female immigration had its own domain after 1919 with the advent of the Council of Women, but it was also effectively cut off from the mainstream of Canadian political life. Thus, influence could less easily be brought to bear on the Council from outside. As the work became more efficiently managed, it also became far less personal. It was in the personal sphere that these women had had influence; in the public sphere they had insufficient legitimacy or power.

Although the assumptions about the relationship between female immigration and Empire building that had informed the work of immigrationist reformers since the Victorian period did not entirely change, the practices associated with these assumptions had changed greatly. It was still the work of women to care for women—but no longer especially the work of ladies. Reform work of this type had become far less the special property of women of the upper classes, and far more the work of the government which represented their class (but rarely their gender) interests. As long as immigrants kept coming, the owners of Canadian enterprises stood to benefit, in both the short- and the long-term. And the wives of those owners continued to benefit as employers of domestics. Yet, the loss of control over the female immigration work in Montreal must have represented a personal loss to those ladies who for so many years had made this work an important part of their own lives. The official records reveal little about the views of the women who were the objects of the ladies' services. The ladies would say the women were grateful on the whole (and there are appreciative notes from women, scattered through the files), for after all, their lives were improved; they got jobs, some of them had a wider range of choices in Canada than in Britain. They enjoyed a safe journey, and some support during settlement. Most of them probably still passed their working lives in someone else's kitchen, in service to the families of others. On the other hand, most of us still pass our lives in unpaid service to our own families. The ladies' help did not eliminate the women's class and gender subordination; but then, it was not meant to. That may also be true of many grassroots community projects of our own time.

NOTES

(All sources are from the Public Archives of Canada unless otherwise noted)

1. For example, see Linda Kealy (ed.), *A Not Unreasonable Claim. Women and Reform in Canada, 1880s–1920s.* Toronto: Women's Press, 1979.
2. Van Horne to J. Egan, December 10, 1885, MG28 III 20 Vol. 3.
3. Report of the Minister of Agriculture, Sessional Paper No. 4, 1888, Appendix 47. The percentage assisted would be shown to be much higher if only single female British immigrants were counted. However, the data are not available in that form.
4. RG76 Vol. 113, file 22787.
5. *Montreal Herald*, December 15, 1896. See also RG76 Vol. 48 file 1836, cited hereafter as WNIS or WPIS papers, May 14, 1896.
6. MG28 I Vol. 115. Papers of the National Council of Women of Canada. Annual Report for 1896. In fact, Homes were opened in all these centers in the ensuing years, by local women's groups with some links to national and Imperial networks. The Winnipeg Home was opened by the daughter of the former Lord Mayor of the City of London; in other places there were National Council of Women and other reform connections. All of these Homes received some form of grants from various levels of government. It is interesting to note that the Toronto Home's subsidy from the provincial government was for many years greater than from the federal government. The female immigration network of the late teens and early twenties resembled in many respects the national network envisioned by the WNIS in 1896.
7. WNIS papers, Gillespie to the Department of the Interior, June 30, 1901.
8. WNIS papers, December 4, 1900. See also *Montreal Gazette*, December 10, 1901.
9. *Ibid.*
10. WNIS papers, December 6, 1901.
11. *Montreal Gazette*, December 14, 1897.
12. WNIS papers, January 3, 1902, January 7, 1902.
13. *Ibid.*, January 25, 1902.
14. Annual Report of the WNIS for 1903.

15. *Ibid.*

16. WNIS papers, April 17, 1901, Smart to Society.

17. *Ibid.* The Society had inquired about obtaining a $3 per head "bonus" paid to those Societies sending domestics into the West (Manitoba) or the Northwest Territories, upon certification by the government that these had reported to work. See correspondence between the government and the Society, June 28, 29, 30 and August 3, 1900, *op. cit.* The annual budgets of the Society do not reveal this "bonus" to have been a source of income; it may have been reported in a different form, or there may have been other requirements for its receipt that made it impractical to go after. The latter seems more likely, as by this time if the "bonus" were a useful source of income the Society would have been more actively pursuing it. Moreover, correspondence from the Winnipeg Home suggests a good deal of bureaucratic stringency. Deputy Minister Smart explained to Miss Fowler of the Home that the "bonus" was not a general thing paid to anyone bringing out domestics: "the Department must have absolute control of the work and know what is being done." See May 21 and 26, 1900, Winnipeg papers, RG76 Vol. 138, file 33136. The "bonus" was stopped in 1910 for immigrants whose fares had been paid by charitable organizations, and in 1914 except for those who had a year's experience working as a domestic prior to coming to Canada; it was stopped entirely during the war.

18. WNIS papers, January 30, 1902.

19. Barnard to Laurier, February 12, 1902, Laurier papers. Series A, Correspondence, Vol. 222, pp. 62646–8.

20. WNIS papers.

21. *Ibid.*, August 3, 1905. Oliver had risen rapidly from store owner and editor of a fledgling newspaper (the *Bulletin*) in pioneer Edmonton; for an account of his 1882 involvement in a vigilante group protecting land claims before government surveys regularized the situation in the city, see Margaret Stobie, "Land jumping," *The Beaver*, Winter 1982.

22. WNIS papers, November 20, 1905.

23. *Ibid.*, December 14, 1905.

24. *Ibid.*, December 18, 1905. In subsequent years, precise records were kept as a matter of course, and such information was required to get the grant payments. It was also considered necessary by some Societies and Homes of Welcome groups to do "follow up" work, e.g., to monitor the immigrant woman's activities after her placement. For details of follow up work see B. Roberts, "A work of Empire: Canadian reformers and British female immigration" in L. Kealey (ed.), *op. cit.*

25. WNIS papers, Scott to Deputy Minister, January 2, 1906.

26. *Ibid.*, January 2, 1906, January 5, 1906. Another possible funding source opened up in 1913: the Society was authorized to collect an employment agent's commission (paid to Canadian government employment agencies by the government) for placing a servant in a job. (The fee was $2 per

placement). The fee does not seem to have played a large part in Home funding. For correspondence see, for example, WNIS papers, May 8, 1913.

27. Department of Interior memo, August 12, 1892, RG76 Vol. 687, file 320, cited hereafter as Corneil papers; WPIS-Montreal to Department of Agriculture, June 1, 1888, Corneil papers.
28. *Ibid.*, Memo, Department of Agriculture, January 28, 1890.
29. *Ibid.*, Quebec Society to Department of Agriculture, May 28, 1888.
30. *Ibid.*, Memo, January 23, 1893.
31. *Ibid.*, February 22, 1891.
32. *Ibid.*, December 28, 1892.
33. *Ibid.*, Montreal Society to Department of Agriculture, June 1, 1888. On British sending agencies see Suzann Buckley, "British female immigration and Imperial development," *Hecate: Women's Interdisciplinary Journal*, January 1977, and Barbara Roberts, "A work of Empire: Canadian reformers and British female immigration" in Linda Kealey (ed.), *op. cit.*
34. Corneil papers, Quebec Agent to Department of Interior, January 27, 1893.
35. *Ibid.*, Memo, August 26, 1892.
36. *Ibid.*, February 27, 1893.
37. *Ibid.*, Department to Corneil, February 23, 1893.
38. *Ibid.*, Memos, March 3, 1893, March 7, 1893.
39. *Ibid.*, Macpherson to Deputy Minister, July 28, 1893.
40. *Ibid.*, Corneil to Deputy Minister, February 2, 1894.
41. *Ibid.*, Doyle to Deputy Minister, February 6, 1894, February 8 1894.
42. *Ibid.*, September 11, 1896.
43. *Ibid.*, Clay to Deputy Minister, November 6, 1896.
44. *Ibid.*, Doyle to Deputy Minister, May 21, 1901.
45. *Ibid.*, Advocat Anger to Minister of the Interior, May 17, 1906.
46. *Ibid.*, Memo, May 21, 1901, and du Tremblay to Superintendent of Immigration, December 22, 1904.
47. *Ibid.*, Scott to Agent Doyle, May 19, 1903.
48. *Ibid.*, December 22, 1904.
49. *Ibid.*, March 30, 1905, March 30, 1906, July 21, 1906.
50. *Ibid.*, May 31, 1905, March 17, 1906, July 3, 1906, July 13, 1906.
51. *Ibid.*, BWEA to Department of the Interior, June 17, 1914.
52. *Ibid.*, Bishop to Department, February 25 1915.
53. *Ibid.*, Page to Department, July 1, 1914, and August 19, 1908.
54. *Ibid.*, December 14, 1915.
55. For the struggle between male- and female-dominated reform groups over the work in Montreal, see B. Roberts, "Sex, Politics and Religion: Controversies in Female Immigration Work in Montreal, 1880–1920," *Atlantis*, Fall 1980, pp. 25–38.

Native Women in Reserve Politics:
Strategies and Struggles*

Jo-Anne Fiske

Introduction: Indian Reserves and the State

Native communities differ from other Canadian communities in three important regards: first, their community government, usually an elected council, has minimal powers of administration and in all respects is subject to rulings of the federal government as authorized through the Department of Indian and Northern Affairs (DINA); second, community life is associated closely with residence on Indian reserves, that is, land held by the state on behalf of individual Indian groups or bands; and third, because the land base of the reserves is either inadequate or impoverished in natural resources, the majority of native communities suffer chronic unemployment, impoverishment, and dependency on state-controlled welfare.

Analysis of the political processes in reserve communities suffering economic and social deprivation has led Larsen to conclude that internal political influence is gained by individuals acting as "middlemen," or power-brokers, between the state and their community. Specifically, he argued that the power of an individual or an elected council rests on the ability to control the scarce resources that circulate from the state.[1] These resources include funds for community administration, grants for community development projects and temporary job creation schemes, and subsidized housing for band members resident on the reserve. A larger power base cannot be created by the band council because the

*An earlier version of this paper, entitled "Women and the Political Process," was presented at the 1987 meetings of the Canadian Sociological and Anthropology Association. I wish to thank Evelyn Légaré, John McMullan, Sheva Medjuk and Daiva Stasiulis for their comments on earlier drafts.

community is bound to the state by the practices of "welfare colonialism" or "wardship."[2] In consequence, competition for political office revolves around the struggle to control the same few resources. Individuals or organizations who are not members of the council and who do success-fully compete for office directly challenge the influence of the council. If their success endures over long time periods they, like the council, become mediating agents who redistribute highly desired goods gained from outside of the community. In rare cases, these individuals or orga-nizations may become so successful that they emerge as rival structures to the council with the ability to sway the political process.

Regrettably, studies of the "middleman" role of power-brokers in com-munity politics have focused only on the actions and strategies of elected councillors who in many native communities are predominantly male. To my knowledge there are no comparable studies of women's struggles to gain access to the same kinds of resources and hence to influence community decision-making. The purpose of this paper is to describe a community in which women do exercise control over critical community resources and hence, quite apart from the band council, shape com-munity decision-making. The paper provides a case study of women's participation in the politics of a Carrier Indian reserve in central British Columbia. I argue that in this case women have obtained and sustained public influence partially because they have formed voluntary associa-tions that have access to critical political resources controlled by the state. I suggest that voluntary associations have the attributes of polit-ical "teams:"[3] they are led by a core of elite women and have members bound to the core by ties of family loyalty and followers whose support is gained by the leaders' careful distribution of scarce goods. Further, I argue that the political interventions of women's voluntary associations alter the political process in two significant ways. First, they place new emphasis on political issues, which women see as central to their ability to carry out their traditional feminine responsibilities as nurturers and providers. In so doing, new networks of alliances, which are essentially between women, emerge to challenge established political practices. Sec-ond, once they gain control over sufficient political resources, the associ-ations become rival structures to the council. This rivalry will exist even when the associations are linked directly to individuals holding political office.

My interest in Carrier women's political strategies is long standing. When I lived in central British Columbia I often heard that women, more often than men, ran the reserve communities. My earlier research analyzed the impact of colonial schooling practices on women's lives. It confirmed that female leadership was vital to community life.[4] Later, I decided to pursue the question further as my doctoral research. I explored the extent and perceptions of women's public influence and leadership in one Carrier community.

During my field work, I worked with band members on research for their land claim and for related struggles to protect their rights to natural resources. I had daily contact with female elders who were respected for their cultural knowledge, skills in the bush, and political abilities. I attended activities organized by the women's associations and learned of women's experiences and struggles to improve their social and economic conditions.

Village Life and Political Organization

The Carrier Indians are located in the Nechako plateau of central British Columbia where they are settled in a number of small reserve villages. Once dependent upon a mixed economy of subsistence bush production (fishing, hunting, gathering) and wage labor, they now rely primarily upon unearned income and bush subsistence. The Carrier are plagued by underemployment. The private sector offers very few employment opportunities. On the reserve, work is limited to a handful of positions in small businesses. While small-scale logging or saw milling operations exist on some reserves, these cannot offer regular employment to all who seek work.[5] Employment in the nearby white communities is rare and insecure. In many of their reserve communities, job opportunities are restricted to positions created by the needs of state bureaucracy: a handful of administrative and clerical positions, community service roles, seasonal bush labor, and seasonal state-funded job creation schemes. The community described here suffers from all these factors. It has no employment through reserve based-businesses. In the absence of state job creation schemes unemployment can exceed 85%. In short, theirs is an economy of dependency characterized by social assistance, state-controled employment schemes, and intermittent casual labor performed for the dominant population.

The division of domestic and subsistence labor is predominantly along gender lines. Women perform the bulk of domestic duties, gardening, salmon fishing, and food processing. Men hunt, trap,[6] fish occasionally, and assist women with their work. But for the most part, women and men work independently of one another. Women control the organization of their work and the distribution of surplus food resources. Men commonly, but not always, hunt without women, and they personally select their own male hunting companions.

The extended family of three or four generations is the critical unit of production and consumption. Whether the main source of income is state transfer payments, pensions, social assistance, etc., or a combination of wages, unearned income and subsistence production, economic resources are shared amongst closely-related kin. At the same time, individual resources are not common spousal property. Spouses personally handle their incomes and ownership of such items as cars, trucks, and boats. Pensioners and workers, for example, independently manage their incomes, which they share with kin as they choose. Women's unearned income, social assistance and family allowance, is an important political resource since women assume financial responsibility for dependent members of their extended families.

Family loyalty is at the heart of the kinship system and community politics. Families are ranked vertically. Those who have claims to traditional rank and high status are politically prominent. Although village factions are identified with prominent families, membership of any unit cannot be identified unequivocally. For each alleged faction there exists an undisputed core of two or three closely related families, but the core's following is hard to pinpoint. Small, economically weak families and individuals pragmatically forge alliances within these factions, which they legitimize by claiming kinship, affinal, or friendship ties with the core families. Acclaimed kinship ties, which can be activated through any of one's grandparents, are complicated by the fact that most families are related to the factional cores in one way or another. Hence, allegiances are fluid, ambiguous, and negotiable.

For political and administrative purposes, the local level of government is the band chief and council. The council hires band administrators and a clerical support staff. As well, it appoints a number of advisory committees, commonly composed of members of the leading families and band elders, to guide the decisions of the council and the administrative staff. Women and men occupy elected and appointed office. In keeping with the higher number of male reserve residents, it is common to find more men than women on the council. Nevertheless, at public band meetings, held by the elected council, the sex ratio is often reversed. Women come to represent their families and households in the absence of their husbands and adult sons. Wives and husbands speak out individually and no opinion takes priority over the other.

Council authority is delegated by the federal government and limited to minor decisions and administrative by-laws. Fiscal control remains in the hands of the DINA, which has direct control over the band resources, capital funds, and administrative budgets. Reserve resource exploitation requires licencing by the DINA and economic development occurs only with state assistance. In short, the band councils are a parapolitical structure directly encapsulated by the state system—they are "partly independent of, and partly regulated by, larger encapsulating political structures."[7] Their authority is limited to community administration and subject to the discretionary powers of one state bureaucracy, the DINA.[8]

The chief and council function as middlemen to the federal government and its funding agencies. Jobs and community funds circulate from state officials and are distributed by the chief and council and the administrators, who act as patrons in an economic system that has few opportunities for expansion. In effect, office holders publicly manage resources that in other circumstances would be private property or individual concerns. For example, the provision of new housing, the renovation of existing housing, or the expansion of community facilities are all tied to state-controled job creation and community improvement schemes. Similarly, the quest for personal goods, household furnishing, children's clothing, amenities for the elderly, etc., is a public not a personal matter since band members must compete for a share of the social assistance funds and services.

Given that desired goods are insufficient to meet everyone's needs, allegations of unfair distribution abound. Accordingly, chiefs, councillors and administrators are drawn into factional disputes and regularly denounced for favoritism. Individually or collectively, office holders are challenged in one of two ways: they can be removed from office or they can have their areas of influence taken from them. The latter event is rare and occurs only when other institutions, voluntary associations or small family-based businesses for instance, compete successfully for state funds and gain control over community developments which generate jobs. Moreover, these other institutions persist only when they can continue to compete successfully against the band council for the same political resources.

An important political resource for Indians is their ideology,[9] which in this case rests on the ideal of "looking after the people." Traditionally, Carrier women assumed responsibilities as family heads, usually in co-operation with a male peer. Currently, women's domestic responsibilities are undifferentiated from community obligations. Women are expected to share their surplus food, to assist young people, and to intervene in the domestic disputes of others in an effort to restore harmony. Furthermore, women are expected to provide care through the assumption of community service roles such as health workers, drug and alcohol counsellors, child care workers, and the like. Among Carrier bands, serious political actors are known as good providers—persons able and willing to support others through sharing scarce goods and by providing job opportunities. Pragmatic politics must be justified as fulfillment of moral responsibilities. This offers women a unique ideological resource, namely accomplishment of their traditional nurturing roles within the context of political action, as the changing dynamic of the women's voluntary associations illustrates.

Women and their Voluntary Associations: Domestic Priorities and the Struggle for Community Services

Women's voluntary associations[10] were first introduced to the Carrier by the church as auxiliaries to the church hierarchy and as community groups dedicated to maternal health and child care. It was not until about 1944, when Indian women across the West formed provincial associations, that Carrier women's groups gained autonomy from church authority and forged inter-reserve networks. Carrier women, like other Western Indian women, formed local chapters of the Native Mothers' Guild[11] to deal with domestic crises, to provide guidance to young mothers, and to improve community services essential to domestic well being.

According to its earliest members, the Native Mother's Guild was initially apolitical; members restricted their activities to individual family needs, confining themselves to a narrow interpretation of their motto, "for home and country." Nevertheless, as time passed, the women found they could not meet their domestic goals without political action. In order to care successfully for their families, they needed new community services: water and sewer systems, improved medical care, electricity, and the like. The quest for these services brought the women into confrontation with the reserve administration, the DINA, and the provincial and federal governments. Understandably, the guild's delegates voiced their concerns as women—as mothers and daughters charged with the nurture of infants and the care of the elderly. One woman described her experience:

> We went to the guild's meetings wherever they happened. I spoke out for our dying babies. What could we do? Our elders were crawling through the snow to get to the outhouse. We fought for water and sewer. We had typhoid then, and T.B. too, it was taking our people. That's what the Native Mothers' Guild was for. All over, the Indian women got together to do something for their children.[12]

The political strategies of the Native Mothers' Guild matured during the 1960s. Involvement in the Native Mothers' Guild resulted in political training for women. An entire cadre of women gained experience in a variety of strategies of lobbying, inter-community activities, and in bringing their influence to bear on the male leaders of their home reserve. In the words of one guild member:

> The men weren't organized like the women. We could stand up to the band council. We spoke for the families and they had to listen. The trouble makers went against us but they couldn't go nowhere. We were all pulling together and then they had to listen.

When the band council lost sight of the struggle for community services as key political issues with respect to its negotiations with the federal and provincial governments, the Native Mothers' Guild did not falter. They petitioned the band council for essential services and lobbied the regional and federal offices of the DINA independently of the elected band council. Letters requesting community services were sent from the Native Mothers' Guild to the regional and federal offices of the DINA. Remembering this action a guild member says:

> That's why they call me a motor mouth. I spoke out when I had to. The men weren't speaking up in public, just talking to themselves. They didn't show no interest in getting to Ottawa. We sent petitions right there and our delegates to talk for us. The Native Mothers' Guild were doing the business for the council.

Disenchantment with the band council grew and led the Native Mothers' Guild to support two of their members as candidates for elected council. This action was remarkable for two reasons. First, women directly challenged the competence of the male-dominated council on grounds of moral accountability. They argued that council apathy and male indifference were responsible for the band's failure to obtain water and sewer systems. Second, their candidates came from two prominent families (identified throughout as Alpha and Beta) commonly perceived as opposing factions. With both women acting as representatives of the same organization and advancing the same causes as council members and as women, however, this band election had the effect of integrating the community rather than exacerbating factional tensions.

Following their initial political success, the Native Mothers' Guild became more confrontational in their tactics. They used the local and national media to draw attention to their needs and became more prominent in negotiations with the state. In the 1970s the highway that slices through the village came under increasingly heavy use. When the provincial government refused to pave the highway within the village limits and denied financial compensation for the expropriated land, the band set up road blockades. Female elders, the symbolic figures of maternal concerns, traditional wisdom and social leadership, were stationed at the front. Although this action was supported in principle and in practice by the band council and involved persons of all ages and both genders, it was conceived and organized by members of the Native Mothers' Guild, who informed the governments of their intentions by letter and brought the matter to the local media.

During the same period, the Native Mothers' Guild extended its sphere of action to include government funding that would not be controlled by the band council. The Native Mothers' Guild obtained funds from a variety of federal government departments (Health and Welfare, Canada Manpower, and the Secretary of State) for community building projects. This was a double blessing for all concerned. The community acquired urgently needed facilities and temporary jobs were made available to men:

> We got jobs for the men that way. They built our crafts centre and then we got the laundrymat. We could give the men jobs with our money.

The Native Mothers' Guild had found a new way of providing for family needs through the provision of community facilities, which would be used primarily by women and children, and the creation of male employment, an urgent need in most families:

> None of our men had jobs then. They were turning to drink. There's always trouble in families if the men don't work.

Control over state-funded projects was critical to women's political struggles. Now women could establish client patron relations with the men they employed. Moreover, as individual women were linked to the successful projects of their association, they gained prestige in the community. Their ability to create jobs was seen to be a new and significant way in which women could provide for the needs of others, in particular for their families. Two important consequences followed: individual women gained greater credibility as community leaders, and the association itself came to be openly viewed as a women's political organization.

In sum, women were motivated to political action by their need to fulfill their traditional responsibilities. Acquisition of water and sewer systems, for example, had been necessary to their efforts to care for their community. In turn, the realization of their initial political goals supplied the rationale for further public interventions. Their pragmatic strategies transformed the nature of their actions from a struggle with the state for community improvement to an internal confrontation over women's political opportunities.

Female Unity and Sexual Politics

In the 1970s the Native Mothers' Guild became a central agent in dealing with the discrepancy between a traditional idealized respect for women and the reality of gender tensions generated by the election of women to the band council. When a woman, a guild president, was elected chief, she found herself facing opposition from men who felt she had usurped a male role. The most dramatic expression of their resentment occurred when a number of men, hired by the council, resisted the need to take orders from a woman. In her words, the men hired to build the new dance hall went "on strike." What started as a dispute over favoritism in the hiring process, was transformed into a complaint about a woman "taking over a men's business." Supported by the Native Mothers' Guild, the chief rose to the challenge by organizing the women to work on the hall roof. She recalled:

> Then them guys quit on us, halfway. And the roofing was supposed to start. That morning they say, "We're on strike," they told me. Boy I ran around. I pick up all the women . . . and we threw the shingles up on the roof. And we all had hammers. And we start to work. We must have had about six strips. Halfway we were. . . . And over they come. The women are busy hammering. About 3:30 somebody comes up. [He] comes up . . . "Gee, we'll go back to work. We just get mad. . . ." Part of that roofing the women did just to show we are able-bodied too.

The council election of 1974 provides a further illustration of the political tensions between women and men. According to both the written records on file at the regional DINA office and the accounts of the women involved, the nominations and election process of that year were characterized by visible hostility between a handful of men and a larger number of women, who in the end had their social and political rights represented by the Native Mothers' Guild.

The issue was in the first instance straightforward. A dispute arose over the exclusion of a woman's name from the ballot. The female candidate complained that her name failed to appear on the ballot despite her having been nominated at the public meeting according to correct procedures. A review by a DINA agent failed to resolve the dispute as no record of her nomination could be verified. From that point, the dispute escalated into one of gender politics. The elder electoral clerk signed an affidavit swearing his records were full and correct and stated that women "had no place" in the council. For support, he obtained affidavits from two other men, his social peers. In response the angered candidate, supported by the Native Mothers' executive, pursued her position with the requisite affidavits of her testimony.

The attack on women's political rights united the women. Personal differences between members were quickly, if temporarily, bridged. Within the Native Mothers' Guild, executive members of opposing factions rallied to support the candidate. They defined the behavior of the men as the acts of "trouble makers" who did not understand election procedures and who were unworthy of their positions. Having gathered strong community support, they successfully petitioned the DINA to call for new nominations. In the end the united Native Mothers were not only able to have the election results overturned, but also in the subsequent electoral process, to elect a number of female candidates.

In short, the Native Mothers' Guild had established itself as a competitor in the political process. Building on their successful lobbying for community improvements and the demonstrated ability of their leaders, the association was able to draw women together in order to confront tensions and structural limitations perceived to be imposed upon them by men. In consequence, male attacks on women's rights to political office were deftly averted.

Family Loyalty and Factional Politics

At this time the Native Mothers' Guild association was the only voluntary organization on the reserve and therefore the only social institution to provide a focus of solidarity for women. Nevertheless, in the absence of outside challenges, its leaders divided and entered into political competition with one another. Having achieved personal prominence and greater prestige for their families, the leaders, who were core members of the two opposing factions, were able to secure elected and appointed positions for their sons and daughters. The political rivalry of the leaders led to internal disputes over use of the guild's funds and resources. These disputes led to further tensions linked to the factional competition for seats on the band council.

Although the two factions were well matched teams, feelings often ran high when one or the other was perceived to be "in power." Tensions mounted as one faction (Alpha) gained a majority of council seats and appointed its members to the key administrative positions. Allegations of favoritism brought against Alpha included their distribution of the guild's resources as well as those of the council. In 1978 tensions between the two major factions came to a dramatic head. Women's social relationships were torn asunder as the two prominent leaders confronted one another in bitter recriminations following the tragic death of a son in each of their families. The schism between the two families spilled through the entire village as the bereaved families found themselves struggling for loyal supporters.

A year later, this factional conflict was exacerbated. A small logging company, owned and operated by Beta, had been licenced by the DINA to harvest timber from the reserve lands. The operation had proceeded successfully until international timber rates fell and the company was forced to re-negotiate stumpage fees with the band council. The council rejected requests for lower stumpage fees when disgruntled band members, urged by the Alpha faction, petitioned the DINA to enforce the original agreement. Without explanation, the DINA seized this chance to terminate the timber licence and foreclose on the company's loans. The company folded and lost all of its assets. Its employees turned to social assistance.

When the DINA terminated the logging licence, the resulting tensions were turned inward on a fragile community. The local elite was unable to take control over community affairs. Tensions mounted to a crisis point and ended any semblance of social cohesion within the Native Mothers' Guild. In consequence, the feuding families escalated their bitter dispute. The Beta faction gained control of the elected council and fired the band manager, a core member of the Alpha faction and a longstanding member of the Native Mothers' Guild, and replaced her with a woman of their own family. Alpha women then withdrew all support from their local chapter of the Native Mothers' Guild and established a new voluntary association, The Elders' Sacred Circle.

With the appearance of a second association, the voluntary associations became clearly aligned with family politics. In many respects they took on the attributes of opposing political teams locked in a struggle for political resources and loyal followings. Whereas the Native Mothers' Guild had defined its presence as an association of women devoted to family and community, the new association presented itself in the traditional role of elderly women, wise advisers to the young. While its stated policy was to represent all elders (its membership list includes elderly men), executive positions were held by Beta women, specifically those women who had been active leaders in the Guild, had been band councillors, or had been on advisory committees to the council. Significantly, the band manager (whose mother was instrumental in founding the new organization) and her husband became key figures in the decision-making process of the Elders' Sacred Circle. They attended all executive meetings and met with the elders to advise them on strategies and programs and to undertake the paper work and negotiations necessary to secure state funds.

With a key family member holding the position of band manager, the society gained marked advantages. Funding applications and development proposals, for example, were required to pass through the administrative offices for council approval before arriving at the funding agency. Yet at the same time, the Elders' Sacred Circle remained independent from the elected council. Hence, the women who ran it were free to act as they thought best with respect to proposed services, economic activities, and hiring practices.

By 1984 the Elders' Sacred Circle was the second largest employer on the reserve. It had secured funds for children's cultural activities, Carrier language classes and cultural workshops; for travel to cultural events throughout the province; and for constructing a new cultural center. By then it had eclipsed the Native Mothers' Guild. It became the more active of the two voluntary associations, experiencing greater success in obtaining government funds, and therefore enjoying greater visibility in the community. The success of this association was reflected in changes in the band council and administrative staff. Beta dominated both. In fact, the majority of permanent personnel hired by the band council were from this kin group as were those who benefited from summer employment programs.

Of course, the Native Mothers' Guild did not disappear as a political force. Rather, it reverted to its original goals, to provide care for needy families and to promote community interests. It took the lead in raising funds for a new church and continued to raise money and gather goods for families facing unexpected emergencies such as household fires. It withdrew from such overt political issues as competing for community development grants and seeking job creation funds. No doubt, recognizing their immediate disadvantages in this competition, the Guild leaders rejuvenated their ideological political resource, their responsibility to nurture and to promote domestic wellbeing in the context of a harmonious community. The two factions continued their rivalry; one drawing upon its ability to enlist a following by extending its patronage relations, the other rebuilding its reputation for community involvement and commitment to traditional, domestic responsibilities.

Now that the women's voluntary associations were clearly aligned with factional interests, neither could promote the specific interests of women. Clearly, they had become associations *of* women *for* family advancement. But women had created a special sphere of influence for themselves in the community political arena. Apart from their baseball team, which did not have the political influence of women's associations, men had no voluntary associations. Thus, following the bitter factional disputes of 1978, men had neither the same opportunities to influence public opinion nor to represent village interests in negotiations with state agents. Only women were able to do this effectively. Moreover, their local political disputes destroyed neither their commitment to the community as a whole nor their determination to struggle with the state on issues critical to native women. Women of both associations continued their struggle for community improvements. At the same time elite women of the two factions continued to meet outside the community as members of the same provincial association. Beyond the conflicts of the local political arena, women remained united in their common struggles against the state.

In sum, Carrier women's voluntary associations constitute a parapolitical structure advantageous to women generally and to individual, elite women particularly. Elite women further their political aspirations, and those of male kin, by dispensing patronage to male and female followers and by advancing the very real needs of family and community. Women's political ambitions, however, are constrained by a political contest fought out between kin-based factional interests. In this situation, women's position vis-à-vis men has less relevance than the bonds of kinship.

Conclusion: Analyzing Women's Community Politics and Power

This account of Carrier women's political strategies has emphasized the intervention of the state into native community politics. Three salient features of state/community relations need to be highlighted. First, the native community is bound to state authority by the practices of welfare colonialism, which subjects all community management to the extraordinary, discretionary authority of the DINA. Personal and community economic dependency necessitates high degrees of state involvement at the same time as it limits the scope of the parapolitical system of voluntary associations. The state-sponsored political structure and its rivals ultimately rely upon a single source of political power: economic resources derived from the state. Although women's voluntary associations may gain public support through their manipulation of ideological resources, they cannot limit themselves to this strategy. As we have seen, the Native Mothers' Guild entered the political arena when it provided a moral critique of the all-male elected council. Women expressed their criticism according to their traditional responsibilities as providers and caregivers. In turn, this enabled women to defeat men's efforts to prevent them from holding elected office.

The bases of the guild's power, however, lay in their access to state-controlled resources. Like the band council, the guild assumed the role of power-broker, distributing from the state to the community. The strong position of the Native Mothers' Guild eventually was challenged by a second voluntary association because it too effectively manipulated scarce resources. Yet without these community assets, the women's position would have been considerably weaker. If the federal government ceased its programs for community economic development, the women's associations would have lost one of their key power bases and the role of broker would have reverted solely to the council, which has always had access to resources through its dependency upon the DINA.

Second, the political limitations women face are exacerbated by the process of local-level politics. Local political action is never wholly independent. Individuals and groups outside the range of local relationships are vital to the political process and are directly involved in their outcome.[13] More importantly, local relationships are "multiplex."[14] Individuals are bound together by an interweaving of multiple kin relations and common interests that create contradictory obligations and personal affiliations.

Women in politics cannot avoid factional in-fighting. Disputes are created and maintained by the state administrative structure and its promotion of competition for scarce resources. Access to state-controlled resources permits them to fulfil their primary responsibility to their family through provision of desperately needed jobs. Women who seek political office require a loyal constituency, and when elected they find themselves partisan to that faction. They must deliver favors unequally and this more narrow partisanship undercuts the mediating role of women's voluntary associations. Consequently, factional interests take precedence and women's voluntary associations lose their broader, collective, feminine responsibility for community wellbeing. Internal divisions, ruptures and fissures follow. Cooperation declines and without the agreement and leadership of elite women, the membership drifts and splits as individuals withdraw or align themselves with one faction or the other.

Third, while Indian politics is a parapolitical subsystem encapsulated by state authority, voluntary associations are themselves further encapsulated by the apparatus of the band council and its administration. Women's parapolitical subsystems are doubly subordinate. They are secondary to a community administration that is directly dependent on the state. Herein lies the irony of the situation: voluntary associations can only attain autonomy from the elected band council by successfully competing with it for state resources, while at the same time, their leaders manipulate the same state resources in order to gain entry to the council.

The survival of the associations depends upon successful mediation of this contradiction. They may muster their ideological resources to counter unsatisfactory administration of their community and thus vitiate their dependence on state resources, or they may initiate action against the state and thus gain the moral support of their community. Neither course is free from political pitfalls. Success in either direction threatens to divide women against women.

NOTES

1. Tord Larsen, "Negotiating Identity: The Micmac of Nova Scotia," in Adrian Tanner (ed.), *The Politics of Indianness: Case Studies of Ethnopolitics in Canada*, Institute of Social and Economic Research, Memorial University of Newfoundland, Social and Economic Papers No. 12, St. John's Newfoundland, 1983, p. 107.
2. Adrian Tanner, "Introduction: Canadian Indians and the Politics of Dependency," Adrian Tanner (ed.), *op. cit.*, p. 2.
3. F.G. Bailey, *Stratagems and Spoils: A Social Anthropology of Politics*. Oxford: Basil Blackwell, 1969, pp. 28, 45.
4. Jo-Anne Fiske, *And Then We Prayed Again: Carrier Women, Colonialism and Mission Schools*, M.A. Thesis, University of British Columbia.
5. The single exception to this is the Tanizul Timber Ltd. of the Stewart Trembleur Band, which has a large tree-farm licence and is a secure source of employment for the surrounding communities.
6. Opportunities to trap are constrained by large-scale resource exploitation and settlement, which have destroyed animal populations in many areas, and by the need for levels of capital investment unavailable to most band members. In the band under discussion only a handful of traplines can now be utilized. The majority of these are leased to other trappers due to the owners' lack of capital.
7. Bailey, *op. cit.*, p. 12.
8. Tanner, *op. cit.*, p. 19.
9. Larsen, *op. cit.*; Tanner *op. cit.*, p. 33.

10. Fictitious names are given to the women's associations in order to protect band and personal identities.
11. See note 10.
12. All quotations are taken from interviews with women actively engaged in women's voluntary associations.
13. Marc J. Swartz, "Introduction," Marc J. Swartz (ed.), *Local-Level Politics: Social And Cultural Perspectives*. London: University of London Press, 1969, p. 1.
14. *Ibid.*

"Making Democracy Practicable":
Voluntarism and Job Creation[*]

Susan Heald

Introduction

From 1981 to 1984 I participated in a project funded by the Local
Employment Assistance Program (LEAP)[1] of the federal government of
Canada. "LEAP provides funds to individuals, groups or organizations
to create ongoing businesses which will provide jobs for the chronically
unemployed."[2] According to the way LEAP was organized at that time,
each project involved three groups of people: the sponsor group, the
project officer, and the target group. In general terms, the sponsor
group was a group of local citizens, preferably skilled in some aspect of
the project, who were willing to donate their labor to the development
of the project, and to be answerable for the use of funds. The project
officer was an employee of the Employment Development Branch of the
federal government, and was responsible for ensuring that the sponsor
group obeyed all LEAP regulations and worked within the terms of the
contract established between LEAP and the sponsor group. The target group was the group of people the project was designed to hire;
the sponsor group was responsible for determining who this would be,
within the general limits set by LEAP. Our particular project involved
the establishment of a natural food restaurant staffed by women that
would eventually be worker-owned. The natural food restaurant was the
only one of its kind located in the city of 110,000 people.

In this paper I will argue that the relations set up in and through

---

[*]Many people have read and provided helpful comments on earlier drafts
of this paper. I would like to thank Philip Corrigan, Marian McMahon, Mary
O'Brien, Harry Smaller, Leila Simonen, Deborah Harrison, Claire Levesque,
Kari Dehli, Jake Muller and Roxana Ng.

this project contributed to *Canadian state formation*. To talk about the state as "in formation" means that it cannot be seen as having "immutable boundaries,"[3] nor even as being fully formed. Rather, we need to see the state as always in the process of formation, always able to change and, perhaps most importantly, to grow. Job creation projects can in one sense be seen as one more way of expanding what is meant by the state. This expansion should be understood in two senses: we must expand the way we understand "the state"; at the same time, the state in a sense expands its boundaries through people's involvement in job creation programs. These ideas will be elaborated throughout the paper.

In this paper, I will first outline the general theoretical understanding of state formation important to my analysis here. I will then describe some of the relationships involved in our project and discuss the nature of job creation programs in Canada. This latter discussion enables me to examine one aspect of the program: that of voluntarism. Canadians are asked to volunteer in support of many efforts to improve community life and services; job creation is one of them. We volunteer for many different reasons, in many different ways, and with many different results. I hope to show that one of the effects is how "the state" accomplishes its work through us.

Method

As a participant in this project I had no thought at the time of writing a paper about it. In fact, it was only after one year and a thousand miles had separated me from the project that I began to think about writing this paper, in response to an assignment for a university course on the state. Consequently, the information contained herein is based on memory, and on written documents produced at the time (such as minutes of meetings, letters to and from the project, etc.). As such, this is by no means an "objective" paper. The project involved three years of effort. The confusion, anger and pain can, perhaps, be better understood by this undertaking, but they cannot be made to go away and I have made no effort to hide them. I (one of my "I's") was there, am here on these pages. Yet, mine is not an isolated case. As we come to understand the state as a very real part of our identity formation, it becomes impossible to set ourselves apart from an analysis of our experiences and the state.

In reading this paper, it must be understood that I am writing from the standpoint of *one person*, whose location in this project was as a member of the *sponsor group*. From this location I can lay no claim to understanding the experiences of any other, differently-positioned persons, nor even of all the members of the sponsor group, although I know some would agree with the analysis presented here. This analysis is thus partial and provisional: the focus is on aspects of the complex relationships involved in state formation, and not aimed at providing a comprehensive account of the project, the LEAP program and people's experience of both.

Like any experience, mine is not strictly verifiable nor replicable, and my analysis of it cannot be the same as my living it. Still, through analyzing the set of relations which were involved in this one project,[4] I hope to move towards understanding both *how* the state is organized, and how it organizes us. In writing this paper, then, I have a dual purpose: to try to make some sense of my experience (in a way which may help others to make sense of theirs), and to subject state theory to examination in the light of this experience. This is a huge undertaking which obviously cannot be completed here. What follows should be seen as a set of glimpses and glimmers of understanding wherein theories of state power are illuminated by my experience and vice versa.

The State

Much literature on the state seems to agree that the *result* of the activities of this thing we call "the state" is the maintenance and organization of our subjection to class rule. However, there are several problems with the way the state is formulated in demonstrating these results. Central for me is the tendency to see the state as a kind of animate being which controls our lives. This kind of discussion centers on attempts to decide who is and is not a part of the state, and to examine how it works (which often make it seem conspiratorial). In this discussion, the state remains "out there," separate from the "real lives" of most people. This points to a second central problem: the tendency to see people—particularly women—as products of other forces, of others' actions and desires. This, of course, is not solely a feature of state theory; nonetheless, again and again this kind of theory deprives us of our motivation, power, action, and resistance.

One way of attempting to avoid some of these problems is to try to see the state as a set of relations and practices in which we *all*, more or less, participate. This participation is usually not so much demanded as invited: The term I have come to use is "summoned." How we are summoned, and who in particular is summoned, become central questions.

Corrigan, Ramsay and Sayer have described the state not as a structure, but as ". . . a complex of social forms *organized* so that it inflects all relations and ideas about relations in such a way that capitalist production, and all it entails, becomes thought of and lived as natural."[5] "The state" is also a *concept* ("something conceived in the mind," according to Webster) which may not necessarily correspond to an identifiable set of structures. As Varda Burstyn says, the state:

> ". . . is a generalization and abstraction. It sums up and schematizes a system of relations, structures, institutions which, in industrialized society, are vast, complex, differentiated, and as an inevitable result, contradictory a well."[6]

Burstyn's four components (relations, structures, institutions and forces) can be collapsed into the concept of "relations," since "structures, institutions and forces" are all expressions of relations between people and/or things. This understanding is consistent with Marx's formulation in the *Grundrisse* that society itself ". . . does not consist of individuals but expresses the sum of interrelations, the relations within which these individuals stand."[7]

In general, I am trying to understand the state not so much as an institution or set of institutions but as a set of *relations* set up by, in, and through those institutions.[8] Thus, we can speak of state formation as a set of relations that are always being formed and reformed in various contexts. These relations may be between persons or things, but what is central is that they are *experienced*, potentially in different ways by different people. The next section, which describes some of the relations in our project, may help to make this clear.

Relations
Through our project[9] relationships involving numerous government and agency representatives were created. I am going to outline some of them here, to show how the state comes to organize us in numerous ways which often seem insignificant and "natural." While each relation on its own may appear simple and unproblematic, in combination they construct and restrict what it is we are able to do, or to even imagine doing.[10]

In the first place, those involved in the project—the sponsor group, the target group and the project officer—took up positions in relation to each other which were structured by the (real or apparent) demands of the LEAP program. These positions were often problematic and contradictory: Members of the target group were required to present themselves as—at one and the same time—unable to get a job yet able to do *this* job. Sponsor group members were to be able to operate a successful business and yet not be identified as *business people*. The LEAP project officer (I will call him Chris) represented LEAP to us. We were rarely given written rules and guidelines; we were required to follow them as they were presented to us by the project officer. Yet, it was the task of the sponsor group, not the project officer, to communicate with the staff—the target group. Whatever opinions of LEAP we (the sponsor group) might have, we had to convey LEAP's demands and instructions to the staff, and try to ensure that they were carried out. Furthermore, it was our responsibility to translate "what actually happened"[11] at the restaurant into a language which LEAP (or Chris) could hear and understand. This was usually done in the form of statistics and budget figures. Individuals, events, opinions and experiences disappeared. The state also tended to disappear, and to be expressed instead as "Chris says . . . ," "Susan says . . . ," and so on. At the same time, this invisible state could be referred to when necessary, so that again and again we were told "LEAP says, wants, demands . . ." "LEAP" was both "Chris" and no one.

The sponsor group had many other tasks which established a set of relations with a much larger network of persons and institutions. As the sponsor group, ten of us agreed to be responsible for the funds (ultimately close to three quarters of a million dollars) which the project received, while ensuring that none of it went into our own pockets. To reduce our personal liability, we entered into arrangements with other government agencies to become a legitimate corporation. In these instances, our responsibility appeared to be to "the public": we were to ensure that taxpayers' money was well-managed.

Since this was a *job-creation project*, our potential employees needed to be defined by the appropriate authorities as "unemployed" and therefore already involved with those organizations which have the power to define individuals in this way. We had further specified that we wished to give priority to single-parent women, and this meant that prospective employees were usually already connected to other government agencies which dealt with and defined "single parents." In most cases, this connection also gave these women access to government funds, such as social assistance. Complex sets of rules about the availability of such funds had to be taken into account if and when the women acquired one of the newly-created jobs.

The decision to hire single-parent women was not entirely ours: LEAP had identified general target groups—women, native and disabled persons —and project sponsors were required to hire from these groups. Thus, there is another set of less obvious relations whereby statistics are collected and used to define certain people as belonging to "disadvantaged groups."

As women, we were identified by LEAP as a target group—a group unable to find jobs. That some of us were employed, well-educated, and so on, enabled us to find special favor with the funders, who saw us initially as "a smart bunch of women." The fact that we were not expected to be capable meant that when—in their terms—we *were*, we could be more successful within the structures which were set up. At the same time, these attitudes contributed to a continual push-pull in expectations: we were to be competent and subservient at the same time.

Meanwhile, the targeting of women as a disadvantaged group was also important to us: it constituted the raison d'être for our involvement in the project. We felt a commitment, as feminists, to participate in initiatives which might improve women's situation in Canada. LEAP's program appeared in part as an answer to some of the criticisms and demands we had made about women's participation in the labor force. That the program managed to appear this way while doing little to correct the situation[12] is part of the complex reality of the state that we are trying to unravel here.

As a business, we entered into another set of relations with state organizations, including consumer and corporate affairs, health and building requirements, liquor licensing, and so on. In addition, LEAP wanted to be sure that if anyone was ever to share in any profits, it would only be target group members; thus, we were told that a worker-owned structure was desirable. While this was perfectly consistent with the aims of our group, the task of producing a shareholders' agreement which would reflect our desires and ideas, comply with the regulations of the Business Corporations Act (which were changed at least once during the time we were working on the agreement), and satisfy LEAP, proved exceedingly difficult. The difficulty was that funding would only be given to corporations whose structure was acceptable to LEAP. But when we asked for LEAP's guidelines to help us draft the shareholders' agreement, we were told that there were none. Meanwhile, the production of the agreement (the result of hours of unpaid labor) was essential for LEAP to decide on the acceptability of the project.

Once the agreement was drafted, it would have a fictitious status for several years, because the federal government retained a lien on all assets of the business until one year after funding ended. To complicate matters further, a worker-owned structure was somewhat inconsistent with a structure where a board of directors (the sponsor group) was ultimately responsible for the fiscal management and hiring practices of the business. A complex transition period thus had to be built into the shareholders' agreement. Anyone who has ever tried to mould a worker-owner agreement into a law designed for privately-owned businesses will know that it is difficult enough without these additional requirements.

Faced with the realities of trying to produce a document which would meet all these requirements, we often floundered. When we persisted, we were faced with the problem of finding and keeping a manager capable of developing a successful business and moving towards a situation of worker ownership. This was a constant problem.

I do not want to suggest that any of this is impossible, or that other groups have not successfully manoeuvred their way through these obstacles. What I am suggesting is that 1) the state sets up and is manifested in these relations; 2) we enter into these relations partly in pursuit of our own goals; and 3) these relations—which are somewhat different for every project—are clearly too complex for anyone to have actually *planned* them such that they would have the effect of perpetuating and forming the state.

Although I am not suggesting a conspiracy, I will go on to examine certain aspects of how job creation programs were instituted in Canada. The institution of these programs illuminates the processes through which state formation takes place.

Job Creation Programs

"When economic conditions are such that employers are hesitant about expanding their business," a pamphlet entitled *The Government of Canada and the Working Person* tells us, "the federal government introduces incentives and programs designed to encourage potential employers to create jobs and thus reduce the number of unemployed."[13] That these incentives and programs do little to affect the economic conditions that have influenced employers' hesitancy in the first place is not stated. The use of the phrase "reduce the *number* of unemployed" is instructive here. It is the *statistics* on unemployment with which political parties—as one manifestation of the state—seem to be concerned, not the *people* who are unemployed nor the reasons for unemployment. Thus, what is important is to be able to appear in the official statistics as having reduced the number of unemployed. This appears as one *raison d'être* of job creation: numbers are shifted into new categories and the problem appears to be solved.[14]

Around the western world, direct job creation programs are considered "measures of last resort."[15] Canadian programs have been considered models for other countries and are noted for their emphasis on assisting specific social groups at the same time as they are attempting to counter seasonal unemployment. The practice of "targeting" has meant—among other things—that the market principles usually guiding employment are by-passed.[16] This is not without significance: employers use the programs to subsidize wage costs, but—at least in the private sector—rarely consider the people working in these programs "proper" employees nor consider them for permanent positions.[17] Participation for many people ". . . is simply a short interlude in an otherwise constant period of unemployment,"[18] because the programs do very little to affect the general unemployment situation and because the jobs are stigmatized.[19] The round of job creation programs begun in Canada in 1971 and modelled thereafter around the world,[20] represented, in the words of one Canadian official, ". . . a conceptual change. . . . [T]he new programs encouraged the jobless to develop and accept administrative responsibility for worthwhile community projects. . . ."[21] In short order, there was a movement towards requiring "community"—that is, "voluntary"—groups to participate in the development and administration of job creation programs. This was not a particularly new approach to state activities: the 1951 Massey Report, which resulted in the establishment of the Canada Council, called for the Council to encourage Canadian arts "through the appropriate voluntary organizations."[22] Further, the Report's authors, ". . . consider that the relation of voluntary effort to governmental activity is the focal point of the work of this Commission . . . the democratic form of government is made practicable through the work of voluntary organizations."[23] It is important that we begin to understand *how* (and why) the state summons "volunteers," "citizens" and "communities" in this way, and the effect this has.

It has already been suggested that one effect of our response to this summons is to expand what the state is understood to be, who is considered a part of it, and how this understanding and incorporation can sometimes work. A reading of Hansard makes it clear that this is no mere paranoid claim. In introducing the Opportunities for Youth Program, Pierre Trudeau made the point most eloquently:

> The government believes as well that youth is sincere in its efforts to improve society and that young people are anxious to work and to engage in activities which are intended to make Canada a better place in which to live. The government proposes therefore to encourage young persons to direct their energy, their imagination and their altruism into projects which are beneficial to the entire community. The opportunities for youth program will combine the resources of the government with the resource-

fulness of youth. . . . There is work to be done; there are tasks to be performed; there are experiences to be gained. There is a whole country to be explored. There is a generation desirous of improving the world in which it finds itself. This summer will challenge us all to accomplish these ends.[24]

Less inspirational, but more to the point, Otto Lang said of another program:

The local initiatives programs really invite persons from one end of the country to the other in municipalities and other responsible organizations to apply their vast ingenuity in joining in the solving of the job creation problem and in producing the best possible result.[25]

Unemployment became something that you or I could do something about. Job creation programs became one way of accomplishing community improvement schemes. It is significant that the timing of the introduction of these programs roughly corresponded to a period of increasing agitation for jobs and social services for women. Apparently, both could be provided through job creation projects, and so many women took up the offer; we heeded the summons, and made "democracy"—or rather class rule—"practicable."

Not only are local individuals and groups being summoned to participate in the activities of the state, but they are expected to do so as volunteers. This is a concept which requires some examination.

"Volunteers" and "Voluntarism"

The problem with theories which have been labelled "voluntaristic" is that they attribute too much to human agency. Similarly, the notion of "volunteering" serves to reinforce the idea that we are free to choose certain activities. One is reminded of Marx's use, in a different context, of the word *vogelfrei*, "literally 'as free as a bird', i.e., free but outside the human community and therefore entirely unprotected and without legal rights."[26] Marx also uses "free" when referring to the proletariat in the double sense of being free from possession of land and free of anything left to sell but their labor power, so that really ". . . he was no 'free agent' . . . the period of time for which he is free to sell his labor-power is the period of time for which he is forced to sell it. . . ."[27] Similarly, I want to question the notion of "free choice" embedded in the idea of "volunteering," and also consider the extent to which volunteer labor is outside the work community, and therefore without rights or protection.

In North America today, added to the notion of "freely chosen" is that of "unpaid work." This implies and reinforces the idea that this work is not and should not be part of the paid work force. It appears as making possible those things the individual wants to do in the society. As residents of a town where many women were seriously under- or unemployed and where good food was hard to get, we "volunteered" to be on the sponsor group because we wanted to change those two facts. We were not compelled, we "cared."[28] The London Edinburgh Weekend Return Group provides one analysis of how this works under the foreboding heading "Caring makes the (capitalist) world go round."

> In a sense, the social worker or nurse or teacher is in a similar situation at work to that in which she is (and others are) as mother or lover at home. She loves and cares because she is human. But that loving and caring is doubly exploited. It seems to involve her in unpaid and unfair amounts of work in the home. And it causes her to accept underpaid and often heartbreaking work outside. Yet if she resists, she risks hurting herself and those she cares about, merely to ruffle the state a little.[29]

This was part of our own logic for becoming involved. While it would probably be untrue to cast the people who gathered together to form the restaurant board of directors as all wanting to "ruffle the state a little," most of us would identify ourselves in one way or another as part of the "counter-culture." Certainly we all "cared";[30] and like everyone else, we all had assumptions—mostly unstated—about how the world works and how we could work to affect change. These assumptions, too, are a part of the state: many of the relations we experience (including, for example, schooling and our participation in the job creation program) function to educate us about our participation in change. In Foucault's terms, these relations have "effects of veridiction," by which he means: ". . . codifying effects regarding what is to be known."[31]

The notions of job creation as a way of solving unemployment and enabling useful community work, and of voluntary action as a way in which "ordinary citizens" can contribute to this solution, work together with other "effects of veridiction" such that certain people find themselves "summoned" to participate. In doing so, we—in the words of the Massey Commission—make democracy practicable. At the same time, we accept a set of constraints about *who* we will represent *how*, and how we will represent *ourselves* in the process.

"Making Democracy Practicable" or "Marching Past the Inspection Booth"

The kinds of contradictions outlined here are played out in thousands of places and ways every day. Thousands of community groups present themselves to hundreds of government (federal, provincial, municipal) funding agencies for an inspection process which, the groups hope, will lead to funding. Some of these groups, like ours, were created specifically to enable a funding application for a specific project. Others are groups which continue from year to year by virtue of their ability to garner government grants. These groups often know that they must change their goals or their program, or think up a new aspect of their endeavor to meet the guidelines. These guidelines, as we have seen in the case of job creation projects, are not always clear and are changed frequently.

All groups share an involvement with a kind of voluntary action which is, in a sense, enforced by law. In the case of LEAP projects, a sponsor group is required. In other situations organizations must be registered as a non-profit corporation and/or have a federal charitable tax exemption number to receive government assistance. To incorporate, a number of unpaid individuals must agree to at least *say* that they are supervising the activities of the organization. Increasingly, funding organizations are requiring evidence of board involvement, as indicated by fund-raising activities, thus demanding more volunteer time.

Preparation of funding applications is a time-consuming process carried out by volunteers or staff who are usually very poorly-paid. The granting agencies are staffed by well-paid, well-educated people. Applications are evaluated at least in part on their neatness, completeness, and sophistication.[32] Passing the inspection process successfully thus requires forms of self-presentation which may have little to do with the vital work of the organization.

In the end, many are left wondering '*si le jeu en vaut la chandelle*'.[33] Organizations cannot proceed without funds, yet the aims cannot be accomplished if the individuals involved are always busy preparing grant applications. Spending hard-won dollars on glossy brochures and other evidence of "sophistication" often seems neither appropriate nor necessary. Presenting ourselves in certain ways to satisfy funders can change how individuals see themselves and their organization; sometimes the very acceptance of funds involves compromises that change original aims beyond recognition.[34] Job creation projects can swell the size of an organization from one or two staff persons to five or ten for a few months, disappear for a season and return with new criteria. If they reappear too soon, groups may not be able to hire the same people because they no longer meet the criteria as "chronically unemployed." Continuity is impossible, and much unpaid labor is often lost during the glut of paid staff. These are just some examples.

The contradictions are enormous, yet groups continue to march past the inspection booth. It is a ragged march, for we seem not to hear the drummer. Poulantzas suggests that there are a set of discourses directed at the dominant classes which ". . . the masses do not manage to hear."[35]

Conclusion

Yet, the problem cannot be that we are deaf, nor stupid. The "smart bunch of women" who began this project remained so to the end, although we all came to feel disillusioned and disempowered. The restaurant was unable to generate enough revenue to warrant continued belief that it would become self-sufficient, and so it was closed less than two years after it opened. The result of our struggle to operate within the relations established by the state was "failure." Other groups may experience failure in other forms: failing to get grants, failing to "manage" the organization properly, failing to keep staff from becoming "burned out." These failures can be explained in a variety of ways, and the truth probably always lies in a combination of factors. What I want to consider here are two of the ways in which this failure can be *experienced*. Frequently, we feel the failure to be the result of personal inadequacies, or of human capacity in general. For myself, at least, combined with a variety of ideas about what went wrong with our project was a sense of my own inability to overcome the obstacles—to fly in the face of adversity, as it were, and make it work. At another level, in trying to make sense of the pain of failure, we may begin to wonder whether it is humanly possible to do the things we were trying to do. This connects with the second way of understanding failure: To see the *forms* as impossible. In our project, this was focused around the efforts to achieve worker-ownership. It became possible to locate the failure in the fact that traditional business practices, organization and division of labor are superior to the alternatives.

In this sense, then—sadly and cynically—even in our failure we serve to "make democracy practicable." To the extent that a central project of the state is to normalize and naturalize the way things are,[36] the failure of alternatives can serve to reinforce current social forms and ideas about human capacities. Persons who once situated themselves as wanting to "ruffle the state a little" feel ruffled themselves, sometimes to the extent that they give up. Democracy is more practicable when people are more convinced of the efficacy of the system as it is.

I do not want to oversimplify. Clearly, we are most often aware that there are forces beyond our control, that the things which make funding applications and funded projects successful are complex and interwoven. We do not simply blame ourselves and give up. I have endeavored to point to some of the many ways in which our complex identities as

Canadian women in the 1980s have been interwoven with the state. We are identified by the state in ways which make it possible for us to *choose* to respond to the summons and participate in the relations which form the state. In this process, the state becomes a part of who we are, and we become part of the state. There is no way, I am arguing, to bracket off "the state" and analyse it separately from the individuals who have learned what it is to be a human being within the politically organized processes of subjection we have learned to call "the state."

Afterword: Auto-Critique, Work in Progress

I. August, 1986. In this work, I find myself continuing to be caught— although I have struggled not to be—in a determinist formulation in which persons and practices are either dominant or subordinate, never oppositional, never creative. In some ways, this is because the particular project left many of us in the sponsor group with little but negative feelings. I think it is also because in trying to understand "the state" as part of who and what we are, I/we have failed to mark out new boundaries for the concept.

In addition, there is a serious problem with language. How does this "thing" which is not a "thing" do anything? How can we say "The State"—even paying attention to the way the word "the" suggests a set of boundaries we are assumed to take for granted—without making it a "thing"? Analyzing relations instead of individuals or institutions assumed responsible for their/our actions—while I would want to continue to argue its importance—may move too far away from a recognition of the fact that these practices are not entirely self-perpetuating: the web of complex relations which has been identified in this paper was in fact set up by a set of real individuals and real institutions existing in the real material world of central Canada in the 1980s.

And so, I am still going in circles, yet still committed to the work. For me, several things remain to be done: to expand the analysis of the history of job creation projects in Canada; to explore accounts of others' experiences with these and other state-funded projects and programs (and this appears to be a growing area of interest for feminist work, in particular), and to explore—and expand or correct—the notion of "in and against" the state. In the end, the hope is to be able to point to some ways in which we can better control the effects of funding practices on our organizations. I have tried to show how our failures are embedded in a vast web of practices and relations, but this is insufficient if we cannot see our way through them. For now, I am operating on the belief that understanding the problem is some kind of step towards its solution.

However, the real project is to try to see how different persons can be summoned differently to participate in the process of governance, and how they may, from time to time, answer the summons while dancing to a different drummer.

II. August, 1987. Two years have now passed since the first draft of this paper was written; three since the restaurant was closed. Two other restaurants and a computer store have come and gone in the old restaurant location, making some of us wonder to what extent our financial problems were due to the location. The beautiful hand-made furniture and prized cappuccino machine now reside, rather ironically, in a place dominated by men, who play cards and watch TV to while away long afternoons at tables where once we dreamed brave dreams. Occasionally, friends and I will venture in to drink cappuccino and reminisce. During a recent visit to the town I was greeted warmly by one former staff who now works in a donut shop, and another who is finishing her university degree.

Although the restaurant is closed, my experience of it does not remain the same. Experience can be re-written if a new discourse presents itself, enabling us to explain our experience to ourselves in a different way.[37] To some extent, that was how this paper came to be written at all: a certain discourse about "the state"[38] allowed me to begin a kind of "micro-physics of power": a way of understanding my experience of the restaurant.

Today, new discourses offer new explanations. Two are central for me: one is methodological and the other theoretical. At a theoretical level, I have come to question the kind of "neo-Gramscian tendency to expand the state"[39] to which I fall prey in this paper. According to Lorna Weir, this literature on the state has acted as a counter-weight to the notion of class—especially production relations—by inserting the state as yet another determinant of social relations. Hegemony is seen as totally a state product and totally ideological. In examining what she calls the "state-is-everywhere people," Weir makes clear that a concept with no boundaries around it is meaningless. The project of boundary-finding is ongoing; many people have recognized that redefinition is necessary, but boundaries are still needed.

Methodologically, I have come to see that a much clearer account is required of the "I" in this paper. Who is the woman who both wrote this paper and experienced the events described therein? How can a writer engage with both the circumstances in which she does her work and the fears and desires which motivate the writing? The need for such an engagement is clear: feminist writers have shown again and again that the search for "objective social science" is not only futile, not only masculinist, but detrimental to women.[40] Furthermore, efforts to move beyond the determinist/voluntarist dualism (which has captured so much space in academic debate) have led to an examination of the notion of "subjectivities," and to a critique of the liberal/progressivist notion of "individual." Our subjectivities are seen to be multiple rather than unitary, changeable rather than fixed, and above all, locatable in the interplay between (unconscious) desire and available discourses rather than in a coherent core.[41] The "I" who writes, then, is someone quite other than the "I" who wrote two years ago, when coherence appeared the ultimate goal of analysis.

But it is not just to demonstrate our lack of coherence that we write about ourselves. A new kind of autobiographical writing is required;[42] one which lets us look at the interplay of psychoanalytic, discursive and structural features in our own lives, and thereby learn something about the society in which we live and work.

NOTES

1. This program no longer exists; in fact, it ceased to exist before the change of governments and while the restaurant was still being funded by the program. Although no reason for the changes to the government job creation programs was ever given to us, the discussion in this paper points to some of the contradictions which were, perhaps, not only too much for those of us on the receiving end, but for the government as well.
2. Employment and Immigration Canada, *Annual Report*, 1980.
3. Nicos Poulantzas, *State, Power, Socialism*. London: Verso, 1978, p. 16.
4. Roxana Ng, "Immigrant Women and the State: A Study in the Social Organization of Knowledge." Ph.D. Thesis, Department of Education, University of Toronto, 1984, provides an interesting, parallel analysis of another employment project.
5. Philip Corrigan, Harvie Ramsay and Derek Sayer, "The State as a Relation of Production," in Philip Corrigan (ed.), *State Formation and Marxist Theory*. London: Quartet, 1980, p. 10.
6. Varda Burstyn, "Masculine Dominance and the State," *The Socialist Register*. London: Verso, 1983, p. 46.
7. Karl Marx, *Grundrisse*, 1858. London: Penguin, 1973, p. 264.
8. See also the Introduction to this volume.

9. It is worth noting that the very fact that we were, to the government personnel, a "project" at the same time as we were expected/expecting to be a "business" in itself pinpoints a major contradiction in job creation projects funded by the state.

10. Imagination is significant here. It is important to remember that state control does not always manifest itself by restricting us from realizing our desires. More often, restrictions are not recognized because it is our capacity to desire, to imagine social forms and human capacities beyond what we now know which is restricted. See Philip Corrigan, "Doing Mythologies," *Borderlines*, No. 1, 1984.

11. See Dorothy E. Smith, "No One Commits Suicide: Textual Analysis of Ideological Practices," *Human Studies* 6, 1983, pp. 309–352.

12. In fact, the general unemployment situation is not "solved" in this process; women, and LEAP's other target groups, benefit little from the mere *appearance* of action.

13. Canadian Unity Information Office, *The Government of Canada and the Working Person*. Ottawa: Minister of Supply and Services, 1984, p. 9.

14. In a similar vein, it could be noted that the recent rash of "Life Skills" programs further shifts "the problem": it is not that there are no jobs, but that people do not have the skills to get them!

15. See, e.g., Michael P. Jackson and Victor J.B. Hanby (eds.), *Work Creation: International Experiences*. Westmead, England: Saxon House, 1979.

16. Detlev Karsten, "Reflections on the West German Experience with Direct Job Creation,"in Jackson and Hanby, *op. cit.*, pp. 87–100.

17. See Jackson and Hanby, *op. cit.*; Employment and Immigration Canada, *Evaluation of Challenge '85 Summer Employment/Experience Development [SEED] Program Element*. Ottawa: Program Evaluation Branch, Strategic Policy and Planning, 1985.

18. Jackson and Hanby, *op. cit.*, p. 9.

19. This was made most clear to me when I went to the bank in a period when we were considering ending our connection to LEAP to ask for a business loan. A year earlier, during a period of extensive press attention to the restaurant, sparked mainly by the Chamber of Commerce's concern that the federal government shouldn't be funding businesses in this way, the terms "target group," "employment disadvantaged," "sole support mothers and the disabled" were mentioned frequently. Apparently my bank manager had absorbed much of this, since he merely gave me a confused look and explained that we could not be treated as a regular business, because we didn't have regular employees. We were ineligible for a business loan.

20. Jackson and Hanby, *op. cit.*, p. 7.

21. Michael J. Francomb, "Job Creation in Canada," in Jackson and Hanby, *op. cit.*, p. 60.

22. See Robin Endres, "Art and Accumulation: The Canadian State and the Business of Art," in Leo Panitch (ed.), *The Canadian State: Political Econ-*

omy and Political Power. Toronto: University of Toronto Press, 1977, p. 423.

23. *Ibid.*, p. 424.

24. House of Commons Debates, March 16, 1971, p. 4287–4288.

25. *Ibid.*, October 14, 1971, p. 8699. Note should be taken that, only months after the first direct job creation programs were entered into, Lang could speak of "the job creation problem" as a fact.

26. Ben Fowkes, translator's note, in Karl Marx, *Capital*, Vol. I. New York: Vintage Books, 1977, p. 896.

27. *Ibid.*, p. 415.

28. "Volunteering" and "caring" have historically been women's domain; substantial work is being and remains to be done regarding the significance for women of this fact. See, e.g., Janet Finch and Dulcie Grove (eds.), *A Labour of Love: Women, Work and Caring.* London: Routledge and Kegan Paul, 1983, and papers by Bullock, Dehli and Roberts, in this collection.

29. London Edinburgh Weekend Return Group, *In and Against the State.* London: Pluto Press, 1980, p. 27.

30. For some this caring mainly related to the problem of making good food available to themselves, their families and friends. Seen in the context of the political and economic reasons why we do *not* have good food, this is a potentially radicalizing concern. In the late 1970s, Canada's People's Food Commission helped many people make these connections; see the Commission's National Report, *The Land of Milk and Money*, Toronto: Between the Lines, 1980. However, put as it so often is in the context of personal health which could be improved through better nutrition, this is a concern which reinforces liberal, individualistic values. It is probably no accident that such a fuss is made by state offices about "fitness"—it focuses both interest and responsibility on individuals and consumes time and energy in personal pursuits which ignore the causes of our ill health.

31. Michel Foucault, "Questions of Method: An Interview with Michel Foucault," *Ideology and Consciousness* 8 (5), 1981.

32. I was once guaranteed a grant the instant I submitted the application because, I was told, I had included all the requested information. The granting organization's representative had not had time to *read* the information— did not even appear to be going to—but *it was there* and that, apparently, was an improvement over other applications! I had passed the inspection.

33. Literally, "if the game is worth the candle." Although this is not an expression that is used very often any more, it does serve to remind us that there are many ways of counting the costs of participation in various "games." One of the more concrete ones is to consider the cost of the candles needed to light the area in which the game is played. Unfortunately, there seem to be few such tangible ways of calculating the costs of participation in the funding game.

34. Toronto peace and disarmament groups, for example, were embroiled in a

controversy around some of these issues; see Stephen Dale, "Politics at the peace core," *NOW*, May 30 – June 5, 1985.

35. Poulantzas, *op. cit.*, p. 33.

36. See Corrigan, 1984, *op. cit.*; and Philip Corrigan and Derek Sayer, *The Great Arch*. London: Basil Blackwell, 1985.

37. This, at least, is the argument of some post-structuralist theory; see, e.g., Chris Weedon, *Feminist Practice and Poststructuralist Theory*. Oxford: Basil Blackwell, 1987; Julian Henriques, *et al.*, *Changing the Subject*. New York: Methuen, 1984; Biddy Martin, "Feminism, Criticism and Foucault," *New German Critique* 27, Fall 1982, pp. 3–30.

38. Mainly that of Philip Corrigan; see Corrigan and Sayer, *op. cit.*; and inspired by Foucault, see "Questions of Method," *op. cit.*; also *Discipline and Punish*. New York: Vantage, 1979.

39. Lorna Weir, Talk at the Marxist Institute. Toronto, February 1987.

40. See, e.g., Gloria Bowles and Renate Duelli Klein (eds.), *Theories of Women's Studies*. London: Routledge and Kegan Paul, 1983; Sandra Harding and Merrill B. Hintikka (eds.), *Discovering Reality: Feminist Perspectives on Epistemology, Metaphysics, Methodology and Philosophy of Science*. Dordrecht: D. Reidel, 1983; Angela McRobbie, "The Politics of Feminist Research: Between Talk, Text and Action," *Feminist Review* 12, 1982, pp. 46–57.

41. In addition to the above, see Valerie Walkerdine, "Sex, Power and Pedagogy," *Education* 38, Spring 1981, pp. 14–24; and "Video Replay: Families, Film and Fantasy," in Victor Bergen, James Donald and Cora Kaplan (eds.), *Formations of Fantasy*. London and New York: Methuen, 1986, pp. 167–199.

42. See Valerie Walkerdine, "Dreams from an Ordinary Childhood," in Liz Heron (ed.), *Truth, Dare or Promise: Girls Growing Up in the Fifties*. London: Virago, 1985, pp. 63–77; Madeleine Grumet, "Bodyreading," *Teachers College Record* 87 (2), 1985, pp. 175–193; Carolyn Steadman, *Landscape for a Good Woman*. London: Virago, 1986; Marian McMahon, "Return of the Repressed: Writing/Righting the Past," M.A. Thesis, Department of Education, University of Toronto, 1987; Susan Heald, "State Regulation and Cultural Organizations: Being the Northern Woman," Ph.D. Thesis, Ontario Institute of Studies in Education, University of Toronto, 1988.

State Funding to a Community Employment Center
Implications for Working with Immigrant Women*

Roxana Ng

Introduction: Community Services and the State

During the 1960s and 1970s, the federal government created programs to provide funding to grassroots community organizations under the general rubric of "citizens' participation."[1] This began notably with the Company of Young Canadians (CYC). Analysts have characterized this form of funding from the state to potentially dissident groups, such as women, ethnic minorities, youths, and the economically disadvantaged, as a means of social control.[2] Community activists, on the other hand, argue that government funding to grassroots community activities was gained through political struggle, and that therefore community work is an agent for social change. There is evidence to support both sides of the debate.

Today, in spite of government cuts in social spending, most community groups continue to be reliant on state funding for their operations and services. To suggest that funding is only a means of social control does little to illuminate, especially for progressive organizations, how to work in the interest of disadvantaged groups in a harsh economic climate. Meanwhile, funding requirements and procedures are constantly created and revised, which make the tasks of obtaining and maintaining state funding increasingly complicated, time-consuming, and difficult. In this paper, I want to examine concretely how state funding affected the work organization of one such group so as to better understand the limits and possibilities of working within the confines of state funding.

---

*An earlier version of this paper entitled, "State funding: implications for work with immigrant women," was presented at the 1986 Workers and Their Communities Conference in Ottawa. I am grateful to Jake Muller and Gillian Walker for comments on previous drafts.

The focus of my study is on a grassroots community employment center which provided job counselling and placement services for non-English speaking and black immigrant women in a large metropolitan city. The center began as an experimental project developed under the sponsorship of another community group working with immigrant women. The project was very successful. And since the project staff were able to demonstrate a need for specialized employment services, they decided to break away from the sponsoring group, to set up an independent organization to help immigrant women with employment related problems.

The opportunity to conduct first-hand observational work on the employment center came about as a result of my involvement, as a paid community worker, researcher, and volunteer, in what can loosely be called the "immigrant community."[3] At the end of 1980, I had just finished a study on immigrant housewives with a community group,[4] and was in the process of identifying a project for my dissertation research. I wanted to find out *how* immigrant women were consistently organized into the lowest strata of the occupational hierarchy.[5] Meanwhile, my colleagues working in the immigrant community suggested to me that I might wish to document the struggles of grassroots community groups in promoting and bettering the status of immigrant women in Canada. The employment center was recommended to me as one such group which had won a major battle in pressuring the state to provide funding for it to continue advocacy work with immigrant women. For me, the center was a strategic entry point for investigating the question I wanted answered, because it was situated at the critical interface between government policies and actions regarding immigrant women, and the reality of immigrant women in the labor force.[6]

When I began conducting field research on the center, it had just been incorporated as a non-profit voluntary organization, and was at the end of its first year of funding under the federal Employment and Immigration's Outreach Program. At this time, the employment center had four full-time staff: an Italian counsellor who also acted as the coordinator, three counsellors dealing with Spanish-speaking, Chinese-speaking, and black women respectively. As and when funding permitted, additional counsellors and receptionists were hired on a temporary basis to alleviate the workload. It had undergone considerable structural and other changes as a result of the incorporation and funding processes. Thus, I was in an excellent position to document the changes and developments of the center resulting from these processes.

In addition to observing how the staff did their daily work, I had access to all the documentary materials (including funding proposals, correspondence, financial records, employers' and clients' records) of the center. As I became familiar with the staff, I was invited to attend staff meetings. But I never attended board meetings. From time to time, I volunteered to act as a counsellor for Chinese and Vietnamese clients when staff shortages occurred. Thus, I gained an encompassing picture of most of the work processes involved in the center.[7]

The discussion presented here is based on observations, interviews with the staff, analysis of documents, as well as my own participation in compiling different kinds of records. In analyzing the center's work organization, I treated it as a component in a larger institutional context; i.e., I attempted to discover its relationship to the state and the labor market.[8] In this way, I discovered how it played a part in mediating and organizing relations between immigrant women and their employers on behalf of the state. What became clear is that although in appearance the employment center remained an independent community group, in actual fact its functions were part of the coordinated activities of the state. I will return to this point after examining the center's funding process.

* * *

A unique and important feature of the employment center was its advocacy work; that is, the counsellors continually attempted to negotiate for higher wages and monitor working conditions on behalf of their clients. Although this was not explicitly stated in the by-laws of the center, it was reflected in its first objective: "To place immigrant women in *meaningful* employment and to help them with employment related needs" (my emphasis). The placement and referral services were seen as corollary to the first objective:

> For the objectives aforesaid to carry on the activities of a job placement, referral and counselling service and other activities as the need arises.[9]

The center's advocacy capacity was crucial in improving the work situation of many immigrant women in the city. Most of these women worked in the non-unionized sectors of the paid labor force where the enforcement of labor standard legislation was the weakest.[10] Although the scope of the center's activities was limited due to its size, its monitoring role was important in serving as a check on unfair business practices in the city. Because of the center's intimate relationship with the state, through its funding structure and referral system, frequent violations of employment standards by employers could be communicated by employment counsellors to the relevant government departments. Thus, theoretically at least, the employment center could exert a certain degree of pressure on employers to guarantee reasonable wage levels and working conditions for its clients.

What I witnessed during the fieldwork period, however, was the shift of the center's work from advocacy on behalf of its clients—on behalf of labor—to provision of services to both employers and clients. Advocacy became progressively less important in contradistinction to the center's expanding capacity to service employers by placing its clients in available job openings. As well, the center experienced increasing conflicts and tensions among its members: between board and staff members; between staff who disagreed on policies for dealing with the center's clients; between staff critical of each other's counselling styles, etc.

One significant current ran through this period of the center's history: instead of receiving another year's grant from the federal Outreach Program with the appropriate annual increases, Outreach signed a series of three-month interim contracts with the center at the previous year's level (i.e., with no increase in salaries or operating expenses). This funding situation persisted throughout the period of my research there.

How are we to understand the rising tensions within the center and its concomitant decrease in advocacy work? Given the precarious character of the funding situation during this period, to what extent did it affect the operation of the center? How are we to understand the changing relation between the employment center and the state? Indeed, how is the role of "the state" to be understood in light of the employment center's experience? These are questions which this paper seeks to answer.

The Funding Process of the Employment Center

The Outreach Program was established as a short-term program within the federal Department of Employment and Immigration as a result of a cabinet decision in 1972. The stated objective of the Program, according to various documents of Outreach, was:

> To improve, with the help of community-based agencies, the employability and employment of individuals who experience special difficulties competing in the labor market and who are not able to benefit effectively from the services offered by their CEC (Canada Employment Centers). The essential purpose of Outreach is to complement, and effectively extend, regular services of the Commission to such groups.

Under this general objective, several target groups, including women, were chosen to be administered within the jurisdiction of the Outreach Program.

In applying for funding from the Outreach Program, then, the employment center entered into a legal agreement with the state to produce a "product" for the state. The legal agents responsible for ensuring the production of this product were the board of directors, who were the body that signed the legal agreement between the center and Outreach, and were therefore legally liable for the funds for this "product." In effect, the state sub-contracted a governmental function to a community agency by providing funding to the agency. In return, the community group had to conform to certain requirements stipulated by the funding program. The contract, signed between Outreach and the employment center, became legally enforceable, and effectively transformed and reorganized the work process of the center. This transformation took place at the point when the contract was drawn up.

When we examine the objective of the employment center, as stated in the 1980–81 funding proposal, and the contract drawn up between Outreach and the center, we see that the services provided to immigrant women now had to be measured in quantitative terms. The objective as stated in the original funding proposal was as follows:

> To serve immigrant women, and especially immigrant women of Chinese, Italian, West Indian and Spanish speaking origins, with their employment-related needs. This has been accomplished through individual counselling.

In the contract between Outreach and the employment center, the objective of the center was altered slightly to read:

> To improve, *in measurable terms*, the employment and employability of immigrant women who have experienced difficulty entering or re-entering the labor market. Special emphasis will be given to employment services for individuals and groups of women of Chinese, Italian, West Indian and Spanish speaking origins. (My emphasis)

Further to this agreement, three major conditions were required by the funding program of the employment center in order for it to obtain continual funds. These requirements are: (a) the proper management of the center; (b) the production of a "documentary reality"[11] of immigrant women as clients; and (c) the demonstration of "cooperation" between the center and the Department of Employment and Immigration. What will become visible in the following account is that these requirements penetrated the work organization of the center and altered its mode of operation in a gradual yet dramatic fashion. This change created a great deal of stress on the center which manifested itself in a variety of ways. It only became discernible, however, when the tension led to such serious cleavages among its members that they could no longer be contained within existing organizational arrangements. In other words, the new funding arrangement had rendered a previously egalitarian and more-or-less collective work organization inoperable and created a new form of organization within the center.

* * *

The major concern of the state, in making funds available to community groups, is that the funds are administered properly (i.e., in ways which accord with the project proposal and guidelines of the particular funding program) and that there is no mismanagement of funds by the project. To achieve efficiency and uniformity within the Department of Employment and Immigration, which includes the various funding programs within its jurisdiction, standardized bookkeeping procedures are developed and followed by all the funding programs.

Before I proceed to describe the record-keeping system required and developed by the employment center, I want to draw attention to the importance of documents in providing for organizational action in the state apparatus and other larger organizations. This is quite self-evident once we think about how state bureaucracies are organized: in records and files, legislation, press releases, orders-in-council, interdepartmental memoranda, and various kinds of information systems.[12] One of the notable features of the employment center was the huge volume of documentary materials it had to produce for the purpose of maintaining continual funds from Outreach. Indeed, the documentary process (re)organized the division of labor within the employment center, and served to articulate its functions to the coordinated activities of the state.

Specifically, in terms of the requirements of Outreach, while the overall budget for the center was approved on an annual basis, the administration of funds was subject to monthly review and negotiation. This presumably allowed the funding program to monitor the use of funds much more closely than giving the center a lump sum. In order to obtain its monthly operating expenses, a Monthly Financial Report (MFR) had to be filled out by the coordinator and submitted to Outreach through the local CEC office. When the MFR was approved by Outreach, a cheque for the following month's expenses was issued.

To generate the appropriate financial information for the MFR, an internal record-keeping system had to be developed which included forms to keep track of: working hours of staff, their benefits, overtime, as well as bookkeeping details such as the balance between the center's expense account and the bank account, and so on. (Diagram 1 summarizes the kinds of documents required by Outreach and the concomitant record-keeping system developed within the center to generate the information required.) All in all, the requirement of the MFR effectively generated a rather elaborate internal record-keeping and information retrieval system previously unknown to the center. The coordination of this information system and record-keeping procedures took time away from counselling and other work with immigrant women. The coordinator's time increasingly shifted from working with clients to administration and coordination.

In addition to the bookkeeping practices, another way for the funding program to monitor the performance of the center and the situation of immigrant women in the labor force was through the production of statistical and qualitative data. This was done through two sets of reports: the Quarterly Statistical Report (QSR) and the Semi-annual Narrative Report (SNR). Again, each of these reports necessitated additional record-keeping devices within the center. (See Diagram 1.) To calculate some of the information required in the QSR, for example, three additional sets of documentary processes were involved:

1) An application For Employment (AFE) form, to be filled out by each client who visited the center. This also constituted the employment counsellors' record on their clients; 2) a Clients' Record Book (CRB), which constituted the center's overall record on all its clients. The categories of information in the CRB corresponded to those requested by Outreach. The required information was entered into this book by each counsellor on a monthly basis. The coordinator then calculated the overall totals of client in-take by the appropriate categories provided by Outreach from the CRB; 3) each counsellor had to fill out a daily Service Sheet (SS), which recorded the types of services she performed, both to clients and to employers. Again, the totals of these services were tabulated by the coordinator on a weekly and monthly basis for the QSR (Quarterly Statistical Report) requested by Outreach.

The point to note here is that the requirements for statistical and other information by the funding program were not just external to the center, to be compiled on a quarterly or semi-annual basis. They necessitated the development of an internal record-keeping system, the maintenance of which became part of the daily routine of the center. This is how the funding process penetrated the internal work organization of the employment center.

Diagram 1

The Record-Keeping System of the Employment Agency*

Internal record-keeping devices		Documents submitted to the funding program
Revenue Canada Taxation TD1 form		
Manual for CPP deductions	Payroll Record (PR)	Monthly
Manual for UIC deductions	Bank Reconciliation (BR)	Financial
Attendancy Sheet (AS)	Receipts and Disbursement Record	Report (MFR)
Application for Employment (AEF)	Clients' Record Book (CRB)	Quarterly Statistical
daily Service Sheet (SS)	weekly and monthly Summary of Services	Report (QSR)
		Semi-annual Narrative Report (SNR)

* Note how the requirements of the funding program generated an elaborate record-keeping system internal to the employment agency.

The third condition placed on the center was that it had to demonstrate "cooperation" with the programs and staff of the Department of Employment and Immigration. Cooperation could be established by mutual referral of clients between the center and the CEC offices. It would also include referral of the center's clients to job training and ESL (English as a Second Language) programs offered through the Department. This kind of cooperation was monitored documentarily in the QSR. In actual fact, since many of the clients of the center were sponsored[13] or illegal immigrants, and/or did not have the required language or educational qualifications, the majority of them would be ineligible for these programs.

There were other ways, however, to demonstrate cooperation. One way was to establish an amiable working relationship with Employment and Immigration officials, notably the CEC project officer and Outreach consultant. (Diagram 2 outlines the structure of accountability affecting the employment center.) This generally included compliance with demands made by Department officials in addition to the MFR (Monthly Financial Report), such as extra statistical and other information on clients or the operation of the center. For example, it would not be uncommon for the Outreach consultant, the official from Outreach responsible for overseeing the employment center, to phone the coordinator and ask her to compile a report on the breakdown of the types of businesses which made use of the center's services for a certain period (e.g., in the last three months). Receipt of the following month's cheque would be contingent upon the completion of this report. Although this kind of information was available, its compilation was cumbersome and took time away from counselling. It disrupted the regular routine of the center, and occasionally led to resentment of the coordinator by other counsellors because she was the one to elicit the information from them.

Finally, as part of the funding agreement between Outreach and the center, Employment and Immigration officials could and did pay regular visits to the center to ensure its smooth running. They could ask to see the internal records of the center, and their visits, though not frequent, put a certain amount of pressure on the staff.

Because of the structure of accountability within the Employment and Immigration bureaucracy, delay in the administration of monthly and yearly funds was built into the whole process. (The right-hand column of Diagram 2 outlines the approximate time line for different tasks to be completed.) When the monthly cheque was delayed, for instance, it was up to the ingenuity of the coordinator to figure out how to pay the rent and other bills, and it could throw the daily routine of the center into temporary turmoil. When there was a delay in the approval and allocation of the annual grant, such as when the 1981–82 budget was renewed on the three-month basis, the center could plunge into a deep financial crisis.

The above account does not describe all the documentary processes involved in the employment center's operation. However, it does give a sense of what was involved for a community group to maintain its funding from the state. The development and maintenance of records for funding purposes became a specialized task in and of itself.

Effects of the Funding Process
This kind of funding arrangement with the state had serious repercussions on the internal organization and relations of the employment center, and on its effectiveness in carrying out advocacy activities. Two notable effects of the funding process, which I will discuss in this section, are changes in the center's mode of operation and problems in staffing.

Diagram 2

Structure of Accountability

Location of Individual	Rank and Position of Individual	Tasks and Respon- sibilities of Individual	Appropriate Time Frame**
Employment and Immigration Regional Office*	OUTREACH ⟵ PERFORMANCE	–oversees center's overall performance –checks and approves reports from center –assesses and approves fund- ing proposal(s) of center –issues cheques to center for monthly expenditures	4th week of month
Local CEC Office*	CEC MANAGER	–checks reports from center –approves reports –forwards reports to Regional Office	3rd week of month
Local CEC Office	CEC PROJECT OFFICER	–receives reports from coordinator –checks reports and super- vises bookkeeping of center –oversees center's operation –ensures cooperation be- tween agency and other CEC programs	2nd week of month
Employment Center	COORDINATOR	–gets various records from staff –compiles various reports –submits reports to CEC Project Officer –coordinates center's operation	1st week of month
Employment Center	EMPLOYMENT COUNSELLORS	–record Attendancy Sheet and Service Sheet –make summary of clients' records in Clients' Record Book	

* Extra information on aspects of the center's operation can be requested at any time by any of these levels.

** This is the time frame for the compilation of the Monthly Financial Report (MFR) and the issuance of the following month's expenditure cheque by Outreach

↑ = reports to

The major change was an emerging hierarchy within the employment center. This occurred before the center officially received funding from Outreach, when it was incorporated in anticipation of receiving funding from Employment and Immigration.[14] In the incorporation process, a board of directors was established. Whereas these people were volunteers working in an advisory capacity to the center prior to incorporation, they were now the legal body within the center responsible for its financial well-being. In relation to the Outreach Program, they became the internal representatives of the state in ensuring the proper administration of the center. This changed status created tension between board and staff members, especially during periods of intense negotiation for funding renewal between Outreach and the employment center. The staff were resentful of being excluded from this process, and of the fact that extra demands were put on them to produce additional information for funding purposes. Relations at the center deteriorated to such an extent that many board and staff members eventually resigned.

In terms of the routine organization of the employment center, a fundamental change which took place gradually as it came under Outreach funding was an internal differentiation of a previously more-or-less homogeneous work process. Prior to Outreach funding, the four counsellors shared similar tasks and responsibilities, and they all had a fairly sound knowledge of the overall operation of the center. Their work consisted mainly of employment counselling and placement of the clients, which included some time-consuming advocacy activities, and making contacts with employers to solicit "job orders" for placement purposes. Although one counsellor was given the title of "coordinator" due to funding and other requirements, the administrative component was a small part of the total work process, which was shared among the staff during the early periods.

As a result of the expanding activities of the center and its transition from an experimental project to a more tightly controlled funding program, the work process of the center underwent an internal fragmentation. With the drastic increase of paper work (i.e., a more complicated bookkeeping system, compilation of statistical and other information) and demands for cooperation with Employment and Immigration staff, it became more and more difficult for the center to maintain an equal division of labor. The coordinator found herself absorbing more and more of the administrative tasks to the exclusion of counselling and other work with clients. In addition, she also took on a supervisory role vis-à-vis the other counsellors. She had to ensure that the rest of the staff would fill out their Service Sheets (ss) and other forms punctually and correctly so that she could get the administrative part of the work completed on time for the Monthly Financial Report (MFR). An implicit hierarchical division of labor developed.

The change from a "collective" to a "hierarchical" division of labor should not be treated merely as a matter of principle; it was a practical arrangement appropriate to this kind of grassroots community organization. Unlike large organizations where internal policies were recorded in documentary form, a collective manner of work was an integral part of policy development within the center. This was generally done in weekly staff meetings and informal discussions among the counsellors, where they went over particularly difficult cases and devised solutions on a collective basis. One example would be to set a minimum acceptable wage level for a particular category of work within the center, such as private domestic service. This was an area of work where potential employers contacted the center with a wide range of hourly wages and work requirements. The staff meeting would be a place where the various issues, such as hourly wages and acceptable working conditions, could be discussed and debated to arrive at a set of guidelines for the counsellors to screen potential employers for the center's clients. It would also be a place where counsellors brought up difficult cases, such as whether and how to guide a client through a nasty fight with an employer (e.g., when a client was dismissed unjustly by an employer). Again, out of the discussions in staff meetings, the counsellors arrived at a policy in dealing with certain types of cases. As well, they provided each other with much needed emotional and practical support for these trying situations. Although the coordinator tried to maintain a collective working style with the changing structure of responsibilities, at times she had to put pressure on the other counsellors to submit their records on time, and it created a rift between her and the rest of the staff.

More significantly, with the unstable funding situation and frequent delays in monthly cheques from Outreach, the staff meetings were increasingly taken up with discussions of financial problems to the exclusion of discussion of the actual services and activities of the center. The counsellors were caught up in their own predicaments. Since advocacy work took time, energy and support from other staff members, it became more and more difficult for individual counsellors to take it up as a routine part of the counselling process. While the informal way of policy formation had previously enabled the employment center to be responsive to its constituency without being bounded by complicated guidelines and stipulations characteristic of large bureaucratic organizations, this method of resolving problems broke down completely during a funding crisis. The consequence of this is that counselling practices became individualized and *ad hoc*. Individual "styles" of working, rather than overall center policies, came to dominate the counselling and placement process. The center's activities became the general provision of services to employers and clients, rather than advocacy work for clients.

The precarious funding situation also led to much staff turnover. While this was a somewhat common feature of the employment center's history, the situation was particularly acute during periods of funding instability. During my research at the center, for example, the position for the Chinese counsellor was opened three times, as people moved onto other jobs with higher salaries and more permanent funding arrangements. As a result of the funding situation, the recruitment of staff also presented itself as a difficulty. When hiring was carried out, members of the center—board and staff—attempted to identify and hire someone with the kinds of qualifications needed by the center and who shared the center's commitment to advocacy work. However, recruitment was usually done under fairly rigid time constraints. If the center spent too long on the hiring process, the unspent salary might have to revert back to Outreach, or the center might face the possibility of losing the position altogether. Under these circumstances, "cultural" criteria (i.e., ethnic background and language proficiency) became the dominant criteria for selecting an incumbent, rather than the incumbent's commitment to grassroots advocacy work and political orientation. Constraints around the hiring process and the relatively low salary precluded careful discrimination of the available candidates, and occasionally the center might end up with a counsellor whose viewpoint was incompatible with the objectives of the center. The counselling and placement work, for this counsellor, became merely a job to be executed, rather than a means of fighting for the rights of immigrant women in the work place.

Although it is true that those counsellors who did not share the goals of the center would move quickly on to other prospects, and the positions would once again be open to other applicants, every time a staff member left, the work of the center was thrown into temporary disarray. The extra work load had to be absorbed by the remaining counsellors, who were already under a great deal of pressure with their existing responsibilities. Clients might have to be turned away when the work load became intolerable, which in turn would affect the overall placement rate of the center, a crucial consideration in maintaining Outreach funding. Thus, every small problem, for a group this size, could potentially become a crisis if not handled properly. But the proper handling of these kinds of situations required planning and a great deal of thought, which in turn took an enormous amount of time and energy and disrupted the normal routine of the center. The funding process, therefore, not only reorganized the work process of the center, in many ways, it dis-organized the work process and seriously undermined its advocacy capacity.

Larger Implications

The story of the employment center illuminates some of the contradictions of engaging in struggles on behalf of disadvantaged groups. Members of the center fought hard to gain funding for provision of special services to immigrant women. But once the center succeeded, it also entered into a contractual and collaborative relationship with the state to provide services in ways which did not necessarily reflect its original intent. Funding demands further led to a reorganization of the internal relations and work processes of the center which undermined its capacity to engage in advocacy work for immigrant women.

I want to conclude this paper by discussing some implications of the employment center's experiences for understanding "the state" and how to work practically as an activist and analyst. Throughout this paper, I have used the term, "the state," in a standard usage as if it was unproblematic. In this common usage, the state is seen to be a machinery or a set of apparatuses[15] which, although not monolithic, nevertheless performs different functions for the dominant classes on behalf of capital; funding is a means for oppressing and corrupting community groups. The implicit assumption is that the state is somehow over and above us. In the case of the employment center, we saw how the funding requirements of the state penetrated its internal organization so that some of its members became part of the administrative processes of the state. *They* were the ones who carried out the activities of ruling.

From this experience (and from other stories in this collection), it is clear that the notion of the state as a set of apparatuses, standing above and apart from us, is inadequate in understanding how the state works. Following more recent re-examinations of the state, I think it is much more appropriate to conceptualize the state as a set of social relations which (a) legitimizes certain courses of action, thereby rendering other (alternate) forms of action illegitimate; and (b) organizes how people relate to one another. What is important to grasp is that these social relations are relations of power.

The emergence of a hierarchical division of labor into board and staff (further divided into coordinator and counsellors) indicates how relations within the employment center were transformed as a result of the incorporation and funding procedures. Furthermore, the center's ability to work with immigrant women came to depend upon the performance of services and production of documents in certain ways for Employment and Immigration. Some work, such as advocacy, was no longer seen to fall within the mandate of the center by virtue of the way in which the contract between Outreach and the center was drawn up. What can be seen is that through its funding arrangement, members of the employment center entered into certain relations with one another and their clients. Thus, it is more useful to think of community struggles as being "in and against the state," rather than completely outside it.[16]

Central to holding the mandated courses of action of the state in place are documents. From the above account, we saw how important documents were in managing the financial affairs and work processes of the employment center. Indeed, it can be argued that the center's activities became the coordinated functions of the state in and through this documentary mode of action: in its By-Laws, by a legally-binding contract, through the generation of various records organized around the budgetary process. These kinds of documentary procedures were not taken seriously by members of the center. In the words of the coordinator, they just wanted to get them "over with" so that they could get on with the "real" work (i.e., working with immigrant women). It was only in negotiation with Outreach for a new contract and when Outreach began to require more and more written information to make funding decisions that some members realized the importance of documents in displaying the center's work and providing for a measurement of its accountability and effectiveness. (Other members, those involved in direct services, remained resistant to and resentful of the imposition of this documentary organization. Some even suggested manufacturing the statistics to which the board was violently opposed. This became another area of contention within the employment center.)

In the light of this analysis, I believe that recognizing the crucial role of documents in affecting organizational actions is a step forward for state-funded community groups. Similar to other negotiations, documentary requirements can also be negotiated, although this can best be done at the outset of funding negotiations. Given the legal enforceability of the contract between the group and the funding program, an activity like advocacy can, and perhaps must, be included in the contractual agreement to preserve its centrality in the service delivery mandate of the group. Furthermore, an in-depth grasp of the financial and budgetary processes is essential for groups to discover how to work creatively while relying on state funding. In the Vancouver Women's Health Collective (now defunct), for example, the "paper work" was shared by all collective members; firstly, this took pressure off any one individual to specialize in this work to the exclusion of doing other work, and secondly, all members gained a working knowledge of this aspect of the Collective's work organization.[17]

I want to state emphatically that it is impossible to have a formulaic approach to state funding. Funding programs and their requirements vary considerably. Even within programs, administrative procedures may differ from region to region, sometimes even from one office to another. Some Secretary of State programs, for instance, have less stringent requirements for record-keeping, but lobbying and good personal relations with funding officers (e.g., constant verbal reports and visits) may be crucial to the funding process. In other words, the question of how to develop a viable economic survival strategy (while remaining faithful to one's intent and objective) can only be worked out practically in relation to the specific situation of a particular group. It cannot be drawn up as a set of generalized principles and procedures because funding programs are targeted for different purposes and therefore have different requirements.

Finally, I want to end by reflecting on my role as an analyst in relation to the groups with whom I work. It is clear that the analyst is not in a position to "tell" a group what to do, or to develop a recipe for community struggle. This can only be done by the groups engaged in particular struggles themselves. As an outsider pursuing my study on the employment center, however, I was in a better position to separate the structural problems (resulting from funding and other constraints) from the personal relations which became increasingly entwined as the story of the employment center unfolded. As I see it, the analyst's responsibility is to make visible the structural constraints within which groups have to operate. In identifying existing sources of contradictions, the analyst can assist groups to develop ongoing analysis of new areas of struggles and change. In the above account, we saw that services provided by the state are not just means of social control; they also represent the battles fought and won by working people. At the same time, we saw how members of the center participated in courses of action which led to their own oppression and to changes in the original intent of the center. Ultimately, analyses of these contradictory processes can enable us to discover how the state works to constrain and limit the actions of working people. More importantly, they can help us assess the strengths and weaknesses of various community actions and movements, so that we may work more effectively to transform the conditions of our lives.

NOTES

1. I do not mean to suggest that state funding to community organizations only began in the 1960s. Roberts' work (in this collection) on the Montreal immigration agencies at the turn of the century certainly indicates that funding to voluntary groups occurred in earlier periods of the Canadian state formation. However, the current wave of state funding on a large scale, relatively speaking, is a result of the rediscovery of poverty in spite of the post-war boom, which took place in Canada as well as in other western industrialized nations such as Britain and the U.S. See John Edwards and Richard Batley, *The Politics of Positive Discrimination*. London: Tavistock Publications, 1978.

2. See, for example, Martin Loney, "A Political Economy of Citizen Participation," in Leo Panitch (ed.), *The Canadian State: Political Economy and Political Power*. Toronto: University of Toronto Press, 1977.

3. Elsewhere, I have argued that the so-called "ethnic" or "immigrant" community is the product of administrative and political processes. It makes sense to speak of an ethnic community only from a ruling perspective; it has little reality and relevance in people's daily experiences. See Roxana Ng, "The Social Relations of Citizens Participation in the Chinese Community," paper presented at the Canadian Sociology and Anthropology Association (CSAA) annual meeting, May 1978; and "Constituting Ethnic Phenomenon: An Account from the Perspective of Immigrant Women," *Canadian Ethnic Studies* 8(1), 1981, pp. 97–108. In this paper, I rely on this understanding of the term, but do not explain in detail how the "immigrant community" is socially constructed.

4. Roxana Ng and Judith Ramirez, *Immigrant Housewives in Canada*. Toronto: Immigrant Women's Center, 1981.

5. One important area of inquiry concerning immigrant women which came to my attention was the fact that they were consistently found in the lowest strata of the occupational hierarchy, working in jobs in private domestic services, sweat shop operations, and assembly lines. See Sheila Arnopoulos, *Problems of Immigrant Women in the Canadian Labour Force*. Ottawa: Advisory Council on the Status of Women, 1979; Roxana Ng and Tania Das Gupta, "Nation Builders? The Captive Labour Force of Non-English Speaking Immigrant Women," *Canadian Women's Studies* 31(1), 1981, pp. 83–89. While the "problem" of immigrant women in the labor force has been a topic of much discussion in recent years, how they come to be organized into the structural locations in the labor market which they occupy has not been a subject of systematic investigation. This question formed the basis for my Ph.D. dissertation research.

6. Roxana Ng, "Immigrant Women and the State: A Study in the Social Organization of Knowledge." Ph.D. Thesis, Department of Education, University of Toronto, 1984. The financial assistance of the Social Sciences and Humanities Council of Canada and the Ivey Foundation of the University of Toronto for this research is gratefully acknowledged.

7. I should mention that not all staff members had a total picture of the center's operation. The counsellors, for example, took little responsibility for the paper work, and were unclear as to what was involved. Board members had little knowledge of the daily routine of the center. Whatever knowledge they had was mediated and communicated by the coordinator. As will be seen, the lack of understanding of the overall work organization by members led to much tension. I would argue that much of members' inability to gain a fuller picture of the center's complete operation was the result of a heavy workload for all concerned, which was directly related to underfunding. However, as members were caught up in the immediacy of their respective tasks in their particular work locations at the center, it was difficult for them to make the connection between their experiences and larger structural processes.

8. This method of analysis has been called "institutional ethnography" by Smith. See Dorothy E. Smith, "Institutional Ethnography: A Feminist Method," *Resources for Feminist Research* 15(1), March 1986, pp. 6–12. For a detailed discussion of my analysis, see my doctoral thesis, *op. cit.*, pp. 36–52.

9. Article II of the By-Laws of the employment center.

10. See Sheila Arnopoulos, *op. cit.*

11. The term, "documentary reality," comes from Dorothy E. Smith, "The Social Construction of Documentary Reality," *Sociological Inquiry* 44(4), 1974, pp. 257–268. She points out that "facts" presented and mediated by documents (e.g., in news accounts) do not reference what actually happened. They must be seen to arise out of the social organization of the production of documents. For example, while drawing on real events in the world as a resource, news accounts actually reference the organization of news production, and not simply the events as they took place. See Nancy Jackson, "Describing News, Toward an Alternative Account." M.A. Thesis, Anthropology and Sociology, University of British Columbia, 1977.

    In terms of my study, statistical information on immigrant women required by Outreach certainly doesn't tell us very much about their lived experiences. Nevertheless, this documentary information was treated by the state as if it referred to the labor market reality of immigrant women.

12. For a discussion of the centrality of documentary processes in the work of organizations, see Smith, 1974, *op. cit.*; Dorothy E. Smith, "Textually Mediated Social Organization," *International Social Science Journal* 36(1), 1984, pp. 59–75; Nancy Jackson, "Class Relations and Bureaucratic Practices," paper presented at the CSAA annual meeting, Montreal, 1980.

13. The Immigration Act divides landed immigrants into three categories: independent, nominated, and sponsored or family class immigrants. (This classification does not include refugees, who belong to a separate category and have different statuses from landed immigrants.) Sponsored immigrants are considered dependents, who enter the country under the sponsorship of ei-

ther an independent immigrant, or someone who already resides in Canada (e.g., a husband or close relative). Since they are not expected to join the labor force, they are excluded from many state subsidized programs, such as job and language training, which are available to independent immigrants. In actual fact, many sponsored immigrants, mostly women, do enter the labor market because of the financial circumstances of immigrant families. This partially accounts for the needs for special services for immigrant women.

14. Officially, incorporation of a community group is not required by Outreach. According to Outreach guidelines, "any local, non-profit organization, association or group, whether formally recognized or not, may sponsor an Outreach project (individuals may be considered as sponsors in certain circumstances)." Unofficially, however, incorporated bodies were favored by both the government and private funding bodies because of the formal structure of accountability built into a corporation. Anyway, this was the structure adopted by the employment center in its attempt to secure funding.

15. Some examples of this view on the state include: Ralph Miliband, *The State in Capitalist Society*. London: Quartet Books, 1969; Nicos Poulantzas, *State, Power, Socialism*. London: Verso, 1980; Leo Panitch (ed.), *The Canadian State: Political Economy and Political Power, op. cit.*

16. This phrase was first used by the London-Edinburgh Weekend Return Group, *In and Against the State*. London: Pluto Press, 1980. Recent re-examinations of the state have added important insights in re-conceptualizing the relation between the state and grassroots movements. See, for example, Patricia Morgan, "From Battered Wife to Program Client: The State's Shaping of Social Problems," *Kapitalistate* (9), 1981, pp. 17–39. It seems much more appropriate to view the state as the embodiment of struggles between classes. See Nicos Poulantzas, *Political Power and Social Classes*. London: Verso, 1978; Cynthia Cockburn, *The Local State*. London: Pluto Press, 1977; Sue Finlay, "Struggle within the State: The Feminist Challenge to Hegemony," unpublished manuscript, Department of Political Science, Carleton University, 1982.

17. Nancy Kleiber and Linda Light, *Caring for Ourselves: An Alternative Structure for Health Care*, Health and Welfare Canada, April, 1978.

The State Funded Women's Movement:
A Case of Two Political Agendas

Alicia Schreader

Introduction: Background and Theoretical Discussion

Throughout the past eighteen years, women's demands for justice and equality have forced a reaction from the political state of most Western industrialized societies. In Canada, the reaction of the state was swift, and thoroughly consistent with liberal democratic methods of intervention and social reform. Thus, in 1967, a Royal Commissioned inquiry into the status of women was established, followed by the creation within government of no less than five representative bodies for women's affairs. Over the years, numerous special advisors have produced many documents, publications and policies, all intended to redress the newly-recognized condition of female inequality. Most significantly, the state instituted a vast program of funding feminist political activity, and services such as rape crises centers and shelters for battered women.

When we examine the historical development of the women's movement, what emerges is a pattern of consistent cooperation between the state and the movement to address women's inequality. The relationship established is, in its concrete form, a *funding relation*, which is distinct and amenable to analysis.

Not all feminist groups, however, have passively submitted to state interventions in their political affairs. In February 1983, the Saskatchewan Action Committee, Status of Women (SACSW) voted unanimously to terminate 1983–84 negotiations with the Secretary of State's Women's Program. Their dramatic action was motivated by a growing sense of alarm over government demands for greater accountability from funded groups. Particularly unnerving to SACSW was the Program's insistence upon reserving the right to approve the political strategies of funded groups.[1]

In a subsequent communique to the feminist community, SACSW raised two critical issues. First of all, they asserted the need for feminists to remain autonomous from state-defined agendas, since our primary responsibility is to women, not government. Second, they voiced the growing concerns of many feminists by asking: what has been the effect of a decade of state funding on the women's movement?

My interest in the consequences of state intervention developed while I was a graduate student in Social Work at Carleton University. I was particularly intrigued by the question of ideology, which, for many, had come to signify either a mechanistic reflection of the economic base of society, or, deliberate manipulation of reality by the ruling class. Neither explanation offered any satisfaction. To investigate this problem I undertook a study on the Secretary of State Women's Program. Analyzing the workings of this Program provided me with a basis for developing a richer, detailed understanding of how state intervention promotes the ideological takeover of small organizations.

Over the years I have engaged in many debates with other feminists as to why the state funds a movement committed to radical social change. Moreover, at the time when I was conducting this study, I was struck by the inability or unwillingness of feminists to think in anything but conspiratorial terms. This reliance upon conspiracy theories had resulted in a perception of the state as monolithic, unified and threatening. But what was more significant was that feminists had thus far neglected to systematically analyze the *process* of state intervention into popular movements. Thus, while the effects of intervention, such as deflection of progressive goals, defusing of issues and co-optation, were increasingly noted, little was understood about how state functioning had promoted these undesirable outcomes. Equally misunderstood was how contradictions in the movement itself had provided significant opportunities for political co-optation to occur.

Piecing the process of co-optation together requires some knowledge of the structures and processes of the state. Such knowledge is essential if progressive movements are not to be rendered powerless in the face of state attempts to control and define popular struggle.

Conceptualizing the State

Before proceeding to an examination of the Women's Program, a brief review of theories of the state will provide the basis for further analysis. The predominant liberal view holds that the state is equivalent to the government. The state is perceived to be above the conflicts of society, acting as a neutral regulator of public life. Particular Marxist views perceive the state as more complicated than this. First of all, it is conceived as a class state, which serves the interests of capitalism and maintains each succeeding generation of workers in subordinate relationship to the interests of capital. Marxists consider the state to comprise not only government, but also the many agencies and institutions involved in governing and in the reproduction of dominant class relations.

Italian Marxist Antonio Gramsci understood the practice of ruling to involve the active, social construction of reality, which he termed ideological hegemony. Gramsci further contended that the maintenance of state power depended upon the state's capacity to repeatedly organize social consensus. Ideological hegemony was considered by Gramsci to be an *organizing principle* for a combination of dominant world views which "is diffused by agencies of ideological control and socialization into every area of social life."[2]

However, the state's attempt to organize social consensus on any given issue is not a process to which all people passively submit. Many will organize to struggle against the state, and their struggles can potentially transform some features of the state and how it operates. Class struggles and women's struggles have historically shaped and been shaped by the state. Thus, the state does not simply, *do things to* the women's movement but rather, in the course of interaction both sides have been molded and transformed.[3]

Understanding the state in this way is analytically useful. It provides us with a way of thinking about the state and hegemony not as static "things," but as active processes. To take it a step further, when we consider hegemony, we are considering the many forms and processes which embody the state, and which act continuously and in concert to impede non-capitalist forms from below. We can expand our analysis further, by recognizing that state ideology is also a process, or more specifically, that it comprises a set of practices as well as a set of ideas. State ideological practices produce particular kinds of problem definitions, needs and methods for dealing with them. These practices are observed to bring into existence certain types of activities and social relations to the exclusion of others.

Furthermore, within the state there prevails a bureaucratic discourse, which manifests a particular structure of social relations, and establishes a practice of ruling *within* the boundaries of the discourse. This practice serves to pattern state personnel and organize their activities, in addition to forcing outsiders to relate in the terms established by the discourse. Bureaucratic discourse and state ideological practices thus provide limited and institutionalized channels which appear to limit the range of possible politics. In general, as Göran Therborn points out, radical protest has been forced to use these channels and in so doing, contributes to their reproduction.[4]

The Women's Program

These processes will now be examined more concretely in terms of the Secretary of State Women's Program. The Women's Program provides an interesting study because significant contradictions developed when feminists were hired to run it. Data for my study were gathered through an extensive analysis of Program documents, funding guidelines, and policy papers. Much additional insight into the operation of the Program was gained through extensive interviews with Program staff. An insightful analysis provided by Sue Findlay, former Director of the Women's Program, contributed much to an understanding of the structure of the Program.[5]

Established in 1972, the Program is situated in the Citizenship Branch of the Secretary of State, whose mandate is "provision of support to voluntary organizations to promote more effective citizenship as well as the development of special citizenship programs for disadvantaged groups."[6] The Women's Program provides two types of funding. Project grant funds are given to women's organizations for the purpose of enabling women to develop skills, coordination, knowledge of women's issues and decision-making abilities. Operational grants are available primarily for national and provincial women's organizations to enable them to provide coordination for action or human and technical resources on status of women issues. In the late 1970s the Program also began to encourage action by major institutions to promote equal representation of women in their decision-making structures.

Since the Program's inception, its principal goal—to increase women's participation in the decisions affecting their lives—has remained constant. However, although the Program has not changed conceptually, there have been dramatic changes in funding patterns. In the early 1970s, much funding was provided to small, locally-based radical feminist groups, whereas by the late 1970s it was predominantly national and traditional women's groups who were being funded. This transformation can be partially attributed to changes in the operation of the Program, but is also partly the result of how the women's movement has developed. That is, increases in the Program's budget required a partial shift towards funding larger projects and organizations, and the radical groups funded initially were not organizationally prepared to undertake projects at the national level.

Three components of the Women's Program will be examined here. First of all, the limitations inherent in the state's hierarchical structure will be discussed, with an emphasis on how this affected both the development and operation of the Program. Second, an analysis of the character of bureaucratic discourse is provided, specifically those mechanisms employed which transformed the advocacy role of staff into one of mediation. Third, the Program's predominant notion of citizen participation is examined, since this comprises the ideological framework into which women's demands are being contextualized. The argument made here is that as an operational concept, citizenship performs objective "work," determining processes and activities both in the Program and among funded groups.

State Structure: The Limitations of Hierarchy

The task of locating and specifying the nature of a particular state apparatus requires that one know its relationship to other state apparatuses, and recognize its relative power within the intrastate hierarchy. The Women's Program ranks among the lowest and least powerful in the hierarchy.

The low status of the Women's Program is a reflection of the general subordinate position of women in society. This becomes evident if we examine the way social interests are represented within the state. The state must forge a workable, if contradictory, unity among competing social interests, since it must represent not only a plurality of capitalist interests, but also those of subordinate social groups. Ultimately, the manner in which contending interests get represented in the state is a product of much negotiation and compromise.

The significant feature of state representation, as Rianne Mahon points out, is that it is structural and hierarchical.[7] Since it is hierarchical, not all interests are represented *equally*. Furthermore, the claims of "interest groups" do not possess authority in their own right, since authority is vested in the state department which is developed to represent them. The structure and forms of the state can thus be viewed as a concretization of social struggle, where the very existence of the Women's Program represents a *compromise* made to the vocal demands of women for social recognition and equality. Development of this and other programs for women represent what Nicos Poulantzas has referred to as an "unstable equilibrium of compromise."[8] Programs for marginalized groups are similarly marginalized in the intrastate negotiation process. The position and authority of the Women's Program resulted in limited scope for Program staff to represent the interests of women within this process. This is apparent from the limited mandate of the Program, which includes the provision of material support and leadership to women's groups, but has absolutely no social impact on the economic and social forces which maintain women's inequality. Those women hired to staff the Program soon became aware that they were expected to contextualize women's interests to make them consistent with the "larger interests" of government.[9]

The larger interests of government are generally defined by authoritative state branches such as the Department of Finance. This department constitutes the seat of power of the hegemonic faction of the ruling class, and through its domination of the budgetary process, Finance gives coherence and form to the larger, that is, economic, interests of the state. In the past ten years the latest version of the "national interest" to be determined by the Department of Finance comes in the form of "fiscal restraint" and cutbacks in government spending. Of course, the concept of cutbacks translates into a rather selective practice that does not interfere with government spending to promote the interests of capital.

Fiscal restraint has, however, resulted in significant changes in the operation of the Women's Program, and its internal processes of accountability have undergone radical transformation. As one former staff member commented, "One could practically give the money out oneself in 1972 (but) by 1980 there were a series of layers through which approval had to go, a very formalized procedure in terms of what kind of information had to be presented, financial (information), etc."[10]

Fiscal restraint is an ideological process which forms the basis for stringent budgetary practices and evaluations of "cost-effectiveness," where these practices are assumed to be beneficial in and of themselves. Restraint can be understood as part of an intrastate thrust towards cost-effectiveness developed under the mantle of scientific management and rationalization of centralized budgetary control which has coincided with the introduction of "program-performance-budgeting-system" into the state apparatus.[11]

Within the Women's Program cutbacks have resulted in rigid internal accounting and administrative procedures, while simultaneously creating significantly greater control over funded groups. Strict budgeting has also limited the resources available for travel by Program staff and thereby inhibited contact with funded groups. State control over the activities of funded groups was increased when the nature of funding was changed from provision of grants to that of "contributions." In accepting a contribution a group enters into a contractual agreement to undertake specific activities acceptable to the Program, whereas acceptance of a grant carries no such obligations.[12]

Project spokeswomen have pointed out the deleterious consequences of fiscal restraint measures for their organizations. The most obvious effect has been increased competition among women's groups for scarce funds: "This competition has placed the government in the position of developing an increasingly tight means of sifting and sorting those groups worthy of limited Women's Program funds."[13] Government demands for increasingly complex methods of bookkeeping and reporting, with flowcharts, priority charts and excessive credibility criteria, far exceed the capability of most volunteer, community-based groups. Further, the government requirement that groups undertake quantitative evaluations of their performance places an emphasis on statistics as a measure of success or failure. Consequently, quality of work and the value women place on their own growth and development are not perceived to be relevant measures of success.[14]

The funding levels of low ranking programs such as the Women's Program are unilaterally determined by the authoritative state branch through its control of the budgetary process. Women's groups are then forced to compete for whatever resources have been deemed adequate to meet women's interests. The authoritative branch, Finance, is empowered to limit concessions to subordinate social forces and, as we have seen, exercises this power through its ideological practices based on fiscal restraint.

Bureaucratic Discourse: From Advocacy to Mediation

It should be recalled that the structure of representation within the state does not permit direct representation of would-be advocates. Instead, because the bureaucracy carefully controls the work of state personnel, representation is carried out by structures rather than by individuals. Furthermore, independent initiatives and behavior of would-be advocates are rigidly controlled by the prevailing administrative discourse, which expresses and reflects "a particular structure of relationships, a set of discursive relations that produces the rules, defines the objects and constitutes the events of study."[15] Discernible methods are actively employed within the bureaucracy that serve to transform advocates into non-threatening administrators. These methods, which will now be explored, were clearly operating in the Women's Program and served to bring Program activities more closely into line with the goals of management.

In the prevailing atmosphere of cooperation between women and government that followed the Royal Commission on the Status of Women, a number of organizations, advisors, councils, task forces, etc. were established, all of which were designed to represent women's interests within policy making and the program development processes of government. But while these actions demonstrated the government's political commitment to women, it is important to note that such a commitment does not automatically translate into policy proposals. In fact, an assessment of the past decade reveals little by way of concrete policies for women.[16] Inside government, action on specific issues and policies has apparently been difficult to initiate, despite the fact that government recruited active feminists as staff for various women's programs.

Recruitment of staff from the women's movement created major contradictions for the government, but in 1972 this was an unavoidable dilemma. At that time there was only one woman in the senior executive category and fewer than 20 in the category below, this being the range from which to select a program director and staff. Among women in the public service who might have been eligible in terms of "management" experience, all were deficient in their knowledge of women's issues. Women's programs in the various branches of the state required staff who could be credible with the women's movement, but who were also familiar with the public service and committed to its perspective.[17]

Women hired to staff the Women's Program quickly discovered that their required role was not that of advocate but of mediator. The mediation role was accomplished through the demand to contextualize, justify and rationalize the Program into the then-current ideological forms: "the just society," "national unity," and so on.[18] This idea of "national unity" was a key one in government at that time and deserves some elaboration. The concept of "national unity" has operated within the liberal ideology of pluralism, permitting the state to be seen as responsive to organized, vocal "interest" groups. It permits the most diluted version of protest to be represented, since many interests must be accounted for.

From the foregoing discussion, it is clear that any advocacy aspirations of staff were, over time, subordinated, and conformity was enforced through the organization of work, which was strictly controlled by management. Throughout this process managerial authority was vigorously reasserted and the involvement of staff with the women's movement became increasingly circumscribed. One former director, a well-known feminist, was admonished for her "unprofessional" inclination to identify too closely with the "client" group. Rules and regulations emerged which clearly contradicted the staff's concept of their work, including the creation of job descriptions and performance evaluations emphasizing supervisory and administrative skills, while diminishing the skills of planning and program implementation. Women in the Program, whose dedication to feminist principles included a commitment to feminist process, were eventually forced to operate hierarchically, and this served to limit their collective autonomy and resistance to management goals.[19] Throughout this period of worker-management struggle, the energies of staff were diverted and expended in fighting the structures and satisfying an endless array of new requirements.

For a short time the Women's Program operated as an alternative feminist model, a coherent and rationally-based opposition force within the state apparatus. Following International Women's Year, and with rumors abounding over the death of the women's movement, there were few pressures from outside the state to guarantee support for the Program at the political level. More recently, the Program has been fully assimilated into bureaucratic process and managers have replaced advocates with administrators. A feminist enclave no longer exists within the state apparatus. Although this and other state women's programs may still offer some resistance in mediating the contradictions inherent in demands for equality, in general women's demands are now clearly mediated through the overall concerns of the state.

It is evident from the above description that conflicts emerging in the course of representation are contained by the bureaucratic process, while being misrepresented as conflicts over method and technique. Rules and regulations are a given and the *science* of personnel management requires that contradictions be resolved by changing individuals. This reflects a central characteristic of the bureaucratic discourse which creates certain types of relationships among people and eliminates others. In the ideological context of personnel management it is not thinkable that workers should participate in the direction of their work:

> The definition of the "best results" of bureaucratic activity can only be defined from the point of view of the bureaucracy itself; 'human resources' have only a function, not a point of view.[20]

Thus, in a bureaucratic context the feminist experimentation described above would be incomprehensible and, while it may not be expressly forbidden, the terms of the discourse simply leave no room for it. Knowledge is also restricted, reduced to the form of information, and filtered and contextualized so that it fits rationally into the system. Relevant knowledge is that which expands the existing realm of techniques, and thinking is limited to what is routine, useful and completely predictable.[21]

The principle techniques of patterning staff through performance evaluations, job descriptions, enforcement of the hierarchical order and managerial authority are integral to the bureaucratic process. Patterning is also accomplished through ideological concepts embedded in the discourse, including notions of "professional" conduct, proper administrative functioning and, indeed, the hierarchical arrangement itself. But what is significant about patterning is that it is a decisive factor in social reproduction and in the reproduction of the state apparatus.

Citizen as an Ideal Creation

In the course of performing their daily activities state personnel recreate class relations in a practical and routine manner. Activities are largely shaped by the predominant conceptual framework and a prevailing selectivity in any department determines what information will be processed. Distinct methods arise for defining and dealing with problems. Citizenship provides the liberal conceptual framework for the Women's Program. This notion of citizenship needs clarification before we proceed to examine its practical consequences.

T.H. Marshall has traced the origins of the welfare state to the evolution of individual citizenship in the form of equal civil and political rights. Citizenship is a status, bestowed upon those who become full members of a community.[22] This concept gives formal recognition to the gap which may exist between the existence of rights and their actual utilization or enjoyment. Predictably, there is a notion of ideal citizenship premised on the "drive" towards equality through the full exercise of individual political rights. Marshall postulates that with the full development of political rights vast changes could be brought about within capitalism, mitigating its worst excesses and eliminating poverty.

Citizenship provides a theoretical, and, as it turns out, a political justification for the welfare state. This is apparent from the presuppositions inherent in the notion of citizenship: social advancement is the norm; unfairness and inequality are accidental and due to temporary conflict or chance; inequality is only temporary. Further, as Ginsberg points out, "The welfare state is thus conceived as the crucial apparatus, though incomplete, for putting individual citizenship and the unity of the nation before class loyalty and organization. . . ."[23]

But we can also think of citizenship as an ideological practice and as an example of what has been referred to as conceptual imperialism. Dorothy Smith has pointed out that the creation and control of concepts is integral to the social construction of knowledge and an essential component in the practice of governing.[24] The social construction of concepts such as citizenship can be analyzed as a moment in the overall process of shaping people's experiences into an appropriate form, in which they can then be articulated into the predominant institutional arrangement of the state. In order to understand how concepts are practices we must analyze them using two procedures. The first procedure involves examining what the concept brings into existence and what kinds of phenomena it organizes. Secondly, one must locate the concept in the social relations which it serves to identify. The concept can then be explored as a "work process" and one which provides for a particular course of action.[25]

In ideological terms the status of citizenship is attained through effort on the part of the individual. The state is thus able to operationalize and promote individual citizenship by promoting citizen participation in community development. Citizen participation has the unintended, but nevertheless real consequence of organizing particular constituencies of people—notably women, native peoples and francophones—into "interest groups" in order to promote their participation in the democratic process of a pluralist society. This approach, which dominates the thinking of the citizenship branch of the Secretary of State, is premised on the identification of unequal participation among these constituencies in the political and social structures affecting their lives. Lack of adequate participation at this level is cited as the *reason* for the unequal status of these groups. In short, the objective of citizenship programs is to help women and other "disadvantaged" groups achieve equal political rights within the existing social order. Thus, in the Women's Program, groups are funded which have as their focus the coordination of action and provision of resources for the purpose of improving women's "status." Women's groups are funded to enable them to develop political skills such as lobbying, preparing briefs and forming delegations. Funding is also provided for projects designed to influence and change social attitudes by providing information and educational materials on issues pertaining to women. This type of work is primarily directed at legislative and policy reform, and at the creation of a public and institutional atmosphere favorable to the social advancement of women's rights.

A major theme in the Women's Program literature is the idea that women's voluntary associations have always been active in the promotion of human rights. Furthermore, "concern of women's groups for human rights and women's rights has always been expressed through dialogue with government."[26] The Program assumes a leadership role in educating groups on the issues affecting women and how best to "dialogue" with government. This leadership function spans the range from production and distribution of educational materials to the overt practice of helping groups to formulate their project proposals and thus to assure funding. Each year the Women's Program makes funding decisions based on its priorization of issues, which provides a powerful incentive for groups to address their projects to these same issues. This, coupled with the practice of helping groups formulate proposals, implies that women's groups are being substantially constrained in their own autonomous development.

The most conspicuous effect of the type of "representation" provided by the Women's Program to women's organizations is that it essentially shapes the latter into a politically appropriate form, as an organized interest group skilled in the methods of liberal democracy. Once organized in this form, groups are then capable of being articulated into the dominant processes of the state. Citizen participation as a conceptual practice accomplishes two significant actions. First of all, it establishes women as citizens. As a category, the notion of "citizen" obscures a great deal about inequality and removes women's difficulties from their gender-specific context. Having removed women's experience of social, political and economic marginalization from the context in which it acquires meaning, this ideological practice then attributes women's marginalization to their low status. Women's lack of participation is essentially transformed into an image problem rather than a logical consequence of how their lives are structured. The second action accomplished by the ideological process is a transformation of effect into cause. The knowledge that women are actively oppressed, indeed oppressed by state practices, is not a type of knowledge which could be either created by or admitted into the process.

What we have begun to uncover is a practice which can only legitimate a singular, narrow understanding of women's marginalized social condition and which can only provide for a limited social course of action. Political issues raised by women are deflected and forced into appropriate categories and forms made available by the ideological process.

One major contradiction resulting from this process is apparent in the funding guideline which requires that voluntary labor be contributed to funded organizations. In ideological terms, the process of developing one's full potential as a citizen includes the self-sacrifice inherent in performing voluntary labor. Such a requirement completely disregards women's often tenuous relationship to paid labor, and as a practice contributes to the reproduction of women as a class for whom the performance of unpaid labor in the "voluntary sector" can be assumed, and is acceptable.

From the foregoing discussion, we can begin to discern how the concept of citizen participation as an ideological practice organizes the concrete activities locating people in the relations of ruling in a particular way. Another aspect to be noted is how the idea of citizenship constructs the identity of the individual around some community and then establishes him/her in an abstract relationship to the nation-state. The emergence of "social rights" and expanded political citizenship for people thus creates an artificial separation between their rights at the point of production and their "political" rights as citizens.

Conclusion

This work has hopefully provided a preliminary analysis of the methods and processes operating in a particular state program which promotes the reproduction of our present social order. The capacity of the state to organize hegemony is partly dependent on the structuring of adequate responses to the vocal demands of organized people. The challenge of feminism to the legitimacy of the liberal democratic state has prompted the formation of various women's programs within the state apparatus. Representation of women's issues through the bureaucratic and ideological processes of the state serves to mediate and ultimately redefine these issues into a form which does not pose a threat to the hegemony of liberal ideology.

The state's "need," for lack of a better word, to mediate organized women's issues and activities and articulate them to its institutional and ideological framework creates significant contradictions for both the state and the women's movement. In the process of developing a credible Women's Program, the state was forced to recruit directors and staff from the movement itself. Women hired to staff the Program were committed feminists who considered their role to be one of advocacy and who represented a considerable challenge to state efforts to contain women's demands. These women engaged in an active struggle to challenge the form and content of bureaucratic practices, which, for a time, interfered substantially with the capacity of the state to organize hegemony.

We have also investigated, through a concrete example, the relationship between formal institutional practices and the activities of ordinary individuals. Uncloaking this connection and examining its dimensions in the funding relation described above provides a framework for feminists both in the state and in funded groups to analyze how they are participating in the reproduction of women's subordination. From the perspective of Marx, there is no rule without the activities of ruling and "there is no class without the activities by which it is constituted."[27] Concretely, this means the relationship between the activities of individuals and the social reproduction of the relations of ruling is determinate and available for our examination.

The discrepancy between the ideological forms of the state and women's experience of oppression has created considerable conflict for feminists. This contradiction enhances the mistrust of the state already prevalent in some sectors of the women's movement. This mistrust, compounded by bureaucratic practices, isolates feminists working inside the state from the women's movement. This is evidenced by actions of other feminists, such as those in the Saskatchewan Action Committee, who have occasionally rejected state funding rather than have their concerns mediated and co-opted by state ideological practices. But one is left to ponder the necessity of co-optation. As the leading contemporary site of class struggle the state is to some extent historically shaped by movements from below. Even more to the point:

> It does a disservice to both women and our understanding of the structuring, ordering and ruling of society to regard ourselves as having been merely passive victims of historical, social and political processes controlled by a conspiracy of men.[28]

One is led to ask whether or not it would be in the interests of feminist organizations to reject state funding and build an alternative funding base. This is a complicated question with no clear answer, but the writer can suggest a way to think about it. First of all, state funding should be recognized as a legitimate gain for women, and evidence of the impact of struggle. As we have seen, funding carries a risk of co-optation, but it has also permitted feminists to engage in numerous political activities and to deliver badly-needed services to women in crisis. The essence of co-optation is one of progressive groups being induced to buy into a state defined agenda with the illusion of having secured power. On the contrary, real power lies in our political clarity and ability to challenge the political positions of the state.

NOTES

1. Saskatchewan Action Committee, Status of Women, *Communique*, March 18, 1983.
2. Carl Boggs, *Gramsci's Marxism*. London: Pluto Press, 1976, p. 39.
3. Patricia Morgan, "From Battered Wife to Program Client: The State's Shaping of Social Problems," *Kapitalistate* (9), 1981, p. 17.

4. Göran Therborn, *What Does the Ruling Class do When it Rules?* London: Verso, 1980, p. 164.
5. Sue Findlay's work on the state and the women's movement, as well as her analysis of the mediation role of the Women's Program, includes "The Politics of the Women's Movement: Lobbying Our Way to Power," unpublished paper, Department of Political Science, Carleton University, Ottawa (no date), and "Struggles Within the State: The Feminist Challenge to Hegemony," unpublished paper, Department of Political Science, Carleton University, Ottawa, 1982. Sue also kindly provided direction in personal communications.
6. *Ibid.*, p. 6.
7. See Rianne Mahon, "Canadian Public Policy: The Unequal Structure of Representation," in L. Panitch (ed.) *The Canadian State*. Toronto: University of Toronto Press, 1977, pp. 165–198.
8. The terms of this "unstable equilibrium" are discussed in N. Poulantzas, *Political Power and Social Classes*. London: Verso, 1978a, p. 192.
9. Findlay, 1982, *op. cit.*, p. 6.
10. Interview with Nancy Lewand, former Director of the Women's Program, Secretary of State, October 6, 1983.
11. For a critical analysis of this "systems" approach, see Ian Gough, *The Political Economy of the Welfare State*. London: Macmillan Press, 1979.
12. Interview with Nancy Lewand, former Director of the Women's Program, Secretary of State, October 6, 1983.
13. Saskatchewan Action Committee, Status of Women, *op. cit.*
14. See Ng in this collection.
15. Kathy Ferguson, "Feminism and Bureaucratic Discourse," *New Political Science* (11), Spring 1983, p. 53.
16. See for example, "As Things Stand," by the Canadian Advisory Council of the Status of Women, Ottawa, 1984.
17. Findlay, 1982, *op. cit.*, p. 4.
18. *Ibid.*, p. 6.
19. *Ibid.*
20. Ferguson, *op. cit.*, p. 57.
21. *Ibid.*
22. T.H. Marshall, *Class, Citizenship and Social Development*. New Jersey: Doubleday Anchor, 1965, p. 92.
23. Norman Ginsberg, *Class, Capital and Social Policy*. London: Macmillan Press, 1979, p. 39.
24. Dorothy Smith, "The Ideological Practice of Sociology," *Catalyst* 8, 1974.
25. See for example, Gillian Walker, "Burnout: From Metaphor to Ideology," *Canadian Journal of Sociology* 11(1), 1986, pp. 33–55.
26. Secretary of State Women's Program, "Pressure for Change: The Role of Canadian Women's Groups," notes prepared for discussion at the United Nations International Seminar, September 7, 1974.

27. Quote taken from Roxana Ng, "Immigrant Women and the State: Toward an Analytic Framework," paper presented to the Western Anthropology and Sociology Association annual meeting, Saskatoon, 1982, p. 3.

28. Gillian Walker, "Recognizing the State: The Dual Relation of Women and the Professions," paper presented at the Canadian Sociology and Anthropology Association meeting, Vancouver, 1983, p. 3.

Part 3:

Community Struggles and State Regulation

Management of Urban Neighborhoods Through Alinsky-style Organizing:
Redevelopment and Local Area Planning in a Vancouver Neighborhood[*]

Jacob Muller

Introduction

This inquiry critically analyzes the hidden social relations which exist between community organizing and urban government. Community organizing here refers to Alinsky[1] and those who advocate his way of organizing. In Canada this includes neighborhood activists such as Keating.[2] Four aspects of Alinsky-style organizing within the urban context are selected for analysis. These are: the pre-defined neighborhood as the starting point of organizing by the organizer; the organizer's concern with helping residents to take on local issues in order to build a strong organization; the conflict tactics used by the neighborhood organization to recruit more members; and the decline of an organization after a few years. These characteristics of Alinsky-style organizing are examined within the administrative practices of those who manage urban government.

For the purpose of this analysis, Cockburn's[3] understanding of urban government, the "local state," is adopted. Urban government refers to those individuals who manage the city in order to "reproduce the conditions within which capitalist accumulation can take place."[4] According to Cockburn, managing urban government involves packing people and functions (such as houses, shops and offices) closer together in order to speed up the movement of capital from the moment of production to consumption and back to investment.[5]

---

[*]This is a revised paper which was originally published as "Management of Urban Neighborhoods Through Alinsky-style Organizing: An Illustration from Vancouver, Canada," *Community Development Journal*, Vol. 20, 2, 1985, pp. 106–113.

The aim here is to show how the Alinsky-style of organizing in the neighborhood became part of a management strategy for ruling the city. The emphasis is on the organizational processes of this relation. Describing these processes within their historical and social conditions of the urban setting locates this analysis within the framework outlined by Marx and Engels in *The German Ideology*[6] and elaborated upon by Smith.[7] The analysis proceeds by treating the four theoretical features of Alinsky organizing, not as "factors" or "indicators," but as practical matters to be investigated. They are taken as descriptions of everyday activities whose social dynamics are discoverable. This inquiry seeks to reveal the organized social processes which produce these features of organizing and their relation to managing the city. Methodologically, I proceed by re-embedding these features in the social relations of their historical context and not by abstraction.

Illustrations of the argument I advance come from research conducted in one of the neighborhoods of Vancouver, the Kitsilano residential area. Here, an Alinsky organizer helped create an organization which was active from 1972 to 1976. This organization advocated conflict tactics to achieve its aims, organized demonstrations to create a powerful mass organization and generally appeared to threaten management at city hall. When we examine the actual social conditions, a different picture emerges. It shows that this kind of organizing does not fundamentally threaten the management of urban government. Rather, such organizing enhances the ability of the city to administer the neighborhood. How this can be so is the problem investigated.

I came to recognize the problem through my involvement with this local organization. As one of its members and a resident of the Kitsilano neighborhood my experiences of Alinsky organizing were first hand. In a way, it was my original participation and support which gradually led me to reject this way of organizing because the Alinsky method obscures much of the existing administrative processes through which such organizing takes place.

Alinsky Organizing of the Neighborhood: Inside the Local State's Administrative Framework

There are two general organizational processes which located Alinsky-style community organizing within the local state's administrative framework. These included the acceptance of the management-stipulated boundary and the neighborhood organizations of the area. By taking these features for granted, Alinsky organizers start their activities within local government's administrative framework.

The existence of an urban neighborhood means that it has already been defined as such by those who administer the city. The neighborhood is part of the administrative process of city government. City councillors and bureaucrats, as well as the organizer, thought and worked with such an understanding. For example, the organizing of the Kitsilano residents was limited to the geographical boundaries of the waterfront in the north, Burrard Street in the east, 16th Avenue in the south and Alma Street in the west. This is an area already identified as Kitsilano in civic documents on re-zoning by-laws, development permits, planning proposals and the like. The start of organizing is specifically located within the administratively defined neighborhood of the city.

Not only did the Alinsky organizer and managers of urban government share geographical boundaries, they also worked with various neighborhood organizations which existed within the residential area. The social composition of the administratively defined neighborhood unit was the context within which the Alinsky organizer strove to build a large grassroots organization. For the organizer, the aim was to unify various existing organizations into a larger one in order to act in collective self-interest.[8] Those managing urban government, however, have had a much longer involvement with neighborhood organizations. As Cockburn[9] has argued, the neighborhood is ground which has been prepared over a long historical period by the local state through its routine administrative practices. The organizing of the neighborhood originates within an already socially formed and constituted setting.

An examination of the relationship between Alinsky organizing activities within Kitsilano and the political process in Vancouver prior to the 1972 civic election is revealing. The Alinsky organizer helped a number of residents who were fighting unwanted development to form themselves into a local group. Various housing pockets of older, single family homes containing working-class families, seniors, students and teachers were being allowed to deteriorate by developers in order to build "attractive" condominiums or luxury apartment highrises.[10] Redevelopment was encouraged by the then business-oriented mayor and councillors from the Non-Partisan Association (NPA) which dominated the city decision-making process. The NPA was being challenged at the poll by a newly formed civic political party called The Electorate Action Movement (TEAM).[11] What the highly educated TEAM candidates offered to voters was a way to integrate citizens' protest by advocating local area planning (LAP), a platform which the NPA did not have. Consultation was envisaged[12] with citizens becoming part of the administrative bureaucracy in the neighborhood. Kitsilano was one of the neighborhoods targeted for local area planning[13] when TEAM came to dominate Vancouver city council in 1972. Alinsky-style organizing developed in this climate of a newly elected urban management "TEAM" committed to neighborhood planning. Protests by evicted residents were targeted against developers through demonstrations directed at city hall to prevent redevelopment. It is in this context that such organized protests against unwanted development projects must be understood.

Channelling Issues and Organization Building for Social Reproduction

Both the method of organizing and the kind of organization Alinsky organizers created served to reproduce the civic structure at the neighborhood level.

With regard to the structure formed to oppose development, the Alinsky organizer helped to create an organization whose leaders saw themselves as "speaking on behalf of the residents of Kitsilano." This organization, however, was not drastically different from the established organizations, such as the prodevelopment Kitsilano Ratepayers' Association, which also claimed to speak for Kitsilano residents. The name chosen for the new organization, the West Broadway Citizens' Committee (WBCC) is also significant. It was named in the fall of 1972 after West Broadway Avenue in Kitsilano where a number of homes were to be expropriated for parking space.[14] This name delineated the parameters of the organization, so that the residents came to identify it in relation to the very civic bureaucratic constructs the organization was set up to oppose. Further, the WBCC organizational structure also mirrored the civic structure. This served to reproduce relations of ruling within the local community organization.

With regard to organizing methods, the West Broadway Citizens' Committee stimulated resident opposition to unwanted development projects by undertaking a number of protest activities.[15] The organizer and leaders of WBCC sought to group residents and organizations under their banner by using Alinsky-style conflict tactics as a recruitment strategy. This increased WBCC's membership, but alienated WBCC from the other established Kitsilano organizations, such as the ratepayers' association, which were fundamentally opposed to such confrontational activities. Since the leaders and organizer of WBCC did not consider it possible to recruit these established organizations, they concentrated their efforts on mobilizing other groups and the unaffiliated residents. But the concept of a mass-based organization, which included the divergent interests of business, professionals, as well as working-class people, did not fundamentally challenge the assumptions of capital accumulation through "development" at the neighborhood level.[16]

Organizationally, WBCC was a classic example of an open, hierarchical, multi-class neighborhood organization.[17] Its meetings were advertised in Kitsilano, and any and all residents were encouraged to attend. Its membership was a mix of organizations and residents who were senior citizens, teachers, workers, professionals and local merchants. The leadership consisted mostly of members with middle-class backgrounds. Its structure consisted of an elected executive, staff (including the paid organizer), various sub-committees and the general membership. On a greatly reduced scale, and with considerably more informality, this kind of community organization mirrors the organization of Vancouver's city government. Indeed, the form and structure of WBCC served to reproduce the existing system and the way it was managed at the local level.

Advocates of Alinsky-style organizing argue that uncontrollable militancy and violence are necessary to achieve concessions for the working class.[18] In fact, the *kind* of conflict undertaken by WBCC posed no fundamental threat to managers of the city.

Alinsky-style Conflict Fosters Participation in the Local State's Administrative Apparatus

While the Alinsky organizer advocated the use of conflict tactics and protest demonstrations to achieve the local organization's aims, a critical analysis of the strategies of WBCC reveals something less radical. On the whole, the organizers used strategies and tactics which were relatively easy to regulate by the neighborhood organization and by the local state. They remained within the sphere of acceptable neighborhood activities. While not necessarily acceptable to managers of the city, these pressures (e.g., demonstrations, press conferences) were well within the bounds of traditional protest group tactics.[19] For example, WBCC leaders organized a one day demonstration against the Canadian federal government's Central Mortgage and Housing Corporation (CMHC) to demand that a senior citizen highrise apartment being proposed for Kitsilano be replaced by a low-rise project. The objective was to tie up CMHC's operations for that day by having WBCC members "visit" their office en masse and phone CMHC continuously to request information on available housing programs. This activity was directed at a personalized target (in this case, the local office manager), and was relatively easy to coordinate and control. It did not question or challenge the intimate relation between developers and the local state.

Not only was the kind of conflict easy to manage by the organization;

it was also manageable by city councillors. The way that Vancouver city council dealt with the WBCC's protest and hostility among local organizations, who were either pro- or anti-development, was to involve all interested Kitsilano organizations in local area planning (LAP). All issues relevant to neighborhood development were now addressed in LAP meetings. The objective of LAP was to produce a neighborhood plan for Kitsilano. By participating in LAP, WBCC became the one dissenting voice among other organizations which favored more development. Its participation conveyed the message to WBCC members that WBCC was effective in preventing massive redevlopment in Kitsilano. And when WBCC leaders could not prevent redevelopment through LAP, members withdrew from the organization and protested to city council directly. City council simply referred the members back to LAP, thereby further isolating the organization.

Local area planning was an important social control mechanism for city council. First, development issues pertaining to the neighborhood were "decentralized" through LAP. Second, LAP created a procedural buffer between city council and local neighborhoods concerning development issues. When under pressure from Alinsky-organized protest, the managers of the local state simply reasserted the use of appropriate channels for residents to deal with development issues, in this case, through LAP.

The different administrative procedures at city council's disposal made it relatively easy for the local state to regulate Alinsky-style conflict tactics and the local organization initiating them. The aim of the local state was to manage local conflict and not to eliminate it.[20] Indeed, the protest activities described here produced interest and involvement by residents in the administrative structure, thereby legitimizing the process of capital accumulation within a liberal democratic state. The radical neighborhood organization served to channel potentially unorganized discontent into a manageable form.

The Decline of Alinsky Organizing

After a few short years, neighborhood organizing initiated by WBCC declined. The organizer left the neighborhood, the local organization faded away.[21] Life in the neighborhood went on.

There has been much debate among neighborhood organizers and analysts as to the reasons for the decline of radical community and neighborhood organizing.[22] Here I focus on the demise of Alinsky organizing within the context of urban government activities. Neither the threat of Alinsky organizing in the neighborhood to have the civic decision-making process decentralized, nor the lack of adequate funding led to the gradual demise of organizing. Organizing declines when managers of the local state consider such work completed.

Alinsky organizers, such as Keating, maintain that their efforts to decentralize the civic power structure and bring it into the neighborhood is threatening to the urban management decision-making process.[23] My analysis shows that Alinsky organizing in fact provided the managers of the local state with cooperative albeit vocal participants at the neighborhood level. As long as Alinsky organizing serves to rouse residents and foster the impression of responsiveness by city managers to neighborhood issues, there is no real need to decentralize. The temporary disruption created by this kind of organizing, which generates resentment by other resident groups in a neighborhood, provides city council with a rationale *not* to decentralize.

In the case of Kitsilano, TEAM defined the problems of citizens' protest against unwanted development between 1972 and 1976 as a lack of adequate local planning. Local area planning provided a way for citizens' groups in Kitsilano to participate with management to produce a neighborhood plan. After Kitsilano LAP had generated a plan, its work for council was considered finished, despite the unsatisfactory outcome of the plan which allowed for the redevelopment of over half of the residential area. WBCC and its successor—a tenants' union called Renters' United for Secure Housing (RUSH)—were no longer necessary to the work of city council. When local participation and the work of the local state were achieved, organizing eventually faded away. In Kitsilano, we see that the completion of the government-defined objectives led to the demise of the Alinsky organization as urban management continued fostering capital accumulation.

A further critique of Alinsky organizing is its inability to arouse the majority of residents. In the case of WBCC, a simple count of its membership list showed that it was never able to mobilize more than two percent of the approximately 40,000 residents of Kitsilano. An examination of the 1975 Kitsilano Community Resource Board election results (when the WBCC put forward and had elected its slate of candidates) shows the total resident support to be just below five percent. The WBCC organizers did mobilize far more people between 1972 and 1976 than all the other more established organizations could claim combined. They could not, however, claim the involvement of the majority of local residents. Indeed, such radical activity provided an acceptable level of contained protest by an active, vocal minority of residents, serving to legitimize city council's effort in dealing with that conflict.[24] The managers of urban government achieve the containment and eventual elimination of protest, which makes city councillors' policies look responsive and benevolent.

While, organizers explained the decline of their efforts as due to a lack of funding,[25] the immediate question is why a lack of funding should be so crucial. Seeking state funding to sustain a neighborhood organization which claims to threaten the state is absurd. Indeed, government funding inevitably transforms an organization to serve the development of capitalism.[26] Questions about state funding must include *why* the state is funding such organizing during a particular time period. In the case of WBCC, questions like these never appeared problematic; it only became "a problem" in a very narrow sense, i.e., the lack of money to sustain a salaried organizer and the operation of the organization.

Conclusion

The aim of this inquiry has been to analyze neighborhood community organizing as part and parcel of the routine management practices of urban government. An Alinsky-based experience has been examined briefly from the start of its organizing efforts through to its decline. It has been asserted that such activity was regulated by the managers of the local state. The conclusion reached is that such an organizing attempt was used to foster "participation" in order to resolve development problems created by city council.

The Alinsky-style organizing of WBCC which involved the participation of an active minority in the planning process, in the end served the continued circulation and accumulation of capital. WBCC's participation in the local state's administrative apparatus of local area planning therefore ensured the stability of the existing decision-making process. WBCC declined because continued development was supported by the other established, pro-development neighborhood organizations which helped local planners draft the massive redevelopment proposals recommended in the Kitsilano neighborhood plan document. Once the "neighborhood plan" was completed for the redevelopment of the Kitsilano area, the Alinsky organizing of WBCC and RUSH became irrelevant to city council. The neighborhood plan was adopted by Vancouver management as "what the local residents want" and thus a development framework for the neighborhood was put in place. This was the administrative method used by Vancouver city council to contain the Alinsky organizing of WBCC.

At the same time that such involvement was produced via this kind of organizing, much was obscured. Issues pertaining to the needs and labor of women in the community, for instance, did not arise as a problem for organizers and members. Similarly, the question of how social class relations are produced and reproduced in everyday life was never taken up. It is only by stepping outside the Alinsky framework that a more comprehensive understanding of such activities can be made.

When Alinsky-style organizing is analyzed within the context of urban government, the hidden dynamics of the local state in regulating protest and discontent in a local neighborhood become evident. These ruling processes of the local state need to be taken into account if we are to be successful in struggling against them.

NOTES

1. See Saul Alinsky, "Community Analysis and Organization," *American Journal of Sociology*, Vol. XLVI, May 1941, pp. 767–808; *Citizen Participation and Community Organization in Planning and Urban Renewal.* Chicago: The Industrial Areas Foundation, 1962; *Reveille for Radicals.* New York: Vintage, 1969; *Rules for Radicals.* New York: Random House, 1972.
2. See Donald R. Keating, *The Power to Make it Happen.* Toronto: Green Tree, 1975; "Looking Back on Community Organizing," *City Magazine* 3 (6), 1978, pp. 36–43.
3. Cynthia Cockburn, *The Local State.* London: Pluto, 1977. More recent efforts of work being done on the local state, following Cockburn, include: S.S. Duncan and M. Goodwin, "The Local State and Restructuring Social Relations: Theory and Practice," *International Journal of Urban and Regional Research*, 6 (2), 1982, pp. 157–185; M. Goodwin and S. Duncan, "The Local State and Local Economic Policy: Political Mobilization or Economic Regeneration," *Capital and Class* 27, Winter 1986, pp. 14–36; W. Magnusson, "Urban Politics and the Local State," *Studies in Political Economy*, 16, Spring 1985, pp. 111–142.
4. Cockburn, *ibid.*, p. 51.
5. *Ibid.*, p. 63.
6. Karl Marx and Fredrick Engels, *The German Ideology.* Moscow: Progress Publishers, 1976.
7. D.E. Smith, "On Sociological Description: A Method from Marx," *Human Studies* 4 (4), 1981, pp. 313–337.
8. See Harry C. Boyte, *The Backyard Revolution.* Philadelphia: Temple University Press, 1980, p. 51.
9. Cockburn, *op. cit.*, p. 159.
10. See Donald Gutstein, *Vancouver Ltd.* Toronto: James Lorimer, 1975.
11. P. Tennant, "Vancouver Civic Politics, 1929–1980," in L.D. Feldman (ed.), *Politics and Government of Urban Canada.* Toronto: Methuen, 1981, pp. 126–147.

12. W. Hardwick and D.F. Hardwick, "Civic Government: Corporate, Consultative or Participatory," in D. Ley (ed.), *Community Participation and the Spatial Order of the City*, Vancouver: Tantalus Research Ltd., 1974, pp. 89–95.

13. A. Horsman and P. Raynor, "Citizen Participation in Local Area Planning: Two Vancouver Cases," in L.J. Evenden (ed.), *Vancouver: Western Metropolis*. Victoria: University of Victoria, 1978, pp. 239–253.

14. M.A. Mitchell and C. Goldney, *Don't Rest in Peace – Organize!* Vancouver: Neighborhood Services Association, 1975, pp. 69–72.

15. D. Ley, "Problems of Co-optation and Idolatry in the Community Group," in D. Ley (ed.), *Community Participation and the Spatial Order of the City*. Vancouver: Tantalus Research Ltd., 1974, pp. 75–88.

16. M. Repo, "The Fallacy of 'Community Control'," in J. Cowley, *et al.* (eds.), *Community or Class Struggle?*. London: Stage 1, 1977, pp. 47–64.

17. Alinsky, 1969, *op. cit.* See also the analysis by R. Bailey Jr., *Radicals in Urban Politics: The Alinsky Method*. Chicago: University of Chicago Press, 1972.

18. Francis F. Piven and Richard A. Cloward, *Poor People's Movements*. New York: Pantheon Books, 1979.

19. G. Drover and E. Schragge, "Urban Struggle and Organizing Strategies," *Our Generation* 13, 1, 1979, p. 68.

20. Cockburn, *op. cit.*, p. 117. See as well Michael P. Smith, *The City and Social Theory*. New York: St. Martin's Press, 1979, p. 259.

21. B. Freeman, "The Decline and Fall of a Community Organization," *City Magazine* 2, 7, 1977, pp. 18–27.

22. D. Roussopoulos, "Reformism and the Urban Question," *Our Generation* 11, 2, 1978, pp. 46–58. A good summary of the debate is provided by W. Magnusson, "Community Organization and Local Self-Government," in L.D. Feldman (ed.), *Politics and Government of Urban Canada: Selected Readings*. Toronto: Methuen, 1981, pp. 61–86.

23. Keating, 1978, *op. cit.*, p. 42.

24. Robert Kraushaar, "Policy Without Protest: The Dilemma of Organizing for Change in Britain," in M. Harloe (ed.), *New Perspectives in Urban Change and Conflict*. London: Heineman Educational Books, 1981, p. 109.

25. Keating, 1978, *op. cit.*, p. 42.

26. See M. Daly, *The Revolution Game*. Toronto: New Press, 1970; Martin Loney, "A Political Economy of Citizen Participation," in L. Panitch (ed.), *The Canadian State: Political Economy and Political Power*. Toronto: University of Toronto, 1977, pp. 446–472; R. Ng, "The Politics of Community Services: A Study of an Employment Agency for Immigrant Women," paper presented at the Canadian Sociology and Anthropology Association annual Meeting in Vancouver, 1983.

The Politics of Minority Resistance Against Racism in the Local State[*]

Daiva K. Stasiulis

Introduction

Prior to the 1970s, most Torontonians viewed their city as one untroubled by racial turmoil. Exclusionary immigration policies had ensured that only relatively small numbers of non-whites were permitted the privilege of entering Canada and settling in its largest city to take up low-wage and relatively menial jobs. While racism formed an integral part of the experience and politics of Toronto's small Black community, it was not a sufficiently large-scale or explosive issue to enter into the political discourse and agenda of municipal government.

The rapid influx of Caribbean and South Asian immigrants during the early 1970s, a product of increased demand for skilled labor and declining supply from "traditional" sources in the British Isles and Europe, made Toronto a more noticeably multiracial city. Alongside the novel appearance of *roti* shops, curry houses and shop-windows displaying colorful Indian cottons, there also developed a disturbing and unfamiliar form of race relations.

The local mass media began to carry frequent reports of racial assaults on city streets and in subways, confrontations between police and Black citizens, and vigorous minority protests against these injustices. These events and their media representation shattered the sanguine view held by many Toronto residents of their city as color-blind and tolerant, if not warmly welcoming of its new immigrants.[1]

One outcome of the collective resistance to racism by Toronto West Indian[2] and South Asian[3] communities has been the emergence of a new

[*]I would like to thank Robert Storey and the editors for their constructive comments on an earlier draft of this paper.

level of "race consciousness" at all levels of state institutions and the creation of a plethora of "race relations" and "visible minority" committees, liaison and consultative structures, programs and commissions. More important than the sheer fact of their existence, however, has been the divergent character of these race-related innovations.

Minority protest and collaboration with receptive officials produced impressive reforms in the Toronto public school system designed to monitor and reduce institutionalized forms of racial discrimination. In contrast, the "reforms" developed in other state institutions, notably in law enforcement, simultaneously contained and heightened minority struggles, fostering contradictory consequences for the divided minority communities.

This paper compares and analyzes the outcomes of campaigns by Toronto Blacks and South Asians to contest racism in the Metropolitan Toronto police force and the Toronto Board of Education. Both of these arenas for anti-racist struggles form part of local state institutions and are therefore ideal for comparative study. For each of the two campaigns, I also examine the conditions under which the anti-racist struggles materialized, and the constraints upon their consequences.

This paper is organized as follows. First, it discusses the problematical nature of the anti-racist movements which formed a turbulent part of Toronto politics in the late 1970s and early 1980s. The next two sections are taken up with analyses of the concerns, strategies and institutional effects of minority struggles against racism in policing and the public school system, respectively. Finally, it concludes with an assessment of the factors accounting for the divergent policy outcomes within policing and educational institutions and certain political lessons that can be drawn from this analysis.

Anti-racist struggles—working class, popular or democratic?

A great deal has been written recently about the "new social movements" and "popular democratic struggles"—a heterogeneous array of socio-political forms of activism against divergent oppressions, based on gender, race, militarism, etc.[4] Some theorists argue that the transformation of advanced capitalist societies in more egalitarian, democratic directions is likely to emerge from a *plurality* of social struggles, with no central or vanguard role relegated to the working class.[5] Other writers sharply reject this claim on the grounds that it ignores the realities of class power and the relationship between consciousness and material conditions and thus lapses into a purely idealist position.[6]

I will not enter into this debate except to aid in clarifying the character of the collective resistance by the Toronto Black and South Asian communities to their experiences of racism. First, it must be noted that the minority challenges to racism were not transparent or unmediated expressions of "working-class struggles," if by that term is meant resistance by some segment of the working class to the authority of capital, and which is understood (at least by some major participants) to further the interests (of some segment) of labor.

Resistance to racism in the Black community was carried out by community development organizations and island associations, some with ideological affinities to black nationalist and liberation struggles in the Caribbean. Within South Asian communities, loosely-based coalitions were formed by religious-cultural associations and a smaller number of political organizations. In both sets of ethnic communities, leaders and activists derived primarily from the professional middle class. That stratum is characterized by high educational status, relative economic security, and flexible time schedules. In addition, the issues of struggle were generally understood in terms of "race" and "ethnicity" rather than "class."

In spite of the middle-class social basis of their leadership, and the self-identification of activists with the idiom of "race" rather than "class," the minority efforts to combat racism in policing and schools connected with wider struggles engaged in by the working class to make these institutions more responsive to the needs of workers. This point, which draws attention to the relationship between class-based struggles and what E.P. Thompson calls "class struggles without class"[7] is an important one and will be elaborated upon in the concluding section of this paper.

The concept "popular democratic struggle," which refers to the organization of "the people" against "the state" or "the large corporations," is also problematic when applied to anti-racist forms of struggle in the Canadian context. As any fifth-generation Black Canadian who is repeatedly interrogated about his or her origins knows, the concept of "the people" denotes "the white Canadian people." The ideological construction of "the people," then, is a historical product of the country's development as a "white settler colony," which fostered decades of racist immigration policies.

Several surveys conducted since the mid-1970s have documented the existence of racist sentiments, especially targetting brown- or black-skinned peoples, among the majority or a significant minority of Toronto residents.[8] In the context of the recession, cuts in social programs and rising unemployment, sections of the working and middle classes came to identify the recent visible minority presence as one cause for their declining economic status. Thus, there exist large segments of the non-dominant classes that not only perceive the presence of visible minorities in their neighborhoods and places of work as illegitimate, but also show antipathy to minority demands for a greater share of diminishing resources.

Though poorly defined as "popular," the anti-racist struggles by minority groups are aptly characterized as "democratic," aimed at producing new or enhanced democratic forms of representation in local state institutions as the means for challenging racial inequality. The desire to democratize and assert popular control over institutions whose growth and bureaucratization had weakened their responsiveness to local concerns provided a key link between the aims of the anti-racist movement and those of other (feminist, gay, working-class) struggles. A growing disquiet was apparent in a significant vocal segment of the population. This provided the anti-racist organizing of the minority communities with a potential connection to a larger popular-democratic struggle. As I argue below, this potential was tapped in the minority campaign against racism in the Metropolitan Toronto police; it served to invigorate that campaign and helped structure its strategies.

The Metropolitan Toronto Police and Race Relations

Sir Robert Peel, founder of the British Police Service, once declared:

> The police at all times should maintain a relationship with the public that gives reality to the historic tradition that the police are the public and the public are the police. . . .[9]

During the 1970s, the mutual suspicion which pervaded relations between the Metropolitan Toronto police force and visible minority communities dealt a severe blow to the dictum of police accountability to the public. The sentiment expressed by many Blacks and South Asians was that their communities had fallen outside the general terms of police accountability and were treated as communities apart from the general public.[10]

An awareness within the Toronto Black community of police bias against Blacks was in part born with the widespread publicization of the Sir George Williams Affair in Montreal.[11] The incipient Black Power movement in Canada, catalyzed by the clash between students and police in 1969, provoked police surveillance of Black organizations by both municipal and federal forces.[12] That same year, a film entitled, "Revolution Underway," linking Black Power movements in the United States to an international communist conspiracy aimed at overthrowing the government, was used in Toronto for training in police work. After meeting with protests from citizen groups, which branded it as racist propaganda, the film was publicly destroyed by then Police Chief, Judge C.O. Bick.[13]

Ten years later, the monthly magazine of the Metro Toronto Police Association, *News and Views*, published two articles making derogatory remarks about a number of minorities, including Blacks, Pakistanis and homosexuals.[14] The fact that senior police officials later defended the publication of the articles (though not the views represented) on the grounds of freedom of expression, further worsened already deteriorated relations between the police and minority communities. Head's (1975) non-random sampling of Black opinion revealed that while over 50 per cent of adults questioned considered that the Toronto police are "generally unfair" in their treatment of the Black population, as many as 75 per cent of Black youths interviewed voiced that opinion.[15]

Arrests for minor infractions of traffic laws, and aggression against South Asians during searches conducted for illegal immigrants, were two police practices condemned by members of the South Asian community. In a 1978 brief to Metro Council, the Indian Immigrant Aid Services also criticized the police for its surveillance of the legitimate political activities of South Asians.[16]

The most common complaint about police practices from the South Asian community, however, pertained to the failure by police officers to provide adequate responses to racial attacks made on community members.[17] This failing was felt to be exemplified by police delays in reaching the scene of racial attacks, refusal to recognize the racial dimension in attacks, unwillingness to seriously investigate racial attacks, intransigence in prosecuting assailants in clear-cut cases, and hostility towards victims to the point of treating them as assailants.

Aggravating the minority communities' disquiet regarding police practices was the lack of sympathy shown by senior officials for the concerns voiced by the minorities. Members of the Board of Police Commissioners responded to minority and public questioning of their credibility by stepping up their verbal attacks on their critics.[18] In addition, both Black and South Asian activists claimed to have been harassed for the strong stand they had taken on police-minority issues.[19]

The anxiety and mistrust engendered by the policies and practices of Metro Toronto police ran high among segments of the West Indian and South Asian community. For these communities, the police shootings of Buddy Evans in December 1978 and Albert Johnson (in his own home) in August 1979 became symbols of the aggressiveness and racism of the

Toronto police. These incidents kindled a sense of solidarity among members of the Black community in particular, and mobilized them to bring pressure to bear on clearly defined institutionalized targets, such as the Metropolitan Toronto Board of Police Commissioners.

Black Communal Strategies

Essentially two strategies were pursued in the Black community's efforts to reform police structures and practices in a manner which would make them more accountable to Toronto's multiracial citizenry. The first, followed by leaders of the National Black Coalition of Canada (NBCC), the Jamaica Canada Association and the Grenada Association, was to work closely with authorities in attempting to ameliorate tensions between the police and the Black community. This entailed providing support and cooperation to Cardinal Carter, the mediator appointed by the Metro Toronto Board of Police Commissioners (a five-person, appointed decision-making body) following the Johnson shooting.[20] Members of the NBCC held a meeting with Premier William Davis to discuss the matter. In addition, the president of the NBCC was involved from the outset in the Liaison Group on Law Enforcement and Race Relations which was established in 1976 to mediate the conflict between the police and visible minority communities (see below).

The Toronto press (chiefly the *Toronto Star*) publicized the views of the moderate leaders and their responses to meetings with government officials and mediators. The moderates hoped that the spectre of an imminent crisis involving widespread violence, promulgated by both the "extremist" elements in the Black community and the far (racist) right, might provoke authorities into providing ameliorative solutions. Referring to the march of an estimated 3,000 Blacks protesting the shooting of Albert Johnson, one spokesperson for the NBCC warned that the march "was the tip of the iceberg. There are elements on the far left and the far right who want violence to explode here. I am aghast. It's a powder keg."[21]

Another, somewhat larger, group of organizations attempted to press for changes in the structures of policing by adopting a mass-based confrontational approach. These organizations regarded the Carter appointment as a defusing mechanism, "a convenient device for cooling down the people's rage while doing nothing."[22] They attempted to activate the support of a broad range of community groups which would directly and collectively put pressure on the Police Board to institute reforms. The United African Improvement Association, the longest-lived organization in the Black community, spearheaded the Albert Johnson Committee

Against Police Brutality. This committee collected funds for the widow of the slain Jamaican, planned benefit concerts and mass meetings, and coordinated rallies and marches.

Other organizations, such as the Black Education Project, preferred to ally themselves with the Working Group on Police-Minority Relations, which formed as a result of complaints regarding police brutality from Metro Toronto's gay community (see George Smith's paper in this collection). This organization consisted of a coalition of reformist alderpersons and trustees, gay community leaders and Black individuals. The two coalitions jointly sponsored a "memorial and benefit concert for Albert Johnson," which drew approximately 1,000 supporters. They also joined with roughly thirty minority and left groups in endorsing a press release formulated by the Working Group which called for the democratization and community control of the Metropolitan Toronto police.[23]

Several marches were organized by the Albert Johnson Committee to dramatize the collective anger and grief of the Black community with respect to the escalation of police violence against minority groups. Early in September 1979, 3,000 people, most from the Black community, participated in an eight-hour, eight-mile protest march, which *Contrast* described as "reminiscent of the civil rights era in the American deep South."[24] On October 14, 1979, a demonstration to oppose racism and police violence, launched jointly by the Albert Johnson Committee and the Sikh-led, Action Committee Against Racism, attracted an estimated 1,200 to 2,000 protesters.[25]

For organizations adopting a confrontational strategy, the decision to spurn attempts to negotiate privately with officials and politicians was a mixture of choice, principle and past experience. Since 1975, at least six special inquiries into complaints of police misconduct had been commissioned by the Metro Toronto and Ontario governments. All six inquiries either explicitly addressed the relationship of racial minorities to policing (Pitman, 1977; Clement, 1980; Carter, 1980) or had direct bearing on this issue (Maloney, 1975; Morand, 1976; Robarts, 1977). The meagre changes produced by the flurry of commissions had convinced many Black groups that senior police officials were resistant to reforms that would make them more responsive to local needs.

An important factor spurring Black organizations to adopt mass protest strategies was the larger political context—e.g., the "mood" of the city with respect of the credibility of the police. A few weeks after the Albert Johnson shooting, the Toronto City Council passed a vote of non-confidence in the Metro Police Board, saying that "it no longer reflected the mentality of an ethnically-mixed community."[26] Moreover, other minority groups, including the highly organized gay community, Sikh and Arab organizations, labor and women's groups, voiced their concerns about misplaced police priorities. These groups, as well as several left political organizations, willingly engaged in alliances and demonstrations through which joint pressures could be exerted.

A survey conducted in October 1979 revealed that the general population of Metro Toronto felt that the Metro police were performing an excellent to good job.[27] The majority (62 per cent) simultaneously felt that "elected representatives of citizens of Toronto" rather than provincial appointees should control and be responsible for police action.[28] As importantly, a sufficient number of minority groups and local politicians were united in their loss of confidence in the decision-makers within the Police Board. The repeated public negative assessments of police leadership, priorities and policies, provided the appropriate climate of opinion to unleash mass protest and provoke the Police Board to respond.

Police Responses to Minority Protest

Although members of the Board of Police Commissioners vituperatively resisted and deflected public criticism of the police force's racist practices by discrediting critics as "vigilantes,"[29] their response also involved the initiation of several structures for resolving conflict. Two such structures, the Police Ethnic Relations Unit and the Liaison Group on Law Enforcement and Race Relations, isolated and acknowledged the problems of "race" within policing and attempted to regain the confidence and cooperation of the visible minority communities.

The Police Ethnic Relations Unit (PERU) pioneered efforts on the part of the Metro Toronto police force to deal with issues defined in ethnic terms. Initially established in 1973 to mediate deteriorating relations of police with the Italian community, the Unit expanded in 1975 and 1977 through the addition of a Black and East Indian section respectively.

During the summer of 1980, PERU consisted of fifteen men out of a force comprising 5,400 members. The types of incidents which the unit was called upon to mediate included name-calling leading to assault, assault causing bodily harm, noise complaints, and violence within schools. Members of the unit also intervened in such "ethnic" conflicts as crowding and parking problems, disputes within South Asian, Caribbean, and other "ethnic" families, and cases involving illegal immigrants. The unit was *not* mandated to mediate disputes involving alleged police mistreatment of minorities or racism in the police force. (Complaints regarding police behavior were directed to another police structure, the Police Complaints Review Board.)

The members of the unit also gave seminars and informal talks about both the work performed by PERU and multiculturalism (sic) to ethnic minorities, members of the general public and police officers at police colleges and stations. In theory, PERU was well-integrated within the structures of policing, and knowledge of the unit's purpose was widespread within the force. One survey suggests a very different reality, with the majority of police officers ignorant of the Ethnic Relation's whereabouts and operations.[30]

PERU has had limited impact on the nature of policing in the city, by virtue of its small size, the junior rank of its officers, and its isolation from the everyday, run-of-the-mill police duties engaged in by the majority of the force. The unit *has* been successful, however, in projecting a positive image to counterbalance the coercive and undemocratic image of the police force as a whole. According to one member of the ethnic squad who had served on the unit for four years:

> It's mainly a *public relations job*. We don't just deal with police problems. It's an educational process. *Our whole thing is to sell the department.*[31]

The commodification of "police good will" in the unit has found its buyers among spokespersons in the minority communities and the press. The unit has received considerable praise from Black community leaders. Community newspapers such as the *Toronto Star* and the Black weekly, *Contrast*, have consistently supported the unit, citing instances of successful mediation of race-related incidents. Thus, the powerlessness of PERU to affect the material practices of policing can be seen as *less* important than its relative success in raising the flagging levels of minority confidence in at least certain elements of the Metro Toronto police force.

Senior levels of the police have recognized the limitations of the unit or any *one* structure in eliminating negative minority perceptions of the police. A second structure, the Liaison Group on Law Enforcement and Race Relations, deserves special attention for its longevity and the considerable official support and finances it has received. Roy McMurtry, a past Attorney General in the Davis Conservative Government, heralded the Liaison Group as the "most promising model for the eighties" and stated that it formed "the focal point of [his Ministry's] involvement in relationships between the police and the visible minorities."[32]

The idea for the development of the Liaison Group on Law Enforcement and Race Relations[33] originated in a seminar held in October 1976, sponsored by two established community agencies and attended by senior police authorities, government officials and human rights commissioners. It was decided that the establishment of local police-minority committees, patterned after similar committees in Britain, would be invaluable in opening lines of communication between visible minorities and the police, and providing forums through which "appropriate police-community responses" to problems could be discussed. Such committees (three initially, with a fourth added in May 1978) were established on a divisional basis in areas with significant visible minority populations and histories of police-minority tensions and overt conflict. The maximum membership of the local committees was set at fifteen persons with a ceiling of six police members and nine community members. The activities of the local committees were overseen by the parent committee composed of representatives from senior law enforcement levels, human rights and cultural state agencies and the two sponsoring organizations.[34]

A salient feature of the liaison structure and the source of considerable disaffection among its minority community members, was the centralization of power at the level of the parent body. Local committees were instructed to seek the approval of the parent body for the minutest aspects of their operations. Another problem which threatened the viability of the project was the reluctance on the part of visible minorities to participate in a structure, regarded with cynicism and decided opposition as "pro-establishment" and "lily-white." The participation of the police also posed difficulties in as much as their occupational socialization and training within a militaristic, authoritarian structure actively discouraged group decison-making and fostered mistrust in the capacity of civilians to evaluate police actions.

Difficulties encountered in the parent and local committees extended beyond those of communication. The adversarial relationship between police and minority group members, carried from the streets and neighborhoods to the committee meetings, colored the project's entire proceedings. Frustration and suspicion, felt by community members over the functioning of the committees, stemmed in large part from the narrow terms of reference developed by the Liaison Group and the lack of autonomy of the pilot committees.[35]

The terms of reference for the local committees directed them to address problems of "race" in isolation from their connections with the dynamics of "class." Yet, the tendency of particular communities to attract a large, aggressive police presence is a product of a complex interaction of class and racial factors including uneven patterns of capital investment, the inferior services provided by the city to working-class neighborhoods, and the necessity of many recent working-class immigrants to seek housing in low-income, high-rise tenements no matter how sterile and inhospitable living conditions are within these "concrete jungles." In both recorded instances where local committees made formal requests to enlarge the scope of their mandate and analyze police-minority relations within a context of problems encountered by relatively powerless, low-income *and* non-white communities, these requests were turned down by the parent body which ruled them outside the local committees' terms of reference. Attempts by one local committee to analyze structured patterns of police-minority relations were also cut short by the refusal of police divisional headquarters to release statistics on racial incidents.

As a result of the impasse reached in the pursuit of community versus police objectives, the committees generally followed a reactive course, examining individual cases of conflict and discussing established police procedures. The use of the committees as mere forums for the explanation (as opposed to the critical scrutiny) of police practices proved unacceptable to community members and several resigned on the grounds that the committees were "pro-police" and had achieved few practical results. A subsequent restructuring of the project (re-named the "Council on Race Relations and Policing") removed all anarchic tendencies of the local committees by simply abolishing them!

The deep fissures between visible minority and police concerns prevented the parent body from playing any political role in the public deliberations over police reform. This meant that during the public discussion on issues having repercussions for police-minority relations (including hiring and promotion practices, composition and autonomy of complaint boards and public accountability of the Police Board of Commissioners), police and civilian members of the parent committee sat in glaring silence on opposite sides of the conference table.

The Liaison Group offered visible minorities quasi-official channels for participation in a dialogue with police. The illusion of equivalence of power and influence and harmony of interests between the two parties could not, however, be maintained in the face of its frequent contradiction by minority experiences of the police "as an occupying army in the visible minority communities."[36]

While the Police Board has offered concessions to minority groups such as less stringent height and weight entry requirements to attract visible minority applicants, it has thus far steadfastly refused to adopt an affirmative action program for visible minorities.[37] The previously all-male, anglo, celtic Board now includes a commissioner who is both female and "ethnic." The Board, however, itself continues to be appointed by the province, rather than be controlled by the democratically elected representatives of the local population. In spite of vigorous lobbying by bodies such as the Citizens' Independent Review of Police Activities for an autonomous, citizen-controlled complaints review board, the police continue to police themselves.[38]

A former coordinator for the Liaison Group remarked that as far as senior police officials were concerned, the project was primarily intended as a defusing mechanism, a "safety valve," where minority groups could "blow off steam in a public forum."[39] The project was developed to meet criticisms with respect to the absence of participation by visible minorities within police structures, while at the same time deflecting their demands for greater police accountability.

Although the Liaison Group originally invited the collaboration of certain Black and South Asian organizations, especially those which eschewed confrontation, its overall effect was to inspire minority combativeness, already fuelled by the police shooting of Albert Johnson and the subsequent acquittals of the police officers involved from charges of manslaughter. The dismissive and even confrontationist response by minority groups to the liaison structure illustrates that such legitimating devices do not always, or automatically, secure the desired results and may, in fact, serve to mobilize rather than quell dissent.

An adversarial stance on the part of Black organizations received support from other sectors of the public. Sources of support included the gay community, organized labor and the women's movement, which organized to resist incursions by the police on their rights to privacy, freedom from sexual harassment and violence, dissent with conditions of employment, and other fundamental civil liberties. These groups provided ready allies for visible minority organizations intent on fighting for the domocratization of the particularly recalcitrant institutions of the Metro Toronto police.

Why was this broad alliance of popular democratic forces unable to wrest concessions whose effect would have been to limit police powers and transfer some measure of control over policing to the local community? In a clearly understated tone, Poulantzas has argued that, "a shift in the balance of forces within the repressive apparatuses poses special, and therefore formidable problems."[40] These special and formidable deterrents to police reforms were starkly evident in the Black community's contestation of racist practices within the Metro Toronto police force.

The task of decreasing racism in police institutions is hindered by their operative "occupational ideology" which is consistent with racist practices and other forms of oppression.[41] At the highest levels of decision-making, the officials are appointed and therefore not directly reliant on an electoral base for their support. The power and financial resources available to these senior, appointed officials are immense and sustained, in comparison with those more sporadically mobilized by the anti-racist and other movements for reform of the police. In fact, the Police Board of Metropolitan Toronto comprises the largest single item of the municipal budget. In 1980, for example, it received 13 percent of the total.[42]

The power and resources of local police structures have become further magnified by the more general restructuring within the Canadian state that has occurred since the mid-1970s to contend with the economic crisis. The retreat by the state from welfare spending has been accompanied by an increase in spending on police, courts and prisons in order to manage the augmenting levels of crisis-induced crime and social tensions, and to impose a new discipline among workers facing diminished living standards.[43] The erosion of the Keynesian welfare state and the bolstering of social control agencies are aided by the growing capacity of neo-conservative ideologies to define political choices. These properties of the larger economic and political crisis, and the recent restructuring of the Canadian state in more authoritarian directions, form part of the real constraints faced by anti-racist and other struggles to hold local police powers in check.

Race Relations in the Toronto Public School System: Beyond Multiculturalism

An examination of the development of the Toronto Board of Education's race relations policy offers a striking contrast to the weak representation of visible minority concerns in policing agencies. The Toronto Board of Education has gone farthest among all local school boards in the larger metropolitan area in both investigating racism within the public school system and in implementing reforms.

The issue of racism first emerged within Board policy discussions during the mid-1970s. An investigation into the quality of education offered to immigrant children led to the adoption by the Board of a new multicultural policy. Most of the recommendations made by the *Final Report of the Work Group on Multicultural Programs* urged reforms in the cultural and linguistic policies of the Toronto Board in order to redress the inequalities in educational access amongst a multi-ethnic, multi-lingual student body. In-service programs were also recommended in order to enable staff to respond to racial incidents. Provisions recommended by the Work Group on Multicultural Programs touched on the attitudinal and overt behavioral dimensions of racism. More importantly, the Report "foreshadowed a number of race relations problems which

. . . [became] painfully evident in the two years [after] the Report was issued."[44]

The pressure on Board officials to address issues of racism emanated from two sources: the growing number of sometimes violent racial incidents occurring in Toronto schools, and the assiduous, sustained work by Black community organizations in putting forward the concerns of Black parents and youth. Chief among these organizations was the Black Education Project (BEP), formed in 1969 by university students to provide services for Black, working-class youth.[45] Like many other politically-conscious Black organizations established during this period, BEP's focus was on education—imparting knowledge of their African roots and culture to Black children, as well as providing upgrading assistance in regular academic subjects.

One of the key concerns brought to the Board's attention by the BEP was the systematic "streaming" or placement of West Indian students in vocational schools and classes designed for "slow learners," a process regarded by parents as consigning their children to futures of social and economic oblivion. Indeed, in Ramcharan's 1974 study of West Indians in Toronto, more than half of the respondents' children enrolled in secondary or post-secondary institutions were attending vocational schools; less than three per cent were attending universities or community colleges.[46]

Another concern shared by both West Indians and South Asians was the content of textbooks and curricula, viewed as denigrating and omitting positive consideration of non-white peoples. *Teaching Prejudice*, a 1971 report on a study of 400 textbooks in Ontario, revealed that non-white groups were frequently referred to as "bloodthirsty, primitive, cruel and savage," in contrast to Europeans depicted as "saintly and refined." Native Indians, Blacks and Asians were rarely referred to in positive ways. The history of Canada's mistreatment of minorities was also, for the most part, omitted.[47]

Pakistani and other Muslim parents raised strong objections to the presence of material, offensive to the Islamic religion, in prescribed Ontario school textbooks. Other material was criticized for conveying an "Oxfam image of the Indian sub-continent," and characterizing South Asians as backward and archaic, encumbered by sacred cows and illiterate peasants, and civilized only by benevolent British colonizers.[48] Such institutionalized denigration of South Asian peoples and cultures, it was feared, would result in grave cumulative effects on the intellectual and emotional development of South Asian children.[49]

Among West Indians, similar criticisms have focused on the inadequate interpretation provided of the history, contributions and lifestyles of Canadian, Caribbean, American and other Blacks, and on racially offensive material in certain works widely accepted as "great literature."[50]

In March 1977, the Toronto Board established a Subcommittee on Race Relations to begin to address the educational issues raised by minority organizations and parent groups. The composition of this committee reflected the growing openness of the Board to community participation in the formulation of policy. Throughout its existence, the committee included two representatives each from Black, South Asian, Korean and Native Indian liaison organizations. The representatives sitting on the liaison committees were not handpicked by Board officials, but rather were chosen through processes initiated and controlled within the communities. In the case of the South Asian committees, elections were held within organizations representing different regional and linguistic groups (Sikh/Punjabi, Gujarati, Bengali, Marathi, etc.) Other members sitting on the nineteen-person committee represented the Board's trustees, teacher and principal associations, the Ontario Human Rights Commission, and the Urban Alliance on Race Relations.

During the nineteen months of its existence, the Race Relations Committee engaged in a lengthy process of consultation with in-school constituencies (students, teachers and administrators) and with a wide variety of community groups. The result of this consultation are detailed in the Subcommittee's Draft and Final Reports. The latter proposed an anti-racist program, making 115 proposals for combatting racism in curriculum, hiring and promotion practices, staff development, the classroom and extracurricular activities. In September 1979, the Board approved the recommendations made within the final report and allocated approximately one million dollars for their implementation over the following five years.

Some of the new policy guidelines, such as those pertaining to review of school curricula, were similar to those already underway within the multicultural program, and thus required "intensification" rather than initiation on the part of the Board. Reforms were launched to correct the dire lack of teaching material on visible minorities, and to develop in-service programs in order to sensitize Board staff to the experiences of racism undergone by members of different racial and ethnic origins. Other changes included the development of course units on race relations in social studies and multiculturalism courses.

The implementation by the Board of these recommendations primarily redressed the institutionalized "ignorance of the cultures and traditions of visible minority groups." The Work Group report explicitly recognized racism to include "not only situations of openly prejudiced personal actions, but also those more subtle organizational programs and practices which provide encouragement and support for racism, albeit unwillingly."[51] Many recommendations were thus intended to "deinstitutionalize" racism.[52]

The Toronto Board's race relations policy was evidence of the Board's inclusive attitude vis-à-vis community groups and its ability to incorporate the expertise and energies of visible minority groups in the direction of constructive, wide-ranging reform. The policy established a new awareness of the reproduction of educational disadvantage for visible minority students through a variety of racially exclusive mechanisms and through the dismantling and appropriation of the skills and strengths associated with students' ethnocultural and class backgrounds. It thus represented a significant advance from the policies of most other school boards which narrowly acknowledged the multicultural composition of the student body, yet denied the double jeopardy of race and class whose capillaries run through the public educational system.

One significant factor accounting for the progressive nature of the reforms was the aggressive and politically astute nature of the pressure brought to bear on access points within the educational institutions by community organizations. Organizations such as the Black Education Project were ideally located to bring the struggle to institute anti-racist reforms onto the terrain of the Toronto Board. The BEP had both established credibility among working-class Black parents and youth through its support of immigration struggles and its extensive program of community services, and won the support of Board personnel through the expertise of its members in multicultural and anti-racist forms of education. Collaboration between BEP and the Board was further promoted when one of BEP's most respected activists accepted a position as a School-Community Relations officer at the Toronto Board of education. Long-term minority access to the Board and a structure for bi-directional communication was institutionalized with the establishment of the Black Liaison Committee in 1974 (later superseded by the Black Parents Organization) and the South Asian Origins Liaison Committee in 1976.

It is doubtful that the astute and concerted minority group pressures would have achieved such positive results in the absence of a receptive climate *within* the Board of Education. Board administrators expressed anxiety over the disruptive potential of racial tensions within Toronto schools and were open to institutional reforms that promised to contain such tensions.

The responsive character of the anti-racist reforms to the concerns of minority, chiefly working-class, parents can be explained by the political and ideological make-up of the Board's elected trustees. As elected politicians, the trustees were more accessible and responsive to their largely working-class, multi-racial and multi-ethnic constituency than were appointed officials. In addition, prior to and immediately following the development of the Board's anti-racist policy, the Left held the balance of power among the trustees. Several trustees had been elected as candidates of the New Democratic Party. The NDP trustees were ideologically inclined to view education as a medium for progressive social reform and an instrument for breaking down inequalities based on class, gender, race and ethnicity. Their predisposition to be responsive to the demands and wishes of community-based organizations worked to the advantage of minority groups courting access to the process of decision-making.

As innovative and comprehensive as the race relations reforms in the Toronto school system were, it is important to acknowledge the limitations placed upon them by both "external" authority structures governing the Board's operations, and factors internal to the Board's politics. One instance recorded in the minutes of the Board is indicative of the manner in which the legal framework of state control emerged to erode some of the more far-reaching of the recommended changes toward community control of education. One recommendation made in the Final Report was to establish an employment and promotions appeals committee with community representation whose purpose would be to adjudicate complaints by teachers of employment-related discrimination. This was retracted quietly after the Board's solicitor advised that delegating the Board's power to third parties was *ultra vires*.[53] The extant structure of authority relations, as codified in Board regulations and the provincial Education Act, sets legal-bureaucratic parameters for race-related reforms, the participation within policy-making of new groups, and the development of local community control over education.

The Board's race relations policy was, additionally, an arena for struggle and contestation, invoking at certain points a polarization of interests between community groups desiring anti-racist reforms and employees within the school system. Many school staff feared that the subcommittee was conducting a "witch hunt" and reacted defensively to the opening up of discussion on race relations. Although willing to acknowledge that racism was a problem in general, they were unwilling to concede the existence of racism within their schools. The recommendation to establish affirmative action programs for the hiring and promotion of visible minority teachers provoked the most widespread anxiety and

fierce opposition—understandable reactions in a context of declining en-
rollments, school shutdowns, teacher layoffs, and general economic dete-
rioration. As a result, the Board's policy with regard to the employment
and promotion of visible minority groups has subsequently been softened
and made less threatening to the majority of school staff. Hiring and
promotion policies for visible minorities now adhere to the "equal opportunity principle" originally rejected by the subcommittee on the grounds
that this measure would not be effective in altering institutional discrimination and would merely guarantee the continued exclusion of visible
minorities.

The Toronto Board's race relations policy can thus best be viewed as
part of an *ongoing* struggle to extend local working-class and minority
group control over educational institutions rather than the *end point*
of such a struggle. One policy is by itself unlikely to subvert the institutionalized and discretionary power of primarily white, middle-class
school staff over minority, working-class children and parents. Moreover,
in the context of increasing attacks on social programs and growing popularity of neo-conservative ideologies, continued vigilance and pressure
on the part of community groups and their allies within the Board are
clearly required to ensure that the progressive bent of the race relations
policy is not dulled in the process of implementation.

Conclusion

The race relations policies which emerged in local state institutions in
Toronto during the 1970s and early 1980s were neither completely "coercive" nor "progressive" in their consequences for minorities. The Toronto
Board of Education's race relations policy provided legitimacy for the
anti-racist concerns of visible minorities, established new vehicles for the
redress of minority grievances and enlarged community control over local
education.

Interventions of this type do not by themselves eradicate the racism
which was revealed in the Board's own investigations to percolate through
virtually all educational practices. They do represent an important first
step in countering the institutional sources for the denigration and subordination of ethnic minorities, through a process that has made educational policy more accountable to local minority communities. Such
successes in the radical democratization of the educational system stand
in sharp contrast to the staunch resistance to anti-racist reforms and
democratizing pressures shown by the Metro Toronto police.

Although not a product of a working-class movement, the advances
made by anti-racist forces within the Toronto public school system are

similar to the objectives of struggles in education by the "larger working class." The basic aim of such struggles is to restructure educational curricula to incorporate the lives and concerns of workers. It must be recognized, however, that in a city settled by immigrants, many with collective histories of racism and colonialism, the lives and traditions of working-class children are far from homogeneous and consist of a set of similar but discontinuous histories. Given that the demands placed by Canadian capitalist development for cheap and appropriately skilled labor have largely been met through immigration, the texture of workers' lives is mediated by particularistic cultures, their pasts and histories of migration. The ethnically and racially differentiated communities of the working class which are commonly perceived as hindering working-class solidarity can provide separate, but reinforcing, sources of refuge and energy for working-class resistance. The strengthening capacities of ethnic community solidarity for such resistance bore fruit in the progressive anti-racist reforms made within the Toronto public school system.

Why did the minority campaign to dismantle racism within the schools secure far greater reforms than the campaign to fight racism in local policing? To be sure, the accomplishments in education were the product of assertive and well-coordinated strategies, supported by an informed and active base within the Black and other minority communities. It is doubtful, however, that these strategies would have achieved such impressive results in the absence of a responsive framework for negotiation and consultation *within* the local educational authority. This was especially true for the left-leaning public school trustees, ideologically predisposed to be responsive to the demands of community groups.

Non-accessibility to popular control of state institutions was blatantly evident in the Black community's contestation of racist practices within the Metro Toronto police force. In spite of the unparalleled assertiveness and astuteness of the Black community's efforts and its success in integrating its activities within a wider campaign to democratize the police, senior officials in charge were able to expend their vastly greater resources to wear down and outflank their opponents. In contrast to the key actors within the local educational institutions, the major decision-makers within policing were appointed officials of the provincial government and thus much less responsive and accessible to local (including minority) communities. In the context of new priorities established in the larger Canadian political economy since the mid-1970s, local police authorities perceived a need to further centralize control so as to better manage the tensions inherent in the crisis. Accordingly, they were unpersuaded by even forceful, popular appeals to vest greater control over the police in the local community.

The minority initiatives examined in this paper suggest the possibility that authentic anti-racist political activity can find a place in state practices without being submerged by state priorities in relation to maintaining accumulation and social harmony. Two political implications can be drawn from the foregoing analysis for minority groups and those supporting struggles for racial equality. First, there is a clear necessity to develop strategies which identify and extend the potential spaces within state bodies for manoeuvring and intervention by anti-racist forces, while recognizing the special and formidable obstructions in seeking access to repressive institutions such as the police.

Second, given that a considerable segment of the Canadian population is indifferent and even hostile to anti-racist goals, any anti-racist movement must treat seriously the need to "universalize" its concerns within a larger, working-class or popular democratic movement to attenuate the multiple sources of oppression within the state and civil society.

NOTES

1. It was these unfamiliar racial tensions in Toronto which evoked my interest and concern upon returning to the city after an absence of three years. I decided to choose as the topic of my doctoral dissertation the efforts by the minority communities to combat racism. Daiva Stasiulis, "Race, Ethnicity and the State: The Political Structuring of South Asian and West Indian Communal Action in Combatting Racism," unpublished Ph.D. thesis, Department of Sociology, University of Toronto, 1982.

2. In the late 1970s, estimates placed the Black population residing in Metropolitan Toronto at 156,000 to 200,000 of which approximately 130,000 to 160,000 were gauged to be West Indian. *Globe and Mail*, January 10, 1978. Although the diverse West Indian population is more appropriately defined in cultural than "racial" terms (e.g., by skin color), it is widely considered to form part of the Black community in Toronto. The coincidence of the efflorescence of international black power movements with the influx of West Indian immigration to Toronto contributed to the "racial" definition of the West Indian population and its organizations.

3. "South Asia" refers to the region comprised by Indian, Pakistan, Bangladesh and Sri Lanka. By the mid-1970s, estimates of the South Asian population in Metro Toronto ranged from 60,000 to 100,000 (or three to five percent of the total population). Sikhs from the Punjab form the largest community; but there are also many Hindus, Muslims, Ismailis (a Muslim group),

Christians and Buddhists, originating from different regions in South Asia, as well as from different countries to which they had previously migrated. Indira Subramaniam, "Identity Shift—Post Migration Changes in Identity Among First Generation East Indian Immigrants in Toronto," unpublished Ph.D. thesis, Department of Sociology, University of Toronto, 1977.

4. Ernesto Laclau and Chantal Mouffe, *Hegemony and Socialist Strategy*. London: Verso, 1985; Jean Cohen, *Class and Civil Society*. Oxford: Martin Robertson, 1983; John Urry, *The Anatomy of Capitalist Societies*. London: Macmillan Press, 1981; see also the special issue on social movements in *Social Research*, 52(4), 1985.

5. Laclau and Mouffe, *ibid*.

6. Ellen Meiksins Wood, *The Retreat from Class*. London: Verso, 1986.

7. E.P. Thompson, "Eighteenth Century English Society: Class Struggle Without Class?" *Social History* 3, May 1978, p. 151.

8. Frances Henry, "The Dynamics of Racism in Toronto," Department of Anthropology, York University, mimeo, 1977; Raymond Breton, "The Ethnic Community as a Resource in Relation to Group Problems: Perceptions and Attitudes," Research Paper No. 122, Centre for Urban and Community Studies, University of Toronto, May 1981. For national surveys of racism, see John Berry, Rudolf Kalin and Donald Taylor, *Multiculturalism and Ethnic Attitudes in Canada*. Ottawa, 1976; Glen Filson, "Class and Ethnic Attitudes in Canadians' Attitudes to Native People's Rights and Immigration," *Canadian Review of Sociology and Anthropology*, 20(4), 1983; Canada, Minister of State, Multiculturalism, "Race Relations and the Law," Report of a Symposium held in Vancouver, April 1982.

9. Quoted in Daniel Hill, *Human Rights in Canada: A Focus on Racism*. Toronto: Canadian Labour Congress, 1977, p. 41.

10. Wilson Head, "The Black Presence in the Canadian Mosaic," Toronto: mimeo, 1975; Bhausaheb Ubale, "Equal Opportunity and Public Policy: A Report on Concerns of the South Asian Canadian Community regarding their place in the Canadian Mosaic," submitted to the Attorney General of Ontario, 1977.

11. In February 1969, a number of students held an illegal sit-in at the computer centre of Sir George Williams University. The purpose of this action was to protest a long-smouldering case of perceived racial discrimination against Black students by a white professor. Subsequent confrontation between the students and an armed Montreal riot squad resulted in the arrest of 96 students (45 of whom were black), the sentencing of three Black students to prison terms, and the institution of deportation proceedings against one of the three interned students. Headley Tulloch, *Black Canadians: A Long Line of Fighters*. Toronto: NC Press Ltd., 1975, p. 137.

12. Soon after a well-attended Black People's Conference in 1971, drawing several black power luminaries from abroad, it was revealed by Toronto Alderman Karl Jaffary that the staff of Metro Toronto's police department

intelligence bureau had been enlarged from 44 to 64. The purpose of the additional staff was to increase surveillance of Black Power and other groups. *Contrast*, March 20, 1971. Police surveillance of the Black community's political activities also involved federal authorities. The RCMP employed Warren Hart, a former FBI agent to provide them with inside information about the political activities of Black and Caribbean organizations. *Contrast*, January 10, 1980; Richard Fidler, *RCMP: The Real Subversives*. Toronto, 1978, pp. 74–75.

13. *Contrast*, March 31, 1969; April 7, 1969.

14. *Contrast*, March 22, 1979; *Globe and Mail*, March 21, 1979.

15. Head, *op. cit.*

16. *IIAS Newsletter*, June-July 1978; Ubale, *op. cit.*, p. 58.

17. Ubale, *ibid.*, p. 59.

18. Winfield McKay, a member of the Police Commission, was quoted in a *Globe and Mail* article (April 1980) as saying, "It is becoming more difficult for officers to discharge their duties fairly because of the continued resentment exhibited by some Blacks towards our police. As a result, their community is in danger of becoming isolated not only from the police but from the white majority."

19. *Islander*, February 26, 1976; *Contrast*, November 28, 1980.

20. *Globe and Mail*, September 7, 1979; *Contrast*, October 4, 1979. "Of the five people on the Commission, three are appointed by the province, one is appointed by Metro Council, and the Metro Chair is a member as a result of provincial legislation. Therefore, only one of the five is a publicly-elected member." Maeve McMahon and Richard Ericson, *Policing Reform: A Study of the Reform Process and Policing Institutions in Toronto*. Toronto: Centre for Criminology, 1984, p. 97.

21. *Toronto Star*, September 9, 1979.

22. *Contrast*, September 6, 1979; *Toronto Star*, September 7, 1979.

23. *Toronto Star*, September 12, 1979.

24. *Contrast*, September 6, 1979.

25. *Contrast*, October 18, 1979. The specific demands of the protest, formulated by the Action Committee Against Racism were worded in excessive, provocative language (e.g., "1. Killer cops be charged with murder.") Certain groups distanced themselves from these inflammatory allegations, thus narrowing the base of support for the October 14 rally.

26. *Contrast*, September 20, 1979.

27. The results of a survey conducted by Goldfarb Consultants revealed that in October 1979, 44 percent of Metro Toronto residents felt that the Metro Toronto police were doing an excellent job, whereas 35 percent felt that they were doing a good job. *Toronto Star*, November 21, 1979.

28. *Ibid.*

29. *Ibid.*

30. P.A. Fowler and P. McLaughlin, "The Police Ethnic Relations Unit," Department of Sociology, University of Toronto, mimeo, 1980.

31. *Toronto Star*, September 15, 1979.
32. Roy McMurtry, "Changing Attitudes for the Eighties," Address delivered to the Liaison Group on Law Enforcement and Race Relations Conference, Toronto, March 8, 1980, p. 1.
33. Much of the material and analyses of the Liaison Group presented here is taken from two sources: two interviews with a Metro coordinator for the Liaison Group, Susan Archibald (On March 18, 1980 and March 16, 1981 after Archibald had left the post); and a report commissioned by the Liaison Group written by a social worker, John Gandy. Gandy's report, completed in September 1979, analyzes data collected from observation of the pilot committees and the parent body over a five month period, January-March 1979, individual and group interviews with members, and minutes of meetings. John Gandy, "Law Enforcement-Race Relations Committees in Metropolitan Toronto: An Experiment in Police-Citizen Partnership." Toronto: Social Planning Council for Metro Toronto, 1979.
34. Gandy, *ibid.*, pp. 51, 66.
35. The mandate handed down from the Liaison Group to the pilot committees consisted of three objectives:
    1. To develop a structure that would increase communication between police officials and visible minority groups;
    2. To provide members of visible minorities with a channel for conveying their attitudes about police pratices to appropriate police officials; and
    3. To provide opportunities to interpret methods and procedures associated with effective policing. Gandy, *ibid.*, pp. 70–71.
36. This was the phrase used by a high profile, moderate spokesperson for the Black community, Dr. Wilson Head, in a presentation by the Urban Alliance on Race Relations to the Parliamentary Committee on Visible Minorities, Ottawa, October 6, 1983. Dr. Head conveyed this experience of six frustrating years working on the Liaison Group project, wherein the police members would rarely permit any discussion of police mistreatment, threatening to walk out of committee meetings if the subject was broached.
37. In 1985, the Police Board refused to adopt an affirmative action program for visible minorities in spite of the fact that the Metro force had less than three per cent non-whites among its 5,395 officers. "Police chief wants to hire minorities," *Globe and Mail*, June 6, 1985, p. 16.
38. With the passage of Bill 68, "An Act for the establishment and conduct of a Project in the Municipality of Metropolitan Toronto to improve methods of processing complaints by members of the Public against Police Officers on the Metropolitan Police Force, 1981," a limited role was provided for citizens in the complaints review process, but initial investigations continued to be undertaken by the police. McMahon and Ericson, *op. cit.*, p. 28.
39. Author interview with Susan Archibald, March 16, 1981.
40. Nicos Poulantzas, *State, Power, Socialism*. London: NLB and Verso, 1980, p. 259.

41. Ian Taylor, *Crime, Capitalism and Community*. Toronto: Butterworths, 1983, p. 49.
42. *Ibid.*
43. *Ibid*; Robert S. Ratner and John L. McMullan, "Social Control and the Rise of the 'Exceptional State' in Britain, the United States, and Canada." In Thomas Fleming (ed.), *The New Criminologies in Canada*. Toronto: Oxford University Press, 1985.
44. Toronto Board of Education, *Draft Report of the Sub-committee on Race Relations*, Toronto, May 1978, p. 2. See also Toronto Board of Education, *Final Report of the Work Group on Multicultural Programs*, Toronto, 1976, p. 37.
45. "The immediate spur to starting the project came from an incident in Alexandra Park [a public housing project], in the summer of 1969. [This incident involved] open conflict between Black and Portugese youth over the use of space at St. Christopher House, and resulted in a high level of police brutality against Black youth." Black Education Project, "The Black Education Project, 1969–1976," Toronto, mimeo, 1976.
46. Subhas Ramcharan, "The Adaptation of West Indians in Canada," unpublished Ph.D. thesis, Department of Sociology, York University, 1974.
47. Garnet McDiarmid and David Pratt, *Teaching Prejudice*. Toronto: Institute for the Studies in Education, Curriculum series No. 12, 1971.
48. S. Sugunasiri *et al.*, "Smarten Up, Indians, and Go Western," in A. Mukherjee (ed.), *East Indians: Myths and Reality*. Toronto, 1978; Ubale, *op. cit.*, p. 88.
49. Ubale, *ibid.*, p. 94.
50. Toronto Board of Education, *Final Report of the Work Group on Multicultural Programs*, 1976, p. 63; Case, *op. cit.*, p. 55.
51. Toronto Board of Education, *Draft Report*, *op. cit.*, p. 8.
52. *Ibid.*, p. 103.
53. Toronto Board Race Relations Committee Agenda, May 22, 1980.

A Grassroots Struggle:
Public Participation in the Eurasian Water Milfoil Issue in the Okanagan Lakes[*]

Melody Hessing

Introduction

The concept of public participation in the decision-making processes of the state is a cornerstone of liberal democracy. Forums such as the public hearing of the administrative tribunal extend public participation beyond the electoral process and enhance citizen access to administrative processes of government.[1] From this pluralist perspective, public participation in the tribunal encourages diversity and balance in the production of decisions. The tribunal is an independent and objective forum. Tribunal members are appointed by government, and considered to be impartial and economically disinterested in the issues at hand. The tribunal is operated according to quasi-judicial procedures, which not only encourage public access, but ensure fairness and a balance among competing forces.

In contrast to this popular liberal image of the public hearing as independent and objective, recognition of the administrative tribunal as an adjunct of the state makes visible a bureaucratic location and professional/technical interface which circumscribe not only its activities, but also the decisions it produces. Although the state acts to initiate and mediate the public hearing, its role is made invisible through ideological hegemonic practices and the complex relations of the administrative structure. How does the state orchestrate the public participation process so as to satisfy both its own needs (legitimation, aggrandizement, social control), while incorporating the often conflicting demands of community grassroots organizations?

[*]My thanks are extended here to Jay Lewis and Jack Warnock of the SOEC for their writing, their grassroots struggle, and their active analysis of political ecology, from which much of this paper is derived.

The experience of the South Okanagan Environmental Coalition (SOEC) in challenging the provincial government's proposed use of herbicides in the Okanagan lakes system is an example of the state's management of public dissent. Between 1978 and 1981, the SOEC was engaged in a number of appeals before the Pesticide Control Appeal Board, the administrative tribunal responsible for the appeal of pesticide decisions. This analysis of grassroots' experience points to an imbalance among competing interests and the relationship among administrative forces which favors the proponent (the provincial government) and works to the disadvantage of community groups. I will demonstrate in this paper how the tribunal elicits and manages participation, and how this understanding of state mediation can redefine the expectations for grassroots involvement.

My own involvement in the South Okanagan Environmental Coalition began in 1977, in conjunction with the activity taking place in opposition to the use of chemical herbicides in milfoil control. As a member of the SOEC, I was engaged in a number of support activities, and was privy to a continual barrage of research, strategy and information sessions, many of which took place in my home. Thus, although much of the data for this paper was gathered from the files and publications of other members of the SOEC, my own observations of, involvement in, and commitment to the organization have also contributed to an understanding and appreciation of the issues.

Milfoil and the Herbicide Issues

Eurasian Water Milfoil (*Myriophyllum spicatum*) is a perennial aquatic plant which first appeared in the Okanagan lakes system of British Columbia within the past two decades. Controversy over milfoil has been directed to its characterization as a "problem," but especially to methods of control. The plant is considered undesirable for a number of reasons. It is regarded as aesthetically unappealing; its decomposition results in shore accumulation of odiferous fragments; its growth restricts water recreation in shallow areas; and it has been accused of damage to the salmonid environment.[2] It is thus viewed as economically and environmentally detrimental, especially in areas like the Okanagan, which are highly reliant on recreation and tourism.

Although the weed is generally regarded as a nuisance, environmental organizations argue that milfoil is not totally harmful. In their view, it provides habitat for fish, filters and improves water, mines nutrient sediments and impedes algae growth. Furthermore, the restricted appearance of the weed to shallow rich environments limits its potential spread. The appearance and increase of milfoil is taken by environmental organizations to be an indication of environmental change or degradation. From this perspective, attention should be redirected from weed control to the reduction or elimination of the process of eutrophication and nutrient enrichment of the lakes.[3]

Milfoil, nonetheless, continues to be generally recognized as a problem, and its proliferation has prompted calls for its containment through a variety of methods. These methods have been the major source of debate. Among the potential methods are biological control, mechanical harvesting, or chemical treatment. The primary conflict has centered around the use of the herbicide 2,4-D (2,4-dichlorophenoxyacetic acid), in milfoil control. The Water Investigations Branch (WIB) of the B.C. Department of the Environment advocated the use of this herbicide in conjunction with other means of milfoil control, as efficient, economic, and safe, and applied for permits for application of this herbicide beginning in 1978.

The use of chemical herbicides in the treatment of Eurasian Water Milfoil has generated considerable opposition from the public. Citizens and public interest groups have cited a number of risks associated with the use of 2,4-D. Their primary concern is the health risk to human beings, based on the mutagenic, teratogenic, and carcinogenic effects of 2,4-D on living organisms.[4] In addition to human health risk, harm to fish and wildlife and damage to agricultural crops have also been cited as potential hazards associated with the use of this herbicide. Critics of herbicide use also note that the debate is an economic issue—2,4-D is one of the most widely used pesticides in North America, and is a $2.5 billion industry. In Canada, it accounts for 25% of all herbicide and pesticide sales.[5]

A Chronology of the Okanagan Lakes 2,4-D Issue

The increase of Eurasian Water Milfoil in the Okanagan lakes system elicited government concern beginning in the 1970s, when the Aquatic Plant Management Program within the Water Investigations Branch (WIB) of the Ministry of the Environment initiated research on the growth of milfoil and the effectiveness of various herbicides. In 1976, an Advisory Committee on the Control of Eurasian Water Milfoil in the Okanagan Lake system was appointed, and endorsed an integrated program of mechanical, hydraulic, biological and chemical control of milfoil. On May 5, 1977, the Province agreed to finance, design, and implement a weed control program in cooperation with local officials. The Advisory Committee held a series of public meetings in the spring of 1977 regarding the milfoil issue. That summer, chemical and mechanical control methods were to be tested in four Okanagan lakes, and more widespread use of 2,4-D was forecast for the summer of 1978.

A citizens' group, the South Okanagan Environmental Coalition (SOEC), was formed in the spring of 1977, following the public meetings of the Advisory Committee. This group challenged the proposed use of herbicides in controlling milfoil, and engaged in political lobbying, public education, research, and networking with other environmental organizations to this end. (In a struggle over milfoil, a water weed, it was only appropriate that a "grass-roots" organization should have been spawned.) In March, 1978, the Pesticide Control Act was proclaimed, allowing for formal public participation, through a system of appeals, to challenge decisions approving proposed applications of pesticides. The Pesticide Control Appeal Board (PCAB) was thus established, and its eight members appointed by government.[6] Later that spring, the Water Investigations Branch (WIB) of the Ministry of Environment was granted permits to apply 2,4-D in four of the major Okanagan lakes. A number of individuals and local and provincial organizations (such as the SOEC, The Society for Pollution and Environmental Control, and the Consumers Association of Canada), appealed fifteen permits to apply the pesticide. The hearings were held in June, 1978, in Penticton. The PCAB upheld four of the appeals (those on Osoyoos Lake), but disallowed the remaining eleven.[7]

In the Fall of 1978, the Minister of the Environment stated that no further herbicide applications would be made on Okanagan and Skaha Lakes. In 1979, the use of 2,4-D was confined to Wood and Kalamalka Lakes at the North end of the lakes system. In both 1979 and 1980, appeal hearings took place in Vernon, with decisions by the Board upholding all the permits requested by the Water Investigations Branch. In 1981, permit applications were made for Osoyoos Lake by the Okanagan Water Basin Board, and upheld by the Board in spite of the SOEC's appeal. In 1982, the PCAB had been replaced by the Environmental Assessment Board. Herbicide control programs had been cut back in the Okanagan area, and no permit applications were made.

During the next several years, herbicide applications were proposed and appealed throughout the province. Although the SOEC lost all of its appeals during this period (1978–81), with the exception of the four overturned in 1978, the SOEC claims that its efforts in opposing the use of 2,4-D have been effective in reducing proposed pesticide applications. Nonetheless, the absence of significant public victories in the appeal process, the lack of a shift in agency policy and the continuing existence of the weed promise further controversy.

The Pesticide Control Appeal Board and
its Administrative Context

Before examining the process of grassroots appeal in the PCAB, let us briefly review the process by which herbicides are approved for use. In general, federal jurisdiction does not contain mechanisms for public involvement in the regulation and administration of pesticide use. Thus, public intervention must be geared towards the *application* of herbicides, which is governed by provincial statute. The British Columbia Pesticide Control Act of 1978 "provides for licensing of all pesticide uses [and] permits the administrator to revoke or suspend a license, permit or certificate when a use is likely to cause an unreasonable adverse harm to man or the environment." The Pesticide Control Branch (PCB) of the Ministry of the Environment administers the act, and its activities include licensing, certification, and the issuing of permits.[8] Proponents of pesticide use must make formal application to the Administrator of the PCB for such use, initiating a process through which public participation may later occur.

The permit application is reviewed by the Administrator of the PCB with the aid of a Pesticide Control Committee.[9] When permits are approved by the Administrator, notice of the impending application must be made by the permit holder. Objections to the proposed application must be filed in the form of an appeal, and it is at this point that the public, in this case, the SOEC and other public interest groups, entered the process. The appellant notifies the Administrator of the Pesticide Control Branch of its objection, and then sends the grounds, or reasons, for the appeal. The PCAB schedules a hearing, the appellant(s) appear(s) before it, and present(s) objections to the proposed herbicide application. Thus, the SOEC's appeal to the Administrator of the Pesticide Control Branch initiated the appeal process of the PCAB. I will turn now to an examination of the appeal process itself.

The Appeal Process

Descriptive accounts of the public hearing process are typically restricted to the formal activities of the tribunal, which in the case of the PCAB, are characterized as "quasi-judicial," or semi-formal. That is, the process of appealing a decision to allow herbicide use follows a "relaxed" form of courtroom-like activities. The procedures typically follow this format: the appellant presents evidence, through submissions and expert witnesses, to the tribunal. Each witness may then be cross-examined by the proponent and then the Board. The proponent (the permit holder) is then given the chance to present evidence, which in turn may be cross-examined by the appellant and the Board. Summations are made by both "sides," and a decision is made by the Board within two weeks of the hearing.

This hearing process is understood to satisfy both legal concerns for procedural entitlement and liberal political concerns for diversity, competition and balance. Public input thus ensures heterogeneity in the process of decision-making by the state, and further provides a balance to the bureaucratic forces involved at prior stages of administration and regulation.[10] As a means of contributing to greater public access, attempts are made by the Board to relax procedures by such means as accepting less restricted versions of evidence. Instructions to prospective appellants explain the process in relatively simple terms. Standardization of procedures ensures fairness in that all participants in the hearing are formally entitled to engage in the same process, irrespective of their interest. Although the hearing is essentially an adversarial forum, the submission—cross-examination—summation process contributes to a dialogue among participants, one designed to mediate competition among differing viewpoints and to afford all interests a similar chance to present evidence. The presumed impartiality of the Board also works to neutralize and balance the proceedings. Hearing procedures are thereby considered to encourage a variety of input, and to mediate and equalize the competition among various interests.

However, when we examine the experience of grassroots organizations such as the SOEC before the administrative tribunal, the formal description of the hearing process becomes inadequate. It fails to recognize the generation, and the social and technical organization, of participation as differentially assumed by participants *and* as forces affecting the decisions of the tribunal. This competitive disadvantage for public interest groups is rooted in systematic social and economic inequalities which remain formally unrecognized by the tribunal. The administrative context of decision-making, and the embeddedness of the appeal structure in the state influence the production of decisions by the administrative tribunal. We can thus view the tribunal as an agent for directing dissent in accordance with class and state interests. I will now describe four aspects of the tribunal process by which the state directs grassroots participation: Preparation, Expertise, Administrative Structure, and Decision-Making.

Preparation for Participation

Participants' preparation for an appeal is largely ignored by the official descriptions of the tribunal. Preparation for intervention is treated as an individual and subjective process. This obscures both its extent and the organizational—and economic—support on which it rests. Preparation for the hearings requires appellants to engage in the following: research; identification of and communication with prospective witnesses; preparation of a brief or submission; communication with government agencies; networking with kindred organizations; and internal organization, which includes fund-raising, task allocation, strategy-setting, and publicity.

Prior to the decision to appeal the use of 2,4-D, research on the "unreasonable adverse effects" of 2,4-D was begun by members of the SOEC, as a means of educating themselves and others about phenoxy herbicides. Coalition members worked for seven months to produce *The Other Face of 2,4-D: A Citizens' Report*, a book on 2,4-D and the phenoxy herbicides. Research was conducted through standard library searches and reviews of the literature as well as by networking with other organizations in North America which opposed pesticide use.[11] Thus, by engaging in and producing this research, the SOEC developed lay expertise on the 2,4-D issue. Connections with other kindred groups were forged through this work, which contributed to practical strategy concerning the struggle against herbicide use.

Research and public education were originally defined as the primary objectives of the organization. This research preparation, however, in conjunction with the establishment of the tribunal, enabled the SOEC to appeal the decision approving the proposed 1978 application of 2,4-D. Although SOEC members were skeptical of their potential success in an administrative tribunal appointed by the state, they decided to launch an appeal for additional reasons:

> First, for our public credibility, we had to exhaust all the proper channels. Secondly, we hoped that we could get some possible court action out of the appeal procedure. Thirdly, this was the very first test of the Appeal Board, and we wanted to demonstrate to the public the realities of these government institutions. Fourthly, we knew that we would have a chance to present our evidence, get some publicity, and strengthen our case with the public. This certainly happened. Finally, we decided it was cheaper to make a long fight at this level than in the courts.[12]

The appellants prepared for their appeal by securing information with which to make their case as to the unreasonable adverse effects of the proposed 2,4-D applications. Research required knowledge of a technical vocabulary, methodology, experiments, cases, and issues, many of which had been discussed in their book. A variety of sources were consulted, including technical/science libraries at universities (for journals, textbooks, encyclopedias), researchers or professors engaged in the production, criticism, and dissemination of such information, and lay information networks. In addition, expert witnesses were identified and secured to testify on behalf of the Coalition. Although the SOEC secured considerable information to prepare itself for the appeal, one major problem for grassroots organizations in gaining access to this material revolves around practical and economic concerns. As an SOEC witness informed the Board:

> . . . You have to recognize that we are full-time in other professions, . . . in the Interior. We don't have staff members. We don't have access to libraries. It's *very* difficult to do a research project in this type of environment up here.
>
> Whenever we had to do research, we've had to go to Vancouver. It takes a lot of effort, and time and money, to get away from a job and go to Vancouver. To go to Macmillan [sic.] . . . Library to find out that half the articles on 2,4-D are checked out and wondering who's got them out. So it's difficult to do that kind of work.[13]

In addition to its actual involvement in the appeal process, members of the SOEC engaged in other activities to supplement their struggle both substantively and financially. As two Coalition spokesmen note:

> The Coalition was continually involved with developing additional tools in their efforts to persuade government that the risks involved with using 2,4-D in the Okanagan lakes were unjustified.
>
> . . . Studies were produced on the economics of the various control measures, the natural decline of Milfoil in North America, and the risk theory involved in pesticide application. Each year when we went before the Pesticide Control Appeal Board, a survey of developments in the field along with an annotated literature search was presented. We analyzed the government program up to that time, using their own data, with strong criticism of our own. These quality research reports were the first line of attack. They were widely circulated to all levels of government, allied organizations and the media.
>
> Numerous other techniques were also brought into play. The extensive artistic talent in the valley was tapped for the production of posters, T-shirts, bumper-stickers, and so forth. Leaflets were printed for public information, while newspaper ads served that purpose and, as well, helped finance our efforts. In spite of the complete use of volunteers, costs ranged as high as $12,000 per year at the height of the campaign. We received hundreds of donations from Okanagan citizens without which the massive public education effort would have been impossible.[14]

From the experience of the SOEC in their struggle, we can see that preparation for an appeal is extensive, costly and demanding in time, energy, and funds. Due to the voluntary basis of participation and lack of state subsidization, the SOEC sought member and public support in order to fund its appeal activities. Motivation to participate was supplied primarily by members' belief of the adverse effects of milfoil application, and their conviction that the appeal hearing, in conjunction with the other activities, could influence the administrative decisions of the state.

The SOEC's ability to generate and sustain appeals over the four years of discussion reinforces liberal notions of civic commitment and points to the democratization of participatory access. However, when we compare the preparatory activities, financial support and motivation of tribunal participants—appellant and proponent—we find differences which are of consequence to the success of their activity in the forum. The proponent, in this case the WIB, is motivated not only by its commitment to an administrative policy, but as well by bureaucratic and economic forces surrounding pesticide application (e.g., expansion or cutback of a program, professional networks). The bureaucratic location and activities of the WIB, such as research and on-site studies of pesticide programs, are relied on by the proponent in preparation for the appeal. Indeed, the requirements for the approval of pesticide applications have served as a preliminary basis for the proponent's tribunal activity. The genesis for tribunal participation is thus imbalanced, with the proponent motivated by economic or bureaucratic interests having both additional incentive and extra means to participate.

In contrast, grassroots or community interests are non-productive and extra-administrative. They tend to be diffuse and self-defined, and to lack a direct economic motivation and basis. The class basis of participation reflects a further imbalance among participants of tribunal activity. Where the proponent's interests (the WIB) are administratively located, grassroots class interests are not directly articulated by the tribunal. Tribunal activity, as I will discuss below, is professional work—favoring the representation of voluntary, middle-class interests. This class membership predisposes middle-class members of the public to take part in the tribunal. However, rather than viewing the tribunal as a domain in which relatively equal (middle) class interests compete, we must recognize that the differential abilities and resources available to competing interests result in a further disequilibrium.

Thus, grassroots groups are practically disadvantaged in their preparation for the appeal, due to their extra-bureaucratic, inadequately funded, and temporary character. Moreover, this disadvantage is obscured by the tribunal's emphasis on procedural entitlement, and its failure to recognize this imbalance as structurally produced and systematically effecting an imbalance among competitors.

Expertise in the Appeal Process

The hearing process is characterized by participants' orientation to and reliance on both procedural and substantive expertise. Expertise is the means by which the competition takes place. Although the PCAB is characterized as a "quasi-judicial" forum, legal expertise may be called on by participants to define, argue, and negotiate the procedures adopted by the tribunal. Members of the SOEC describe their sense of the hearing process:

> An appearance before the Appeal Board is an intimidating and mystifying process for the average citizen. The citizen is faced with nine people who know a great deal about pesticides. Questioning comes not only from the members of the Board, but there is a cross-examination by the lawyers for the permit-holder. There is a courtroom atmosphere, and those daring to question the government are really on trial.[15]

Legal expertise is relied on, especially in doing cross-examination, but as well in the presentation and submission of one's position. Thus, legal expertise is one weapon in the struggle between competing interests. However, retention of counsel is considered by the tribunal to be an option rather than a necessity. When counsel is retained, the appellant must individually assume the cost of this service.

In the 1978, 1979, and 1980 hearings legal counsel was retained by the SOEC through the public advocacy services of the West Coast Environmental Law Association (WCELA), which is subsidized by the legal profession and the state. Legal preparation and support costs such as copying and correspondence, and provision of counsel's accommodation were borne by the appellant. As legal counsel, the WCELA engaged in several activities on behalf of the appellant. They filed the appeal, communicated with the Administrator and the Board, and aided the appellants by preparing witnesses, including both experts and SOEC spokespersons. This process included identification of areas to be examined in the submission, preparation for cross-examination, and strategic organization for making a case.

During the 1978–80 hearings, cross-examination was done both by counsel and by SOEC spokespersons. Grassroots members may see themselves as *capable* of assuming this procedural expertise, and may wish to act as their own procedural experts. Nonetheless, this may detract from the competitive success of their efforts. Mr. Warnock of the SOEC states of his 1978 cross-examination experience: "Obviously, even though I knew the stuff really well, I knew his material, I knew how to get at it, I couldn't do it because I didn't have the experience."[16] After the 1981 hearing in which legal counsel were not present, the SOEC speaker reflected on this experience. Mr. Lewis noted that issues arose during the course of the hearings which might have been negotiated, if not resolved, by the presence of counsel, which he says, "allows you to keep your mind on the case and not have to think about the procedures."[17]

Characterization of the tribunal as quasi-judicial infers procedural access to lay (e.g., non-professional) community groups. The availability of state-subsidized legal advocacy services such as the WCELA indicates relative parity for public interest groups competing in the tribunal. This supports the liberal characterization of the tribunal, by which the competitive inequality among participants is again obscured, as is the professional nature of tribunal activity. While grassroots concerns must be "upgraded" so as to access the forum, this translation can also redefine the aims and methods of political action.

Legal expertise is thus one means by which the state manages the grassroots experience in tribunals, through the provision of statutory regulations as well as the professionalization of the participatory experience. Although legal counsel provides a necessary service for grassroots organizations, concern for procedural skills can diffuse the substantive issues and contribute to the professionalization—and co-optation—of lay participants.[18]

Appellants also depend largely on substantive expertise—knowledge, skills and experience relevant to the issues under consideration by the tribunal. The consideration of scientific and technical issues poses particular problems for grassroots appellants who lack both general and specific knowledge in these domains. Although formal access to the decision-making process is provided by the tribunal, the inaccessibility of technical expertise provides a disadvantage to grassroots organizations in the competitive appeal process.

The professional and technical nature of the hearing process contributes to the imbalance among competing interests. Grassroots organizations, which lack resources and organizational strength comparable to those of government or industry, are placed at a disadvantage in a forum predicated on these skills.[19] Moreover, the lack of recognition of hearing costs as a competitive factor allows participation to be regarded as accessible to all, rather than the product of resources which are unequally distributed. The appellant must bear the cost of sponsoring an expert witness, while if the proponent chooses to use expert witnesses, these costs are absorbed by the state.

In the Okanagan 2,4-D hearings, members of the SOEC presented the bulk of submissions made to the Board, utilizing expert witnesses to testify on their behalf. The appellants selected the experts, and paid for their appearance (travel, accommodation, and where appropriate, honoraria). The difficulty for grassroots organizations in utilizing expert witnesses is not only financial, however, but also a reflection of the struggle against entrenched or dominant administrative positions. As members of the SOEC note, regarding their difficulty in locating appropriate witnesses:

> The Coalition's experience with the involvement of the universities on the Milfoil issue has not been good. To date, only one university professor in British Columbia has come forward in support of the public interest research group's position. . . . Other members of the academic community who were willing to lend their expertise had to be brought in from the United States.
>
> On the other hand, there was no reluctance on the part of a number of professors to become involved on the government's side . . . the Advisory Committee is composed of UBC faculty. Four of the seven members of the original PCAB held UBC faculty positions. Two of the three expert witnesses which the government has brought before the PCAB are from UBC. The answer to this question of why there is persistent university support of government and industry may be that they are not convinced that we are right. Or they may realize that public interest organizations have little money or power. Furthermore, we suspect there is a fear that professors who side with activist groups find it difficult to fund research programs, retain graduate students and get tenure. In British Columbia, it is uncommon to find University faculty taking a strong public stand against a government program. Perhaps this situation is to be expected, but it is discouraging nonetheless for people struggling in remote areas on complex issues.
>
> . . . In Canada, there have been few people in positions of authority who were willing to speak out on these issues. . . . The message is clear. If you speak out strongly on pesticide issues as a professional with confirmed credentials, you do so at risk to your career.[20]

For grassroots organizations struggling over issues which have been scientifically defined, the difficulty in securing experts is not simply a question of funding, but is related to the social and economic organization of technical information. Professional networks link corporate, state and university agencies, and reflect a class structure which may exclude grassroots participants.[21] Indeed, the issues addressed by the tribunal (scientific, technical), the nature of the discussion surrounding them (legal, professional), and the incentive and resources needed to participate, discourage the representation of grassroots interests in the tribunal.

The Appeal Structure

The structure of the appeal, ranging from the legal organization of the tribunal process to the larger administrative context of the tribunal, operates to the disadvantage of grassroots organizations, as the experience of the SOEC illustrates. In the administrative hearing, the legal concept of the "burden of proof" is a primary organizational feature, and refers to the onus placed on the appellant to override the decision approving the proposed pesticide application. Thus, in the PCAB hearings, the appellant must present evidence which persuades the Board that the Administrator erred in approving the proposed herbicide application. Although the onus could be said to have rested with the proponent (the WIB) at earlier stages in the decision-making process (to establish that the proposed herbicide application would not cause an "unreasonable adverse effect" to man [sic] or the environment), the burden of proof now rests with the appellant. From the administrative perspective, this shift of the burden of proof to the appellant represents a balance in the overall decision-making process. However, from the perspective of the grassroots organization, the assumption of the burden of proof at the one and only stage of the regulatory process in which there is any public input provides an imbalance and a disadvantage to the public. The diminished access to resources (information, funding, time, professional networks) of public interest groups further creates a competitive bias against their position.

In 1981, the PCAB issued the following statement regarding this regulatory context:

> Appellants should be aware that the responsibility for registering . . . chemicals for use as pesticides is vested with the Federal Government. . . . It would . . . be the responsibility of the Federal Agency to ensure that the data upon which it bases its decision is reliable. Before a permit is issued, the application is assessed by a Provincial Pesticide Control Committee composed of people knowledgeable in agriculture, forestry, occupational health, and fish and wildlife.
>
> . . . The Board does not have the extensive organization or background experience available to the Federal Government Agency who made the decision to register the chemical. The Board will give considerable weight to the decision of the administrator and the committee, as well as to the decisions of the Federal agency (Agriculture Canada), and . . . substantial and convincing evidence would be required before the Board would (a) disregard a safety decision made by the Federal authority, or (b) in the absence of new evidence or arguments, interfere with the committee regarding unreasonable adverse effect.[22]

Thus, two sets of administrative decisions, those at the Federal (Agriculture) and at the Provincial level (the Administrator of the Pesticide Control Branch and the Pesticide Control Committee), approving the herbicide, support the position of the permit holder. From a pluralist perspective, this administrative structure can be viewed as a system of checks and balances providing for multiple input, in which the proponent has already had to make a case for the safety of the herbicide. These prior levels of government are assumed to act as a regulatory gauntlet.

This appeal structure poses a number of problems for grassroots appellants. The reliance of the Board on prior administrative decisions, coupled with the inaccessibility of the grounds of these prior decisions was presented as a problem during the 2,4-D hearings by SOEC counsel, Greg McDade:

> Every step of this appeal we've been fighting the problem that we have no knowledge of what the administrator considered. We're fighting a secret decision, and we have to always come up with evidence that proves that someone made a wrong decision, without knowing what grounds they made their decision on.[23]

Thus, although the appellant must make a case for the error of the Administrator of the Pesticide Control Branch in issuing the permits (for herbicide application), the data on which these earlier decisions were based are unavailable to the public. Minutes of the meetings of the Pesticide Control Committee which advised the Administrator are unavailable.

In addition, the administrative organization of the appeal process poses additional problems for grassroots participants. Although the pluralist scenario of public participation depicts the regulation of pesticides as governed by checks and balances within the greater legislative framework, a review of state involvement suggests an administrative bias favoring administrative alliances and working to the disadvantage and restriction of public participation.

The pesticide application was initiated by the WIB but evaluated by another branch of the same ministry. Once the permit has been issued, the public's case is heard by the PCAB which has been appointed by the Minister of the Environment. As members of the SOEC note, "The whole process could hardly be seen to be one where the regulator and appeal processes are at arms length in order to provide democratic checks and balances."[24] Although these various bodies may be administratively separate, the existence of bureaucratic networks and professional alliances would promote action in accordance with these interests, and against the appellant. Thus, the existence and weight of previous decisions, and the administrative location and bureaucratic interdependence of the tribunal indicate its propensity to favor the proponent.

Decison Making

The 1978–81 appeals by the SOEC were largely rejected by the PCAB, in favor of the permit holder. The grassroots organization was successful only in 1978, when the Board decided in their favor and disallowed four permits for herbicide use in Osoyoos Lake. Although members of the SOEC had braced themselves for this news, their failure in the tribunal's decisions was difficult to accept:

> The SOEC presented six and one-half days of evidence, using top experts. The WIB testified for three hours, and gave no evidence. People couldn't figure that out. People think these Boards are impartial. They think if they can provide enough evidence, the Board will logically decide on . . . their their behalf, and they're stunned when they don't . . . since we had all the evidence they'd have to decide for us.[25]

Other decisions of the PCAB also reflect a tendency to support the administrative status quo, and to disfavor the appellant. In his examination of the PCAB's decisions during its first years (1978–79), Kellett found that only seven appeals out of forty-six were allowed.[26] An analysis of the 1981 record of the tribunal indicated that all of the 165 appeals were overturned.[27]

From the dominant liberal pluralist perspective, those who make the decisions represent a heterogeneity of interests. They must have some technical understanding of the issues while maintaining a position of disinterestedness. The PCAB purports to represent a diversity of occupational training and experience regarding pesticide use. Board members are appointed by the Minister of the Environment. Of ten Board members, four are UBC professors, three have agricultural occupations, one is a career civil servant, one a forester, and one the president of a chemical company. The Ministry of the Environment characterized this Board upon its appointment as possessing ". . . an excellent balance of academic expertise, practical business and land-use experience, and more extensive knowledge of B.C.'s various regional needs."[28]

From the perspective of grassroots appellants, however, the representation of professional and managerial interests, technical orientation, and lack of lay representation pose problems for the production of balanced decisions. The absence of women on the Board, especially given the potential adverse effects of pesticides on women due to their reproductive capacities, is problematic. The absence of direct representation of labor interests further deprives appellants of an economic basis from which to address state and bureaucratic interests. The indirect representation of entrepreneurial interests also poses a problem. Members of the SOEC have noted an institutional pro-chemical bias: several members are from academic disciplines or organizations which implicitly or explicitly endorse the widespread use of agricultural chemicals.[29] Thus, a critical analysis of the tribunal as state presence reveals potential professional alliances among tribunal members and proponents, a structural predisposition in favor of administrative interests, and a subsequence disadvantage to the grassroots appellant.

Conclusion

The experience of the SOEC in appealing the use of 2,4-D in the Okanagan lakes system through the Pesticide Control Appeal Board demonstrates how the state mediates grassroots dissent. From this example, we can see how public interest groups organize their activities to conform to the state's articulation of the participation process. In the case of the administrative tribunal, as we have seen, public participation is characterized by adherence to professional (legal, scientific and technical) forms of preparation and involvement, demonstrating dependence on procedural and substantive expertise. The hearing activity is dependent on a bureaucratic and administrative context from which grassroots interests are practically excluded on a daily basis, but to which the tribunal grants a formal, specialized, and limited access.

This analysis contradicts the liberal definition of the tribunal. The state has been defined as external to, yet correcting (in a limited manner) the social and economic inequalities of the society. Yet, the failure of the tribunal to acknowledge differentials among competing participants reveals its predilection to act on behalf of entrenched, advantaged, bureaucratic interests. This also supports the characterization of the tribunal as a class apparatus in capitalist society. Thus, the middle-class requirements of public participation, although conducive to the process of tribunal participation, reflect the economically anomalous position of appellants in terms of both incentive and resources, and works to the systematic disadvantage of grassroots organizations.

This analysis does not dismiss completely a liberal interpretation of the tribunal. The SOEC's appeal does display increased participatory access to state administrative forces. The quasi-legal formality of the hearings, and existence of legal advocacy services such as those provided by the WCELA, indicate a movement for equalization of opportunity within the tribunal. The increased interventionist nature of the state in regulatory decisions also is compatible with the liberal characterization of the state as an independent and objective arbitrator.

Nonetheless, contemporary analysis of the state explains this liberal characterization of grassroots participation as limited by structural and instrumental forces. Structural analysis points to the functions of public participation for the state. The ideological hegemonic practices of the state characterize the administrative tribunal in liberal terms—as independent, publicly accessible, and fair, contributing to its legitimation. The increasing power of the state have been described by a number of Canadian writers (such as Doern, Mahon, Panitch and others). Loney, for example, observes the social and ideological control provided by state funding practices of grassroots organizations:

> What Canada has witnessed is not a genuine increase in grassroots democracy but a move to increasingly sophisticated strategies for reincorporating potentially dissident groups into the mainstream of society. Simultaneously, government funding has ensured the domination of ideas and practices which sustain the existing socio-economic order either directly or by maintaining the illusion of a genuine pluralism.[30]

The state has also been perceived by a number of writers as occupying a position of "relative autonomy." From this perspective, the state has some limited independence from class interests, but as Ratner *et al.* note, this "can never be more than relative and limited since the state's continued existence ultimately depends on the revenues generated by capital."[31]

Instrumentalist readings of the tribunal would note the similarities between Board members, proponent, and industry interests,[32] in which, as Ratner *et al.* note:

> . . . a correspondence of class power and state power is said to exist because of the overt similarities in class background, interests, and world-view between those who shape and run the economy and the personnel of the state. . . . [Among these similarities would exist] common class position, close educational ties, family and personal networks, shared ideological perspectives, and close working relationships between the dominant class and intermediary institutions. . . .[33]

This analysis of grassroots participation in a state-managed tribunal has contributed to the theoretical literature by demonstrating how the state operates as a dynamic force in society. From the PCAB, we can understand how the state functions to maintain and expand its own interests, which are primarily those of bureaucratic expansion and social and ideological control. Nonetheless, public accessibility to the forum and grassroots input to the ongoing policy and regulatory processes cannot be discounted as insignificant. Let us turn now to a final assessment of the SOEC's activities in opposition to herbicide use, and generate some lessons for future grassroots activities.

An evaluation of the SOEC's struggle against the provincial government's proposed herbicide applications must of course attend directly to the organization's failure in the tribunal. As I discussed earlier, the bulk of the decisions of the PCAB went against the SOEC, and favored the proponent's use of 2,4-D. However, the SOEC interpreted these results in a number of ways, many of them favorable to its larger grassroots aims. Although the decisions were made primarily against them, the SOEC found that on a number of occasions, most notably in 1978, the bureaucratic nature of the process served to delay 2,4-D applications beyond their seasonal deadline, thereby serving to prevent the applications (see endnote 7). The tribunal process also produced a public accountability process for the WIB which is not characteristic of the routine operation of state agencies. In terms of the public educational process, members of the SOEC felt that their tribunal involvement, and the associated media coverage, was successful in informing the public of the potential dangers associated with herbicide use and in pressuring the provincial government against herbicide use. In addition, of course, members of the organization became more politically skilled in learning about the issues, tribunal procedures, and the larger process of government confrontation.

Thus, although the immediate decisions of the tribunal process have been disappointing to SOEC members, there is a greater success when we evaluate all the SOEC's organizing activities from the perspective of social change. SOEC members attribute this larger political success to their diverse attack on the milfoil issue. As mentioned earlier, appeal through the PCAB was but one method chosen by the SOEC to challenge herbicide use. Research, the publication of that research, and extensive fundraising activities contributed to the publicity of the issues. Perhaps the most forceful tool of grassroots activity, however, was the formation of political alliances:

> We began by presenting the B.C. Medical Association, the Canadian Public Health Association . . . and the B.C. Registered Nurses Association with a stack of studies on 2,4-D. We asked them to take a stand. They all came out against the 2,4-D program. Their opposition to the position of the bureaucrats from the provincial and federal health departments was a major victory in the battle. We also gained the support of two major farm organizations in the Okanagan, The B.C. Grape Growers and the B.C. Fruit Growers. . . .

The Okanagan Labour Councils, local labor unions, and the B.C. Federation of Labour strongly supported our position, even with financial contribution. . . . All the Okanagan Indian band councils supported our position, and actively worked with us on several confrontations. . . . The SOEC and other local groups conducted petition drives. We did careful public opinion surveys which showed strong majority support for our position. As the issue made the headlines and the evening television, the three opposition parties decided that it was good politics to come out against putting 2,4-D in the Okanagan lakes.

By the end of 1978 forty-six organizations had come out against the use of 2,4-D, with only five in favor—four of these being tourist groups. Even the tourist industry changed their position when they concluded that the bad publicity over the 2,4-D program was hurting business.[34]

This analysis demonstrates that the methods and goals of grassroots organizations must take into account the substantial resources, extensive administrative powers, and multiple needs of the state. When the decision to engage in state-supported dissent activities is made, grassroots interests must recognize their material and structural disadvantage. Nonetheless, participation in state-sanctioned activities may promote a measure of social change, contribute to a diversity in the decision-making process, provide a focus around which activities can be based, and be utilized for educational and publicity purposes. Rather than orient *all* their activities to the ends dictated by the state (i.e., tribunal participation), a diversification of activities maintains some degree of grassroots control, "hedges bets," and is less likely to result in complete disappointment and burn-out. Finally, we must remember, as SOEC members comment on their struggle:

What is required are major and deep changes in our society's political and economic structures. Until that occurs, citizen efforts, whether they seem successful or not, are severely limited in scope. That is not to diminish the need for the effort, but merely to remind political ecologists that their ultimate goals must be ones of major political and economic change.[35]

NOTES

1. The electoral basis of public participation central to more traditional democratic theorists such as Schumpeter, Dahl, Berelson and Lipset has been

extended by contemporary theorists to incorporate ideals of participatory egalitarianism and an extended state regulatory power. Doern, for instance, characterizes Canadian political life as possessing a ". . . high degree of individual freedom and market activity within a system of democratically elected government . . . (and is portrayed by) a benevolent competition among interest groups with the state as independent referee removing the excesses of the marketplace." G. Bruce Doern, *The Regulatory Process in Canada*. Toronto: Macmillan, 1978, p. 3.

2. British Columbia Ministry of Environment, Aquatic Plant Management Program, *Some Facts About 2,4-D*. Victoria: 1978.

3. South Okanagan Environmental Coalition, Submission to Pesticide Control Appeal Board. Penticton, 1978.

4. John Warnock and Jay Lewis, *The Other Face of 2,4-D*. Penticton: South Okanagan Environmental Coalition, 1978.

5. John Warnock and Jay Lewis, "The Political Ecology of 2,4-D," *Alternatives*, Fall-Winter, 1982, p. 35. Roberts reports that pressure is being exerted by the chemical industry through advertising, government lobbying and industry involvement in scientific societies to continue and accelerate local demand. T. Roberts, *Pesticides: The Legal Questions*. Vancouver: Legal Services Society, 1981.

6. The Royal Commission of Inquiry into the Use of Pesticides recommended in its final report (1975) the establishment of a board to which decisions of the Administrator of the Pesticide Control Board could be appealed. "The Board was envisaged as a technical board having the 'capacity to hear and assess the merit of technical arguments brought before it'." *Ibid.*, p. 37.

7. These applications were eventually reduced, due to the Judicial Review requested by the SOEC, the subsequent extension in hearings, and the delay in pesticide applications.

8. Although all use of pesticides on public land is technically subject to permit requirements, the use of permits has generally been reserved for large-scale and aquatic public use.

9. The Pesticide Control Committee, according to the Act, is to be composed of representatives of the agriculture, environment, forestry, and health ministries, and other persons deemed appropriate (s. 17).

10. "Public involvement will tend to lessen regulator 'capture' by regulatees, and will therefore produce more 'balanced' decisions. . . . Since the administrative agency must take an objective position, it is necessary for the public . . . to become involved so that some voice apart from the industry's will be heard, and therefore the traditionally 'unrepresented' interests will have an influence on the decision-makers." David Lenny, "The Case for Funding Citizen Participation in the Administrative Process," *Administrative Law Review* 28, 1976, p. 491.

11. See Warnock and Lewis, *op. cit.*, 1982, p. 34.

12. Warnock and Lewis, *op. cit.*, 1978, Addendum 1, pp. 4–5.

13. Pesticide Control Appeal Board, *Proceedings*, 1978, Statement by John Warnock.

14. Warnock and Lewis, *op. cit.*, 1982, p. 36.

15. *Ibid.*, p. 37.

16. John Warnock, Interview, 1982.

17. These included procedural questions with regard to the status of observer/ witnesses in the hearing, the status of evidence submitted to the Board in previous years and the question of re-submission of this evidence, the Board's restriction of cross-examination, and the introduction of evidence by the Board and proponent during cross-examination. Jay Lewis, Interview, 1983.

18. For further discussion of the implications of grassroots' use of legal advocacy services see Linda Christiansen-Ruffman and Barry Stuart, "Actors and Processes in Citizen Participation: Negative Aspects of Reliance on Professionals," in Barry Sadler (ed.), *Involvement and Environment*. Edmonton, Environment Council of Canada, 1, 1978, pp. 77–102.

19. The total resources of 77 public interest groups are under $5 million, in contrast to corporate, trade, and professional lobbies, who in Ottawa alone number 300, with budgets totalling more than $120 million a year. V. Ross, "Cancelled Due to Loss of Interest," *Maclean's*, July 6, 1981, pp. 42–43.

20. Warnock and Lewis, *op. cit.*, 1982, p. 37.

21. See also Dorothy Nelkin, *Controversy: Politics of Technical Decisions*. Beverley Hills: Sage, 1979.

22. B.C. Pesticide Control Appeal Board, "Statement to be Included with Procedures for Hearing Appeals." Victoria, B.C., 1981.

23. Pesticide Control Appeal Board, *Proceedings*. Penticton, 1978. Statement by Greg McDade.

24. Warnock and Lewis, *op. cit.*, 1982, p. 36.

25. John Warnock, in *Pesticides: The Hidden Assassins*, (film), Legal Services Society, 1980.

26. Stan Kellett, "An Evaluation of the Performance of the British Columbia Pesticide Control Appeal Board." Paper written for Law 415, Environmental Control Techniques, UBC, 1980, p. 10.

27. West Coast Environmental Law Research Foundation, Newsletter, 1983–84, p. 5.

28. *Vancouver Sun*, January 4, 1980.

29. Warnock and Lewis, *op. cit.*, p. 37.

30. Martin Loney, "A Political Economy of Citizen Participation," in L. Panitch (ed.), *The Canadian State*. Toronto: University of Toronto Press, 1977, p. 446.

31. Robert Ratner, Johm McMullan and Brian Burtch, "The Problem of Relative Autonomy and Criminal Justice in the Canadian State." Paper presented to the Canadian Sociology and Anthropology Association Meetings, Vancouver, June, 1983, p. 14.

32. Clement notes, for example, that "the corporate elite is very active in both the state and political systems," while Andrew and Pelletier note that the composition of Canadian regulatory bodies possesses a corporate bias. Wallace Clement, *The Canadian Corporate Elite: An Analysis of Economic Power*. Toronto: McClelland and Stewart, 1975, p. 347; and Caroline Andrew and Rejean Pelletier, "The Regulators," in Doern, *op. cit.*

33. Ratner, *et al.*, *op. cit*, p. 10.

34. Warnock and Lewis, *op. cit*, 1982, p. 36.

35. *Ibid.*, p. 39.

Policing the Gay Community*

George W. Smith

Introduction

Near midnight on February 5, 1981, the intelligence bureau of the Metropolitan Toronto Police raided four downtown gay steambaths and arrested more than 300 men as being either keepers or found-ins of a common bawdy-house. The scope and violence of these raids made them a *cause célèbre*. Three years earlier gay people in Toronto had established the Right to Privacy Committee (RTPC) to defend men arrested in Toronto steambaths under the bawdy-house law. A major result of the February 5 raids was that the RTPC became the largest militant gay organization in Canada. Not only did it organize the largest anti-police demonstrations in recent Toronto history, but its work with a group of progressive lawyers, the largest since the Artistic Woodworkers' strike in the early '70s, resulted in court victories for nearly 90% of those charged. The committee ultimately raised over $200,000 to finance this defense effort. From 1980 to 1984 I sat on the executive of the RTPC. For fifteen months immediately after the bath raids, I served as chairperson of the organization. The writing of this paper comes out of my experiences during this period of my life.

While the bath raids created a serious confrontation between gays and the police in Toronto, serious enough, in fact, for Toronto City Council

*My first attempt to formulate the topic of the police came about as a result of an invitation from David Rayside of University College to speak at a conference at the University of Toronto called *1984 in Canada: Authority, Conformity, and the Policing of Citizens*. I would like to thank Dennis Finlay and Tim McCaskell for commenting on earlier drafts of this paper, and Gary Kinsman for providing historical data on the regulation of sex in Canada.

to commission a special study of the problem,[1] the raids themselves were merely a very dangerous crevasse in what, for gay men, was an already uneven and treacherous terrain. For decades the Toronto police, often using entrapment techniques, had arrested men who were engaging, or who the police thought might engage, in homosexual activity. Over a quarter of a century ago, the then Chief Constable of Toronto, John Chisholm, summarized for the Royal Commission on the Criminal Law Relating to Criminal Sexual Psychopaths some of the problems faced by the police in regulating sex in the city:

> Homosexuality is a constant problem for the Police in large centres, and if the police adopt a laissez-faire attitude toward such individuals, City parks, intended for the relaxation of women and children and youth recreation purposes, will become rendezvous for homosexuals. In addition to his immoral conduct, the homosexual requires further Police attention, as he is often the victim of gang beatings, or robbery with violence, and is easy prey for the extortionist and blackmailer. Homosexuals have been stabbed and wounded and in a few cases have even been murdered. The saddest feature of all, however, is that homosexuals corrupt others and are constantly recruiting youths of previous good character into their fraternity.[2]

As the government of Canada prepared to pass the omnibus Criminal Code bill (C-195) in 1969, decriminalizing gross indecency between consenting adults in private, the police grew increasingly alarmed that this change in the law would result in the "spread" of homosexuality, a spread they would have great difficulty containing.

A month after the Canadian Parliament passed bill C-195, homosexuals in New York City staged a three-day riot over a police raid on the Stonewall Inn, a bar in Greenwich Village. This event would be recorded in political annals as the beginning of the modern gay liberation movement. What was important about the Stonewall riots was how this revolt of what were essentially street people could come to mean so much for so many. As a symbol of gay oppression everywhere, it represented gay people's experience with the police as an agency concerned with regulating sex. The same generalized experience also informed and organized, in part, the May 1979 burning of police cars in San Francisco after Dan White, a former policeman, was given only a seven-year sentence for assassinating George Mascone, the mayor of the city, and Harvey Milk, a gay city supervisor. Two years later similar experiences of police oppression led to the demonstrations of resistance in Toronto following the bath raids.

For the majority of Toronto's gay community, the raids were perplexing. Why they were carried out was a matter of constant speculation. One steambath, at least, had been operating in the city for nearly twenty years. According to the managers and owners of these clubs, most were visited by officers from the morality bureau, which oversaw and permitted their operation. The question of why the police had arrested so many people was also raised continually. If "cleaning-up" or closing down the baths was the purpose, this could have been accomplished without arresting hundreds of individuals. Indeed, the bath raids were the largest mass arrest of citizens in Canada since the federal government had declared the War Measures Act to cope with nationalist struggle in Quebec. And finally, why had the police behaved so viciously? The owners of the clubs claimed that over $50,000 in damage was done to their establishments, and those arrested documented in graphic detail case after case of police abuse.[3]

The need to answer these questions was more than a matter of idle speculation. This was particularly true for the leadership of the RTPC, who had the responsibility of forging a politics that could respond publicly to the raids and to their aftermath, while at the same time continuing to organize the resistance of the gay community. As relations between the police and the RTPC unfolded, organizing became not so much an inquiry into the raids themselves, as an on-going research project into the police and the policing of gays in Toronto. At every point, including the production of this paper, it has been a work-in-progress, constantly shaped by the everyday practical activities in Toronto of the police and of gay people, including the RTPC.

Organizing Our Research

A major problem of organizing research of this kind is knowing how to begin. The knowledge which we, as gay people, have of the police arises out of our historic treatment by them as they carry out their work of regulating sex. Among us, accounts of the efforts of the police to administer our sexual lives circulate mostly by word of mouth, although they appear from time to time in the gay media, as well as in gay history and literature.[4] A fundamental property of such accounts is that they arise locally out of our first-hand experience of being policed, and of having our lives controlled and regulated by the authorities. In trying to make sense of what are for us often violent, brutal experiences, these accounts come to be told and recorded from the standpoint of gay people. They describe the reality of gay experience.

What is implicit in our experience of being policed is that the regulation of sex in our society is not only locally, but extra-locally organized. What I mean by this is that the organization of police work is not straight-forwardly comprehensible within the ambit of a local setting—such as being arrested in a bath raid. Rather, our experience on such occasions suggests that our local, face-to-face treatment at the hands of the police is the result of a much more extensive organization located elsewhere. From time to time, and often at a completely unexpected moment, this organization penetrates the local circumstances of our lives, casting them beyond our control. It is precisely this awareness of the opaque, extra-local character of policing that produces within the gay community a continuously elaborated set of speculative accounts as to why the police behave as they do.

In these accounts, police oppression is sometimes seen as the result of the personal bigotry and brutality of front-line officers directly responsible for local law enforcement—a case of "homophobia simple." On other occasions, accounts are constructed around the rationale of "clean-up" campaigns, etc., in which gay people see themselves merely as pawns in a larger political scenario, such as a provincial election. Another account, recently developed in Toronto, is that of a "mini-economy" in which police harassment of gay people is understood as arising out of a peculiar professional symbiosis involving the judiciary, the police, and the legal profession. The arrest and prosecution of gays, according to this explanation, is not fundamentally a matter of eradicating homosexuality, but is rather a self-serving arrangement whereby the judges have an easy day of it handling guilty pleas that are relatively simple to dispense; the police get their clearance quotas, thereby assuring the "efficiency" of their division, bureau, etc.; and the lawyers obtain their sometimes extravagant fees, very often simply for pleading their double-charged clients guilty to the lesser charge.[5]

There are problems, of course, with these kinds of explanations. While the zeal and enthusiasm with which some officers enjoy arresting gays mark them as homophobic, the organization of the mass arrest of over 300 individuals during the bath raids clearly goes beyond personal bigotry. At this point homophobia and heterosexism take on systemic proportions. Similarly, the fact that after the bath raids Roy McMurtry, who was Attorney General and Solicitor General of Ontario at different times during this period, saw no need for a public inquiry, and indicated, implicitly at least, that the provincial government approved of the actions of the police. Mr. McMurtry claimed on the floor of the Provincial Parliament not to have had any advanced knowledge of the raids, let alone to have ordered them to coincide with the impending provincial elections. This was despite the fact that support for gay rights (which under the circumstances was tantamount to support for bathhouse sex) could have proved to be a difficult election issue for the opposition parties—especially for the New Democratic Party (NDP) which in theory supports gay rights as party policy. According to the Tory government's account, the raids were not part of a master plan to win the election. Indeed, Staff Inspector Donald Banks, head of the police intelligence bureau responsible for the raids, testified before the House of Commons standing committee on justice and legal affairs that he, and he alone, was responsible for ordering them.[6] It was precisely these kinds of problems with the speculative character of our explanations of the bath raids that demonstrated the inadequacy of our ability, within the scope of local events, to come to grips with the extra-local organization of police oppression.

As we thought about the problem of how to begin our research, one thing became clear: our interest in the regulation of sex arose out of our generalized, everyday experience as gay people of having our sexuality denied and our lives overrun and sometimes destroyed by the police. Like those in the past who have speculated about why the police behave as they do, we wanted to know how this sort of thing was happening to us. Thus, the basis of our inquiry was neither theoretical nor abstract. Rather, our experience of policing directed us to attempt in a very practical way to address as a problem the relation between gay men and the society in which we live. We wanted our study to assist us in understanding our world with a view to transforming it. Toronto was not the first city where gays had a problem with the police, and the RTPC was not the first organization to attempt to change the way in which the police treated gay people. By the late seventies, in fact, various jurisdictions across North America had proposed a number of solutions to this problem, such as the hiring of gay police, psychological testing to weed out homophobic recruits, gay- police liaison committees, and better in-service training. By the early 1980s, however, it became clear that none of these strategies held much promise for improving gay-police relations. Nonetheless, they provided the context for the political debate around what to do about the police.

Beginning with the experience of having our sexual lives regulated by the authorities, we decided to render this opaque feature of our everyday world problematic.[7] We used the notion of "problematic" to set out a form of inquiry that, starting from the position of individuals in the everyday world, is directed at illuminating how their world is shaped and determined by social processes that go beyond it—specifically in our case, the work of the police in regulating sex. This was to be a study not *of* gay people, but *for* them.

Our Study of the Police

For a number of years, the RTPC gathered data on the police as it was generated day by day out of the bath raids and their aftermath. This work was not initially seen in any technical sense as research. One thing we did, however, was to keep an extensive collection of newspaper clippings. Another was to record raid-related TV coverage on a VCR. Our periodic meetings and discussions in committee with the defense lawyers also supplemented, second-hand, our knowledge of police practice. As the case of the found-ins slowly ground through provincial court, the RTPC executive continued its study of policing, mainly by inviting experts to talk about their experience with and research on the police. Also, as part of the City Council's inquiry into the raids, the Police Chief sent a letter to the Mayor which included an internal report from Staff Inspector Banks to the chief on how the raids were conducted. This report constituted our first primary data on the internal workings of the police. After the 1981 raids, the police continued to raid the baths sporadically. In the spring of 1983, officers from the morality bureau arrested 24 individuals as keepers, found-ins and inmates of a common bawdy-house at the Back Door bath. The RTPC, in defending those arrested in this raid, came into possession of the preliminary disclosure documents provided by the Crown Attorney's office to the defense attorneys as part of pre-trial preparations for those individuals accused in the Back Door case of being "keepers" of a common bawdy-house. These documents, describing the pre-raid investigation of the bath, became the second set of primary data on the internal operations of the police.

It is how we used these documents to carry out our research on the police that I want to describe now. I am going to use the disclosure document's account of the "First Visit" of the undercover officers (i.e., secret police) to the Back Door bath to illustrate our procedure:

> **First Visit**
> Constable Coulis and Procter attended at the premises, entering separately, where they approached the cash area. It was at this location that the officers first saw the accused; who was later identified as [John DOE]. [DOE] was the only employee that the officers saw that night. [DOE] was the one who permitted the officers access to the premises once they had paid the fee for either a room or a locker.
> When the officers first entered the premises they walked around and noted the lay-out of the premises as well as any indecent activity that

was taking place at that time. It was at this time that both officers saw a number of men laying [sic] nude in their private booths with the door wide open. Some of these men were masturbating themselves while others just lay on the mattress watching as other men walking about the hallways. The officers took periodic walks about the premises and they saw that the same type of indecent activity was taking place each and every time. During the course of the first visit the officers made certain purchases from [DOE], who was working in the office area. The office area was equipped with numerous sundry items available to the patrons for a fee: pop, coffee, cigarettes, vaseline and various inhalants. The officers watched [DOE] on two separate occasions when he left the office area to clean rooms that had just been vacated. On each of these occasions, [DOE] walked past a number of rooms that were occupied by men who were masturbating themselves. At no time did [DOE] make an effort to stop these men, or even suggest that they close the door to their booth so that these activities would no longer be visible to other club patrons.

"Social Form" and "Social Relations": A Way of Investigating and Talking about Social Organization

The procedures we used in treating this document as basic data in our research are those which Dorothy Smith has developed and advanced over the past decade as a method of textual analysis. This method takes as a basic premise that the social world in which we live depends for its continued existence on the practices and activities of people. In doing so, it reveals that the documents which people produce and use both *express and co-ordinate* the social forms of these activities.[8] "Social form" is used here to point out and investigate the ways in which people's activities are neither random or chaotic, but rather constitute a particular social relation. The notion of a "social relation," in turn, is used to examine courses of action, developed intersubjectively and inter- twined and extended over time, in which people participate, but which no one person both initiates and completes. For us, the policing of gay people comes to have just such a distinct social form: an institutional relation regulating our sexual lives that is constituted and reconstituted in the routine procedures and practices of the police. To think about policing this way is to see how it is that local events are situated within the structure of more extended social processes.

An important discovery of contemporary sociology, credited to ethno- methodology,[9] is that documents are part of the make-up of social rela- tions. That is, documents only make sense within the social organization of their construction and use. Thus, making sense of the police account of the "First Visit" depends on a taken-for-granted understanding of the organization of a police investigation (i.e., an investigative relation). For example, to understand why the officers reported taking periodic walks around the bath and seeing the same type of indecent activity on each and every occasion requires locating this account in a particular course of action: making an investigation of a bathhouse under the provisions of the *Criminal Code*. It is the *Code's* structure of relevance that provides for the "common-sense" interpretive practices used by police officers (and for that matter, lawyers, judges, etc.) in constructing and reading this account. Its social organization is part of the work of the police because it is procedures involved in enforcing the law that make sense of the officers walking around the bath and reporting seeing the same type of "indecent" activity on each occasion.

Indeed, what the police see as "indecent" activity is organized and experienced very differently by gay men. The social form of gay activity in a steambath is not one of investigating and reporting "crime," but a social relation that aims at producing sexual encounters. It is this to which gay men are oriented. Coulis' and Proctor's activities as police officers, however, are not concerned with having sex. The social organization of their work, oriented to the requirements of the *Criminal Code*, is located very differently. Its *mise-en-scène* is extra-local. While gay men in the bath would describe themselves as engaging in sex, even "hot" sex, and other erotic and eroticizing activities, they would not see themselves as engaging in "indecent" acts. To see what is going on as "indecent," in the sense in which the officers went around observing "indecent" acts, requires the contextual overlay of the *Criminal Code*. Consequently, what comes into view in analyzing the social organization of the officers' account of the "First Visit" is a textually-mediated work process, extra-locally organized, that transforms a scene of sexual pleasure into the site of a crime. It is in this relation that the sexual activities of the bath patrons are transformed into "indecent acts" and an ordinary individual, the bath attendant, eventually becomes "the accused." It is precisely how the "First Visit" account reconstructs a local event in terms of the structure of relevance of police work that displays it as an extra-local organizational accomplishment, and underscores its embeddedness in that organization.

The Social Organization of Gathering Evidence: Inscription

Following this analysis, we took up the next part of our research by attending to the ways in which Coulis and Procter's report is integral to the social relation of "investigating crime" or "gathering evidence" as its context. It is important to keep in mind that in examining the account the police provide of their actions and of what they see, we are not investigating its "truth," but rather its social organization. We are not interested in reading through the text to a set of circumstances that lie behind it and which it is taken as representing. Within the context of "investigating crime" the report of the "First Visit" is a story about bath attendant John DOE, who lets the patrons of the bath masturbate in public. What creates this story are the legal "facts" of the report. These "facts," in turn, are created by the use of inscription techniques[10] that are an essential part of the work of gathering evidence, and therefore internal to the organizational properties of the report. "Inscription" is used here to point out the practices involved in producing an event or object in documentary form as a "fact" about the world. Masturbation becomes the "fact" of "indecent acts," not because of what Coulis and Proctor see as such, but because of what they report. It is only on the basis of what the officers report, rather than on what they see, that the bath is raided, for example. Consequently, "indecent acts," as a legal "fact" about activities at the Back Door bath, only exist as a product of their being inscribed in the report.

This technique is the means by which events in the ordinary world are reconceptualized and entered into documentary reality.[11] The legal "facts" of the report are constructed by the inscription techniques as discursive objects,[12] textually-mediated to the world through the categories of the *Criminal Code*. It is precisely the mediating work of the *Code*, in fact, that makes these "facts" *legal* "facts." These procedures provide a different mapping of the activities and individuals at the Back Door, locating the "indecent acts" and the "accused" on paper, in documents. It is as they are inscribed (i.e., mapped) in a police report as "facts" that these phenomena come to constitute a documentary reality that organizes the *modus operandi* of the police. In other words, it is because the officers *report* (i.e., inscribe the "fact" of) "the same type of indecent activity . . . taking place each and every time" they walked about the premises, for example, that the police raid the bath, and that DOE is arrested, thereby becoming an "accused" slated for trial.

As part of our investigation of inscription we went on to analyze its ideological properties. But before reporting on this part of our research, I want to describe a feature of police inscription techniques central to how a policing relation is able to penetrate our lives as gay men. This is the way in which individuals are transformed into legal "facts" and in the process entered into and held in the on-going institutional relations regulating sex. The institutional relation of policing takes the form of a sequential series of moments, investigation-raid-arrest-trial, organized internally across various institutional sites, where the former intends the latter and the latter, in turn, accomplishes the former. That is, the investigation of the premises intends a police raid which accomplishes the purpose of the investigation; the raid, in turn, intends the arrest of individuals which accomplishes the raid; and so on and so forth. It is the way in which these various moments are knitted together and organized as an internal relation that makes these activities a course of action.

Throughout the report of the "First Visit" the family name of the bath attendant is written into the account in uppercase letters, which not only emphasizes his centrality to the "facts" of the account, but, more importantly, transforms him by this very activity of naming into a "fact," himself, about activities at the Back Door.[13] It is by being transformed this way into a legal "fact" that he is "identified" to the authorities, and thereby caught up and held in the sequential moments of this documentary mode of action. By way of contrast, the individuals masturbating in their private booths are not named, consequently not identified, and therefore not swept up individually into this investigative relation. For the time being, all that is required is to observe and record their "indecent acts" as evidence (i.e., legal "facts") against the bath attendant. What these procedures for naming individuals in the disclosure document display, consequently, is that inscription as a documentary procedure does not merely describe, it picks out, lodges and secures an individual within an investigative course of action. In this way it co-ordinates and concerts an investigative relation, and is an important means by which this extra-local, regulatory relation penetrates the local setting of gay men's lives.

The Social Organization of Gathering Evidence: Ideology

The next part of our study undertook to probe more deeply the social form of these techniques, specifically their ideological and conceptual properties and their legislative context. Following Smith and with an eye to the materialist foundations to our research (i.e., that the social world is constituted in the activities of people) we did not use the notion of "ideology" to reference personal mental states such as beliefs or, put more grandly, a political *Weltanschauung*. Nor did we follow the Mannheimian tradition of ideology as biased knowledge, tainted by class interests or whatever,[14] which is how it is ordinarily used in traditional sociology. Instead, we used "ideology" in a materialist sense to point out the social form of the textually-mediated reporting practices of the police. The procedures we were interested in, of course, were the inscription techniques the police used to construct the "facts" of an investigation.

Figure 1: Smith's Ideological Circle

A		B		C		D
steambath activity	→	encoding	→	"First Visit" report	→[15]	Criminal Code

In the case of the Back Door, these techniques, as I have said, formally transformed a scene of sexual pleasure into the site of a "crime." In this process they come to appear as an "objective" form of knowing, where the analysis and description arising out of them is not articulated directly to the actual social organization of the bath, but instead is constructed in terms of what is important about this setting for the purpose of ruling it (i.e., regulating sex). The organization of this form of knowing involves what Smith calls an ideological circle.[16] The ideological circle is a two-phase process: first, there is an interpretive phase where events are analyzed as documenting an underlying pattern originating in a textual discourse (in this case, the *Criminal Code*'s conception of "crime"—"bawdy-house," "indecent acts," "keeper," etc.); and a second phase where the underlying pattern operates as part of the procedures for selecting, assembling and ordering these "facts."[17] In the Back Door bath case, an ideological circle is produced when the masturbatory activities of the bath patrons are treated as documenting "indecent acts," the *Criminal Code* conception of which is used in the first place to generate this "fact" about these activities. Each is used to elaborate the other. Figure 1 schematizes this form of organization. In Figure 1, the actually social organization of a gay steambath, represented in box A, is transformed by an encoding process, represented in box B, into the legal "facts" of a police report, box C. The encoding process is governed by the interpretive schema of box D, which in this instance is the *Criminal Code*'s conception of a "bawdy-house." What is important is that the account intend the conceptual schema by being read as referencing the phenomenon of the schema.

In the disclosure document the "facts" about the Back Door bath (i.e., "indecent acts," "not stopping individuals from masturbating," etc.) are used to document and "underlying pattern" of a "common bawdy-house." It is, however, how a "bawdy-house" is defined (i.e., conceptualized) in the *Criminal Code* (see Figure 2) that provides the procedures for selecting and ordering these observations (e.g., "indecent acts" + a person in charge who does not stop them = a "keeper of a common bawdy-house") as documenting this underlying pattern. The bath is not a "bawdy-house" as such. The Back Door is only describable as a "bawdy-house" in the report by virtue of how a "bawdy-house" is defined in the *Code*. The legal definition, as referencing an underlying schema of "bawdy-house," and the "facts" of the case are used, in this fashion, to elaborate one another. What is meant here by "ideology" is this circular organization of routine police practice that makes it possible to describe events and individuals located in the everyday world of a gay steambath in the abstract, legal terminology of police work. In this process, the ordinarily pleasurable activity of jacking-off comes to be described as an "indecent act." This transformation is not merely some sort of artful piece of trickery, but rather a procedure essential to administering sex under the *Criminal Code*. The textually-mediated social organization of this ideological circle provides the means of accounting for actual activities going on in the everyday world in terms of the formal categories which co-ordinate objectively, rationally, a ruling apparatus. It is in this sense that the legal conception of a "bawdy-house" is a ruling idea and ideology; the practical means whereby this ruling idea comes to shape people's lives. What is central to this process is how it goes forward on paper; how it takes the form of a textually-mediated relation.

The Social Organization of Gathering Evidence: A Conceptually-Determined Relation

Our research had started out with a view to seeing how it is that local events are situated within the structure of more extended social processes. We took Coulis' and Proctor's account of their "First Visit" to the Back Door bath as an artifact of just such an extended process. Our research began by substructing the lineaments of its social organization. The early stages of our investigation centered on how the report of the "First Visit" was structured by the work of gathering evidence. This led us to focus on inscription as that feature of police work that displays the internal relation between a police report and its organizational context.[18] In turn, our analysis of inscription revealed how police work is organized conceptually, that is, how it takes the form of an ideological practice. Our discovery of the conceptual/ideological form of police practice now made it possible to describe how police work is conceptually co-ordinated and organized by the *Criminal Code*. This located the work of Coulis and Proctor in a broader context. Within this context, however, to describe policing as "gathering evidence" merely begged the question, organizationally speaking. What we had to look

at now was, what does this notion of "evidence" that informs the *Code*
presuppose? This led to the necessity, at least in a cursory way, of
substructing the conceptual apparatus of the *Code* to display the social
form of organization which this document expresses (i.e., its structure
of relevance), and which the police are hired to enforce—in this case, a
heterosexually-organized society where legitimate sexual activity is not
only "decent" (i.e., focused on procreation) but also takes place within
a domestic relation. "Domestic" should not be read here as synonymous
with "marriage," but as intending various social forms that either tend
towards (e.g., pre-marital sex) or approach in one way or another (e.g.,
common-law marriage) married life.

Our first step in this direction, as I have already mentioned, was realizing, through our analysis of the ideological organization of Coulis' and
Proctor's report, how the work of inscription, and therefore, in these
circumstances, ruling practice, begins with concepts. It was to this phenomenon that we now turned our attention in order to explicate the
organizational context of police work. What we found was that legal
concepts, far from being theoretical entities divorced from the practical-
ities of everyday life, constitute a fulcrum from which a ruling apparatus
gets purchase on the lives of those it seeks to govern. Our analysis now
proceeded to examine the way in which legal concepts organize the work
of the police. Here, it is important to keep in mind the work that the
Criminal Code does in transforming legal concepts into procedures. The
Code constitutes a set of procedures and a form of organization.

I pointed out earlier that the social relation regulating sex consists
of a set of sequentialized moments: investigation-raid-arrest-trail. What
I want to illustrate now is how the conceptual features of the bawdy-
house law in particular, and the *Criminal Code* in general, organize this
sequence. More especially, I want to examine how the paperwork involved in gathering the "facts" in the Back Door case articulates the
conceptual features of the bawdy-house law to the various moments
of this regulative relation, in the process organizing and concerting it.
What a bawdy-house is, is a matter of a legal definition and not simply a matter of ordinary usage. This means that the police, following
the procedures of the *Code*, must be sure that the definition applies
to a particular premises before the patrons can be arrested as found-
ins. In other words, the conceptual character of the law, transformed
in this instance into rules of evidence,[19] requires a three-step process:
investigation-raid-arrest, rather than the police simply going out, ran-
domly raiding premises and arresting individuals (if any) having sex
outside of a domestic relation. Thus, the law ordinarily requires an

investigation to precede a raid. In Toronto the investigation of a gay bathhouse can take six months or more.[20] The process of investigation provides, in part, for the organization of secret police units, such as the Morality Squad and the Intelligence Bureau.

This relation between the conceptual character of the law and the organizational moments of this documentary course of action (i.e., investigation-raid-arrest) governs the work of inscription. The "facts" inscribed in the report of the "First Visit" to the Back Door, for example, take as their structure of relevance proving that the premises operated as a common bawdy-house, and that John DOE was a "keeper."[21] (See Figure 2) Again, this is evident from how the names of the men masturbating in their open rooms are not inscribed in the disclosure document. Rather than being used to arrest these men, the evidence of "indecent acts" is to be employed at a future date to justify a raid on the Back Door and to arrest the patrons at that time, whoever they might be, as found-ins of a common bawdy-house. As part of this sequencing of police activities, the law requires that evidence alleging that a premise is being used as a bawdy-house be collected first, before a raid can take place. Thus, the social organization of inscription in Coulis' and Proctor's report, in concentrating on the legal "facts" of "keeping," co-ordinates the work of regulating sex by attending to the organization of a police investigation required by the *Criminal Code*. This underlines how the work of the police is a textually-mediated form of organization.

The Social Organization of Gathering Evidence: A Mandated Course of Action

The way in which the conceptual properties of the *Code* shape the organization of a police investigation is also evident from how the "facts" inscribed in Coulis' and Proctor's report are contextualized by very specific activities on the part of the two officers. It was when they ". . . *approached* the cash area," for example, that they first saw the bath attendant, John DOE. Likewise, it was in *walking around and noting* "the layout of the premises" that the officers saw ". . . a number of men laying [sic] nude in their private booths . . ." and that ". . . some of these men were masturbating themselves. . . ." And of course, it was in ". . . *taking periodic walks about the premises* . . ." that they ". . . saw the same type of indecent activity . . . taking place each and every time." Similarly, the officers *watched* DOE, on two separate occasions, walk past a number of rooms that were occupied by men who were masturbating themselves and make no effort to stop them. This account of the actions of the two officers is obviously a very partial one because it does not describe their personal behaviour: perhaps hitching up their pants, having a smoke, going to the toilet, watching people showering, observing the bath's decor and so on and so forth. Indeed, the activities of Coulis and Proctor described in the account are very different from this sort of personal behavior. The attachment of these activities to the "facts" of the account constitute them as "official investigative activities." These are the activities that Coulis and Proctor engaged in in order to carry out their duties as police officers. They are, for example, the kinds of activities about which they could be cross-examined by a defense attorney in a court of law. The fundamental thing about these activities, as our research went on to examine, is that they are determined by the conceptual features of the *Criminal Code*, in the same way as Coulis' and Proctor's reporting attends to the investigation-raid-arrest moments of a policing relation.

In describing our analysis, I am not suggesting that Coulis' and Proctor's account of what they did and saw is not true. Again, the focus of this analysis is not the truth of this report, but its social organization. What is important about these activities, independently even of whether or not Coulis and Proctor actually carried them out, is that they are required as part of the investigation by the conceptual formulation of the bawdy-house law. I am not claiming that these particular actions are necessarily part of this investigation, but that what is required is that the "facts" be contextualized by some investigative actions or other, depending on the circumstances. If there are no official police actions, as is sometimes the case in employing entrapment techniques, for example, where an officer uses personal behavior (e.g., coming on to someone in a public toilet) rather than official procedures, the officers must then invent an account of their investigative behavior to contextualize the alleged "facts" in the case. Thus, the "facts" of the "First Visit," to be official police "facts," require being contextualized by the appropriate investigative (as opposed to personal) actions on the part of Coulis and Proctor. Whether they are true or not the "facts" must be reported in the context of a "mandated course of action"[22] that is determined by the *Criminal Code*. In this way they become, not Coulis' and Proctor's "facts," but "police facts" that could be reported, for example to the press, as an "objective" account of what went on at the Back Door.

It is Coulis' and Proctor's investigative activities mandated by the *Code* that constitutes, as a feature of their report, their *performing* "the police" as an organization. These are not their personal but their official actions and, consequently, are reported formally, objectively, by being described as independent of their subjectivity. This is done by

Figure 2: Section 179, and 193 of the *Criminal Code*

179.(1) In this Part . . .
"common bawdy-house" means a place that is
   a) kept or occupied, or
   b) resorted to by one or more persons
for the purpose of prostitution or the practice of acts of indecency; . . .

*****

193.(1) Everyone who keeps a common bawdy-house is guilty of an indictable offense and is liable to imprisonment for two years.
   (2) Every one who

   (a) is an inmate of a common bawdy-house,
   (b) is found, without lawful excuse, in a common bawdy-house, or
   (c) as owner, landlord, lessor, tenant, occupier, agent or otherwise having charge or control of any place, knowingly permits the place or any part thereof to be let or used for the purpose of a common bawdy-house,
is guilty of an offence punishable on summary conviction.[23]

inscribing these actions (again, yet another inscription technique), actually performed by two different people, in various areas of the bath premises and at different times, from the standpoint of a neutral third party observing "the officers" conducting their investigation. What is important here is that the production of "objectivity" depends on the "mandated course of action," the details of which, as we shall see below, depend on the conceptual formulation of the *Code*. Thus, the social organization of the factual objective character of the report does not arise from its disengagement from the work of the police, but rather it is precisely the way it uses inscription techniques conjoined with a mandated course of action as a tacit resource of police work that produces its "objective" character. Again, it is the textually-mediated features of police work that concerts the regulative relation of policing sex.

Having identified Coulis' and Proctor's investigative behavior as a "mandated course of action," our research went on to examine the mandated character of their activities, i.e., how they are determined conceptually, legally, by the *Code*. Figure 2 reproduces two parts of the bawdy-house law, sections 179 and 193 of the *Criminal Code*. Notwithstanding that "indecency" is not particularly well defined in the *Code*, it was in meeting the investigative requirement of proving that the Back Door was a "bawdy-house"; that is, a place "kept, or occupied, or resorted to by one or more persons for the purpose . . . of acts of indecency" that Coulis and Proctor "walked around and noted" a number of men lying nude in their private booths with the door wide open, some of whom were masturbating themselves. Similarly, it was through the activity of entering, approaching the cash area, and paying their fee, that Coulis and Proctor found the individual, later identified as John DOE, to be an employee of the bath. Later they watch him "on two separate occasions . . . walk past a number of rooms that were occupied by men who were masturbating themselves," and at no time ". . . make an effort to stop these men." This watching was necessary to the "facts" in the report alleging that DOE was an "agent . . . having charge of [a] place," who knowingly permitted "the place . . . to be . . . used for the purpose of a common bawdy-house." Thus, it is the definition of a "bawdy-house" and the conception of a "keeper," as they are elaborated in the *Criminal Code*, that determine this mandated course of action.

A particular striking example of the conceptual determination of this investigative relation occurred on the officers' "Second Visit" to the Back Door where they reported that:

> Later in the evening both of the officers received their rooms. COULIS attended at PROCTOR's room and heard loud noises emanating from the room directly beside PROCTOR's. Both PROCTOR and COULIS peered over the top of the partition separating the rooms and saw that there were two men engaged in anal intercourse.

What is significant here is that even though the 1969 *Criminal Code* amendments exempt from prosecution homosexual acts that take place in private, Coulis and Proctor saw fit to report on this incident which required them to invade the privacy of two individuals having sex behind a locked door. Indeed, to make this observation the two officers had to scale an eight-foot wall, and there is every reason to believe that they also had to remove the chicken wire covering the ceiling of their room, installed specifically to prevent individuals not only from spying on one other, but more importantly, to protect their valuables.[24] In this instance the officers report the "fact" of "indecent acts" taking place in the "private booths" of the club patrons, as they called them in their first report, even though, technically speaking, the individuals involved could not be arrested for engaging in homosexual activities under these circumstances.

The conceptual underpinnings of the law that guided the officers' investigative activities in this instance are that (1) the bawdy-house law is concerned with "indecent acts," and (2) while homosexual acts between consenting adults in private are exempt from criminal prosecution, they are still indecent and therefore a "fact" relevant to the investigation of the Back Door. An important conceptual feature of the law that supports the treatment of homosexual activity as "indecent" arises out of the *Criminal Code* reforms of 1969. Under these reforms, section 158 of the *Code* does not legalize but merely decriminalizes under very special conditions (i.e., adults in private) homosexual acts. Here is part of the 1969 debate in the House of Commons that led up to this peculiar status for homosexual activity. In it David Lewis, then leader of the NDP, summarizes for the House the intent of the Liberal government's bill:

> The sections which proclaim that homosexuality is an evil act, an undesirable act, remain in the *Criminal Code*. No one who is really dealing with the subject in the kind of objective, honest way in which we were asked to deal with it can suggest that parliament is saying anything other than that this unfortunate deviation from normal behaviour is an undesirable thing.
>
> What is being suggested in this amendment, what the minister and what the majority in this parliament are saying, is that when two adults who are assumed to have enough judgment to understand situations suffer from this kind of emotional or mental illness, or whatever it may be, and engage in it in private without impinging on the rest of the community, without being in a position to affect, warp and distort the moral attitudes of other people, when two adults who are beyond a certain age and are sick with this particular illness do this undesirable act in private, they will not be brought as criminals before a criminal court. This is all this legislation says.[25]

Later in the day, John Turner, the then Justice Minister, reinforced this interpretation of the bill:

> Let me say also that this proposed section does not legalize homosexuality. The legal effect is to exempt from sections 147 and 149 of the *Criminal Code* the particular conduct described in new article 149A. That is the sole purpose of this measure, as was well set out in the very able speech this morning by the hon. member for York South (Mr. Lewis).[26]

Given the intent and thus the conceptual formulation of the law (i.e., illegal, but not criminal in private), it is not strange that Coulis and Proctor saw it to be perfectly appropriate as part of their mandate to invade the privacy of the men in the next room and to report on what they saw. The *Code*'s definition of a "bawdy-house" as a place people

resort to for acts of indecency does not merely provide for their actions,
it shapes them, and in the end makes it possible for Coulis and Proctor
to report their activities as police work.[27]

The Social Organization of a Legal Concept

Although this discussion of the 1969 reforms does not deal directly with
the bawdy-house law, it does provide an insight into the social organization of a legal concept. It is not merely that Coulis' and Proctor's
activities are embedded in the work of the police, and policing embedded in the conceptual formulations of the law, but that legal concepts,
in turn, are embedded in the social organization of a ruling apparatus.
It is this piece of contextualization that we went on to explicate, if only
briefly and somewhat tangentially.

In an earlier section of this paper I quoted part of the brief submitted
by the Chief Constable of Toronto to the 1958 Royal Commission on
the Law Relating to Criminal Sexual Psychopaths. A royal commission
and the briefs it receives from various citizens and professional organizations is but one example of how the social organization of this kind
of conceptual formulation arises out of the discursive interpenetration
of the various sites of managing and administering society. These sites
include, among others, government bureaucracies, professional organizations, public bodies, and of course, legislatures. In the 1968 House
of Common's debates on the amendments to the *Criminal Code*, John
Turner provided, in part, a thumbnail sketch of the social organization
of the new legal (i.e., ruling) concept of homosexuality (i.e., illegal, but
not criminal in private). Defending certain criticism of his bill in the
house, he told the honorable members:

> I do not rely on the opinions of the law officers of the Crown to support the
> opinion I submit to Your Honour and Members of the house. This bill was
> reviewed on two occasions since its original introduction by the attorneys-
> general of the provinces. It has also been considered by the members of
> the uniformity commission. It has also been thoroughly studied by our
> own standing committee as well as the legal profession, representatives
> of the medical profession and Crown prosecutors. These individuals have
> considered and reviewed this particular clause and its predecessor since
> December 21, 1967.[28]

There is good reason to believe that the conceptual formulation of Turner's bill did not begin in this country, but in England with the report in 1957 of the Wolfenden Committee on homosexual offenses and
prostitution.[29] The decade of controversy emanating from the publication of this report before it passed into English law in 1967 culminated

in the highly publicized Hart-Devlin debates—Hart, an eminent philosopher of jurisprudence at Oxford, and Lord Devlin, Justice of the High Court, Queen's Bench.[30] The conceptual point at issue between the two was the possibility of identifying a secular ground for laws relating to morality by distinguishing between public and private behavior. Hart was for, Devlin against, this distinction. According to Hart, homosexual activity that might be considered morally wrong (i.e., indecent) on religious grounds by many people, should not be considered a crime if engaged in in private. Typically, throughout the events leading up to the 1969 reforms in Canada, not a single piece of official evidence was taken from an openly gay person. The laws regulating our sexual lives were drawn up by others located within the matrix of institutional resources used to manage and administer society.

Regulating Sex: A Textually-Mediated Relation

Our research originally began with our generalized experience as gay men of having our sexual lives policed. The course our analysis took was one of sketching an ever-widening/deepening set of contextual circumstances, starting with the activities of Coulis and Proctor, through to the work of making law. Having sketched the lineaments of this organization in one direction, it is now possible to recapitulate it going in the opposite direction. The key to being able to do this is the connective work documents do in a ruling relation—in this case especially, the work of the *Criminal Code*. Starting, then, from within the highest and most powerful administrative context, what we discovered was the institutional relation which in the first instance provided the conceptual framework of the law. In the case of Canada's bawdy-house law (copied from the English statutes and amended in Canada in 1917 to include indecent acts along with prostitution[31]), this relation operates today in much the same way the ruling organization described by John Turner did in 1969. At a national level, its purpose, organized conceptually through the definition of a "bawdy-house" in the *Criminal Code*, is to make illegal any place that individuals might resort to for prostitution or acts of indecency.[32] Within this context, we examined how the conceptual formulation of the bawdy-house law organizes a mandated course of action constituted in the investigative practices of Coulis' and Proctor's work. This displayed how legal concepts co-ordinate and concert the work of the police. Moreover, our analysis showed how this textually-mediated investigative course of action operates, using inscription techniques, to enter and secure individuals in a regulatory relation. Thus, concepts, in the way they shape and determine this process of "enmeshing," display the organizational properties whereby they control those aspects of life which they inform and order.[33] It is in this sense that the conceptual formulation of the *Criminal Code* intends a social form that the work of the police accomplishes (i.e., the enforcement of a heterosexual society where legitimate sexuality is focused on procreative sex within a domestic relation). The bawdy-house law, in this sense, "crystalizes" a social form of life which is both the social organization of its construction and the social organization which its application brings into being. The reproduction of this social form, expressed in the *Criminal Code* and enforced in this instance by the police, is organized as an institutional relation. What I mean here by "institutional" is the way in which the social organization of this conceptual formulation subtends a course of action put together as a series of sequentialized, interconnected moments stretching backwards and forwards through time, knitting together the various institutional sites of ruling: professional organizations, universities, government bureaucracies, royal commissions, legislatures, attorneys-general, the police, courts, defense attorneys, prisons, etc. It is within this context that this institutional, regulatory relation displays its affinity to the social organization of class.

The most significant aspect of this relation is its textually-mediated properties. The documents which organize and hold it together are of various types: the studies of sexologists, dossiers on psychiatric cases, philosophical publications, government reports, interdepartmental memoranda, various Hansards, briefs from medical associations, committee reports from bar associations, government statutes, psychological and sociological studies, police reports, search warrants, arrest records, appearance notices, disclosure documents, case *factums*, court transcripts, and so forth and so on, with the most important, of course, being the *Criminal Code.* These documents not only link the various moments of this relation, they concert it! For example, in the account of the "First Visit" there are two sequences of inscription: the original report of Coulis and Proctor, and the reconstruction of this account in the disclosure document itself. The temporal sequence of this work can be seen in the initial identification of John DOE. ("It was at this location that the officers first saw the accused; who was later "identified" as [John DOE].") Originally, he was just observed (i.e., reported on). It is on the basis of this report, it must be remembered, that the bath was raided. Now, in the disclosure document he is "identified" as the accused, which means that in the interim the raid has taken place, DOE has been arrested and is presently awaiting trial. Two moments of inscription in this relation visible in the disclosure document are: first, writing the police report at the time of the investigation, and second, putting together the disclosure account as part of the preparation for trial. The way in which the category of "the accused" can be used retrospectively in the disclosure account displays how these sequences of inscription and the documents they construct concert this investigative relation by holding together the moments of "investigation" and "raid" while intending the moment of "trial." Thus, the social relation regulating sex is a form of organization in which the activities of the authorities are co-ordinated through time and space by a form of paperwork. What our research demonstrated was that documents and paper work are essential to this social process; texts, in other words, are an active component of social relations.[34] This finding can be expressed more generally by saying that ruling in our society takes a discursive form.

Conclusion

Our research began by rendering problematic our generalized experience of having our sexual lives regulated by the police. Our method of work, keeping to our materialist premises, was to investigate how our world is shaped and determined by social processes that go beyond its scope. Our research, in other words, was an inquiry into the extra-local social relations organizing our lives. For as long as the policing of sex has existed in our society, gay people have speculated about its "cause." The problem up to now with these accounts has been their inadequacy in providing a description of the mediating links between "cause" and "effect." How do we know, for example, that the Tory government of Ontario ordered the 1981 raids as part of a strategy to win the next provincial election? As it stands, this is an unsubstantiated allegation. In it the relation between gays and the police is not grounded empirically, but merely "theorized." Similarly, how is it that, in contrast to other forms of policing (e.g., cases of robbery and murder), the regulation of gay sex is caused by the mental state (i.e., the homophobia) of police officers? When pursued, these accounts fail to provide a concrete description of how various critical sites of ruling involved in regulating sex are articulated to each other. The connection between the mini-economy model, for example, and the actual way in which regulating sex is put together is a mystical one. In setting out to investigate the policing of gays, we did not want our conclusions to have this character. We wanted them, rather, without making any claims for their completeness, to be empirically and therefore scientifically adequate as a description of how the policing of gay men works.

Our empirical investigation began with an examination of an artifact of police work taken from the actual organization of their efforts at regulating gay sex: the report of two officers' first investigative visit to a gay steambath. Our strategy was to substruct this document as a way of revealing the form of social organization that brought it into being. Our approach to this task, however, did not begin from within a social vacuum. As a committee responsible for helping to defend gay men arrested in the 1981 bath raids, we had an opportunity to gain some very routine insights into the day-to-day operations of the criminal justice system. We had at other times occasion to view, as well, the operations of other sites of ruling, for example: Toronto Metro Council's police budget subcommittee, the Metro Toronto Police Commission, and the House of Commons Standing Committee on Justice and Legal Affairs. Usually, in these circumstances we would be making a deputation, presenting a brief, or attending to some other quasi-administrative function. This very practical exercise, however, informed our analysis at many points.

The main findings of our research revealed the textually-mediated character of police work. A primary property of the extra-local relations which impinge on the local face-to-face organization of gay men's lives is their documentary character. It is only the categories of the *Criminal Code* that makes the administration of sex possible. It is the *Code*, in this sense, which organizes the extra-local relations that penetrates our lives with the intent of regulating sex. This analysis stands in stark contrast to our usual accounts of why the police behave as they do. Up to this point, gay people have not examined in any detail how policing is organized in documents as a documentary mode of action. By substructing the investigative report of Coulis and Proctor's "First Visit" to the Back Door bath, our research focused on the secret penetration of gay men's social space by the police. Their investigative activities had none of the physical aspects of a bath raid. Nonetheless, this kind of work typically prepares the grounds for a raid and subsequently the arrest of individuals as keepers, found-ins, or inmates of a common bawdy-house. In the investigative work of the secret police there is none of the harassment, verbal abuse, beatings, and the like that often characterize gay men's treatment by the police. Yet, the actions of Coulis and Proctor in inscribing the "facts" of the Back Door case, enmesh individuals more securely in this relation than might any physical force. What our analysis of the "First Visit" revealed, consequently, is a world behind the phenomenon of the police officer which turns out to be a lot more determined and determining than a physical confrontation between a gay man and an arresting officer.

In locating the "cause" of our harassment and arrest by the police in the physical presence of police officers, we excluded the social organization of their work, primarily because its textually-mediated character was invisible in the phenomenal form of our experience. Thus, what is essentially a form of social organization was collapsed into the bodily manifestation of the police (e.g., the police as homophobic). Similarly, previous suggestions that the "cause" of our harassment, arrests, and beatings by the police resides in "clean-up" campaigns, excludes any account of the social organization that makes this kind of police action possible. Because the fundamental arrangement of the administration of sex is not immediately visible, we also sometimes invent a surrogate organization which we label as its "cause," e.g., "the mini-economy." It is these kinds of theories about how policing works that lead to a general belief on the part of gay people that the police do not treat gays fairly in comparison with their work of regulating sex among the heterosexual population. A good example is the argument that police treat sexual offenses in "lovers' lanes," more leniently than they do those of gay men in city parks or public washrooms. It is this belief that stands behind the demand on the part of some elements in the gay community for more discretion on the part of the police in applying the law; for better gay-police relations, the hiring of gay police, and so on.

At present, Canadian law allows homosexuals to have sex in private without the threat of being arrested, but it discourages any form of organization that might provide for this kind of illegal activity by creating a venue for people to meet each other for sex. It is hardly logical to expect "even handed" treatment of gays and heterosexuals when the law itself is heterosexist and when sex outside of procreation within a domestic relation is "indecent," or even "grossly indecent," and therefore illegal. Even if the police were scrupulous in the application of such a law, gay men and heterosexuals would not be equally free to pursue their sexual lives.

While historically, gay politics has attempted to solve the problem of police harassment by calling for the administering of psychological tests to weed out homophobic recruits, the organizing of gay-police liaison and other similar measures, it has failed to understand what our research has underlined: the central mechanism organizing the policing of gays in the *Criminal Code*. Consequently, getting the police off our backs is not particularly a matter of developing better public relations with police departments, but of changing the law.

The most important feature of the political organization of gay people has, no doubt, been the process of "coming out." Unless individuals come out, there can be no publicly visible community of gay people, and without a public community, gay politics is impossible. In Canada, gay people, especially since the 1969 *Criminal Code* amendments, have believed that legally they are on a par with heterosexuals. What the experience and research of the RTPC has shown is that this is not so. Moreover, the kind of inequality between gays and straights witnessed in the policing of the gay community—where the law is applied equally except that heterosexuals turn out to be more equal than others—is the responsibility of the law and the institutional relations within which it is conceived and written. What gay liberation requires in Canada, consequently, is a transformation in the law. This is not to call for reform, but for revolution. After all, the purpose of a revolution is to change the law.

NOTES

1. A. Bruner, "Out of the Closet: A study of relations between the Homosexual Community and the Police," Report to Mayor Arthur Eggleton and the Council of the City of Toronto. Toronto: City Clerk's Office, 1981.

2. Canada. Royal Commission on the Criminal Law Relating to Criminal Sexual Psychopaths, *Report*. Ottawa: Queen's Printer, 1958, p. 27.

3. D. White and P. Sheppard, "Report on Police Raids on Gay Steambaths," submitted to Toronto City Council, February 26, 1981, pp. 12–14.

4. See as examples: *The Body Politic*, a magazine for gay liberation, Andre Hodges' biography of Alan Turing, *Alan Turing the Enigma*. New York: Simon and Schuster Inc., 1983, chapters 7 and 8, and John Preston's novella, *Fanny Queen of Provincetown*. Boston: Alyson Publications, 1983.

5. It has not been uncommon, historically, for the Toronto police to charge a gay man with an "indecent act" and "gross indecency" for allegedly committing a sexual act "in public." Through a system of plea bargaining, the gay man's lawyer pleads him guilty to the lesser charge—in this case, the "indecent act."

6. Canada. House of Commons, Standing Committee on Justice and Legal Affairs, *Minutes of Proceedings and Evidence of the Standing Committee on Justice and Legal Affairs*, Issue No. 81, Wednesday, May 5, 1982, pp. 23–4.

7. Dorothy E. Smith, *The Experienced World as Problematic: A Feminist Method*, The Sorokin Lectures No. 12. Regina: University of Saskatchewan, 1984.

8. Following Marx's social ontology, artifacts can be said to "express," "bear" or "crystalize" a social relation. This language intends that these artifacts

not be taken as "referencing" the social relations in which they arise, but as constitutive of and constituted by these relations.

9. See, for example, H. Garfinkel, "Good organizational reasons for 'bad' clinical records," *Studies in Ethnomethodology*. Englewood Ciff: Prentice-Hall Inc., 1967, Chapter 6.

10. B. Latour and S. Woolgar, *Laboratory Life. The Social Construction of Scientific Facts*. London: Sage Publications, 1979; M. Lynch, "Discipline and the Material Form of Images: An Analysis of Scientific Visibility," a paper presented at the Annual Meeting of the Canadian Sociology and Anthropology Association, Vancouver, 1983; and Dorothy E. Smith, "Textually-Mediated Social Organization," *International Social Science Journal* 36(1), 1984, pp. 59–74.

11. Dorothy E. Smith, "The Social Construction of Documentary Reality," *Sociological Inquiry* 44, 1974, pp. 257–268.

12. A discursive object is a thing which only exists on paper and which is brought into being using documented procedures for classifying the practices and activities of people, e.g., "crime."

13. Given that the officers did not know the name of the accused during their undercover visits to the bath, DOE's name in the disclosure documents probably comes from the documentation of his arrest.

14. K. Mannheim, *Ideology and Utopia*. New York: Harcourt Brace & World, 1936.

15. This broken line represents the social organization of intending.

16. In developing the analysis of the ideological circle, Smith acknowledges her indebtedness to Garfinkel's description of the documentary method of interpretation, particularly where he analyses events treated as documents of the schemata of a textual discourse. Garfinkel's original work is to be found in H. Garfinkel, *op. cit.*, p. 78–9. Smith's account of the ideological circle can be found in Dorothy E. Smith, "No One Commits Suicide: Textual Analysis of Ideological Practice," *Human Studies* 6, 1983, pp. 309–359.

17. Smith, 1983, *op. cit.*, p. 331.

18. This relation is not structured as two independent activities: investigating crime and then writing a report. Rather, the report is part of the investigation in that the investigation is not complete until the report is written.

19. It is important to keep in mind here that the *Canada Evidence Act* is part of the application of the *Criminal Code*.

20. In his report to the Chief on the 1981 raids, Staff Inspector Banks described how the investigative phase of this operation took six months.

21. One effect of this inscription procedure was that DOE, upon reading the report, came to believe that the police were personally out to get him, when really what they were doing was proving the Back Door to be a bawdy-house. But in order to do that, of course, they had to prove DOE was a keeper.

22. D.E. Smith, "The Active Text: a textual analysis of the social relations of public textual discourse," paper presented at the World Congress of Sociology, Mexico City, August, 1982. Smith describes a mandated course of action as: an instance of a general and important social process by which organizations appropriate as theirs, that is, as an organizational action, the actions of individuals who "perform" the organization.

23. E.L. Greenspan (ed.), *Martin's Annual Criminal Code 1984*. Aurora, Canada: Law book Inc., 1984.

24. Of course, it could have been the case that someone else had ripped the chicken wire away from the top of the wall dividing the two rooms. The two officers, however, reported that immediately after recording this incident, Coulis returned to his room where he too noticed noises coming from a room directly beside his. Again, peering over the partition he saw two men in the room engaged in intercourse.

25. Canada. House of Commons, *Hansard*, April 18, 1969, p. 7696.

26. Canada. House of Commons, *Hansard*, April 18, 1969, p. 7710.

27. This, of course, still raises the constitutional question of whether the bawdy-house law can be used in this fashion to override the right to privacy as guaranteed under section 8 of the *Charter of Rights and Freedoms*.

28. Canada. House of Commons, *Hansard*, April 18, 1969, p. 7710.

29. England. The Committee on Homosexual Offenses and Prostitution, *The Wolfenden Report of the Committee on Homosexual Offenses and Prostitution*. New York: Stein and Day, 1963.

30. H.L.A. Hart, *Law, Liberty and Morality*. London: Oxford University Press, 1963; and Sir P. Devlin, *The Enforcement of Morals: Maccabean Lecture in Jurisprudence*. London: Oxford University Press, 1959.

31. Stuart Russell, "The Offense of Keeping a Common Bawdy-House in Canadian Criminal Law," *Ottawa Law Review* 14, 1982, p. 275.

32. The purpose of the law was underscored when the Ontario Court of Appeal in 1982 extended the definition of a bawdy-house to cover a parking lot where prostitutes and their clients resort to having sex in the clients' cars. R. *v.* Pierce and Golloher, 1982, 66 C.C.C. (2d) 388,37 O.R. (2d) 721 (C.A.).

33. G. Kress and R. Hodge, *Language as Ideology*. London: Routledge and Kegan Paul, 1979, pp. 62–84.

34. Smith, 1982, *op. cit.*

'Piracy', the Capitalist State, and Proactive Struggle:
The Woods Harbour Experience[*]

Donald J. Grady and R. James Sacouman

The "final solution" to the Atlantic Canadian fisheries is now in play. Over the last few years, the Canadian capitalist state has moved decisively, in concert with large fisheries capital, to "rationalize" the East Coast fisheries for the benefit of the region's biggest capitalists and for its own vested interests in anti-democratic state control over actual producers (both workers and petty producers).[1] Thousands of jobs and hundreds of coastal communities are under the axe.

The "Kirby Report" (the 1983 Task-Force on Atlantic Fisheries) has been the most recent instrument—yes, instrument—of this alliance of state and big capital against inshore petty producers and fisheries workers, and against smaller capitalist processors and near-shore vessel owners. In Newfoundland, the federal and provincial wings of the state have salvaged big fisheries capitalists and bankers by buying control over their bankrupt fish companies. In Nova Scotia, the federal and provincial wings of the state have salvaged big fisheries capitalists and their bankers by simply donating millions to these provincial giants without taking control.[2] In both cases, state-led monopolization/salvaging/capitalization have meant numerous plant shutdowns, pogey, and protests by plant workers and by smaller capitalist processors.

But the "dull compulsion" of economic coercion by the state in

---

[*]This paper is dedicated to the fishing community of Woods Harbour, Shelburne County, Nova Scotia—men, women and children, who have taught us more and better about the reality of struggle than either of us had understood. We hope that this telling of their struggle may be a contribution. With family gratitude to Kirby, Marie, Sheldon, Tim Leighton, Gert, Sterling, Davis, Ronnie, and Captain James.

alliance with big fisheries capitalists is only one aspect of the story. What the state is doing in alliance with big fisheries capital is what the latter has failed to do throughout this century: wipe out the inshore fisheries and the semi-proletarian[3] or dependently-independent[4] work-and-lifestyles involved.

Inshore families and communities have been super-exploited throughout this century, and until very recently, by fisheries capital and the federal and provincial wings of the state. It was more profitable, at least in the short-term, to maintain a semi-proletarianized inshore fisheries in dependency, for a sizeable proportion of the catch, than to move to expand capitalist accumulation by large investments in the means of production and by fully proletarianizing a depleted workforce. On the other hand, until confronted by the current crisis which began in the late 1960s, many inshore petty producers of luxury species (e.g., lobster, scallops) in southwestern Nova Scotia had been able to maintain their relative independence, and that of their communities, from big capital and from the state. Beginning in 1968, however, the state moved to control and, where necessary, destroy these successful inshore fishermen and coastal communities.

This paper is an attempt to analyze an ongoing struggle for survival by one such successful fishing community in southwestern Nova Scotia, the "pirates" of Woods Harbour. The co-authors have been working with the people of Woods Harbour and have also acted as "expert witnesses" for the defense at the sentencing hearing of the first eight fishermen charged with piracy in Yarmouth, Nova Scotia. Our approach will be to emphasize and to seek to enhance the pro-active struggle of the people of Woods Harbour against the coercive capitalist state, in favor of the inshore fisheries, and in alliance with other food workers and petty producers.

Our stance leaves us open to charges of bias from supporters of the capitalist state (You betcha!). But more disturbing has been a charge from the Left of our approach being guilty of petty-bourgeois populism, of being narodniki.[5] Our initial response is this:

1) that the Woods Harbour struggle is for community control over a community resource and for worker-owner control over the conduct of its fisheries;
2) that the community of Woods Harbour is seeking alliances with other food workers and petty producers against the state's attempt to isolate and destroy this community;
3) that, in significant part, the failure of socialism in Canada grows from an inability and/or unwillingness to forge alliances between workers and

petty producers; and finally,

4) that socialist democracy must encourage community, worker, and worker-owner control if it is to be democratic.[6]

The Story to 1984: In Brief[7]

Since March, 1983, the 1,058 people of Woods Harbour in Shelburne County, Nova Scotia, have been on trial for organizing and defending their community and way of life. The chief prosecutors have been the Department of Fisheries and Oceans (DFO) and the Canadian legal system. The trial has taken place at several venues: the sea, the wharf, Dennis Point, the Yarmouth court. So far one man has been found guilty of "theft of a Canadian vessel" (piracy) and seven men have changed their pleas from not guilty to guilty before the Nova Scotia Supreme Court. Two further fishermen pleaded guilty before County Court during January, 1984, and five others were charged with theft and mischief.

The Bear Point, Shag Harbour, Woods Harbour Fishermen's Association (BSWFA), the Women's Support Group and the entire community have vowed that no person will serve an hour in jail. As one woman put it: "We're all together. If one goes down we all do." As another said: "The only thing we're guilty of is not giving in to them and their destroying us." To understand the "we" and the "them" requires a brief look back and a hard look ahead at Woods Harbour's struggle to maintain a community and way of life.

Since 1761 the people of Woods Harbour have worked hard in the fishery. Descendants of the original settlers (and a small increment of newcomers) have built a community with two major characteristics: independence and integrity. Their independence grew directly out of the physical and social requirements of the fishery. The fisherman and his family have established a way of life keyed to the resources of land and sea, guaranteed only by their own efforts. As changes in the technology and marketing of fishing placed new demands upon them, they enhanced their capacities for effort and self-reliance. When independence of spirit and action were required, they supplied it. The reputation of fishermen from Woods Harbour and area came to be that when someone from that community was put to the test, integrity and independence were the reliable reply.

Because those in the fishery depend for their survival on the willingness of fellow fishermen and their families to come to the aid of vessels in trouble, a parallel tradition of mutual aid and interdependence has grown up. Principles governing when and how one fisherman or family will help another with gear, cooperate in the location of traps, collaborate with repair, maintenance or construction of boats and/or machinery are well established.[8] As one community member put it: "After all, while we compete for fish, we depend on one another in the face of the sea." Where the Woods Harbour fishery had been weak, however, was in the lack of a collective organization that could effectively express to the state the needs and desires of the community. This weakness has recently been overcome.

During the period of dramatic changes in the offshore and inshore fisheries involving the development of the International Law of the Sea, 1966–1967, the inshore fishermen of Woods Harbour were among the earliest and most successful adopters and adapters of new techniques and new equipment which would allow larger catches. Often these means of enlarging the catch were subsidized by readily available federal and provincial government loans. As the costs of equipment skyrocketed because of these loans, fishermen became greatly indebted to the government in order to "keep up."[9] Yet, since 1968 members of the community have also been called upon to respect increasingly restrictive policies and regulations by the federal Department of Fisheries. On the one hand, inshore fishermen were told to get bigger by going into debt to the state; on the other hand, they were told to abide by fishing regulations and restrictions to which they had never agreed, to cut back their catches, and undermine their livelihood. This pincer movement of easy loans and restrictive rules was, of course, applied not only to inshore fishermen but to companies like Nickerson-National Sea. But while state capital has been used to salvage the larger mismanaged companies, even the most successful of the little guys are being left to drown. And if the most successful can be drowned, then the entire inshore fisheries and the hundreds of communities dependent on it are destined to go under, while the state and monopoly capital take charge.[10]

During numerous discussions with representatives of the DFO, southwestern Nova Scotia fishermen were urged to organize. They were repeatedly told that the DFO could not and would not discuss new regulations with individual fishermen and "unorganized groups" making representations on behalf of segments of the fishery or particular parts of the shore. In response to the requirement that they organize in order to represent their interests and in order to be heard on a variety of issues, including trap limits in the inshore lobster fishery, fishermen from Bear Point, Shag Harbour and Woods Harbour formed their own Fishermen's Association, the area's first real organization of fishermen.

Because the Association was a first and because the community truly believed that the state and the DFO simply did not know, much less understand, the facts of the inshore fisheries, the BSWFA undertook to inform the DFO of exactly how many traps they were setting and where they had been fishing since trap limitations were first set in 1968. BSWFA representatives also made it clear that there had been *no (zero) overfishing in terms of stock depletion of the resource* during that time period. Instead of responding to the fishermen's candor by opening negotiations with the BSWFA over limits and regulations, the DFO used these volunteered charts to center out the Woods Harbour fishermen for harassment. The facts of no real overfishing, i.e., depletion of stocks, were swept aside. Most members of both the Association and the Women's Support Group now saw themselves as having been extremely naive. The DFO was not interested in honesty and grounded evidence. The DFO was interested in making an example out of them, meting out exemplary punishment, thus teaching all inshore fishermen and coastal communities to defer to the Department's power and expertise. The DFO is now seen as nothing but Canada's second largest police force—the "fish police" as they are known in Woods Harbour.

DFO representatives from Yarmouth and Barrington began rigorous enforcement of trap limitations in the BSWFA area around March 15, 1983. DFO enforcement programs, provocative and damaging methods of inspection, and incidents of arbitrary imposition of abusive authority created an environment of suspicion and hostility which exploded at Dennis Point in Pubnico Harbour on May 11, 1983. Between March 15 and May 11, both untagged and properly tagged gear were confiscated, destroyed, or misplaced by DFO enforcement officers. Boats were boarded and lobstering efforts disrupted. Stan Dudka, the DFO's senior "trouble shooter," was brought in to "handle the problem" by attempting to intimidate BSWFA area lobstermen. On one occasion, fishermen arriving at the wharf in Woods Harbour from a full day's work reported that they were taunted by Dudka with his comment that: "By the end of the season, we'll have you on your knees kissing our asses for favors."

The DFO was not listening at all to the newly organized group. The BSWFA and Women's Support Group organized two peaceful delegations to DFO offices in Yarmouth during April 1983. On one of these two occasions, the protesters were met by more than 20 specially equipped RCMP officers in crowd control gear. DFO officials at the Yarmouth office were unavailable to meet with community members. The BSWFA also took the DFO to federal court requesting an injunction to prevent DFO's search and seizure methods. That case was to have been heard in Ottawa on May 13, 1983.

On May 11, a Woods Harbour fishermen noticed the DFO hauling a neighbor's traps without the neighbor's knowledge. He got on the radio, let nearby boats know what was going on and said that he was going to follow the DFO into their wharf to protest. By general account, more than 40 vessels and upwards of 200 people (including community members who arrived by car), followed him to Dennis Point in Pubnico Harbour. At Dennis Point, after a morning of discussion and heated exchanges, and under the watchful eyes of two RCMP officers (and DFO cameras), two vessels were damaged—one to the point of sinking. Woods Harbour, through its representatives, was charged with piracy, a charge unprecedented in Canadian judicial history.

On May 13, the federal court ruled against the BSWFA request for an injunction against DFO activities since, in the court's view, the fishermen did not come to the case "with clean hands." Having been blocked in all ways, Woods Harbour had finally exploded with reactive dynamite. One DFO official and even Premier John Buchanan have since acknowledged that fishermen were being harassed in such a way that some major incident "had to happen."

Woods Harbour was shocked but solid. Virtually everyone recognized that they had been set up to react, and admitted that anyone in the community could have been directly involved. Many felt guilty for not being arrested even if they had not been there; they could have been there, and some felt they should have been at Dennis Point wharf. Maybe now they would get their day in court, a chance to tell the world what was going on. At any rate, they would make sure that nobody went to jail.

Initially, the Yarmouth Crown Prosecutor, under advice from the Office of the Provincial Attorney General in Halifax, decided to charge individuals under the piracy provisions of the Criminal Code (76a)—maximum sentence, 14 years. Supreme Court Justice R. MacLeod Rogers requested and was assigned the fishermen's case, even though it was not his session in Yarmouth and despite the fact that in the past he had often prosecuted fishermen in the area as a Crown Attorney working with the DFO. In the first trial, the accused lobsterman was found guilty by judge and jury. Questions were raised about the trial proceedings, particularly about Justice Rogers' charge to the jury and his characterization of crown and defense witnesses. Prospects for the remaining seven defendants (who included three members of the BSWFA executive) were seen as quite ominous. Things were not looking bright.

Quite unexpectedly a way out of impending jail terms appeared. In response to pleas from local notables, the Attorney General's Office advised the Yarmouth Crown Prosecutor to offer the fishermen's attorneys a "deal." The "deal" was that if the accused pleaded guilty, expressed regret, agreed to pay restitution for the damaged vessels and supplied more names of participants who would also plead guilty, then they and the new names would receive suspended sentences with terms of probation involving community service. The accused were given 24 hours to agree to the deal or face the prospect of further convictions with likely (and lengthy) jail terms. At an emergency meeting of the BSWFA, the Association decided to accept the "deal." About 40 people volunteered to be guilty and a short list of 10 names was provided to the Crown. Criteria for the BSWFA's selection were primarily that the next group of defendants be composed of experienced fishermen and solid community workers. The Crown selected the final five to be prosecuted from this list.

Throughout the construction of the "deal," the fishermen consistently expressed their objections to being forced into a compact of silence with the judicial system and the DFO. They recognized that failure to accept the terms dictated would make all those charged vulnerable to the same experience of justice and the same outcome that had occurred in the first trial before Justice Rogers. The Association and the Women's Group defined the deal as a crude form of "judicial blackmail" and bitterly resented this distortion of justice. To their credit, they faced this prospect united. As one fishermen put it: "They didn't give us much choice but to stick together and swallow the rotten thing whole."

The remaining seven of the original eight went to court during October 1983 and changed their pleas from "not guilty" to "guilty" of "piracy." Word got around about the "deal" in the area and in the rest of the province. Sentencing of the original eight was seen to be preordained. And so it would have been, except that a Yarmouth lawyer not directly involved in the case made the terms of the "deal" public at a meeting of the Yarmouth Town Council three days before the sentencing hearing.

The *Yarmouth Vanguard* duly reported this on the front page of its Wednesday, December 14, 1983 edition. Sentencing of the original eight was completed by noon the next day. Justice Rogers commented critically on the prior revelation of the "deal" and added an additional year of probation and an additional 100 hours of community service to the terms of the probation.

In Woods Harbour, the agenda of community struggle remained the same: defense of the area's inshore fishery and protection of the future of independent, family-based fishing for the next generation of Woods Harbour fishermen.

DFO efforts to isolate and stigmatize the BSWFA as a renegade group had failed. People in other fishing communities of Nova Scotia, the Atlantic Provinces and the West Coast sent telegrams and letters of support; so did representatives of organizations like the Maritime Fishermen's Union (MFU), the Canadian Farm Survival Association, along with other North American and European groups. The commitment of those involved in Woods Harbour has deep roots in a tradition of independence and integrity, and efforts to quiet their protests with strong enforcement measures and stern legal imposition served only to strengthen their resolve.

The BSWFA has itself given support to a number of fishermen's and farmers' protests.[11] In ongoing meetings with the DFO and other fishermen's groups, the BSWFA continued to show itself to be militant and uncompromising *vis-à-vis* the state's attempts to divide and conquer. The BSWFA's strategy won some concessions on replacement tags for the spring season. After two lengthy meetings of the Lobster Advisory Committee, the DFO agreed, contrary to its previous assertions, to supply all District 4A lobstermen with 35 request replacement tags. Other organizations, in particular the Maritime Fisherman's Union District 9, have much to learn from the BSWFA. In terms of militancy and analysis in southwestern Nova Scotia, the BSWFA acts as the union and the MFU District 9 acts as an association.

Woods Harbour in Praxis to 1984

We have addressed two tasks: providing the general framework with which the goals of capitalist state policy for the Atlantic fishery have challenged the survival of inshore fishermen and their communities; and recounting the specific struggle of the BSWFA as a leading exemplar of how this conflict, with all elements of the juridico-political system, is being carried out. In this section we examine the material gathered to 1984. We illustrate the repertoire of techniques for carrying forward the goals of the BSWFA and Women's Group (influence) and those of the Department of Fisheries and Oceans (social/state control). Influence represents the efforts of emergent groups to achieve goals focused upon the wants and needs shared by class- and gender-rooted individuals, and social control represents the requirement that the interests of an established socio-political class and gender order be maintained, preferred, and, where required, imposed upon all others.[12] In essence, the dichotomy between influence and social control closely approximates that between oppressed and oppressors, ruled and rulers.[13]

Reviewing events in BSWFA's struggle with DFO, examples of actions representing each of the following tactical categories can be derived:

A. Under Influence
1. Constraints:
EXAMPLES:
  (a) The threatened one day blockade of tourist ferry traffic in and out
      of Yarmouth Harbour in May 1982 by fishing boats mainly from the
      Bear Point, Shag Harbour, Woods Harbour area. The demand at
      this time was that the DFO implement a plan to improve wharf facil-
      ities in Woods Harbour. A last-minute telex from Romeo LeBlanc,
      Minister of Fisheries in Ottawa, approving the wharf construction
      project obviated the blockade. The Woods Harbour "fleet" was
      already steaming for Yarmouth when news of the DFO capitulation
      was received.
  (b) Two orderly protest marches to DFO district offices in Yarmouth
      during April 1983. Each effort involved between 75 and 125 people,
      fishermen and families, and was organized and implemented by
      the BSWFA and the Women's Group in an effort to cause the DFO
      to provide a constructive response to long-standing grievances of
      inshore lobster fishermen. Neither effort produced a DFO change
      of policy.
  (c) Incidents at Dennis Point wharf, Pubnico Harbour in May 1983.
      DFO enforcement officers were caught hauling tagged traps for in-
      spection in an area fished by BSWFA boats, broke off for Pubnico
      and exchanged angry threats with fishermen in transit and on
      the wharf—eventuating in the loss of two DFO leased vessels and
      "piracy" charges against BSWFA members. This constraint forced
      the hand of state authority.
  (d) "Going public" with statements to the press, radio and television
      which directly exposed the contradictions within DFO policy and
      practice, DFO violations of their own regulations and guidelines
      (e.g., trap limits, inspection excesses, abuse of enforcement au-
      thority, misreporting of negotiations). The BSWFA was particu-
      larly committed to exposing the abuse of judicial independence and
      equality before the law represented in the first trial of the accused
      "pirates" (October 1983) and the flagrantly prejudicial imposition
      of the no-jail deal initiated and implemented by government and
      judicial actors during the court process (December 1983–February
      1984). DFO officials repeatedly advised BSWFA representatives not
      to "go to the media" with reports contradicting department press
      releases on negotiations. The BSWFA was specifically warned that
      terms of the deal promised no jail sentences only if Woods Harbour
      maintained silence and remained compliant to those terms. Need-

less to say, Woods Harbour kept up relentless pressure by exposing DFO duplicity in constructing and then reneging on the "deal."

2. Inducements:

EXAMPLES:

(a) Voluntary provision of charts indicating the location and number of traps set by Woods Harbour-based fishermen to DFO officials (October 1982). In supplying this information the fishermen anticipated that the DFO might, upon review, revise its trap limit policy to meet the demonstrated and legitimate requirements for economic survival of the Woods Harbour group. Mr. Jim Melanson of the DFO Halifax policy group promised to "get back" to the lobstermen in a few days. The DFO did not, and the material supplied was employed by fisheries enforcement the following spring (April and May 1983) in the "crack down" on Woods Harbour traps. As late as May 7, 1984, DFO officials were quoted as determined to continue strict enforcement practices where the Department has "cause and reasonable and probable grounds" to suspect violations. The same sources admitted that such grounds for action "more commonly come" from anonymous informers and are difficult to check.[14]

(b) Formation of the BSWFA in March–April 1983 by Woods Harbour lobstermen in direct response to complaints from DFO officials in Barrington and Yarmouth that they could not negotiate with "unorganized individuals seeking to represent the needs and interests of communities of fishermen protesting departmental policy or offering solutions to difficult situations. Ironically, the subsequent role of the BSWFA as a continuing thorn in the side of the fisheries bureaucracy grew directly out of organizational demands set out to serve the convenience of decision-makers. It is clear now that the DFO did not expect the inshore fishermen to be able to get together or to demonstrate a capacity to press their case—especially *against* the department and government and *with* other groups in the public arena.[15]

(c) Formulation by BSWFA of the central terms of the "moratorium" agreement with DFO Yarmouth and Halifax which effectively "defused" the explosive situation in Woods Harbour following the confrontation at Dennis Point, Pubnico (May 1983). In the immediate aftermath of these events, BSWFA membership authorized the association executive to persuade DFO officials to call a temporary halt to enforcement throughout all of district 4A (from the Shelburne County line to Digby) so that any untagged traps could be landed without reprisal. DFO estimated that approximately 11,000 traps were brought ashore, along the full district coastline. Everyone involved, including BSWFA and DFO agreed that the "moratorium" played an essential role in reducing the high probability of confrontation between lobstermen and enforcement officers.

(d) Long-term participation by BSWFA representatives in the meetings of the Lobster Advisory Committee established by the DFO in 1982 as a "sounding board" for officials to gather the views of lobstermen from communities and groups throughout district 4A. Although clearly designed to collect views rather than to negotiate issues, the Committee was manipulated by DFO officials from Halifax to authenticate their own policies. And while such action on the part of DFO officials encouraged division of interest among fishermen from different ports with varying (and not always complementary) short-term needs, the BSWFA still saw this committee as an arena for building a broader basis for cooperation among lobstermen in the development and management of resources (e.g., for an opening of the fishery to the next generation, for mobilizing a demand that the DFO present an evidenced basis for random policy initiatives, and for establishing the right of fishing communities to an effective role in generating as well as implementing regulations). The BSWFA made notable gains from its participation in the Lobster Advisory Committee on both fronts—forging links with other communities and carrying its case from that committee to the public arena.[16]

3. Persuasion:

EXAMPLE:

(a) Prior to the formation of a formal BSWFA organization in the spring of 1983, groups representative of the Woods Harbour community made repeated submissions to DFO (locally in Barrington, at the district level in Yarmouth, and through district offices to supervisory and policy personnel at the regional level in Halifax). The content of much of this communication was intended to educate the DFO to the damaging effects of current and proposed enforcement of "dead letter" regulations, and to elicit changes in the serious threats to the economic survival of sincere fishermen. Some Woods Harbour members thought such efforts unlikely of success but worth the effort as a test of the reliability of fisheries officials. In retrospect, it is clear that the initiative was doomed both because the DFO was determined to carry through on its own policy, and because the fishermen's attempt to tell the truth on the issues and about their own practices was seen as dangerous and provocative naïveté by experienced bureaucrats.[17]

(b) The public forum held at the Barrington Passage Secondary School in October 1982 during which DFO officials sought to justify the "improved" lobster regulations (involving tag limits and strict enforcement). Fishermen from all over the area (including Shelburne, Cape Sable Island and Woods Harbour) made determined efforts to provide a reasonable and informed basis for DFO to "review and revise" its imposed course of action without achieving any reliable indication of government "good faith." Most fishermen (and their families) went away feeling that they had been heard but not "listened to."

(c) In this summary group, we include all of the "official" representations, appeals, and requests for timely intervention addressed by the BSWFA to elected representatives at all levels of government including: the Federal Minister of Fisheries, the Premier and Minister of Fisheries of Nova Scotia, Federal MPs, both opposition leaders and the relevant party critics of the federal DFO, Provincial MLAs, provincial opposition spokespersons, and mayors and council members of Municipal and County jurisdictions. The best that can be said of this process is that in making their case to political officials, the BSWFA exhausted available channels of redress, while satisfying itself and its community that no responsible public official can later claim that he/she failed to lend assistance because he/she was unaware of the nature of the problem.

B. Under Social Control

1. Sanctions:

EXAMPLES:

(a) Exemplary and punitive application of DFO inspection powers in a particularly abusive fashion off Woods Harbour (late April to May 11 1983). During the 1984 Spring season, more subtle tactics involving the running down of trap buoys and lines rather than hauling traps to destruction had been used to continue the DFO's grim determination to break the BSWFA—or at least to provoke a further physical confrontation by wearing down and frustrating lobstermen.

(b) Criminal charges including "piracy" as well as the lesser offenses of theft over $250 and "mischief to public property" against a total of 15 members of the BSWFA. The charge sheet in the hands of the state continues to include terms of "good behaviour" over those with suspended sentences, open files investigating the roles and identity of alleged "associates," and the possibility of further charges on the basis of self-provided information from five "volunteer pirates" as part of the "deal." DFO officers busied themselves with a deliberate policy of singling out for persistent and harassing inspections those Woods Harbour fishermen who alleged violations of fisheries regulations (March–May 1984).

(c) The "deal" constitutes the most powerful sanction against the BSWFA, the Women's Group and the Woods Harbour community. By implicating the BSWFA as a "party" to the deal, the government used the courts as a form of "judicial blackmail" on the community. Since the fishermen involved represented the community, they continued to serve as hostages for their own "good behavior" over the next three years, as well as sureties that all BSWFA members would comply with the laws and their extensions in DFO regulations. Although the pledge of silence imposed by the government as a condition of the deal has not kept the sordid history of the deal from modest public attention, the fact remains that shutting down the court proceedings as a potential arena for embarrassing public revelations has been largely successful to date.[18] As in the first two instances used under sanctions, the deal represents a particularly venemous form of attempted repression.

2. Insulation:
EXAMPLES:
(a) Government efforts to insulate and thus isolate the BSWFA began early with a DFO tactic of "layer-caking" access to policy makers within the region. At the outset (1981–1982) local DFO officials sought to perpetuate the myth that all problems could be solved "in the field" at the local wharf level. When the new "enforcement policy" was floated locally in 1982, similar efforts were made to enter discussions at the informal group level in the Yarmouth District office. Only when fishermen broadened their demands and defended their organization through late 1982 and early 1983 was a regular channel opened to the regional office in Halifax. Even after a full year of open conflict and public debate, Halifax officials worked hard to keep the BSWFA from any endorsed, face-to-face negotiations with ministerial grade officials of Fisheries and Oceans in Ottawa. The BSWFA has patiently and skillfully done an end-run around insulating efforts by seeking to work through federal parliamentary fisheries committees and representatives. But, with the ordained conviction of true believers, the DFO bureaucrats continue to block channels under their departmental control. Ottawa receives representation from the BSWFA but considers acknowledgment a fulsome response.

(b) The establishment of the so-called Lobster Advisory Committee—
a group with authority to discuss but no reliable mandate to effect
regulations—is a DFO designed instrument of insulation at two levels: between fishermen and government policy-makers and (more
dangerously) among groups and communities of fishermen in that
district. By clearly identifying that the BSWFA is to be treated as a
rabble of renegade, selfish and dangerous malcontents, the DFO has
signalled to potential BSWFA allies (especially, the Maritime Fishermen's Union District 9) and other community representatives that
they would be well-advised to keep a healthy distance between
their aims and those of the "notorious, self-confessed pirates" of
Woods Harbour. While the device is easily seen and appreciated
for what it is by all concerned (including the DFO), its deliberate
and cynical use persists. It remains to be seen whether fishermen
outside Woods Harbour will openly reject efforts at insulation by
the state authorities. At the same time, it is obvious that no one
fishing for a living is under any illusion about the patently false
claim that the only people violating trap limit regulations live in
Woods Harbour. The resource in this case is unity, and it is being
brought to bear despite the best efforts of the DFO.[19]

3. Persuasion:
EXAMPLES:
(a) While persuasion remains available as an analytic category, it is a
largely inoperative tactic in the DFO's Woods Harbour effort. The
reason for this empty space is quite simple; categorical untruth has
always received little credit in the community. The long-standing
experience of fishermen with fisheries authorities has given little
basis for the minimal level of trust required to make a fisherman
available for persuasion.[20]

As we have learned and insisted, the fundamental desire of Woods
Harbour women, men and children is to be left sufficiently to their own
efforts to make a livelihood from the sea, to pursue their family and community purposes in peace. Given the fundamental institutional duplicity
of the DFO, its economic and political masters and the ancillary support
of the judicial system, the only marvel is that this entire awe-inspiring
"cathedral of hypocrisy" persists in pursuing its message of authoritative
persuasion. To our knowledge there are no takers in Woods Harbour.

In our terms, what is unfolding in the efforts of the BSWFA since its
founding is a determined attempt to develop an effective combination of
constraints, inducements and persuasions required to defeat the capitalist state's destruction of the inshore fisheries.[21]

Despite the obvious physical preponderance of the DFO in steel ships, weapons and enforcement personnel, the BSWFA has achieved its best results when its members have mobilized clear constraints. This was the case in the blockade threat (May 1982), in the disciplined resistance to arbitrary search and seizure (Spring 1983), and in the scrupulous invigilation, denunciation, and denial of legitimacy employed by BSWFA vessels at sea (Spring 1984). In May 1983, the DFO did provoke a BSWFA response which temporarily provided the state with a "rationale" for "punishment." Despite consistent DFO provocations during the Spring of 1984, on the other hand, the BSWFA met the challenge of choosing when, where and how to implement constraints.

Similarly, when influence advocates indulge too heavily in efforts to induce authoritative compliance, they risk erosion of their own solidarity mobilization without assurance of authoritative compromise. As was especially the case in the generation of the Lobster Advisory Committee, the DFO saw BSWFA participation as an opportunity to introduce the state's program of insulation. Nevertheless, BSWFA efforts at turning local, regional and national attention upon the distortions of fisherman's positions by the DFO demonstrate a use of inducements which go over the heads of state bureaucrats in the direction of demystifying and demasking the state.

Finally, persuasion directed at a real adversary holds minimal promise —unless, as the BSWFA demonstrated, lobbying of different echelons of state authority can be used to "peel back" layers of potentially crosscutting political interest. Exhausting the channels of redress provided by the "formal freedoms" and "rights" of an oppressive system may also play a useful role in embarrassing authorities, and in debunking the illusory myths of presumed redress. At this level, as we suggested, the state's formulation and imposition of the "deal" have suggested more promise for BSWFA mobilization than for DFO sanction and insulation.

Conclusion

At the current state of proactive struggle in Woods Harbour, it would be premature to offer any more than the tentative prescriptions laid out thus far.[22] But from the strength of purpose, tenacity, and community solidarity already demonstrated to date by the BSWFA, the Women's Group and the people of Woods Harbour, it is appropriate to acclaim how far these practitioners of proactive class struggle have progressed in advancing the fight against their antagonists in state authority, and in mobilizing support from other class and community allies.

Central proactive mobilization processes have been addressed and need to be further addressed by the BSWFA, the Women's Group and the community. A leadership of and from the class-community solidarity base, that acts as the best expression of that base is, in our view, a major strength of the BSWFA. That leadership now needs to extend itself further among the membership; more members need to become active and regularly involved. The basis of unity of the BSWFA and Women's Group is clear cut, uncompromising, and practised in terms of its expression of class interests with inshore fishermen and small farmers. Solidarity links with other uncompromising petty producers need to be further extended and deepened. Other organizations have a great deal to learn from this insurgent upstart; the BSWFA's stance requires extended solidarity. Finally, the BSWFA has already made some links with similarly "uncompromising" working-class organizations. These links need to be further developed and solidified through a network of communication and organization.

It also should be said, in this more academic context, that intellectuals committed to linking their mental work with proactive class struggle ought to rethink the clockwork components of their left dogmatism. Claims that require rethinking and practical renovations are, among others: 1) producers must be inevitably wiped out by the capitalist state and capitalism; 2) only purely proletarian struggles count; and, 3) socialism can be built without working-class alliances with petty producers, rural women and rural communities. Surely a central error of left intellectuals in Canada who would be "organic," who would practise a socialist strategy aimed at a world of equality, extended democracy and popular class liberation, is the failure to theorize, organize and practise strategies where the lived experiences of all the non-ruling classes are central to that struggle. Despite our failures, community-and-class rooted struggles, of course, continue. Because of our failures, alliances aimed at equality, democracy and popular class liberation will take longer than we, in our heads, want.

Postscript

Since the events analyzed above, the pattern of struggle over the state's commitment to "rationalize and control," i.e., destroy, the inshore fisheries has both broadened and deepened.

From the Spring of 1984, the BSWFA has operated under continuous state sanctions. A variety of charges—including Criminal Code violations involving alleged assaults, obstructions, and interferences with RCMP and Fisheries Officers attempting to inspect lobster traps in the waters off Woods Harbour and at dockside—have been laid against eight fishermen. DFO sweeps have resulted in several dozen charges under the Fisheries Act. In a large number of cases, violations have been alleged against fishermen named in a DFO "hit list" of spokesmen for the BSWFA. For example, in one case begun in 1985, four charges of assault and obstruction were laid against one BSWFA member who had played a leading role as a fishermen's representative on the federal Lobster Advisory Committee. Found not guilty of these charges in provincial court in May 1986, the case has been appealed to the Nova Scotia Supreme Court.

State efforts to continue the insulation of the BSWFA from its allies among inshore fishermen have continued with little success. As the crisis of survival in the fisheries has extended to other sectors—like the scallop, crab, and herring fisheries—a growing body of opposition to state plans is emerging and the militancy of the BSWFA is becoming infectious. The pages of regional fisheries newspapers like the *Atlantic Fisherman* and local journals like the *Guardian* have begun to reflect widening resistance from other sectors. By now, neither the state nor its DFO auxiliaries appear to have much faith in persuasion as an effective tactic for winning over fisheries communities to the virtues of their own elimination.

Pursuing their strategy of mobilizing as much support as possible, the BSWFA has used state-designed occasions such as a DFO-sponsored Lobster District 4A Management Seminar in January 1985 to challenge DFO "management options" and to strengthen fishermen's resolve to push back the federal effort to control unfairly, and thus destroy, their livelihood. Through the state-sponsored and largely manipulated or ignored Lobster Advisory Committee, in conversations with DFO officials in Yarmouth and Halifax, in public forums such as community meetings and radio talk shows, BSWFA efforts at demythologizing and demystifying state legitimacy continue to play a role in forwarding the process of community and class struggle. On the other hand, while BSWFA participation in the Lobster Advisory Committee has prevented the DFO from pushing through unacceptable trap limits, the DFO has steadily pulled back from debate in the Committee, pushing controversial agenda items up the bureaucratic chain of command from Yarmouth towards Halifax and Ottawa.

The BSWFA, of course, continues to confront the state legally through the courts and in parliamentary committees. During a long evening session of the Parliamentary Committee on Fisheries and Forestry (June 5, 1984), a BSWFA delegation provided detailed evidence of the DFO's arbitrary and excessive enforcement practices and of violations of the independence of the judiciary through DFO and Nova Scotia governmental participation in the "deal" which subverted a fair hearing of the original charges of piracy.[23] At a second meeting in the Fall of 1985, the BSWFA delegation convinced the Committee to hold hearings into the issues raised "at the earliest possible moment."[24]

The BSWFA has secured a careful legal briefing on the merits of a constitutional challenge to DFO practice, including dimensions of "judicial blackmail" raised by the "deal." The BSWFA is also in support of efforts by individual fishermen who have challenged the DFO "sector management" rationale for catch restrictions in other fisheries, and the Department's efforts to place new "waiver requirements" on fishermen seeking boat construction loans from the Fisheries Loan Board. In the face of state coercion, the community of Woods Harbour has been consciously exhausting all "legal" options.

While it most emphatically cannot be said that the Woods Harbour struggle will be won tomorrow, we can assure those who seek to learn from this vital, many-pronged, and ongoing expression of solidarity against tremendous odds, that the power of popular class liberation will not ultimately be denied.

NOTES

1. "Petty producers" is the usual term employed to refer to independent/dependent commodity producers who are neither, strictly speaking, working class nor bourgeois, being both workers and owners of means of production. The term, as will be obvious in our treatment of it, definitely does not connote any lack of importance or pettiness.
2. R. Williams, "The Restructuring That Wasn't: The Scandal at National Sea," *New Maritimes* 2(7), 1984, pp. 4–8. L.G. Barret, and A. Davis, *Floundering in Troubled Waters.* Halifax, Gorsebrook Institute for Atlantic Canada Studies Occasional Paper No. 1, St. Mary's University, 1983.
3. R.J. Sacouman, "Co-operative Community Development Among Nova Scotian Primary Producers, 1861–1940." In N.B. Ridler (ed.), *Issues in Regional/Urban Development of Atlantic Canada.* Saint John: University of New Brunswick at Saint John Social Sciences Monograph Series, 2, 1980, pp. 11–26; M.P. Connelly, and M. MacDonald, "Women's Work: Domestic and Wage Labour in a Nova Scotia Community," *Studies in Political Economy* 10, 1983, pp. 45–72; R.J. Brym, and R.J. Sacouman, *Underdevelopment and Social Movements in Atlantic Canada.* Toronto: New Hogtown Press, 1979.

4. R. Williams, "Inshore Fisherman, Unionization, and the Struggle Against Underdevelopment Today," in Brym and Sacouman, 1979, *op. cit.*, pp. 161–175.

5. B.D. Fairley, "The Development of Capitalism in the Fishing Industry in Newfoundland: A Critique of Narodism in the Atlantic Canada." Unpublished M.A. Thesis, Department of Political Science, Queen's University, 1983 and "The 'Metaphysics' of Dualism and the Development of Capitalism in the Fishing Industry in Newfoundland." Paper presented at the annual meeting of the Atlantic Association of Sociologists and Anthropologists, University of New Brunswick, 1984.

6. For a somewhat alternative line of argument concerning populism that also stresses the need for working-class alliances with small-scale worker-owners, see J.F. Conway, "The Nature of Populism: A Clarification," *Studies in Political Economy* 13, 1984, pp. 137–144, and A. Finkel, "Populism and the Proletariat: Social Credit and the Alberta Working Class," *Studies in Political Economy* 13, 1984, pp. 109–135.

7. This section is a slightly less journalistic version of D.J. Grady, and R.J. Sacouman, "Guilt by (Fishermen's) Association: The State Versus the Woods Harbour 15 + 1043," *New Maritimes* 2(6), 1984, pp. 4–6 and *Canadian Dimension* 18(2), 1984, pp. 4–6. For more on the Story, see A. David, and L. Kasdan, "Bankrupt Government Policies and Belligerent Fishermen Responses: Dependency and Conflict in Southwest Nova Scotia Small Boat Fisheries." Paper presented at the Marginal Regions Seminar, Gregynon, Wales, August 1983; D.J. Grady, "'Big Media' and 'Small Harbours': Distortions of the Community Struggle in Southwestern Nova Scotia," *Atlantic Fisherman* 1(1), 1984, p. 7, and K. Nickerson, "'Piracy' and Grassroots Unity: Coastal Communities on Trial," *New Maritimes* 2(2), 1983, pp. 4–5.

8. A. Davis, "Property Rights and Access Management in the Small Boat Fishery: A Case Study from Southwest-Nova Scotia," in A. Hanson and C. Lamsen (eds.), *Fisheries Decision-Making: Perspectives on East Coast Canadian Policy Setting and Implementation.* Halifax: Department of Ocean Studies, Dalhousie University, 1983.

9. On the general explosion of inshore fishermen's indebtedness to the federal and provincial governments and the directly related skyrocketing of costs of equipment, see Davis and Kasdan, *op. cit.*

10. A.G. Gray, "The Offshore Small Boat Fishery of South West Nova Scotia." Unpublished M.E.S. Thesis, Dalhousie University.

11. K. Nickerson, *op. cit.*

12. In fact, most of our material here will under-represent and under-rate the Women's Support Group's vital work. The principal reasons for this are: the DFO and its operations directly discount, treat as redundant, other members of fishing communities who are not fisher*men* and discussions of state-community interactions are male-dominated. Any paper on precise,

solidarity-building processes of mobilization within Woods Harbour and between Woods Harbour and other neighboring coastal communities would necessarily document the leading role of the Women's Group.

13. In this task we will utilize concepts and categories first introduced by William A. Gamson, in *Power and Discontent*. Homewood, Ill.: Doresey Press, 1968, and most recently applied in W.A. Gamson, B. Fireman, and S. Rytina, *Encounters with Unjust Authority*. Homewood, Ill.: Doresey Press, 1983.

14. *Halifax Chronicle Herald*, May 7, 1984, p. 27.

15. More could (and will) be said later regarding the specifics of BSWFA organizing. For the moment at least, this area may be best left to the knowledge of membership and community—and the imagination of state authorities.

16. See, for example, press report in *New Maritimes* in March 1984, *Halifax Chronicle Herald*, April–May 1984 and CBC radio and television coverage, March 21, April 24 and May 7, 1984. Given the BSWFA's development of the Lobster Advisory Committee as a resource, it is currently an open question whether this dimension has shifted categories from inducement to constraint. One thing is quite certain; the DFO is increasingly nervous that the BSWFA may be in the process of turning the state's creation against its original purpose of "domesticating" the South Shore dissidents and demonstrating the futility of "resistance" to all other members of the Atlantic inshore fishery.

17. Paul Sutherland, DFO Director of Fisheries Operations for the Scotia-Fundy region (including southwestern Nova Scotia), made this point clearly in conversation with a BSWFA representative and D.J. Grady on May 7, 1984. Sutherland referred to the need to "quiet things down" and persuade the BSWFA to be "more realistic" in response to the "political facts of life in the fishery." He was particularly annoyed that the BSWFA had "gone to the media with stories" about the Department's enforcement practices in southwestern Nova Scotia.

18. For reports on the "deal" as an illustrative case of state ventures into social control, see Grady and Sacouman, 1984, *op. cit*. Oblique discussion of the deal as an aspect of the Woods Harbour story was contained in a CBC broadcast, *Inquiry*, April 4, 1984, and the CBC *Journal*, May 7, 1984. As one fisherman commented: "Well, finally the lid is off the garbage can at last!!"

19. The obverse of the DFO's tactic of isolation is the BSWFA's continuing effort to bring pressure to bear from other regional, national and international groups, e.g., support received from MFU #9, Nova Scotia Federation of Labour, CLC, West Coast Fishermen's Associations, Canadian Farm Survival Association, and the American Farm Movement. Allen Wilford's recent volume, *Farm Gate Defense*, gives a clear and solidary endorsement of the work of the BSWFA, commenting on shared problems and cooperative action by Canadian farmers and fishermen: ". . . because we're all in this

thing together," A. Wilford, *Farm Gate Defense*. Toronto: N.C. Press, 1984, p. 200.

20. As one BSWFA member put it: "We all know what Stan Dudka stands for—head, neck and heels—and it's all lies."

21. What is of particular interest in the Woods Harbour struggle is the strength of community solidarity, organizational commitment and group determination operating in the otherwise lopsidedly unequal balance of forces at work. When compared to many other efforts by relatively small groups to challenge state power in the Canadian context, Woods Harbour is extremely strong in depth and determination. Davis and Kasdan, *op. cit.*, have taken a more pessimistic view of the prospects for success by the Woods Harbour community.

22. For an approach to understanding social bases, mobilization processes and success/failure in cooperative settings, see Sacouman, *op. cit.*

23. Minutes of Proceedings and Evidence of the Standing Committee on Fisheries and Forestry, House of Commons, Issue No. 21, June 5, 1984.

24. *Ibid.*, Issue No. 54, October 30, 1985.

Conclusion

Community Class Struggles
and State Formation

Roxana Ng and Jacob Muller
with Gillian Walker

Introduction

In compiling this collection, we have attempted to display various forms
of organizing efforts at the "community" level and their differential treatment by different levels of "the state": from women's work in the Native
Mother's Guild in a native community in British Columbia (Fiske), to
fishermen's organizing in Nova Scotia (Grady and Sacouman), to criminalization of bath houses in the gay community in Toronto (Smith). The
papers show that what can be described as "community organizing" is
very diverse; it covers a wide range of activities, from women organizing
for state reforms, as in the case of female immigrationists (Roberts) and
middle-class mothers in Toronto schools (Dehli), to reaction and resistance to state intervention in community life in various ways (Muller,
Stasiulis, Hessing, Smith, Grady and Sacouman).

One major message derived from these stories is that both community-
state relations and practices are contradictory. As Dehli and Muller
demonstrate, community activities are not always progressive and do
not always serve the interest of all community members. Similarly, state
responses to demands from below are not unitary. At times, they are
extremely oppressive and coercive, as indicated by treatments of gay
men in Toronto and fishing communities in Atlantic Canada (Smith,
Grady and Sacouman). At other times, experiences such as those of
the Eurasian water milfoil issue (Hessing) and reforms in race relations
in the Toronto Board of Education (Stasiulis) seem to indicate that
grassroots struggles can find a place in state reforms. Frequently, state
programs and practices are shaped by interactions between state officials and pressures from below, as in the case of the Secretary of State

women's program (Schreader) and the Community Employment Strategy Program (Christiansen-Ruffman).

For the actors engaged in these struggles, the courses of action and choices available are never straight forward or simple. These actors are constantly caught in dilemmas which force them to reassess their activities and sometimes even to change the direction of their struggles. The outcome of these struggles are not one-sided victories or failures. Neither "the state" or "the community" has the complete upper hand. The studies included here show that the processes of the struggles themselves are just as important to document and analyze as the outcomes, because they tell us about our mistakes and how we change in the course of our struggles.

Based on the foregoing studies and analyses, a number of questions about community organization and the state, and the relation between the two, can be raised. What kind of conceptualization of "community" and "the state" would be adequate to account for the diversity of people's experiences in different kinds of organizational contexts? What is the precise relationship between "community" and "the state"? And how may we understand and more productively explore gender, sexual, racial and class dynamics in the struggles we have documented in this collection?

Recommendations on Method

The diversity of experiences documented here suggests that we have to develop a different *method* of investigating and understanding "the community" and "the state," and their relation to each other. As we already stated in the Introduction, in the social sciences as well as in everyday usage, "the community" and "the state" are commonly treated as distinct analytical categories and phenomena which designate activities occurring in separate domains. Similarly, terms such as "class," "gender," and "race" are used as analytical categories referencing different phenomena. The term "class" is used to designate the economic domain and objective features of socio-economic life. Gender and race are used to designate aspects of the social and subjective domains. Their relationship to each other can only be derived from analytical schema designed to discover their correlation as variables.

Thus, for example, gender and ethnicity are relevant to studies of social class only if they intersect in the schemata which analysts have constructed to classify certain groups of workers or certain sectors of the population. The state is relevant to researchers of community studies only if certain government policies or programs impinge on the particular community or group they are investigating.[1] In these procedures, the interconnection of certain forces (community-state relations, gender and race dynamics) in the shaping of everyday experiences is left unexaminable.[2]

Some analysts in this collection raise questions about the common usages of these concepts. Walker, Heald, Ng, Schreader, and Muller render problematic notions of "the community" and "the state" as opposing categories in the organization of social life. Stasiulis suggests that considering the struggle against racism apart from "class struggle," as it is traditionally defined in orthodox Marxism, simply does not provide an adequate account of the "new social movements" of which the struggle against racism is a part.[3] While dealing with very different topics, Roberts' and Dehli's analyses show that the category, "women," is internally differentiated by class and ethnicity. Bullock's study shows that the term, "community care," masks women's labor in the family in caring for handicapped children.

Implicit in these studies, then, is a methodological critique of standard examinations of "community," "the state," "class struggle," and so forth, and a recommendation for a different conception of social reality which can deal with the totality and complexity of social experiences. In this conclusion, we would like to put forward a different way of understanding these concepts which can take account of the interconnection and the diversity of people's experiences in everyday life. We suggest that they be treated as *social relations* which have to do with how people relate to each other through productive and reproductive activities.

Our understanding is derived from Marx and Engels' discussion of the materialist method, in which they state that in analyzing the social world, we must constantly keep in mind that it is comprised of "real individuals, their activity and the material conditions under which they live."[4] We argue that Marx's conception of class is more than a mere economic category; it refers to people's relations to the means of production. It is the expression of a process, the result of which is the transformation of sectors of society.[5] When we talk of class, we are referring to a process which indicates how people interact with their material environment and with each other in a given historical moment. They construct and alter their relation to the productive and reproductive forces of society using whatever means they have at their disposal. Although Marx's primary concern is with class relations, a similar understanding can be applied to gender and race relations. Thus, we see that family and kinship (which ethnic theorists consider the primary bases of ethnic group formation), as well as sexuality, are means people deploy to exert their domination or overcome their subordination in any given society.

This understanding of how gender, race and class relations operate is born out by the studies in this collection. For example, Roberts' study shows that in order to consolidate their power within the state apparatus, ruling-class men took over immigration matters which were started by upper-class women. Stasiulis' and Grady and Sacouman's research displays how Blacks and fishermen deploy their racial, ethnic and community ties to resist the domination and oppression by (mainly) white ruling-class men. The conceptualization put forward here, then, brings class, gender, race and community into a relation of necessary interconnection; it does not fragment or isolate them in social analysis.

Rethinking "Community" and "State" as Relations

Following from this understanding of "class as relations," we challenge the commonly held notion of "the state" as a set of apparatuses which stand over and above communities. In such a view, ruling activities are seen to be the repressive and oppressive practices imposed on "the community" by the state. While it is true that "the state" generally refers to the multiplicity of institutions and departments which administer and coordinate the activities of ruling, we also wish to advance the notion of the state as the central constituent in the developing relations of capitalism in Canada. As such, this set of relations did not appear overnight. It was constructed through time, by complicated and extensive struggles of people grouped together by their differing relationships to the emerging dominant (in Canada, capitalist) mode of production.[6] It follows that "communities" and community protests are the other side of the same coin: their emergence and decline has to do with extensive struggles of people grouped together by their differing relationships to the dominant mode of production which manifests and asserts itself in different localities.

Thus, people don't enter into relationships and interactions with either "the state" or "the community." The state and the community are themselves products of people's activities and creations as people group together to struggle for or against domination. Here is how Marx and Engels put it:

> The social structure and the state are continually evolving out of the life process of definite individuals, but of individuals, not as they appear in their own or other people's imagination, but as they really are, i.e., as they operate, produce materially and hence as they work under definite material limits, presuppositions and conditions, independent of their will.[7]

The formation of the state in Canada occurred during the consolidation of British and French rule (and the struggle between the two) through immigration and colonization. The constitution of a community is directly related to the way that a particular struggle is waged. Hence, we have "ethnic communities," the "gay community," the "business community," as well as communities bounded by geographic boundaries. As Walker's historical examination of "community" and "community economic development" reveals, the separation of "the state" from "the community" has to do with the separation of politics and the economy from civil society. As capitalism develops, "community" comes to be identified with the good and the benevolent; "the state" comes to be seen as a neutral entity which is open to influence and pressure by different constituency groups in the community.

In Canada, the separation of the state from the community becomes increasingly solidified with nation building. Implicit in the task of nation building is a gender division of labor. In examining the work of upper-class women from Britain between 1880 and 1920, Roberts divides the work of nation building into two aspects. The first had to do with developing the infra-structure of the economy: the building of a nation-wide transportation system, the development of a manufacturing base and a commodity market, etc. This was the domain of men. The second aspect had to do with the building of the human nation: the development of a population base in Canada. Women reformers were the active organizers of this aspect of nation building. To ensure the white and Christian character of the nation, these women worked relentlessly to organize the emigration of working-class girls from Britain to serve as domestic servants and wives in the new colony. They were the first people to establish immigration societies in major cities in Canada to take care of new immigrants. Similarly, Dehli's research on school reforms in Toronto at the turn of the 20th century shows that middle-class mothers from (mainly) British background worked hard to introduce and enforce a set of "correct" (read middle-class) mothering practices on working-class immigrant women through the school system. In these studies, we find that gender, ethnicity/race, class dynamics are intertwined with the construction of the state and community.

As ruling-class men consolidated their power in the state apparatus, they also began to take over and incorporate women's work into the state. Thus, Roberts finds that by 1920, control over immigration and the settlement of immigrants had shifted from the hands of the family, and to the mediation of relations between the economy and civil society, namely, in the community. This is what Bullock discovers when she examines the ideology of "community care." She finds that community care is in effect the work women do, without pay, when the state attempts to shift its funding priority away from social responsibilities.

As the character of corporate capitalism changes in relation to changing economic requirements, both in Canada and globally, the management and regulatory systems in the state also change. Increasing unemployment and social dissension make it necessary to develop new ways of containing and accommodating marginalized sectors of the population. Thus, in studies by Christiansen-Ruffman, Fiske, Heald, Ng and Schreader, we see the development and extension of the state apparatus into local communities through funding and employment programs. These programs further fragment the already marginalized groups (women, immigrants, and native people), creating new divisions and contradictions within these groups.

The Relations of Ruling

What these studies demonstrate is that the activities of ruling do not take place merely in the formal state apparatus. They penetrate relations in community life. In effect, ruling involves various administrative practices and modes of management which occur at different sites: in governmental departments naturally, but also on the reserve (Fiske), in residential neighborhoods (Muller), in community groups (Heald and Ng), as well as through organizing forums which solicit a variety of interests, including business and grassroots input (Hessing).

In an advanced capitalist social formation such as the one we have in Canada, many of these administrative forms are routinized and entrenched as part of "the normal way of doing things," not just in governments, but in community groups as well. Thus, both Heald and Ng find that while funding to community and women's groups represented gains for these groups, the procedures required by funding programs and developed by the groups themselves became an oppressive force within the groups. These procedures structured the relations among group members such that an internal fragmentation occurred. Some group members became the enforcers of class rule. Even radical neighborhood organizing, as Muller's analysis of an Alinsky-style organization in Vancouver reveals, does not pose a fundamental challenge to the local state. It can be seen that these administrative and managerial processes are reproduced at different sites in different manifestations both within the state and in the community.

However, since ruling also has to encompass different and competing interests, the administrative and managerial activities developed to deal with these interests are not, and cannot be, uniform. Thus,

Christiansen-Ruffman finds, in her examination of the federal Community Employment Strategy Program implemented in Labrador, Nova Scotia, and Prince Edward Island, that the policies of one level of government might be interpreted and enacted quite differently by another level of government in different provinces.

This reality of class rule in a liberal democratic state means that space can be created to accommodate interests from below. Hessing finds that grassroots environmental groups could attempt to interfere with the otherwise unchecked use of 2,4-D in the Okanagan lakes. Schreader finds that the establishment of the Women's Program within the federal Secretary of State department was a response to pressures from the women's movement. Although ultimately class rule prevailed, subordinate groups were able to make gains in the short-run. Certainly, these efforts served to heighten people's awareness of the issues involved and of the possibility of pushing beyond existing boundaries which constitute the state and the community.

On the other hand, if protests from below pose or become a threat to bourgeois hegemony and Canadian nationalism, which is rooted in Anglo-patriarchal heterosexual conformity, then these attempts will be violently suppressed. Stasiulis' comparative study shows that while anti-racist struggles within the Toronto Board of Education could be accommodated, they were resisted in the Toronto police force. Similarly, Toronto's gay community has to put up with constant harassment by the police, as Smith's discussion on policing the gay community reveals. The marginalization and criminalization of homosexuals is legitimated by the legal system and enforced by the police, the courts, and other regulatory institutions. Finally, when petty commodity producers', in this case fishermen's, interest clashes with the interest of the capitalistic fishing industry, it is militantly suppressed by the Department of Fisheries and Oceans (DFO) and the courts.

The various studies in this collection, documenting the variety of organizing attempts in the community and within different levels of the government, begin to pinpoint the possibilities and limits of working within the confines of a liberal democratic state such as the one we have in Canada. The diversity of these experiences are directly attributable to the changing requirements in the development of capitalism in Canada over time. Capitalist developments fragment people's experiences (e.g., by separating politics and the economy from civil society), while homogenizing other processes at the same time (e.g., by creating and routinizing management systems which are administered in similar ways at different sites). We emphasize that these processes are enacted in *social relations*, which are embodied in ordinary everyday activities.

The Documentary Mode of Action

Many papers in this collection directly or indirectly describe the way in which documentary processes play a key role in mediating the relation between the community and the state. We especially want to draw attention to the centrality of these processes in coordinating ruling activities and in facilitating the enforcement of class rule at different sites. From the case studies, it becomes clear that it is through documents that ruling penetrates local groups and communities.

Smith's analysis of the police investigative report on bath houses shows precisely how provisions in the *Criminal Code* organize the activities of the police department in its investigation; they shape the way in which policemen select and interpret people's interactions in a bath house. Hessing's study shows that in order for people's experiences to be admissible as evidence and proof in a tribunal, they have to be presented in a particular language and format. Heald and Ng describe how the production of various kinds of data (e.g., financial information and performance evaluation), in particular documentary formats, is key to community groups' ability to obtain and secure government funding, which also ties these groups to the apparatus of ruling. Indeed, it can be said that in contemporary societies, ruling is encoded largely in documentary processes such as in legislation, orders in council, interdepartmental memoranda, and contracts.[8]

It is through documentary processes of various kinds that ruling can take place simultaneously at different sites, not simply in the formal state apparatuses, but also in local communities, such as in an isolated native reserve (Fiske), and in community groups (Ng and Heald). Thus, it is no longer meaningful to refer to the state as if it stands over and above us. Indeed, if we participate in administering some kind of documentary process, we are implicated in the activities of class rule, because the documentary mode of management penetrates local settings, and connects them ultimately to the larger managerial contexts of corporations and different levels of the government.[9]

Community Class Struggle

What is the implication for community class struggles of the understanding of community and the state we put forward above? It is clear that the commonly held notions of the state as standing over and above individuals in civil society, and the community as representing the good and the benevolent sphere of social life, are inadequate to account for how "ruling" takes place and has consequences for people's lives. We have used the term, "ruling," here to point to the management of people which takes different forms and which occurs simultaneously at different sites, both in the formal state apparatus and in the community. Modes of ruling change over time in response to changes in the requirements for capitalist accumulation and responses to struggles from below. In contemporary society, ruling has come to be encoded in documents; this is one way in which ruling activities penetrate community life. In struggling for change, therefore, we have to be aware constantly of how forms of ruling alter and develop to capture and incorporate different segments of the population.

Having gained some understanding of how ruling works in modern society, we need to develop alternate forms of resistance and ways of organizing social life. This will be a difficult task, because we don't have many blueprints to follow. But we know that these forms of resistance cannot be uniform because our experiences, as men and women, as majority and minority group members—as people situated in different locations divided by age, gender, race, sexual orientation and class—are not the same. We need to develop multiple strategies, at our different locations, for coping, surviving, and resisting forms of ruling imposed from the outside as well as from within.

Given the pervasiveness of documents in our daily work and documents' ability to enforce class rule in an organizational setting, we feel that activists must seriously analyze the role documentary processes play in sanctioning certain courses of action and rendering illegitimate other courses of action in the context of their own work, as recommended by Ng and Heald. We suggest that this is a new terrain of struggle in contemporary reality. A deeper understanding of documentary processes and how they work can open up new possibilities in defining new areas of autonomy for people in subordinate positions, as noted by Smith in the conclusion to his analysis. One such struggle, as Heald suggests in her "Afterword," is to develop a language which would describe more accurately her experience of being "in and against the state."[10] Elsewhere, Muller has suggested developing a language for the people with whom one works, rather than making use of the managerial language which has become so much a part of our everyday vocabulary.[11]

The transformation of social life for subordinate groups under capitalism is a long and tedious process. As demonstrated by the studies in this collection, we can never take our own mode of organization for granted, because class rule, through different kinds of documentary and other processes, has a way of transforming our practices. Thus, working toward change involves a constant analysis of the forces which oppress us, as well as a critical assessment of our own practices. In particular, we have to confront and grapple with the contradictions we experience in different work sites, and attempt to understand the dynamics which generate these contradictions.

This collection of papers has posed a challenge to how we think about "the community" and "the state." We suggest that the way in which these concepts are traditionally defined have restricted our ability to look beyond the confines of what constitute "the community" and community development. It has restricted our ability to develop resistance and build alliances across traditionally defined community boundaries. In closing, we want to emphasize the fluidity of the boundaries between communities and the state. How these boundaries are defined and constituted must be a subject of critical exploration at all times. Furthermore, we need to assess and learn from the organizing experiences of other progressive groups frequently not included in the community development literature. We can learn from feminist, gay and lesbian struggles, struggles by the disabled, struggles by native nations and ethnic groups, as well as struggles waged by subordinate groups in developing nations. These struggles can inform and inspire us to develop alternate forms of organizing and resistance, which will bring us a step closer to the larger movement toward a truly democratic society.

NOTES

1. For examples of such studies on class relations, see Alfred Hunter, *Class Tells. On Social Inequality in Canada*, 2nd ed., Butterworths, 1986; and various writings by the leading American Marxist scholar, Eric Olin Wright. A noted example of Wright's work, which has been used extensively, is "Class boundaries in capitalist societies," *New Left Review*, 98, 1976, pp. 3–41. For examples of works on the community and the state, see the citations in the Introduction.

2. For a more extended discussion of the problems of standard approaches to gender, race, and class, see Roxana Ng, "Conceptual difficulties of the interrelation of gender, race/ethnicity, and class—a discussion," a lecture given at a course on "Critical Philosophy of Science," University at Bergen, Bergen, Norway, May 1988.

3. This is also the position of Ernesto Laclau and Chantal Mouffe, *Hegemony and Socialist Strategy*. London: Verso, 1985, and John Urry, *The Anatomy of Capitalist Societies*. London: Macmillan Press, 1981.

4. See Marx and Engels, *The German Ideology*. New York: International Publishers, 1970, p. 42. This method has been elaborated by contemporary theorists such as Dorothy E. Smith, *The Everyday World as Problematic: A Feminist Sociology*. Toronto: University of Toronto Press, 1987; and Derek Sayer, *Marx's Method: Ideology, Science and Critique in Capital*. Sussex: The Harvester Press, 2nd Printing, 1983.

5. This understanding of Marx's notion of class is eloquently explained by Harry Braverman in *Labor and Monopoly Capital. The Degradation of Work in the Twentieth Century*. New York: Monthly Review Press. See also E.P. Thompson, *The Making of the English Working Class*. Middlesex: Penguin, 1963.

6. See Mary McIntosh, quoted in Corrigan and Derek Sayer, *The Great Arch. English State Formation as Cultural Revolution*. Oxford: Basil Blackwell, 1985.

7. Marx and Engels, *op. cit.*, pp. 47–48.

8. In sociology, ethnomethodologists were the first to take documentary features in contemporary society seriously as an area of empirical investigation. See the works of Harold Garfinkel, *Studies in Ethnomethodology*. Englewood Cliffs, N.J.: Prentice Hall, 1967; Staton Wheeler (ed.), *On Record: Files and Dossiers in American Life*. New York: Russell Sage Foundation, 1969, and Don Zimmerman, "Fact as a practical accomplishment," in Roy Turner (ed.), *Ethnomethodology*. Middlesex: Penguin, 1974, for example. For a discussion specifically on the role of texts in ruling, see Dorothy E. Smith, "Textually mediated social organization," *International Social Sciences Quarterly* 36(1), 1984, pp. 59–75.

9. For another example which displays the pervasiveness of documentary processes in the organization of a local setting, see Jacob Muller, "Ruling through texts: developing a social service training program for a community college," *Community Development Journal*, 24(4), 1989, pp. 273–282.

10. London Edinburgh Weekend Return Group, *In And Against the State*. London: Pluto Press, 1980.

11. Jacob Muller, *op. cit.* See also the work by the Progressive Literacy Group, *Writing on Our Side*. Vancouver: Progressive Literacy Group, 1986; and Richard Darville, "The language of experience and the literacy of power," in J. Draper and M. Taylor (eds.), *Adult Basic Education: A Field of Practice*. Toronto: Culture Concepts Inc., forthcoming in 1989.

Bibliography

ABRAMS, P. (ed). 1978 *Work, Urbanism and Inequality*. London: Weidenfeld and Nicolson.

ACKELSBERG, Martha A. 1983 " 'Sisters' or 'Comrades'? The Politics of Friends and Families." in I. Diamond (ed), *Families, Politics and Public Policy*. London: Longman.

AHLBRANDT, Jr., Roger S. 1984 *Neighbourhoods, People and Community*. N.Y.: Plenum Press.

ALINSKY, Saul. 1941 "Community Analysis and Organization." *American Journal of Sociology*, Vol. XLVI, May, pp. 797–808.

1962 *Citizen Participation and Community Organization in Planning and Urban Renewal*. Chicago: The Industrial Areas Foundation.

1969 *Reveille for Radicals*. New York: Vintage.

1972 *Rules for Radicals*. New York: Random House

ANDREW, Caroline and Rejean PELLETIER. 1978 "The Regulators" in G. Bruce Doern (ed), *The Regulatory Process in Canada*. Toronto: Macmillan.

ARMOUR, Leslie. 1981 *The Idea of Canada and the Crisis of Community*. Ottawa: Steel Rail Educational Publishing.

ARMSTRONG, Patricia. 1983 *Labour Pains: Women's Work in Crisis*. Toronto: The Women's Press.

ARNOPOULOS, Sheila M. 1979 *Problems of Immigrant Women in the Canadian Labour Force*. Ottawa: Advisory Council on the Status of Women.

BAILEY, F.G. 1969 *Stratagems and Spoils: A Social Anthropology of Politics*. Oxford: Basil Blackwell.

BAILEY, R. Jr. 1972 *Radicals in Urban Politics: The Alinsky Method*. Chicago: University of Chicago Press.

BARRETT, L. Gene. 1983 "Uneven Development, Rent and the Social Organization of Capital: A Case Study of the Fishing Industry of Nova Scotia, Canada." Unpublished PhD. thesis, University of Sussex.

BARRETT, L. Gene and Anthony DAVIS. 1983 *Floundering in Troubled Waters: The Political Economy of the Atlantic Fishery and the Task Force on Atlantic Fisheries*. Halifax: Gorsebrook Institute for Atlantic Canada Studies. Occasional Paper No. 1, Saint Mary's University.

BARTON, Stephen E. 1977 "The Urban Housing Problem: Marxist Theory and Community Organizing." *Review of Radical Political Economics*, Vol. 9, 4: 16–30.

BEAR, Leroy Little, Menno BOLDT, and J. Anthony LANG (eds). 1984 *Pathways to Self-determination: Canadian Indians and the Canadian State*. Toronto: University of Toronto Press.

BERELSON, B.R. 1954 *Voting*. Chicago: University of Chicago Press.

BERRY, John; Rudolf KALIN and Donald TAYLOR. 1976 *Multicultural Attitudes in Canada*. Ottawa: Ministry of Supply and Services.

BLACK EDUCATION PROJECT. 1976 "The Black Education Project, 1969–1976." Toronto, mimeo.

BLAU, Joel. 1980 "The Consent of the Served — Some Notes on the Literature of Citizen Participation." *Catalyst*, 5. Toronto, Ontario.

BLUESTONE, Barry. 1982 "Deindustrialization and the Abandonment of Community" in J.C. Raines, *et al.* (eds), *Community and Capital in Conflict*. Philadelphia: Temple University Press.

BLUESTONE, Barry and Bennett HARRISON. 1980 *Capital and Communities*. Washington, D.C.: The Progressive Alliance.

BODIE, Bertrand and Pierre BIRNBAUM. 1983 *The Sociology of the State*. Chicago: University of Chicago Press.

BOGGS, Carl. 1976 *Gramsci's Marxism*. London: Pluto Press.

BORIS, Eileen and Peter BARDAGLIO. 1983 "The Transformation of Patriarchy: The Historic Role of the State" in I. Diamond (ed), *Families, Politics and Public Policy*. London: Longman.

BOWLES, Gloria and Renate Duelli KLEIN (eds). 1983 *Theories of Women's Studies*. London: Routledge and Kegan Paul.

BOWLES, Samuel and Herbert GINTIS. 1986 *Democracy and Capitalism*. New York: Basic Books.

BOYTE, Harry C. 1980 *The Backyard Revolution*. Philadelphia: Temple University Press.

BOYTE, Harry C. and Sara M. EVANS. 1984 "Strategies in Search of America: Cultural Radicalism, Populism, and Democratic Culture." *Socialist Review*, Vol. 14(3), pp. 73–100.

BRANDWEIN, Ruth A. 1982 "Toward Androgyny in Community and Organizational Practice." in A. Weick and S.T. Vandiver (eds)., *Women, Power and Change*. Washington, D.C.: National Association of Social Workers, Inc.

BRAVERMAN, Harry. 1974 *Labour and Monopoly Capital. The Degradation of Work in the Twentieth Century*. New York: Monthly Review Press.

BREINES, Wini. 1982 *Community and Organization in the New Left: 1962–1968*. N.Y.: Praeger.

BRETON, Raymond. 1981 "The Ethnic Community as a Resource in Relation to Group Problems: Perceptions and Attitudes." Research Paper No. 122, Centre for Urban and Community Studies, University of Toronto.

BRIGHT, Charles and Susan HARDING (eds). 1984 *Statemaking and Social Movements*. Ann Arbor: University of Michigan Press.

BRITISH COLUMBIA, Ministry of Environment. 1978 "Some Facts about 2,4-D." Victoria: Aquatic Plant Management Program.

BRUNER, A. 1981 "Out of the Closet: A Study of the Relations between the Homosexual Community and the Police." A report to Mayor Arthur Eggleton and the Council of the City of Toronto. Toronto: City Clerk's Office.

BRYM, Robert J. and R. James SACOUMAN. 1979 *Underdevelopment and Social Movements in Atlantic Canada*. Toronto: New Hogtown Press.

BUCKLEY, Suzanne. 1977 "British Female Immigration and Imperial Development." *Hecate: Women's Interdisciplinary Journal*, January 1977.

BULLOCK, Anne. 1986 "Community Care of Severely Handicapped Children at Home: A Moment in the Organization of Women's Work." Unpublished Thesis, School of Social Work, Carleton University, Ottawa.

BULLOCK, Anne and Marie L. CAMPBELL. 1986 "Community Care: An Analysis of Gendered Ideology-Bound Ruling Practices," Paper presented to the Canadian Sociology and Anthropology Association (CSAA) Meeting, The Learned Societies Conference, University of Manitoba.

BUREAU OF MUNICIPAL RESEARCH. 1921 *White Paper No. 47*. Toronto.

BURSTYN, Varda. 1983 "Masculine Dominance and the State" in Ralph Miliband and John Saville (eds), *Socialist Register, 1983*. London: Merlin Press.

CAMPBELL, Marie. 1985 "Managerialism: A Class Phenomenon in Nursing." Paper presented to CSAA Session Marxian Analysis of Professional Occupations. The Learned Societies Conference, University of Montreal, May 29.

CAMPFEUS, Hubert (ed). 1983 *Rethinking Community Development in a Changing Society*. Guelph, Ont.: Ontario Community Development Society.

CANADA, Employment and Immigration Commission. 1977 *Community Employment Strategy 1976–1977*. Ottawa: Supply and Services Canada.

1980 *Annual Report*. Ottawa: Supply and Services Canada.

1985 *Evaluation of Challenge '85 Summer Employment/Experience Development [SEED] Program Element*. Ottawa: Population Evaluation Branch, Strategic Policy and Planning.

CANADA, House of Commons. 1969 *Hansard*. Ottawa: Queen's Printer.

1982 *Minutes of Proceedings and Evidence of the Standing Committee on Justice and Legal Affairs*. Issue No. 81, Wednesday, May 5th, 1982.

CANADA, Minister of State, Multiculturalism. 1982 "Race Relations and the Law." Report of a Symposium held in Vancouver, April.

CANADA, Royal Commission on the Criminal Law. 1958 *Report of the Royal Commission on the Criminal Law Relating to Criminal Sexual Psychopaths*. Ottawa: Queen's Printer.

CANADIAN UNITY INFORMATION OFFICE. 1984 *The Government and the Working Person*. Ottawa: Supply and Services Canada.

CASTELLS, M. 1983 *The City and the Grassroots*. Berkeley and Los Angeles, California: U. of California Press.

CAWSON, Alan. 1982 *Corporation and Welfare*. London: Heinemann.

CAWSON, Alan and P. SAUNDERS. 1983 "Corporatism, Competitive Politics and Class Struggle" in R. King (ed), *Capital and Politics*. London: Routledge and Kegan Paul.

CHEKKI, D. (ed). 1979 *Community Development: Theory and Method of Planned Change*. New Delhi: Vikas.

CHRISTIANSEN-RUFFMAN, Linda and Janice Wood CATANO. 1986 "Resistance to Consumer Participation among Health Planners: A Case Study of BONDING'S Encounters with Entrenched Ideas and Structures." *Resources for Feminist Research*, Vol. 15(1), pp. 21–23.

CHRISTIANSEN-RUFFMAN, Linda and Barry STUART. 1978 "Actors and Processes in Citizen Participation: Negative Aspects of Reliance on Professionals." in B. Sadler (ed), *Involvement and Environment*, Vol. 1. Edmonton: Environment Council of Canada, pp. 77–102.

CLARK, David B. 1973 "The Concept of Community: A Re-examination." *Sociological Review* Vol. 2(3), pp. 397–416.

CLASTRES, Pierre. 1977 *Society Against the State*. New York: Urizen Books.

CLEMENT, Wallace. 1986 *The Struggle to Organize*. Toronto: McClelland and Stewart.

1979 "Property and Proletarianization: Transformation of Simple Commodity Procedures in Canadian Farming and Fishing" in Wallace Clement (ed), *Class, Power and Property: Essays on Canadian Society*. Toronto: Methuen.

1975 *The Canadian Corporate Elite: An Analysis of Economic Power*. Toronto: McClelland and Stewart.

COCHRANE, Honora M. 1950 *Centennial Story: The Board of Education for the City of Toronto, 1850–1950*. Toronto: Thomas Nelson and Sons.

COCKBURN, Cynthia. 1977a *The Local State: Management of Cities and People*. London: Pluto Press.

1977b "When Women Get Involved in Community Action." in M. Mayo (ed), *Women in the Community*. London: Routledge and Kegan Paul.

COHEN, Jean. 1983 *Class and Civil Society*. Oxford: Martin Robertson.

COHEN, G. Marjorie. 1987 *Free Trade and the Future of Women's Work*. Toronto: Garamond Press.

COHEN, Youssef, *et al*. 1981 "The Paradoxical Nature of State-making: The Violent Creation of Order." *American Political Science Review*, Vol. 75(4), pp. 901–910.

COLLIER, Ken. 1984 *Social Work with Rural People*. Vancouver: New Star Books.

CONNELLY, M. Patricia and Martha MacDONALD. 1983 "Women's Work: Domestic and Wage Labour in a Nova Scotia Community." *Studies in Political Economy*, 13, pp. 137–144.

CORRIGAN, Paul and Peter LEONARD. 1978 *Social Work Practice Under Capitalism: A Marxist Approach*. London: MacMillan Press.

CORRIGAN, Philip (ed). 1980 *Capitalism, State Formation and Marxist Theory*. London: Quartet Books.

1984 "Doing Mythologies." *Borderlines*, 1 (Fall), pp. 20–22.

CORRIGAN, Philip; Harvie RAMSAY and Derek SAYER. 1980 "The State as a Relation of Production" in P. Corrigan (ed), *Capitalism, State Formation and Marxist Theory*. London: Quartet Books.

CORRIGAN Philip and Derek SAYER. 1985 *The Great Arch*. London: Basil Blackwell.

COWLEY, J., *et al*. (eds). 1977 *Community or Class Struggle?* London: Routledge and Kegan Paul.

CRAIG, G.; N. DERRICOURT and M. LONEY (eds). 1982 *Community Work and the State*. London: Routledge and Kegan Paul.

CROWLEY, Terry. 1980 "Ada Mary Brown Courtice: Pacifist, Feminist and Educational Reformer in Early Twentieth Century Canada." *Studies in History and Politics*, pp. 75–114.

DAHL, R.A. 1956 *A Preface to Democratic Theory*. Chicago: University of Chicago Press.

DALY, M. 1970 *The Revolution Game*. Toronto: New Press.

DARVILLE, Richard. 1989 "The Language of Experience and the Literacy of Power" in J. Draper and M. Taylor (eds), *Adult Basic Education: A Field of Practice*. Toronto: Culture Concepts Inc., forthcoming.

DAVIS, Anthony. 1983 "Property Rights and Access Management in the Small Boat Fishery: A Case Study from Southwest Nova Scotia" in A. Hanson and C. Lamsen (eds). *Fisheries Decision-Making: Perspectives on East Coast Canadian Policy Setting and Implementation*. Halifax: Department of Ocean Studies, Dalhousie University.

DAVIS, Anthony and Leonard KASDAN. 1983 "Bankrupt Government Policies and Belligerent Fisherman Responses: Dependency and Conflict in the Southwest Nova Scotia Small Boat Fisheries." Paper presented at the Marginal Regions Seminar, Gregynon, Wales, August.

DAWLEY, A. 1976 *Class and Community*. Cambridge, Mass.: Harvard University Press.

DELHI, Kari. 1984 "Community Work and Schooling in the Toronto Board of Education." Unpublished Master's Thesis, Ontario Institute for Studies in Education, University of Toronto.

1983 "Out of the City Trenches: Some Notes on Analysis of and Practice in Communities." Unpublished Ms, Toronto: Ontario Institute for Studies in Education, Dept. of Sociology in Education.

DEVELOPMENT PLANNING ASSOCIATES LIMITED. 1978a *Labrador Straits Community Employment Strategy*. Prepared for the Canada Employment and Immigration Commission, the CES Coordinators, and the Communities in Labrador Straits, 4 Vols.

1978b *Evaluation of the Community Employment Strategy in Prince Edward Island*. Prepared for the CEIC and the Joint Federal-Provincial Manpower Needs Committee for P.E.I. 5 Vols.

1978c *Evaluation of the Community Employment Strategy in Nova Scotia*. Prepared for the CEIC and the Nova Scotia CES Research and Evaluation Committee, 6 Vols.

DEVLIN, Sir P. 1959 *The Enforcement of Morals: Maccabean Lecture in Jurisprudence*. London: Oxford University Press.

DIAMOND, Irene (ed). 1983 *Families, Politics and Public Policy: A Feminist Dialogue on Women and the State*. London: Longman.

DI NORCIA, Vincent. 1984 "Social Reproduction and a Federal Community." *Socialist Studies/Etudes Socialistes: A Canadian Annual* pp. 196–210.

DOERN, G. Bruce. 1978 *The Regulatory Process in Canada*. Toronto: Mac-Millan.

DOWNS, Anthony. 1981 *Neighbourhood and Urban Development*. Washington, D.C.: The Brookleigh Institute.

DRAPER, James A. (ed). 1971 *Citizen Participation: Canada, A Book of Readings*. Toronto: New Press.

DROVER, G. and E. SCHRAGGE. 1979 "Urban Struggle and Organizing Strategies." *Our Generation*, Vol. 13(1), pp. 61–71.

DUNCAN, S.S. and M. GOODWIN. 1982 "The Local State and Restructuring Social Relations." *International Journal of Urban and Regional Research*, Vol. 6(2), pp. 157–185.

EDWARDS, John and Richard BATLEY. 1978 *The Politics of Positive Discrimination: An Evaluation of the Urban Program, 1967–77*. London: Tavistock Publications.

EICHLER, Margrit. 1983 "Women, Families and the State" in J. Turner and E. Lois (eds)., *Perspectives on Women in the 1980s*. Winnipeg: University of Manitoba.

EISENSTEIN, Zillah. 1983 "The State, the Patriarchal Family, and Working Mothers." in I. Diamond (ed), *Families, Politics and Public Policy*. London: Longman.

ELSHTANI, Jean Bethke. 1983 "Antigone's Daughters: Reflections on Female Identity and the State" in I. Diamond (ed), *Families, Politics and Public Policy*. London: Longman.

1984 "Reclaiming the Socialist-Feminist Citizen." *Socialist Review* Vol. 14 (2), pp. 21–27.

ENDRES, Robin. 1977 "Art and Accumulation: The Canadian State and the Business of Art" in Leo Panitch, (ed), *The Canadian State: Political Economy and Political Power*. Toronto: University of Toronto Press.

ENGLAND. The Committee on Homosexual Offenses and Prostitution. 1963 *Wolfenden Report of the Committee on Homosexual Offenses and Prostitution*. New York: Stien and Day.

ENGLEHART, K.G. and M.J. TREBILCOCK. 1981 *Public Participation in the Regulatory Process: The Issue of Funding*. Working Paper No. 17. Ottawa: Economic Council of Canada.

EPSTEIN, Steven. 1987 "Gay Politics, Ethnic Identity: The Limits of Social Constructionism." *Socialist Review*, Vol. 17(3&4), pp. 9–54.

FAIRLEY, Bryant D. 1983 "The Development of Capitalism in the Fishing Industry in Newfoundland: A Critique of Narodism in Atlantic Canada." Unpublished M.A. thesis, Department of Political Science, Queen's University.

1984 "The 'Metaphysics' of Dualism and the Development of Capitalism in the Fishing Industry in Newfoundland." Paper presented at the Annual Meeting of the Atlantic Association of Sociologists and Anthropologists, University of New Brunswick.

FERGUSON, Kathy. 1983 "Feminism and Bureaucratic Discourse." *New Political Science*. 11, Spring.

FIDLER, Richard. 1978 *RCMP: The Real Subversives*. Toronto.

FILSON, Glen. 1983 "Class and Ethnic Differences in Canadians' Attitudes to Native People's Rights and Immigration." *Canadian Review of Sociology and Anthropology*, Vol. 20(4), pp. 454–482.

FINCH, Janet. 1984 "Community Care: Developing Non-Sexist Alternatives." *Critical Social Policy*, Issue 9, Vol. 3(3), pp. 6–18.

FINCH, Janet and Dulcie GROVES (eds). 1983 *A Labour of Love: Women, Work, and Caring*. London: Routledge and Kegan Paul.

FINDLAY, Sue. 1982 "Struggle within the State: The Feminist Challenge to Hegemony." Unpublished Ms, Dept. of Political Science, Carleton University.

n.d. "The Politics of the Women's Movement: Lobbying Our Way to Power." Unpublished Ms, Dept. of Political Science, Carleton University.

FINKEL, Alvin. 1984 "Populism and the Proletariat: Social Credit and the Alberta Working Class." *Studies in Political Economy: A Socialist Review*, 13, pp. 109–135.

FISHER, Robert and Peter ROMANOFSKY (eds). 1981 *Community Organization for Social Change: An Historical Perspective*. Westport, Conn.: Greenwood Press.

FLYNN, Rob. 1983 "Co-optation and Strategic Planning in the Local State" in R. King (ed), *Capital and Politics*. London: Routledge and Kegan Paul.

FORM, William H. and Delbert C. MILLER. 1960 *Industry, Labor and Community*. N.Y.: Harper and Brothers.

FOUCAULT, Michel. 1981 "Questions of Method: An Interview with Michel Foucault." *Ideology and Consciousness*, 8, pp. 3–14.

FOWLER, P.A. and P. MCLAUGHLIN. 1980 "The Police Ethnic Relations Unit." Dept. pf Sociology, University of Toronto, mimeo.

FREEMAN, B. 1977 "The Decline and Fall of a Community Organization." *City Magzine*, Vol. 2(7), pp. 18–27.

GAILEY, Christine Ward. 1985 "The State of the State in Anthropology" *Dialectical Anthropology*, Vol. 9(1), pp. 65–89.

GAMSON, William A. 1968 *Power and Discontent*. Homewood Ill.: Dorsey Press.

GAMSON, Wm. A., B. FIREMAN and S. RYTINA. 1983 *Encounters with Unjust Authority*. Homewood, Ill.: Dorsey Press.

GANDY, John. 1979 "Law Enforcement — Race Relations Committees in Metropolitan Toronto: An Experiment in Police-Citizen Partnership." Toronto: Social Planning Council for Metro Toronto.

GARFINKEL, Harold. 1967 *Studies in Ethnomethodology.* Englewood Cliffs, N.J.: Prentice-Hall.

GARFINKEL, H. 1967 "Good Organizational Reasons for 'Bad' Clinical Records" in H. Garfinkel, *Studies in Ethnomethodology.* Englewood Cliffs, N.J.: Prentice-Hall.

GINSBURG, Norman. 1979 *Class, Capital and Social Policy.* London: MacMillan Press.

GLENDENNING, Caroline. 1983 *Unshared Care: Parents and Their Disabled Children.* London: Routledge and Kegan Paul.

GOODWIN, M. and S. DUNCAN. 1986 "The Local State and Local Economic Policy: Political Mobilization or Economic Regeneration." *Capital and Class,* 27 (Winter), pp. 14–36.

GOUGH, Ian. 1979 *The Political Economy of the Welfare State.* London: MacMillan Press.

GRADY, Donald J. 1984 " 'Big Media' and 'Small Harbours': Distortions of the Community Struggle in Southwestern Nova Scotia." *Atlantic Fishermen,* Vol. 1(1), p. 7.

1979 "No Parking: Citizen's Resistance to the Imposition of Government Planning on Nova Scotia's Eastern Shore." Paper presented to the Atlantic Association of Sociologists and Anthropologists, Halifax.

1974 "Politics without Power: Where the Wasteland Begins for Canada" in David J. Martin (ed), *Proceedings of the Conference on Resource Constraints and Human Responses.* Thunder Bay: Lakehead University.

1972 "A Systems Approach to Political Socialization: Learning as a Struggle." Paper presented at the Annual Meeting of the Canadian Sociology and Anthropology Association, Ottawa.

GRADY, D.J.; N. MacLENNAN and J. MULLER. 1975 "Grassroots Influence and Authoritative Social Control: Halifax Municipal Elections of 1971" in Sadatal Dasgupta (ed), *Issues in Urban and Rural Settings of Atlantic Canada.* Charlottetown: U.P.E.I. Press.

GRADY, D.J. and J. SACOUMAN. 1984 "Guilt by (Fishermen's) Association: The State Versus the Woods Harbour 15 + 1043." *New Maritimes,* Vol. 2(6), pp. 4–6 and *Canadian Dimension,* Vol. 18(2), pp. 4–6.

GRAHAM, Hilary. 1983 "Caring — A Labour of Love" in Janet Finch and Dulcia Groves (eds)., *A Labour of Love: Women, Work and Caring.* London: Routledge and Kegan Paul.

GRAMSCI, Antonio. 1971 *Selections from the Prison Notebooks.* New York: International Publishers.

GRANT, Wyn. 1983 "Representing Capital: The Role of the CBI" in R. King (ed), *Capital and Politics*. London: Routledge and Kegan Paul.

GRAY, Allan G. 1983 "The Offshore Small Boat Fishery of Southwest Nova Scotia." Unpublished M.E.S. thesis, Dalhousie University.

GREENSPAN, E.L. (ed). 1984 *Martin's Criminal Code*. Aurora, Ont.: Canada Law Book, Inc.

GROVES, Edith L. 1925 *The Kingdom of Childhood*. Toronto: Warwick Brothers and Rutter.

1932 *Everyday Children. A Book of Poems*. Toronto: The Committee in Charge of the Edith L. Groves Memorial Fund for Underprivileged Children.

GRUMET, Madeleine. 1985 "Bodyreading." *Teachers College Record*, Vol. 87 (2), pp. 175–193.

GUBERMAN, Nancy. 1985 "Behind Recent Social and Fiscal Policy in Quebec: A Redefinition of Motherwork by the State." Paper prepared for the Workshop on Motherwork, Val Morin, Quebec.

GUTSTEIN, D. 1975 *Vancouver Ltd.* Toronto: James Lorimer.

HANMER, Jalna. 1977 "Community Action, Women's Aid and the Women's Liberation Movement" in Marjorie Mayo, (ed), *Women in the Community*. London: Routledge and Kegan Paul.

HARDING, Sandra and Merrill B. HINTIKKA (eds). 1983 *Discovering Reality: Feminist Perspective on Epistemology, Metaphysics, Methodology, and Philosophy of Science*. Dordrecht: D. Reidel.

HARDWICK, W. 1974 *Vancouver*. Don Mills, Ont.: Collier-MacMillan Canada Ltd.

HARDWICK, W. and D.F. HARDWICK. 1974 "Civic Government: Corporate, Consultative or Participatory" in D. Ley (ed), *Community Participation and the Spatial Order of the City*. Vancouver: Tantalus Research Ltd.

HARMSTON, F.K. 1983 *The Community as an Economic System*. Ames, Iowa: Iowa State University Press.

HART, H.A.L. 1963 *Law, Liberty and Morality*. London: Oxford University Press.

HARTSOCK, Nancy C.M. 1985 *Money, Sex and Power*. Boston: North Eastern University Press.

HEAD, Wilson. 1975 "The Black Presence in the Canadian Mosaic." Toronto, mimeo.

HEALD, Susan. 1988 "Women and Cultural Production: Subject and Subjection." Ph.D. Thesis, Dept. of Education, University of Toronto.

HENRIQUES, Julian; Wendy HOLLOWAY, Cathy URWIN, Couze VENN and Valerie WALKERDINE (eds). 1984 *Changing the Subject: Psychology, Social Regulation and Subjectivity.* London: Methuen.

HENRY, Frances. 1977 "The Dynamics of Racism in Toronto." Department of Anthropology, York University, mimeo.

HILL, Daniel. 1977 *Human Rights in Canada: A Focus on Racism.* Toronto: Canadian Labour Congress.

HODGES, A. 1983 *Alan Turning the Enigma.* New York: Simon and Schuster.

HOLLOWAY, John and Sol PICCIOTTO (eds). 1978 *State and Capital: A Marxist Debate.* London: Edward Arnold.

HORSMAN, A. and P. RAYNOR. 1978 "Citizen Participation in Local Area Planning: Two Vancouver Cases." *Vancouver: Western Metropolis.* Victoria: University of Victoria.

HOUSTON, Susan. 1982 "The 'Waifs and Strays' of a Late Victorian City: Juvenile Delinquents in Toronto" in Joy Parr (ed), *Childhood and Family in Canadian History.* Toronto: McClelland and Stewart.

HOWE, Carolyn. 1986 "The Politics of Class Compromise in an International Context: Considerations for a New Strategy for Labour." *Review of Radical Political Economics*, Vol. 18(3), pp. 1–22.

HUNTER, Alfred A. 1986 *Class Tells. On Social Inequality in Canada.* Toronto: Butterworths. 2nd Edition.

JACKSON, Michael P. and Victor J.B. HANBY. 1979 *Work Creation: International Experiences.* Westmead, England: Saxon House.

JACKSON, Nancy S. 1980 "Class Relations and Bureaucratic Practice." Paper presented at the CSAA annual meeting, Montreal.

JESSOP, Bob. 1982 *The Capitalist State.* New York: NYU Press.

KARSTEN, Detlev. 1979 "Reflections in the West German Experience with Direct Job Creation" in M.P. Jackson and V.J.B. Hanby (eds), *Work Creation: International Experiences.* Westmead, England: Saxon House.

KEALEY, Linda (ed). 1979 *A Not Unreasonable Claim: Women and Reform in Canada, 1880s–1920s.* Toronto: The Women's Press.

KEATING, Donald R. 1978 "Looking Back on Community Organizing." *City Magazine*, Vol. 3(6), pp. 36–47.

1975 *The Power to Make It Happen: Mass-based Community Organizing: What It Is and How It Works.* Toronto: Green Tree Publishing.

KELLETT, Stan. 1978 "An Evaluation of the Performance of the British Columbia Pesticide Control Appeal Board." Vancouver: Paper written for Law 415, Environmental Control Techniques.

KEYES, Michael J. 1980 *The Politics of Guysborough Community Employ-ment Strategy Association [CESA] 1975-1980: An Experiment in Rural Job Creation and Retention.* M.A. Thesis in Public Administration, Dal-housie University.

KING, R. (ed). 1983a *Capital and Politics.* London: Routledge and Kegan Paul.

1983b "The Political Practice of the Local Capitalist Association" in R. King (ed), *Capital and Politics.* London: Routledge and Kegan Paul.

KLEIBER, Nancy and Linda LIGHT. 1978 *Caring for Ourselves: An Alter-native Structure for Health Care.* Health and Welfare Canada.

KNOP, Edward. 1987 "Alternative Perspectives on Communist Impacting: Toward Complementary Theory and Application" *Sociological Inquiry,* Vol. 57(3), Summer, pp. 272-291.

KORNBLUM, William. 1974 *Blue Collar Community.* Chicago: University of Chicago Press.

KRAUSHAAR, Robert. 1981 "Policy without Protest: The Dilemma of Or-ganizing for Change in Britain" in M. Harloe (ed), *New Perspectives in Urban Change and Conflict.* London: Heineman Educational Books.

KRESS, G.F. and R. HODGE. 1979 *Language as Ideology.* London: Routledge and Kegan Paul.

LACLAU, Ernesto and Chantal MOUFFE. 1985 *Hegemony and Socialist Strat-egy.* London: Verso.

LAND, Hilary. 1978 "Who Cares for the Family." *Journal of Social Policy.* Vol. 7, Part 3, pp. 257-284.

LARSEN, Tord. 1983 "Negotiating Identity: The Micmac of Nova Scotia" in *The Politics of Indianness: Case Studies of Ethno-politics in Canada.* Institute of Social and Ecomnomic Research, Memorial University of New-foundland: Social and Economic Papers, No. 12. St. John's, Newfoundland.

LATOUR, B. and S. WOOLGAR. 1979 *Laboratory Life. The Social Construc-tion of Scientific Facts.* London: Sage Publications.

LEES, R. and M. MAYO. 1984 *Community Action for Change.* London: Routledge and Kegan Paul.

LEGAL INFORMATION SERVICES. 1980 *Pesticides: The Hidden Assas-sins.* Vancouver: Legal Services Society.

LENNY, David M. 1976 "The Case for Funding Citizen Participation in the Administrative Process," *Administrative Law Review,* Vol. 28, pp. 490-494.

LEVINE, Helen. 1983 "The Power Politics of Motherhood" in J. Turner and E. Lois (eds), *Perspectives on Women in the 1980s.* Winnipeg: University of Manitoba Press.

LEY, D. 1974 "Problems of Co-optation and Idolatry in the Community Group" in D. Ley (ed), *Community Participation and the Spatial Order of the City*. Vancouver: Tantalus Research Ltd.

LIPKY, M. 1980 *Street-Level Bureaucracy*. New York: Russell Sage Foundation.

LIPSET, Seymour Martin. 1960 *Political Man*. Toronto: Doubleday.

LOFLAND, Lyn. 1975 "The 'Thereness' of Women: A Selected Review of Urban Sociology" in M. Millman and R. Kanter (eds), *Another Voice: Feminist Perspectives on Social Life and Social Science*. New York: Anchor Press.

LONDON EDINBURGH WEEKEND RETURN GROUP. 1980. *In and Against the State*. London: Pluto Press.

LONEY, M. 1983 *Community against Government*. London: Heineman.

LONEY, Martin. 1977 "A Political Economy of Citizen Participation" in Leo Panitch (ed), *The Canadian State: Political Economy and Political Power*. Toronto: University of Toronto Press.

LOWE, S. 1986 *Urban Social Movements: The City after Castells*. London: MacMillan Press.

LUSTIG, Jeff. 1981 "Community and Social Class." *Democracy*, Vol. 1(2), pp. 96–111.

LYNCH, M. 1983 "Discipline and the Material Force of Images: An Analysis of Scientific Visibility." A paper presented at the CSAA Annual Meeting, Vancouver.

MAGNUSSON, W. 1981 "Community Organization and Local Self-Government" in L. Feldman (ed), *Politics and Government of Urban Canada: Selected Readings*. Toronto: Methuen.

1985 "Urban Politics and the Local State." *Studies in Political Economy*, 16, Spring, pp. 111–142.

MAHON, Rianne. 1979a "Canadian Public Policy: The Unequal Structure of Representation" in Leo Panitch (ed), *The Canadian State: Political Economy and Political Power*. Toronto: University of Toronto Press.

1979b "Regulatory Agencies: Captive Agents or Hegemonic Apparatuses?" *Studies in Political Economy*, 1, pp. 162–200.

MANNHEIM, K. 1936 *Ideology and Utopia*. New York: Harcourt, Brace and World.

MARSHALL, T.H. 1965 *Class, Citizenship and Social Development*. Garden City, N.J.: Doubleday Anchor.

MARTIN, Biddy. 1982 "Feminism, Criticism, and Foucault." *New German Critique*, 27, Fall, pp. 3–30.

MARTIN, Robert (ed). 1984 "Critical Perspectives on the Constitution." *Socialist Studies/Etudes Socialistes*. Winnipeg: Society for Socialist Studies.

MARX, Karl. 1973 *Grundrisse*. London: Penguin. Originally published in 1858.

1977 *Capital, Volume 1*. Translated by Ben Fowkes. New York: Vintage Books.

MARX, Karl and Frederick ENGELS. 1970 *The German Ideology*. New York: International Publishers. Also published in 1976 by Progress Publishers, Moscow.

MAYBANKS, Sheila and Marvin BRYCE (eds). 1979 *Home-based Services for Children and Families: Policy, Practice and Research*. Illinois: Charles C. Thomas.

McDIARMID, Garnet and David PRATT. 1971 *Teaching Prejudice*. Toronto: Ontario Institute for Studies in Education, Curriculum Series No. 12.

McINTOSH, Mary. 1979 "The Welfare State and the Needs of the Dependent Family" in Sandra Burman (ed), *Fit Work for Women*. New York: St. Martin's Press.

McMAHON, Maeve and Richard ERICSON. 1984 *Policing Reform: A Study of the Reform Process and Police Institutions in Toronto*. Toronto: Centre for Criminology.

McMAHON, Marian. 1987 "The Return of the Repressed: Writing/Righting the Past." M.A. Thesis, Dept. of Education, University of Toronto.

McMURTRY, Roy. 1980 "Changing Attitudes for the Eighties." Address delivered to the Liaison Group on Law Enforcement and Race Relations Conference, Toronto, March 8.

McROBBIE, Angela. 1982 "The Politics of Feminist Research: Between Talk, Text and Action." *Feminist Review*, 12, pp. 46–57.

MEINHOF, Ulrike Hanna. 1986 "Revolting Women: Subversion and its Media Representation in West Germany and Britain." in S. Reynolds (ed), *Women, State, and Revolution*. Brighton: Wheatsheaf.

MEYER, Peter M. 1986 "The Corporate Person and Social Control: Responding to Deregulation." *Review of Radical Political Economics*, Vol. 18(3), pp. 65–84.

MILIBAND, Ralph. 1969 *The State in Capitalist Society*. London: Quartet Books.

MILLER, Mike. 1981 "Community Organization USAP: The View from the Movement." *International Journal of Urban and Regional Research* Vol. 5(4), pp. 565–572.

MINAR, David W. and Scott GREER (eds). 1969 *The Concept of Community*. Chicago: Aldine Publishing Co.

MITCHELL, M.A. and C. GOLDNEY. 1975 *Don't Rest in Peace — Organize!* Vancouver: Neighbourhood Services Association.

MOLLENKOPF, John. 1981 "Neighbourhood Political Development and the Politics of Urban Growth," *International Journal of Urban and Regional Research*, Vol. 5(1), pp. 15–39.

MORGAN, Patricia. 1981 "From Battered Wife to Program Client: The State's Shaping of Social Problems," *Kapitalistate*, 9, pp. 17–39.

MULLER, Jacob. 1989 "Ruling through Texts: Developing a Social Service Training Program for a Community College." *Community Development Journal*, 24(4), pp. 273–282.

MULLER, Viana. 1985 "Origins of Class and Gender Hierarchy in Northwest Europe." *Dialectical Anthropology*, Vol. 10(1&2), pp. 93–105.

MULLINS, Patrick. 1987 "Community and Urban Movements" *The Sociological Review*, Vol. 35(2), May, pp. 347–369.

NATIONAL INSTITUTE ON MENTAL RETARDATION. 1984 News Release. Toronto, September.

NELKIN, Dorothy. 1979 *Controversy: Politics of Technical Decisions.* Beverly Hills: Sage.

NG, Roxana. 1988 "Conceptual Difficulties of the Interrelation of Gender, Race/Ethnicity, and Class — A Discussion." A lecture given at at course on "Critical Philosophy of Science," University of Bergen, Bergen, Norway, May 1988.

1988 *The Politics of Community Services: Immigrant Women, Class and State*. Toronto: Garamond Press.

1987 "Ethnicity, Schooling and the Social Division of Labour: A Response to Jackson" in J. Young (ed), *Breaking the Mosaic: Ethnic Identities in Canadian Schooling.* Toronto: Garamond Press.

1985 "Introduction" to Dorothy E. Smith and Varda Burstyn, *Women, Class, Family and the State.* Toronto: Garamond Press.

1984 "Immigrant Women and the State: A Study in the Social Organization of Knowledge." Ph.D. Dissertation, Ontario Institute for Studies in Education, University of Toronto.

1983 "The Politics of Community Services: A Study of an Employment Agency for Immigrant Women." Paper presented at the CSAA annual meeting, Vancouver, B.C.

1982 "Immigrant Women and the State: Toward an Analytic Framework." Paper presented to the Western Anthropology and Sociology Association meeting, Saskatoon.

1981 "Constituting Ethnic Phenomenon: An Account from the Perspective of Immigrant Women," *Canadian Ethnic Studies*, Vol. 8(1), pp. 83–89.

1978 "The Social Relations of Citizens' Participation in the Chinese Community." Paper presented at the CSAA annual meeting, London.

NG, Roxana and Tania DAS GUPTA. 1981 "Nation Builders? The Captive Labour Force of Non-English Speaking Immigrant Women," *Canadian Women's Studies*, Vol. 3(1), pp. 83–89.

NG, Roxana and Judith RAMIREZ. 1981 *Immigrant Housewives in Canada.* Toronto: Immigrant Women's Centre.

NICKERSON, Kirby. 1983 "'Piracy' and Grassroots Unity: Coastal Communities on Trial," *New Maritimes*, Vol. 2(2), pp. 4–5.

NISBET, Robert. 1966 *The Sociological Tradition*. New York: Basic Book Publishers.

NORTHWAY, E. 1966 *Laughter in the Front Hall*. Toronto: Longman.

NOVOGRODSKY, Charles. 1986 "Together we are Ontario." A Report Prepared for the Ontario Ministry of Education Conference, School Community Relations Department, Toronto Board of Education, Constellation Hotel, Toronto, March 19–21, 1986.

O'CONNOR, James. 1973 *The Fiscal Crisis of the State*. New York: St. Martin's Press.

ONTARIO. Ministry of Community and Social Services. 1984 "Guidelines of the Social Services at Home Program." Operational Support Branch. January.

1983a "Three Decades of Change: The Evolution of Residential Care and Community Alternatives in Children's Services." Policy and Program Development Division. November.

1983b "The Nature and Effectiveness of Family Support Measures in Child Welfare." Policy and Program Development Division. August.

1982 Communications Branch, News Release. October.

PANET-RAYMOND, Jean. 1987 "Community Groups in Quebec: From Radical Action to Voluntarism for the State." *Community Development Journal* Vol. 22(4), pp. 281–286.

PANITCH, Leo (ed). 1977 *The Canadian State: Political Economy and Political Power*. Toronto: University of Toronto Press.

PEOPLE'S FOOD COMMISSION. 1980 *The Land of Milk and Honey*. Kitchener, Ontario: Between the Lines.

PERRY, Stewart E. 1987 *Community on the Way*. Albany, N.Y.: SUNY Press.

PESTICIDE CONTROL APPEAL BOARD 1978–1981 Proceedings, Okanagan 2,4-D Hearings. Penticton, Vernon, B.C.

PIERRE-AGGAMAWAY, Marlene. 1983 "Native Women and the State" in J. Turner and E. Lois (eds)., *Perspectives on Women in the 1980s*. Winnipeg: University of Manitoba Press.

PIVA, Michael. 1979 *The Conditions of the Working Class in Toronto, 1900–1921*. Ottawa: University of Ottawa Press.

PIVEN, Francis Fox. 1984 "Women and the State: Ideology, Power, and the Welfare State." *Socialist Review*, Vol. 14(2), pp. 11–19.

PIVEN, Francis F. and Richard A. CLOWARD. 1979 *Poor People's Movements*. New York: Pantheon Books.

PLANT, Raymond. 1974 *Community and Ideology: An Essay in Applied Social Philosophy*. London: Routledge and Kegan Paul.

POULANTZAS, Nicos. 1978a *Political Power and Social Classes*. London: Verso.

1978b *State, Power, Socialism*. London: Verso.

PRESTON, J. 1983 *Fanny Queen of Provincetown*. Boston, Mass.: Alyson Publications.

PROGRESSIVE LITERACY GROUP. 1986 *Writing on Our Side*. Vancouver: Author.

RAINES, John C. 1982 "Economics and the Justification of Sorrows" in J.C. Raines, *et al.* (eds), *Community and Capital in Conflict*. Philadelphia: Temple University Press.

RAINES, John C., *et al.* (eds). 1982 *Community and Capital in Conflict: Plant Closings and Job Loss*. Philadelphia: Temple University Press.

RAMCHARAN, Subhas. 1974 "The Adaptation of West Indians in Canada." Ph.D. Thesis, Department of Sociology, York University.

RATNER, Robert S. and John L. McMULLAN. 1985 "Social Control and the Rise of the 'Exceptional State' in Britain, the United States and Canada" in Thomas Fleming (ed), *The New Criminologies in Canada*. Toronto: Oxford University Press.

RATNER, Robert S., John McMULLAN and Brian BURTCH. 1983 "The Problem of Relative Autonomy and Criminal Justice in the Canadian State." Paper presented to the CSAA Meeting, University of British Columbia, Vancouver.

REITZES, Donald C. and Dietrich C. REITZES. 1987 "Alinsky in the 1980s: Two Contemporary Chicago Community Organizations." *The Sociological Quarterly*, Vol. 28(2), pp. 265–283.

REPO, M. 1977 "The Fallacy of 'Community Control'" in J. Cowley (ed), *Community or Class Struggle?* London: Stage 1.

REYNOLDS, Sian (ed). 1986 *Women, State and Revolution.* Brighton: Wheatsheaf.

ROBERTS, Barbara. 1980 "Sex, Politics and Religion: Controversies in Female Immigration in Montreal, 1881–1921." *Atlantis*, Vol. 6(1), Fall, pp. 25–38.

1979 "A Work of Empire: Canadian Reformers and British Female Immigration" in L. Kealey (ed), *A Not Unreasonable Claim: Women and Reform in Canada: 1880s–1920s.* Toronto: The Women's Press.

ROBERTS, Tim. 1981 *Pesticides: The Legal Questions.* Vancouver: Legal Services Society.

ROSS, E. 1983 "Survival Networks: Women's Neighbourhood Sharing in London Before World War One." *History Workshop*, Vol. 15, pp. 4–27.

ROSS, V. 1981 "Cancelled Due to Lack of Interest." *MacLean's*, July 6, pp. 42–43.

ROUSSOPOULOS, D. (ed). 1982 *The City and Radical Social Change.* Montreal: Black Rose.

1978 "Reformism and the Urban Question." *Our Generation*, 11 (2): 46–58.

SACOUMAN, R. James. 1980 "Semi-Proletarianization and Rural Underdevelopment in the Maritimes." *Canadian Review of Sociology and Anthropology*, 17 (3), pp. 232–245.

1978 "Co-operative Community Development Among Nova Scotian Primary Producers, 1861–1940: A Critical Review of Three Cases" in N.B. Ridler (ed), *Issues in Regional/Urban Development of Atlantic Canada.* Saint John: UNBSJ Social Science Monograph Series, Vol. II.

SASKATCHEWAN ACTION COMMITTEE on the Status of Women. 1983 Communique (dated March 18).

SAUNDERS, Peter. 1981 *Social Theory and the Urban Question.* N.Y.: Holmes and Meier.

SAYER, Derek. 1983 *Marx's Method.* Brighton, Sussex: Harvester Press.

SCHLOSSMAN, Steven. 1976 "Before Home Start: Notes Toward a History of Parent Education in America, 1897–1929." *Harvard Educational Review*, Vol. 46(3), August, pp. 436–467.

1981 "Philanthropy and the Gospel of Child Development." *History of Education Quarterly*, Fall, pp. 275–299.

SCHUMPETER, J.A. 1942 *Capitalism, Socialism and Democracy.* New York: Harper and Row.

SCULL, Andrew. 1984 *Decarceration: Community Treatment and the Deviant: A Radical View.* 2nd Edition, London: Polity Press.

SEABROOK, Jeremy. 1984 *The Idea of Neighbourhood*. London: Pluto Press.

SHANLEY, Mary Lynden. 1983 "Afterword: Feminism and Families in a Liberal Polity." in I. Diamond (ed), *Families, Politics and Public Policy*. London: Longman.

SHORT, J.R. 1984 *The Urban Arena: Capital, State and Community in Contemporary Britain*. London: MacMillan Press.

SIMMONS, Harvey. 1982 *From Asylum to Welfare*. Toronto: National Institute on Mental Retardation.

SMITH, Dorothy E. 1987 *The Everyday World as Problematic: A Feminist Sociology*. Toronto: University of Toronto Press.

1985 "Women, Class and the Family." in *Women, Class, Family and the State*. Toronto: Garamond Press. Also in: R. Miliband and J. Saville (eds)., *The Socialist Register*. London: The Merlin Press.

1984 "Textually Mediated Social Organization." *International Social Science Quarterly*, Vol. 36(1), pp. 59–75.

1983 "No One Commits Suicide: Textual Analysis of Ideological Practices." *Human Studies*, 6, pp. 309–352.

1982 "The Active Text: A Textual Analysis of the Social Relations of Public Textual Discourse." A paper presented at the World Congress of Sociology, Mexico City.

1981a "Institutional Ethnography: A Feminist Method." Paper presented to the Conference on the Political Economy of Gender Relations, Toronto. [Published in *Resources for Feminist Research*, Vol. 15(1), 1986.]

1981b "On Sociological Description: A Method from Marx." *Human Studies*, Vol. 4(4), pp. 313–337.

1979a "A Sociology for Women" in J.A. Sherman and E.T. Beck (eds), *The Prism of Sex: Essay in the Sociology of Knowledge*. Madison: University of Wisconsin Press.

1979b "Women and the Politics of Professionalism." Unpublished Ms., Ontario Institute for Studies in Education, Dept. of Sociology.

1977a *Feminism and Marxism: A Place to Begin, A Way to Go*. Vancouver: New Star Books.

1977b "Some Implications of a Sociology for Women" in N. Glazer and H.Y. Waehrer (eds), *Woman in a Man-Made World*. Boston: Houghton-Mifflin Company.

1974a "The Social Construction of Documentary Reality." *Sociological Inquiry*, 44, pp. 257–268.

1974b "What it Might Mean to do a Canadian Sociology: The Everyday World as Problematic." *Canadian Journal of Sociology*, Vol. 1(3), pp. 363–376.

1973 "Women, the Family and Corporate Capitalism" in Marylee Stephenson (ed), *Women in Canada*. Toronto: New Press.

1972 "The Ideological Practice of Sociology." Paper presented to the Department of Sociology, Queen's University. [Published in *Catalyst*, No. 8, 1974.]

SMITH, Michael P. 1979 *The City and Social Theory*. New York: St Martin's Press.

SOUTH OKANAGAN ENVIRONMENTAL COALITION. 1978–1981 Submissions to the Pesticide Control Appeal Board. Penticton, Vernon, B.C.

STASIULIS, Daiva. 1982 "Race, Ethnicity and the State: The Political Structuring of South Asian and West Indian Communal Action in Combatting Racism." Ph.D. Thesis, Department of Sociology, University of Toronto.

STEEDMAN, Carolyn. 1986 *Landscape for a Good Woman*. London: Virago.

STEVENSON, Paul. 1983 "The State in English Canada: The Political Economy of Production and Reproduction." *Socialist Studies/Etudes Socialistes Annual*.

STEWART, R. 1982 "The Offense of Keeping a Bawdy House in Canadian Criminal Law." *Ottawa Law Review*, Vol. 14.

STOBIE, Margaret. 1982 "Land Jumping." *The Beaver*, Winter 1982.

SUBRAMANIAM, Indira. 1977 "Identity Shift — Post-Migration Changes in Identity Among First Generation East Indian Immigrants in Toronto." Ph.D. Thesis, Dept. of Sociology, University of Toronto.

SUGUNASIRI, S. 1978 "Smarten Up, Indians and Go Western" in A. Mukherjee, (ed), *East Indians: Myths and Reality*. Toronto: Published for Indian Students Assoc. at University of Toronto Press by Indian Immigrant Aid Services.

SWARTZ, Marc J. 1969 "Introduction" in Marc J. Swartz, (ed), *Local Level Politics: Social and Cultural Perspectives*. London: University of London Press.

TANNER, Adrian. 1983 "Introduction: Canadian Indians and the Politics of Dependency" in Adrian Tanner (ed), *The Politics of Indianness: Case Studies of Native Ethnopolitics in Canada*. St. John's Newfoundland: Institute of Social and Economic Research, Memorial University of Newfoundland. Social and Economic Papers No. 12.

TASK FORCE ON ATLANTIC FISHERIES. 1983 *Navigating Troubled Waters: A New Policy for the Atlantic Fisheries*. Ottawa: Supply amd Services Canada.

TAYLOR, Ian. 1983 *Crime, Capitalism and Community*. Toronto: Butterworths.

TENNANT, P. 1981 "Vancouver Civic Politics, 1929–1980" in L.D. Feldman (ed), *Politics and Government of Urban Canada*. Toronto: Methuen.

THERBORN, Goran. 1980 *What Does the Ruling Class Do When It Rules? State Apparatuses and State Power under Feudalism, Capitalism, and Socialism*. London: Verso.

THOMPSON, E.P. 1978 "Eighteenth Century English Society: Class Struggle Without Class?" *Social History*, 3, May.

1963 *The Making of the English Working Class*. Middlesex: Penguin.

TORONTO BOARD OF EDUCATION. 1976 *Final Report of the Work Group on Multicultural Programs*, Toronto: Author.

1978 *Draft Report of the Sub-committee on Race Relations*. Toronto: Author.

TORONTO HOME AND SCHOOL COUNCIL. 1936 *The Story of the Toronto Home and School Council Through the Years 1916–1936*. Toronto: Author.

TROY, Kathryn. 1985 *Studying and Addressing Community Needs: A Corporate Case Book*. N. Y.: Conference Board, Inc.

TULLOCH, Headley. 1975 *Black Canadians: A Long Line of Fighters*. Toronto: NC Press Ltd.

TURNER, Joan and Emery LOIS (eds). 1983 *Perspectives on Women in the 1980s*. Winnipeg: University of Manitoba Press.

TURNER, Roy (ed). 1974 *Ethnomethodology*. Middlesex: Penguin.

UBALE, Bhausaheb. 1977 "Equal Opportunity and Public Policy: A Report on Concerns of the South Asian Community Regarding their Place in the Canadian Mosaic." Brief submitted to the Attorney General of Ontario.

URRY, John. 1981a *The Anatomy of Capitalist Societies*. London: MacMillan Press.

1981b "Localities, Regions and Social Class." *International Journal of Urban and Regional Research*. Vol. 5(4), pp. 455–474.

URSEL, Jane E. 1984 "Toward a Theory of Reproduction." *Contemporary Crises*, 8, pp. 265–292.

WALKER, Gillian A. 1985 "Community Economic Development: Self-Help Capitalism or Oppositional Base?" *SPAN: Canadian Review of Social Policy*, 13, pp. 65–71.

1986a "Burnout: From Metaphor to Ideology." *Canadian Journal of Sociology*, Vol. 11(1), pp. 35–55.

1986b "Working Paper: Capitalism and Community." Unpublished Ms., School of Social Work, Carleton University.

WALKERDINE, Valerie. 1981 "Sex, Power and Pedagogy." *Screen Education*, 38, Spring, pp. 14–24.

1985 "Dreams from an Ordinary Childhood" in Liz Heron (ed), *Truth, Dare or Promise: Girls Growing Up in the Fifties*. London: Virago.

1986 "Video Replay: Families, Films and Fantasy" in Victor Bergen, James Donald and Cora Kaplan (eds), *Formations of Fantasy*. London and New York: Methuen.

WARNOCK, John and Jay LEWIS. 1978 *The Other Face of 2,4-D*. Penticton: South Okanagan Environmental Coalition.

1981 "The Political Ecology of 2,4-D." *Alternatives*, Vol. 10, pp. 33–40.

WEEDON, Chris. 1987 *Feminist Practice and Poststructuralist Theory*. Oxford: Basil Blackwell.

WEST COAST ENVIRONMENTAL LAW RESEARCH FOUNDATION. 1983–1984 "Cases in Brief." *Newsletter*, Winter, p. 5.

WHARF, Brian (ed). 1979 *Community Work in Canada*. Toronto: McClelland and Stewart Ltd.

WHEELER, Stanton (ed). 1969 *On Record: Files and Dossiers in American Life*. New York: Russell Sage Foundation.

WHITE, D. and P. SHEPPARD. 1981 "Report on Police Raids on Gay Steambaths." Submitted to Toronto City Council, February 26th.

WIKLER, L. and D. HANUSA. 1980 "The Impact of Respite Care on Stress in Families of Mentally Retarded Children." Paper presented at the American Association of Mental Deficiency. San Francisco.

WILFORD, Allen. 1984 *Farm Gate Defense*. Toronto: NC Press.

WILKIN, David. 1979 *Caring for the Mentally Handicapped Child*. London: Croom Helm.

WILLIAMS, Raymond. 1986 "Towards Many Socialisms." *Socialist Review* Vol. 16, pp. 45–65.

WILLIAMS, Rick. 1984 "The Restructuring that Wasn't: The Scandal at National Sea." *New Maritimes*, Vol. 2(7), pp. 4–8.

1979 "Inshore Fishermen, Unionization, and the Struggle against Underdevelopment Today" in R. Brym and J. Sacouman (eds), *Underdevelopment and Social Movements in Atlantic Canada*. Toronto: New Hogtown Press.

WILLISTON, Walter. 1971 *Present Arrangements for the Care and Supervision of Mentally Retarded Persons in Ontario*. Ontario Department of Health.

WILSON, Elizabeth. 1977 "Women in the Community" in M. Mayo (ed), *Women in the Community*. London: Routledge and Kegan Paul.

1981 "Women, the 'Community,' and the 'Family'" in Alan Walker (ed), *Community Care: The Family, the State and Social Policy*. Oxford: Basil Blackwell and Martin Robertson.

WIREMAN, Peggy. 1984 *Urban Neighbourhoods, Networks and Families.* Lexington, Mass.: D.C. Heath and Co.

WISINER, Susan and D. PELL. 1981 *Community Profit: Community Based Economic Development in Canada.* Toronto: Is Five Press.

WOLFENSBERGER, Wolf. 1972 *The Principle of Normalization in Human Services.* Toronto: National Institute on Mental Retardation.

WOOD, Ellen Meiskins. 1986 *The Retreat from Class.* London: Verso.

WOODWORTH, W. *et al.*, (eds) 1985 *Industrial Democracy: Strategies for Community Revitalization.* Beverly Hills: Sage publications.

WRIGHT, Eric Olin. 1976 "Class Boundaries in Capitalist Societies," *New Left Review*, 98, pp. 3–41.

YOUNG, Iris Marion. 1986 "The Ideal of Community and the Politics of Difference" *Social Theory and Practice*, Vol. 12(1), pp. 1–26.

ZARETSKY, Eli. 1982 "The Place of the Family in the Origins of the Welfare State" in Barrie Thorne and Marilyn Yaslom (eds)., *Rethinking the Family.* New York: Longman.

1976 *Capitalism, Family and Personal Life.* London: Harper Colophon Books.

ZIMMERMAN, Don. 1974 "Fact as a Practical Accomplishment" in Roy Turner (ed), *Ethnomethodology.* Middlesex: Penguin.